Legal Pitfalls
in Architecture, Engineering, and Building Construction

(With Special Forms)

McGRAW-HILL SERIES IN MODERN STRUCTURES:
Systems and Management

Thomas C. Kavanagh, Consulting Editor

Legal Pitfalls
in Architecture, Engineering
and Building Construction

(With Special Forms)

NATHAN WALKER, LL.B.

EDWARD N. WALKER, LL.B.

THEODOR K. ROHDENBURG, AIA

Second Edition

McGRAW-HILL BOOK COMPANY

New York   St. Louis   San Francisco   Auckland
Bogotá   Düsseldorf   Johannesburg   London
Madrid   Mexico   Montreal   New Delhi
Panama   Paris   São Paulo   Singapore
Sydney   Tokyo   Toronto

Library of Congress Cataloging in Publication Data

Walker, Nathan.
 Legal pitfalls in architecture, engineering, and
building construction.

 (Modern structures series)
 Includes index.
 1. Building—Contracts and specifications—United
States. 2. Architects—Legal status, laws, etc.—
United States. 3. Engineers—Legal status, laws, etc—
United States. I. Walker, Edward N., joint author.
II. Rohdenburg, Theodor Karl, joint author.
III. Title. IV. Series.
KF902.W3 1979   343′.73′078   77-28978
ISBN 0-07-067851-0

1234567890 KPKP 7865432109

*The editors for this book were Jeremy Robinson and Margaret Lamb,
the designer was Naomi Auerbach, and the production supervisor
was Frank P. Bellantoni. It was set in Illumna
by KBC/Rocappi.*

Printed and bound by The Kingsport Press.

This book is dedicated to the New York Chapter of The American Institute of Architects for its outstanding and vital contribution to the improvement of man's environment.

The second edition of this book is dedicated to Nathan Walker (1905-1973), former counsel to the New York Chapter of the American Institute of Architects, who was an authority in the law of architecture, engineering, and building construction. His love for the law was only second to his love for his family.

DISCLAIMER

The second edition of *Legal Pitfalls in Architecture, Engineering, and Building Construction* is designed to present accurate and authoritative information and to reflect the state of the law and regulations as they exist at the time of publication. Major changes may result from future action of commissions, departments of justice, Congress, state legislatures, or the courts.

Legal Pitfalls is written with the understanding that the publisher, the editors, and the authors are supplying guidelines and not attempting to render legal, accounting, or other professional services.

In recent years, the role of women in architecture, engineering, and construction has seen tremendous growth, and this is indeed desirable. However, the terminology in these fields is replete with such words as "draftsman," "workmen's compensation," and "craftsman." In addition, the English language has no neuter personal pronoun. Therefore, where words such as "draftsman" or the pronoun "he" are used, we hope that readers will understand them to refer to persons of either gender.

"If a building, which an architect or other workman has undertaken to make by the job, should fall to ruin either in whole or in part, on account of the badness of the workmanship, or even because of the badness of the soil, the architect and undertaker shall bear the loss, if the building falls to ruin in the course of ten years."

(CODE NAPOLEON, ARTICLE 1792)

Contents

Preface to the Second Edition

The system of laws in this country, and the judicial interpretation of these laws, are not static and immutable, but fluid and dynamic. In order to react sensitively to changing social, political, economic, and technical forces, constitutions are amended, legislators enact new statutes, and courts find new interpretations of constitutions and statutes. Adherence to precedent is valuable in that it makes for an ambient of stability and predictability, instead of one in which a case might be decided one way today and the opposite way in a different court tomorrow. However, precedent is not followed blindly. In the words of one jurist,

The law should be based on current concepts of what is right and just and the judiciary should be alert to the never-ending need for keeping its common law principles abreast of the times. Ancient distinctions which make no sense in today's society and tend to discredit the law should be readily rejected. . . .

Consequently, it was felt desirable to publish a second edition of this book, to expose to architects, engineers, and builders the changing shapes of legal pitfalls in their professional pathways, and to reveal some of the hazards appertaining to new pathways being explored by them in their increasing efforts to find better and more economical answers to society's building needs. The legal protection afforded under the concept of necessity for privity of contract has recently been sharply eroded, resulting in changes in the relationship between professional and builder. The traditional roles of the architect and engineer are expanding into new areas, and a new professional, the construction manager, has entered the building field. Because these changes are relatively recent, there is a scarcity of precedent established by case law. However, it is possible to discern trends in legal decisions, and it is hoped that an awareness of these trends, as discussed in this second edition, will enable the reader to avoid some of those pitfalls which already have entrapped others.

Edward N. Walker
Theodor K. Rohdenburg

Preface to the First Edition

"Every man is presumed to know the law." This proverbially assumed knowledge—or his own lack of it—is cause for qualms and apprehensions on the part of every layman. However, although this presumption of knowledge applies to the criminal law as a matter of public necessity, no such inflexible inference is applicable to the civil law. If it were so applicable, "we would not need lawyers to advise, and judges to decide, what the law is."

It would seem to be fundamental that an architect or engineer, although a professional in his chosen field, should be regarded as a layman in the field of law; and thus he should be afforded the same consideration generally accorded to laymen to whom knowledge of the civil law is not imputed. However, the experienced professional knows that, frequently, a necessity to understand the civil law attaches forcibly, even destructively, to both architect and engineer. He must be cognizant of the laws of the locale where each project is to be erected. Lack of such knowledge could affect adversely the owner, the builder, even the public at large, as well as the professional himself; thus ignorance is no excuse.

Throughout the progress of each commission, from preliminary negotiations with prospective client to the supervision of construction, the professional must have an understanding of the law which may be applicable.

In the preparation of technical documents, as well as in the determination of disputes between owner and contractor, the architect or engineer cannot remain aloof from the law. It constantly haunts him and presents a continuing challenge in his everyday activities.

Not being the beneficiary of a formal legal training, what can the conscientious practitioner do to reduce his risk? There is no simple answer to this question. The only feasible answer, at best partial and subject to obvious limitations, is for him to become conversant, insofar as possible, with legal pitfalls which have entrapped other members of his profession. Such knowledge will enable him to endeavor to avoid a repetition of errors committed by others through lack of understanding of technical facets of the law. Because of the close working relationship between the contractor and the architect or engineer, the contractor, too, must be cognizant of legal pitfalls relating to building construction.

One of the purposes of this book is to make all those engaged in designing or erecting buildings more deeply conscious of the law, and to make them aware of certain legal pitfalls so that they may recognize danger in sufficient time to procure legal advice which may be necessary to safeguard their interests and those of their clients. It is not intended that the layman shall act as his own lawyer. Throughout this book will be found a number of recommendations and suggestions dealing with business aspects. In addition, there will be found recommendations of a legal nature. With respect to the latter, no matter to whom addressed, it is intended that no one will accept or follow them without first consulting an attorney.

The reader will appreciate that it is not possible to expose every legal trench; nor is it possible to attempt to backfill completely those which have been discovered through contact with the experiences of others. It is more helpful and appropriate to uncover those important and prickly pitfalls which experience has shown frequently recur in the daily activities of those who "simply must know."

Then, too, it cannot be overlooked that legal difficulties arise at times because of the incompleteness of written agreements. This incompleteness often stems from a lack of familiarity with special contingencies that may arise, and which consequently are not considered either in the negotiations between the parties or in the written agreement itself.

It would be impossible to include, within this book, forms of agreements covering every conceivable special situation that might develop. However, there have been included some special forms which have been found useful in special situations. These forms are intended to serve a dual purpose: first, to alert the layman to possible contingencies which should be anticipated in the negotiation of business arrangements before they are reduced to binding legal documents; second, to guide the lawyer in the preparation of those documents, the layman knowing full well that his lawyer will experience no difficulty in determining their utility and in making such revisions as may be necessary to cope with any specific problem.

The legal aspects of this book have been prepared solely by Nathan Walker, LL.B. In endeavoring to present the material contained in this volume in a simple style, he has been aided by Theodor Rohdenburg, AIA, who has contributed his technical knowledge and experience as an architect and professor of architecture.

Nathan Walker
Theodor K. Rohdenburg

Acknowledgments

For their help in the preparation of portions of this second edition, we wish to thank Arnold Y. Kapiloff for his legal expertise, Ronald S. Herbst for his assistance and research, and Diane S. Maniscalco for her help in preparing the manuscript.

PART ONE
Legal Responsibilities

CHAPTER 1

Legal Pitfalls in the Owner-Architect (Engineer) Relationship: Agreements

1.1 *Professional Responsibilities in General.* Each of the design profession-als has an obligation to protect the interests of a larger segment of society than that made up of his clients. In addition to his duty to use his technical skill and judgment to protect his client from the consequences of the client's lack of building knowledge, he must be guided by an inflexible sense of fairness in his relationships with contractors and with other professionals and must provide society in general with buildings which are safe and stable.

In the preparation of his plans and specifications, and in the construction administration of the job as well, if either professional has the requisite skill and does not use it, he is chargeable with negligence; and if he does not possess the requisite standard of skill, he is liable because of the lack of it. However, these professionals are not held to absolute accuracy in perform-ing their professional duties, nor do they warrant the perfection of their plans and specifications. The law requires only the exercise of ordinary skill and care in the light of present-day knowledge. They may be charged with the consequence of errors only where such errors have occurred for want of reasonable skill or reasonable diligence.

In soliciting work in his professional field, or in accepting a commission, each such professional represents:

1. That he possesses the requisite skill and knowledge

2. That he will use reasonable care and diligence in the application of his knowledge
3. That he will be guided by his best judgment
4. That he will be honest

Should he fail in any one of these areas, and injury to person or property results from such failure, he may be liable under the law for any damages sustained.

The professional's most obvious and immediate duty, of course, is that owed to his client, as established by contract or law. The client expects him to provide a design which will be suitable for its intended use. The client has a right to rely on his professional adviser to provide a building which will have the requisite structural stability and weatherability to protect the client and his operations from harm, and which will meet the standards set by the community in order to safeguard life, health, and property. Although the appearance of his buildings is a matter of primary concern to the architect, he does not guarantee to produce a design endowed with beauty, nor one which will be in accord with his client's aesthetic tastes.

1.2   Importance of Written Agreement. Generally speaking, the professional is entitled to be paid for the services he provides, whether in the preparation of design studies, working drawings, specifications, or any other services rendered. However, this general rule, like every other rule, is subject to limitations and exceptions. The right of the architect or engineer to compensation presupposes that there is an express or implied contract between him and his client which contemplates that the professional shall render the services which he ultimately performs. Ordinarily, the contract may be verbal. However, in certain jurisdictions, for example, in New York, the contract must be in writing, if it is understood that the services are not to be completed within one year from the making of the contract. On the other hand, this same jurisdiction does not require a written contract, though the services are performed during a period exceeding one year, provided the understanding between the parties does not contemplate a definite period for the rendition of the services. The verbal agreement is the understanding between the parties. The writing is merely evidence of that understanding as a note is evidence of a debt; the indebtedness exists quite apart and independent of the note itself.

1.2.1   Client May Assert that Services Were Free. The principal reason for insisting upon a written contract for professional services is that an oral agreement, made during conversation, may not leave both parties with the same understanding of its terms and conditions.

One young architect, just starting his professional career, arranged to provide plans and specifications and supervise the construction of a building, without the precaution of having a written agreement with his client. Before construction was completed, a difficulty arose between them, and the architect was discharged. Forced to sue for payment for preparing plans and specifications, the architect testified that his client had expressly agreed to pay him well for his services. However, the client testified that the architect had solicited the job, saying that it would be a great help to him in starting out in his business, and had offered to do all the architectural work without any charge whatsoever. Though the architect was awarded judgment, there can be no assurance that under comparable circumstances the same favorable result would follow.[1]† Each case rests upon its own factual foundation, and the verdict of a jury never can be predicted.

1.2.2   *Death of Client May Bar Proof of Oral Agreement.* Another important reason for requiring the client to sign a written agreement is that in case of his death, the professional may be barred from testifying as to the transaction with his deceased client, as a result of which he may not be able to prove the understanding arrived at with his client. In certain jurisdictions a partisan witness is prohibited from giving his version of a transaction with another who is deceased, since when death silences one, the law will silence the other.

In a recent transaction a professional's client suddenly died owing the professional a very substantial sum of money. No written contract had been signed. The executors of the owner's estate resisted the claim because of the absence of a written contract. Though the professional had knowledge of all the facts, he ran the risk of losing his case. Considering the grave legal dangers that arise in a situation where the architect's or engineer's claim is not supported by a written agreement, it is difficult to understand why so many professionals are willing to take a chance. Even though the client's word may be deemed to be as adequate as his bond, nonetheless, his death may destroy the "bond."

1.2.3   *Danger in Starting Work before Contract Is Signed.* A more common mistake, also resulting in a loss to the architect, is to start work on a commission before an agreement has been signed. A single instance, except in detail, is typical of many. An architect sent a written agreement to a prospective client for a large residence, meanwhile starting work on the basis of an oral authorization. Although several reminders failed to evoke more than promises to return the signed agreement "as soon as I find time," the architect completed the preliminary drawings and asked for a conference to discuss them. The client requested deferment of the conference, pleading his wife's illness. It finally appeared that the wife's illness was more severe than had been thought, and the client decided not to build at all—and not to pay his architect, as no written agreement had been signed. Such instances occur so frequently that the architect is well advised to say, "No, I

---

† Superscript numbers appearing in the text are keyed to corresponding numbers which will be found in the back of the book under "Case References." Such references include the titles of reported cases and citations, with minor exceptions.

have not started sketches yet, but I am anxious to start. Will you please send back the signed agreement so that we may begin to study this interesting project?"

1.3 Necessity for Stipulating Compensation. Where there has been no request for services, the architect or engineer may not recover compensation unless his services are accepted. One who officiously prepares sketches in the hope of securing employment is regarded in the eyes of the law as being a mere volunteer who may not claim compensation unless his services subsequently are accepted by the client. A request by an owner for services, followed by the rendition of the services, creates an obligation to pay. Assuming that the architect or engineer is not a mere volunteer, he is entitled to be compensated. In the absence of any understanding regarding the specific amount of his compensation, the law will imply an obligation on the part of the client to pay the reasonable value of his services. If the reasonable value of his services is disputed, and resort to law is necessary, the professional may testify to the nature and scope of the services rendered, the extent of responsibility assumed, his customary charges for similar services, and such other matters as may be pertinent. But then, unfortunately, he would be obliged to entrust the duty of appraising the value of these services to the sagacity of a judge, jury, or arbitrator whose award may very well be a sum less than the customary compensation. This incalculable risk is one which must be borne by a professional who omits to arrive at a definite understanding with his client as to his compensation.

1.3.1 Professional's Compensation May be No Greater for Remodelling than for New Construction. An architect in Pennsylvania discovered, to his chagrin, the cost of failing to be definite. He had entered into a proper written contract to perform architectural services, in connection with a proposed addition to an existing bank building, for a fee of 5 percent of the cost of construction. During the progress of the work, the owner decided to remodel the interior of the original building, and the architect was asked to work on this as well. However, no new written contract was made, and although it is not unusual for an architect to charge a higher fee for services in connection with remodelling work than for new construction work, nevertheless, when on completion of the work the client was billed at the rate of 10 percent for the remodelling, he refused to pay more than 5 percent. Forced to sue for his fee, the architect found that the court upheld the client, holding that where an architect enters upon the performance of other services of the same general character relating to, connected with, or growing out of the original employment, he must show at least an implied contract for a higher standard of remuneration for the one than the other before he can recover anything over the rate of commission (5 percent) originally agreed upon by him.[2]

1.3.2   *Extra Compensation for Additional Services May Be Challenged.* Is an architect entitled to additional compensation for extra services when his contract is silent on this point? At least one court has denied such compensation under these circumstances. In another case, the architect was awarded further compensation for extra services despite the absence of any express agreement to compensate him therefor. The architect agreed to prepare plans and specifications for a building and superintend its construction for a stipulated sum. After accepting plans and specifications prepared under this agreement, the client ordered new plans for an entirely different building on the same site, but on completion of this extra work, refused to pay the architect more than the original sum stipulated in the contract. In this case, the court held that the architect was entitled to additional compensation for the extra work, saying:

> Respondent [Architect] did not agree to make all plans and specifications appellant [Owner] might order in contemplation of the construction of a building, but to make plans and specifications for the proposed building. The only reasonable, sensible construction of that language is that it called for one set of acceptable plans and specifications. That being satisfied, the acceptance of an order for another set was neither within, nor a mere extra incidental to, the original contract.

The accepted order for the second set of plans constituted a new contract having no relation to the work under the written contract, but was governed thereby as to price for the new work; nothing having been said about compensation therefor, the presumption was that the parties comtemplated it would be paid for at the same rate as the original work of the same general nature.[3] In order to avoid any question as to whether the changes involve merely an alteration of the original design or in fact the creation of a new design, it is apparent that the contract always should include a provision for additional compensation to cover changes of any nature. The standard form of agreement contains such a protective provision.

1.3.3   *Unenforceability of Agreement to Agree.* The professional's written agreement with his client should state specifically the amount to be paid or the measure of compensation. If perchance it is not reasonably possible to agree in advance upon the compensation, it should never be stated that "the fee shall be such sum as the parties hereafter shall agree upon," for such an understanding is nothing more than an agreement to agree and usually is considered so indefinite that it is legally incapable of enforcement. But an agreement which is silent as to the amount of compensation is considered in exactly the same light as one which expressly fixes the standard of measure as the reasonable value of the professional man's services, and therefore is enforceable.

1.4   *Agreements with Corporations and Public Bodies.* Even a written agreement clearly indicating a meeting of the minds on this subject will not always insure the payment of compensation. Particular care should be taken when entering into a contract with a private corporation. First, the legal right of the corporation to enter into the contract should be verified. Corporations are formed for certain specific purposes, and legally they may do only those things which are authorized by their charters. Second, even though it has been determined that the corporation has a legal right to make a certain contract, the right of an officer to sign for the corporation should be verified, since in the final analysis it is the directors who normally must approve contracts. Given the opportunity, the professional should obtain a certificate from the secretary or assistant secretary of the corporation, certifying that the officer signing the contract on its behalf was authorized to do so by the directors. If this is not possible, every effort should be made to obtain the signature of the president, rather than a lower-ranking officer, since it is usually presumed that the president of a corporation has the authority to enter into ordinary contracts on its behalf without express authority of the directors.

1.4.1   *Authority of Public Bodies to Act May Be Disputed.* Caution must be exercised when entering into a contract with a public body; agreements which do not come within its charter or enabling act may not be enforced by law, and often the expenditure of public funds must be approved by the voters. This is not necessarily to imply bad faith on the part of these public officials, but sometimes ignorance of their authority.

A municipal board of education entered into an agreement, in the Standard Form of Agreement of the American Institute of Architects, authorizing an architect to prepare preliminary sketches and cost estimates for a new school building, in order to prepare a budget figure for public referendum. Since the voters would have to approve a specific sum of money for the purpose of purchasing land and furnishing a building thereon, it would seem reasonable to assume that the board had the power to incur reasonable expenses for expert aid in determining the amount to be included in the referendum. However, a group of citizens challenged the right of the board to pay its architect, on the ground that the board had failed to earmark in its annual budget any funds to cover the architect's preliminary work and that therefore the public had been denied an opportunity to present objections to this expenditure at the public hearing on the budget.

In another instance, an architect who had performed professional services for a building for which a state was the client found himself in trouble when he attempted to collect compensation. His claim was one of several being resisted by the state on the ground that certain agents of the state had greatly exceeded their authority in making contracts. In this state, under its constitution, the state may not be sued, and it is presumed that those who enter into a contract with the state do so with full knowledge of this legal barrier. The only recourse available to the architect was to present his claim to the state attorney general, in the hope that the latter would make a recommendation to the state legislature for payment of his claim.

1.5 Ambiguous Language. It is essential in preparing an agreement with a client that the architect or engineer exercise extreme care to guard against the inclusion of ambiguous words, which he interprets in one fashion, the other party to the contract may interpret differently, and the court may determine mean something not quite the same as either party understood. The agreement may be modified considerably, or even set aside completely, by ambiguous wording, because if the document is ambiguous or equivocal, oral evidence may sometimes be admitted to ascertain the intention of the contracting parties, and a jury may have to decide what the parties really intended.

1.5.1 Physically Practicable or Financially Practicable? Though the meaning of the word "practicable" is well understood, it has more than one connotation—depending upon the sense in which it is used. At least, so one engineer discovered when his client refused to pay his bill. The client consulted him regarding an expansion to his plant, which the same engineer had designed originally. The client explained the need for additional space, and suggested to the engineer that a 3000-square-foot second story be added to one portion of the original one-story building. As the original building had been erected on filled-in land, necessitating the installation of piles, the engineer thought it possible that a new second story might overload the piles and also might impose too great a load on the existing 8-inch masonry walls.

In view of these physical conditions, the engineer explained in his initial conversation with his client that he was uncertain as to the practicability of erecting the proposed addition; that he felt he must first review the design of the original building, check certain records in the building department, and consider the building code further before determining whether it was practicable to build. He verbally agreed with his client that for complete structural plans he would charge 8 percent of the cost of construction work, but that if it were not practicable to build, he would limit his charge to $250. These arrangements were confirmed by letter signed by the engineer and approved by the owner. The engineer thereafter checked the structural features of the building, made certain computations, reviewed the building code, and consulted with the chief engineer of the building department. As a result of these investigations, he determined that it was physically practicable to support the second story on a crane runway which had been provided in the original building.

Subsequently, the engineer prepared, filed with the building department, and obtained approval of the required structural plans. Bids were taken, and the lowest bid was $35,000. The client refused to proceed with construction, claiming that he did not anticipate spending more than $20,000, and that in view of the cost of construction, as disclosed in the lowest bid, "it was not practicable to build." Accordingly, he refused to compensate the engineer beyond the sum of $250.

The engineer contended that the word "practicable," as used in the agreement between the parties, meant practicable physically, rather than practicable economically, as urged by the owner. Since no attempt was made in the written agreement to define the word "practicable," which is a word of only general import, the document was ambiguous. Because it was ambiguous, oral evidence was admissible to explain what the parties meant by the use of that word. In this case the jury, by its verdict, accepted the engineer's interpretation, though the verdict was not unanimous. What is more important is the fact that because of the ambiguity in the use of the language, oral evidence was admissible, and the jury, as the trier of the facts, was allowed to fix the sense in which this word was used. Had the engineer exercised greater care in the preparation of the agreement, he could have made it clear and unmistakable that his compensation would be limited to $250 only if his preliminary investigations disclosed that it was not physically practicable to proceed with this addition.[4]

1.6 *Professional Responsibility when Construction Cost Is Limited— General Rule.* In any building project undertaken in today's society, the money price of the project looms as a large conditioning factor. Whether the owner is a governmental agency, a business corporation, or an individual, there is inherent in his situation a maximum price which should not be exceeded. He looks to his architect or engineer to protect his financial interests, and thinks that the architect or engineer, because of his training and experience, has the power to foretell building costs with substantial accuracy.

If his client is expending public funds voted by referendum, or expending specifically appropriated public funds, the architect or engineer is charged with notice of the maximum price of the project, and to attempt to design approximately within this maximum becomes his contractual duty. If he produces a design for a building costing twice its contemplated price, no matter how appropriate to its proposed function, and no matter how visually appealing, the design is of no value to the client, who probably will refuse to accept it.

If a contract between a private client and architect or engineer calls for a building to cost not more than a restricted amount, the professional, normally, may not recover compensation if the drawings and specifications prepared by him are for a building which will cost substantially in excess of that amount. Although a slight variance between the restricted cost and the actual cost would not prejudice the professional's right of compensation, a substantial variance would be considered a breach of contract.

For example, in a case decided by a court in Texas, it was held that where an architect drew plans for a $75,000 building, instead of a building costing $70,000, the architect had substantially complied with the limit fixed by his contract and could recover his compensation from the owner.[5] On the other hand, a court in another state held that where the cost of construction was 27 percent more than the limit fixed by the architect's contract, the architect had not fulfilled his obligation and was not entitled to be paid for his services.[6]

The general rule referred to above was applied in an action by an engineer against an architect to recover for services rendered. The engineer, who was engaged with the architect in a joint project relating to the design of a high school, overdesigned the electrical and mechanical work, as a result of which it was not possible to bring the cost of construction within the known amount available therefor. Ultimately, the school board was compelled to engage other professionals to redesign the project. The court dismissed the engineer's action.[7]

1.6.1   *Exceptions to General Rule.* It should be emphasized that if an increase in cost results from changes made by an architect or engineer, pursuant to the owner's instructions, the owner cannot escape liability to the professional. Furthermore, where the owner accepts the drawings with full knowledge that they do not meet the restriction as to cost of construction, he must compensate the professional notwithstanding the fact that the cost is substantially in excess of the limitation prescribed by the contract. The acceptance of the documents by the owner may take place, even though a construction contract is not awarded.

For instance, it appeared in a dispute between owner and architect that the lowest bid submitted was far in excess of the cost limitation, and after the owner discovered this fact, he decided to defer construction. However, he suggested that the architect make certain changes in the drawings to overcome objections raised by the building department so that the owner could proceed expeditiously with construction at a later date if he chose to do so. Under such circumstances, it was obvious that he had accepted the drawings and specifications notwithstanding the high bids, and that therefore the architect was entitled to his compensation.

It should be remembered that if the professional's contract imposes a cost limitation, and the lowest bid substantially exceeds the restricted amount, it has been held (unless his contract expressly states otherwise) that he has the absolute right to make reasonable changes in order to reduce the cost to the stipulated sum. Similarly, if he offers in good faith to make such changes but is prevented from so doing by the owner, nevertheless, he may recover his compensation. This appears to be based on the theory that the architect or engineer is not required to go through the idle ceremony of revising the documents under such circumstances. The law will assume that what the architect or engineer had offered to do could have been done, had it not been for the owner's interference.

1.6.2 Coming to Grips with Cost Limitation. In cases of restricted cost where a private owner asserts that there was a limitation as to cost, and the professional's contract is in writing, it has been held that the limitation exists only if it appears in the written contract. That is, one normally cannot contradict the terms of a written instrument by the assertion that there was a condition not found in the written document itself. In a case decided by the highest court in Wisconsin, it was held that a private owner could not impeach the Standard Form of Agreement by claiming that there was an oral understanding limiting cost, since the terms of the Standard Form contained no such limitation.[8] Other courts have permitted such evidence to be introduced on the theory that it explains the intention of the parties involving an essential element of the agreement which was not, but should have been, incorporated therein.[9]

The legal implications of language contained in a written contract are such that seemingly innocent statements may be sufficient to constitute a cost limitation; for example, a contract recites that the board of trustees of a university has appropriated 1 million dollars for the construction of a new dining hall, and desires to engage the architect to render professional services in connection with the contemplated work. The implication is that cost of construction is limited to 1 million dollars. If the architect prepares plans and specifications calling for an amount substantially in excess of this limit, he may not recover compensation, absent acceptance of the drawings by the owner with full knowledge of the actual cost, because noncompliance with the condition referred to constitutes a failure to carry out his contract.

Although it may be unwise for him to do so, the architect has the right to agree to a cost limitation if he so desires. Circumstances may dictate that he must so agree. If his contract establishes a cost limitation, then ordinarily he exposes himself to certain legal risks, as previously observed. The present standard form of agreement between owner and architect recognizes the right of the owner and architect to incorporate in their written agreement a fixed limit of construction cost, which will include a bidding contingency of 10 percent, or such other amount as may be stipulated.

Should the lowest bona fide bid be in excess of the stipulated maximum construction cost, the standard form affords the owner three alternative options: (*a*) to approve an increase in price; (*b*) to authorize rebidding; or (*c*) to cooperate in revising the scope and quality of the project in an effort to reduce the cost. The architect is required in the last case to make revisions without additional compensation.

If the owner exercises option (*a*), no problem will arise. Similarly, if the owner exercises option (*c*), there should be no problem since in this instance his cooperation in making revisions to reduce the cost is required to be to the full extent necessary to achieve the desired result.

However, the conclusion is inescapable that if the owner merely exercises option (*b*), and the lowest bid on rebidding is in excess of the fixed limitation, the architect has not fulfilled his obligation to design within the restricted figure and has breached his contract. Such a result may be unfortunate, but he has agreed to it with his eyes wide open.

For the architect who recognizes the moral aspect of assuming that cost is important to his client and that he has a professional obligation to protect his client's financial interest, but does not wish to incur any risk in his endeavor to satisfy the cost limitation, another approach is possible. He may recite in his contract that he will use his best efforts to design a building costing not more than $_____ (the restricted cost). Also, that if the lowest bona fide bid exceeds said sum by more than 10 percent, he will revise the drawings and specifications without extra compensation, and that if thereafter upon rebidding, the lowest bona fide bid still is in excess of said sum, the owner shall have the option of proceeding with construction and paying the architect his full fee or abandoning construction and paying the architect only for the services rendered to the date of abandonment.

1.7 Guaranteeing Maximum Construction Cost. The dangers inherent in guaranteeing construction costs are plain. One has only to examine the range of contractors' bids, where each bidder is wagering his own financial future on the accuracy of his cost analysis, to realize the foolhardiness of such a guarantee by the architect.

1.7.1 New York Prices Are Not California Prices. The architect must be sure that some innocent statement to the client will not be construed as a guarantee of maximum price. A California architect was visited by New York entrepreneurs interested in building a supermarket. The architect showed these prospective clients several supermarkets he had designed in California, and answered many detailed questions regarding these examples, including their contract prices, as well as the materials and fittings which had been provided for these prices. The architect stated the maximum and minimum unit price costs of these buildings he already had designed, and confirmed these figures in a letter.

The clients authorized the architect to design for them in New York a supermarket like the ones he had completed in California. They indicated their willingness to sign a written agreement and requested the architect to include this letter as a condition of the agreement. As the letter was merely an informative one regarding his California experiences, the architect agreed, thinking that his clients desired in this manner only to stipulate the same materials and fittings for their own job.

New York prices are not California prices, and the low bid on this job was considerably in excess of the California prices noted in the letter. The client charged that these prices, included in the agreement, constituted a written guarantee, and sought to evade any payment whatsoever to the architect.

1.7.2 *Professional's Responsibility for Accuracy of His Estimates.* Another legal facet worthy of consideration is one which involves a claim by an owner against a professional based on the theory that the cost has been negligently or fraudulently underestimated. Extreme care and caution must be exercised by the professional in furnishing an estimate to an owner, for if his estimate is grossly erroneous, the law may hold him liable for any damages suffered by the owner, and he may forfeit his compensation if the final cost is substantially in excess of his estimate.

For example, in a case decided some years ago, an owner employed an architect to design and supervise the construction of a hotel. The owner claimed that the hotel, when completed, cost considerably more than the architect's estimate. In the ensuing action, the owner alleged that the architect had been fully informed regarding the financial situation disclosed by the owner's survey, which indicated that a reasonable return on the investment could not be earned by the proposed hotel if its cost exceeded $2000 per guest room, in addition to the fair proportionate cost of the ground floor rental space.

The owner alleged further that the architect had assured it that the cost would not exceed $340,000, which the owner had arranged to borrow for the construction of the building; that cost was of such primary importance that it insisted that there should be no mistake on this point, and accordingly requested the architect to check his cost estimates again and prepare a detailed written statement. Finally, it was alleged that the architect delivered a written estimate, based on his plans for the project of $374,729, and upon his assurance that this represented the outside and maximum figure, the owner decided to go ahead with the project. The construction contract was let on a cost-plus-fee basis, and the final cost of the hotel was approximately $500,000. The court ruled that if the owner's allegations were true, the architect would be liable for damages because the actual cost of the project was greatly in excess of his cost estimate.[10]

In this case, the architect's contract did not contain the customary provision then found in the Standard Form, which read: "When requested to do so, the architect will furnish estimates of the cost of construction, but he does not guarantee the accuracy thereof."† Any such provision furnishes a substantial measure of protection to the architect when the accuracy of his estimate is assailed by an owner.

1.7.3   Silence Not Tantamount to Guarantee. In an interesting case, an architect was charged with having guaranteed an estimate furnished by a builder. Before a cost-plus-fee construction contract was awarded, the owner asked the builder for an oral estimate. The owner claimed that the architect was present, that he assented to the contractor's estimate, and in effect guaranteed it by word of mouth. Ultimately, the actual cost was greatly in excess of the estimated cost. This architect's contract did not contain the standard provision, relating to disclaimer of guarantee, previously referred to. The architect denied that he had guaranteed the estimate, and fortunately for him, in this case the court accepted his denial as being credible. While indicating that the making of such a guarantee by the architect, even orally, would render him inescapably liable, the court here exonerated the architect by finding that he had merely remained silent when the builder gave his estimate. The architect was under no duty to warn the owner against relying on the estimate furnished by the contractor, ruled the court, adding that to impose such a duty on the architect would require him to engage in a dispute with an experienced builder on the subject of cost of construction.[11]

All too frequently the client, after abandoning the project, refuses to pay the architect because the lowest bid exceeds the original budget or an estimate prepared or secured by the architect. Regardless of any verbiage in the contract which negates the idea that the architect undertakes to meet a budget figure or guarantees the accuracy of any estimate, experience dictates that architects should not hesitate to remind their clients, and preferably in writing, that the only manner in which the cost of construction can be ascertained accurately is by taking bids. Such an admonition ultimately should prove extremely helpful in avoiding any dispute which otherwise might be generated because of an owner's understandable disappointment when the bids come in "too high." Furthermore, if a controversy should arise, the written reminders may keep open the door to an amicable solution of the architect's claim.

1.8   Neutralizing Unfair Contract Conditions. Dissatisfaction and expensive litigation often result from the lack of an initial understanding of the rights and duties of the architect. These should be spelled out in the owner-architect agreement, so that the architect does not find himself at the mercy

† The Standard Form now provides that the architect does not guarantee that bids will not vary from any statement of probable construction cost or any other cost estimate prepared by the architect.

of contract clauses which make his right to recover compensation contingent upon the occurrence of conditions which are beyond his control.

In his relations with his client, the architect sometimes is requested to accede to conditions affecting the payment of his compensation, ranging from the not unusual stipulation that a certain percentage of the fee will be payable when certain drawings are "completed and approved" to a great variety of special conditions arising out of the individual client's financial position. Some of these seemingly innocent additions to the agreement may operate later to prevent the architect from collecting his fee.

If a client were to ask, "Would you mind my deferring my first payment to you until I take title to the land? At that time I will have more cash in hand," the architect probably would agree. To do otherwise would seem uncooperative, even churlish—unthinkable to create this impression at the outset, when he is attempting to establish that personal rapport so necessary to a successful project. So he does agree, and there is inserted into the owner-architect agreement a clause to the effect that the architect's fee for preliminary studies will become payable upon the owner's acquisition of the site. Although this arrangement may have been made in good faith, if the owner subsequently does not take title to the site—owing to a defect in title, or to the seller's refusal to convey, or for any other unforeseen reason—the architect's fee never does become payable.

Aside from stiffly refusing his client's request, what may the architect do to protect himself against such contingencies? While being accommodating, he may in his own turn suggest a further clause which will neutralize the owner's suggestion: "I will be glad to cooperate; and it would seem reasonable to set an outside time limit; but in no case later than December 31, 19_____." As the architect is being agreeable, the owner will not want to appear unreasonable, and such an addition usually will be accepted.

The purpose of the architect's addition is to neutralize the possible unfair consequences of the owner's request and to make certain that payment of the architect's fee (or a part thereof) must become due at some time in the future.

Such a neutralizing clause is applicable to a variety of situations. Where the agreement states that the architect's drawings are to be approved by the owner, there is the implication that no compensation will be paid without such approval. If the owner were to decide for any reason that the project should be abandoned, he would be reluctant to pay the architect's fee, even though the agreement stated that the architect is to be paid a scheduled percentage of his fee on account of services rendered up to the time of abandonment. Therefore, if the owner's approval of drawings is an implied condition to payment, the architect should suggest an addition to the agreement that the owner will not withhold approval unreasonably. With such a clause present, the architect will be entitled to compensation if approval is withheld unreasonably.

It sometimes happens that the owner will ask that the agreement stipulate that he will pay the architect "as he receives funds" from a lending institution or from some other source. Were the owner not to receive such payment at all, he would not pay his architect at all. To avoid this situation, the architect should insist that the agreement contain a neutralizing provision, stating that any deferment of payments due the architect is permitted only for the convenience of the owner; and that it is not intended that receipt of above-mentioned funds by the owner is a condition precedent to the right of the architect to be paid. Similar situations may arise in the relationship of an architect and his consulting engineer, or in the relationship of a general contractor and subcontractors, and should be neutralized in this same fashion.

The following is a typical example, demonstrating how to neutralize a condition in the agreement between owner and architect, which otherwise would jeopardize recovery of the architect's compensation. Assume that an owner proposes the following provision:

If for any reason whatsoever a Building Loan Agreement is not entered into between the Owner and the State of New York, or the New York State Finance Agency, the Owner shall not be obligated to the Architect for any fees or other charges payable to the Architect under this Agreement.

To avoid the obvious effect of this provision, the architect simply would add the following words:

except, however, that if such Building Loan Agreement is not entered into through no fault of the Architect, the Owner, nevertheless, will pay to the Architect any fees or other charges payable or accruing to him under this Agreement for services performed and disbursements incurred up to the date that he is notified in writing by the Owner that such a Building Loan Agreement will not be entered into, and that consequently, the Architect should perform no further services.

1.9 *Determining Amount of Compensation.* It is unusual for the prospective client to have knowledge of the customary ways of determining the professional's compensation—or even of the exact services for which this compensation is to be paid. Therefore, it is necessary for the architect, or engineer, to explain at the earliest possible time what services he is prepared to render, and what he expects to be paid for these services. There are four commonly used types of compensation arrangements:

1. Stipulated sum
2. Percentage of cost
3. Professional fee, plus expense
4. Multiple of direct personnel expense

These may not be used indiscriminately, nor should any one of them be used for all types of commissions. Although each type has general advantages and disadvantages, each also has quite specific advantages and disadvantages when applied to a particular project under consideration. The professional must study all the factors involved—human, as well as legal—so that he may make a decision which is truly appropriate in the light of attendant circumstances. Fairness demands that the method selected assure that he be compensated reasonably for the time and effort expended by him on the project at hand.

In computing his fee by any of these methods, the architect or engineer must give serious thought to his probable costs. Unless a detailed estimate is made of the number of technical employees required for the project, their individual salaries, and the probable time to be expended by each of them, any cost figure will be sheer speculation and may result in a serious financial loss. Also, indirect costs must be estimated. Overhead costs—office rent paid, the cost of stationery used, salaries paid to secretaries and clerical workers, and other items of expense which are not directly attributable to any specific job—must be apportioned to the several jobs in the office. Overhead costs will be found to vary from one office to another, and the ratio of overhead costs to direct costs varies inversely with total volume of business.

1.9.1   Indirect Costs. The fee, over and above costs, may be a fixed amount, or a percentage of the architect's or engineer's costs, except that in the case of Federal projects, compensation consisting of cost plus a percentage of cost has been outlawed; cost plus a fixed fee is permissible. The direct costs, including technical payroll, are easily determinable for purposes of interim payments. However, actual overhead costs which constitute a legitimate charge against the job are not computed so easily, until an annual audit is made.

The following method of including overhead costs in interim billing has been used in a Federal project. During the first year of the contract, a tentative overhead figure is established as a percentage of the technical payroll, this percentage being computed on the basis of the architect's previous experience. At the end of the fiscal year, the actual overhead rate for that year is calculated as a percentage of the actual technical payroll and reimbursement adjusted accordingly. During each succeeding year of the contract, the actual overhead rate, computed for the preceding year, is used as a tentative figure, to be adjusted again at the end of the year on the basis of the actual overhead rate for that year.

This method of determining and applying the actual overhead rate obviates the necessity for the professional or his client speculating as to the proper rate. It also may be used in private projects, particularly those which may endure for a number of years—during which annual periods the actual overhead rate may vary substantially. A clause that has been used will be found on page 255.

1.10 *Compensation Payable in Installments.* Whichever method of fixing compensation be chosen, there are certain legal pitfalls to be avoided. It is usual for agreements between the architect or engineer and his client to stipulate that payments to the architect (engineer) shall be made periodically as the services are performed. The importance of providing for the payment of the fee in installments should not be overlooked.

In some jurisdictions, in the absence of a legal excuse, it has been held that a person performing professional services is not entitled to recover his compensation, in whole or in part, until he has performed his services fully and completely.[12] Stated differently, ordinarily the giving must precede the asking. However, where the contract provides that the fee is payable in installments, the architect or engineer is entitled to be paid in the proportions stated in the contract upon completion of the items of service embraced within each installment period. Furthermore, where the compensation is to be paid in installments for the separate items of service, with a price or percentage apportioned to one or more items of service, the contract may be regarded as being severable, as distinguished from entire, so that the professional may recover for one or more items of service, even though he should fail in the performance of other items of service.[13]

1.10.1 *Effect of Entire or Severable Contracts.* No precise or invariable rule can be laid down by which it may be determined whether a contract is entire or severable; it is a question of the intent of the parties, to be discovered in each case from the language employed and the subject matter of the contract.

Thus, in one jurisdiction, an owner-architect contract was held to be a severable contract because it provided for installment payments upon completion of the several parts of the work. However, the trend of authority indicates that such a contract is regarded as being entire. Indicative of the trend are the following cases. One involved alterations to a residence. The contract between the owner and the builder read in part:

All above material, and labor to erect and install same to be supplied for $3,075.00 to be paid as follows:
$150.00 on signing of contract, $1,000.00 upon delivery of materials and starting work,
$1,500.00 on completion of rough carpentry and rough plumbing,
$425.00 upon job being completed.

As the work progressed, the first two stipulated payments were made, but when, on completion of rough carpentry and rough plumbing, the builder asked for the third installment of $1500, the owner would not pay. The builder then stopped work and brought suit for the balance, contending that the contract was severable and that the measure of his damages was the provision in the contract for the installment payment of $1500.

The owner countered that the contract was entire, and that interim payments were not for work already done, but merely advance payments on the contract price. The jury awarded the builder his $1500. However, the appellate court of last resort held that the contract was entire, and that upon the owner's default the builder could collect either the reasonable value of the work which had been finished or, on the contract, for losses equal to the contract price, less payments already made and less the cost of completion.[14]

In the other case, plaintiff agreed to lay and finish floors in an apartment house building erected and owned by the defendant. Plaintiff was to be paid a total of $1350 for its work; 80 percent of that sum, or $1080, becoming due "on completion of laying" thereof. The laying of the floors was substantially completed. The plaintiff received $800 and made demand for $280, being the balance of 80 percent of the contract price. The defendant failed to pay the said sum of $280, and as a result the plaintiff refused to complete the finishing of the floors. Defendant contended that the plaintiff breached its contract by failing to finish the floors, and as a result of the breach, defendant was obliged to engage the services of another contractor to complete the work, at a price exceeding that provided for in the agreement.

Although the defendant breached the contract in failing to pay the sum of $280, the court ruled that since this contract was entire, the plaintiff was not relieved by this breach from full and complete performance of his undertaking, and having failed to complete the contract, was liable for the damages sustained by defendant. After commenting that a contract is divisible when performance is divided into two or more parts with a definite apportionment of the total consideration to each part, the court concluded that this contract was not divisible, but rather entire, stating:

While the performance of the contract in the case at bar is divided into two parts, namely, the laying of the floors, and the "finishing" thereof, there is nothing before us either in the agreement or in the circumstances surrounding it to indicate that the apportionment of the total consideration bears any relation to each item of performance. In other words, there is no proof that 80% of the contract price represents the cost of laying the floors and that 20% thereof represented the cost of finishing. We therefore conclude that such was not the case and that the contract was an entire one. It follows then, as already indicated, that it was incumbent upon plaintiff to complete its undertaking. This it failed to do, and since damages were proved by defendant as a result of that failure, defendant was entitled to a judgment on its counter-claim.[15]

Although the two cases last mentioned involved construction contracts, in a third case, involving the Standard Form of Agreement between owner and architect, the court held that the contract was not divisible, saying:

This basic promise is not broken down into a commitment to pay a certain percent of cost for plans and a certain other percent for supervision. In other words, the promise is unitary in character—a certain overall single total amount in exchange for all the services to be performed by the architect. When we inspect the clauses headed "payments," we find that these provisions relate to times of payment of parts of the fee, without any specific allocation of any part of the fee to any part of the services.[16]

1.10.2 *Rights of Professional upon Client's Default in Payment of Installment.* The Standard Form of Agreement, promulgated by the American Institute of Architects, provides that the architect's fee is to be paid in installments and that the aggregate of such installments shall equal the percentage of the estimated fee upon the completion of each stage of the service, as specified therein.

Although undoubtedly the intention of the Standard Form is to protect the architect and permit him to bill his client as his services progress, nevertheless the form contemplates total services for an agreed total compensation. Consequently, it may be considered to be an entire agreement, rather than a divisible one. If this is the legal effect of the Standard Form, then the question arises, what relief is afforded to an architect whose client defaults in the payment of an installment? The Standard Form provides that in case either party shall default substantially in the performance of his part of the bargain, the other party may terminate the agreement upon giving seven days' written notice of his intention so to do; but as a practical matter, the average architect is unwilling to resort precipitously to such a drastic remedy.

In the absence of an election to terminate the agreement, the architect is faced with a difficult choice—either to continue with his services without collecting his fee and thereby permit the client to magnify the architect's financial problem, or to withhold further services, in which case the client may claim damages against his architect on the theory that the contract is entire, so that the architect had no legal right to withhold his services despite the client's default. The problem is an ever-recurring one and appears to be so serious that many professionals have been advised to include in their agreements a special clause permitting them to suspend or withhold their services until the client has remedied the financial default. A clause that has been used, and which alternatively provides for termination if the default continues for an unreasonable period, is referred to on page 252.

1.11 *Safeguarding Compensation Payable by Foreign Client.* Many professionals today find that their practice is not only interstate but also international. When an architect or engineer undertakes a commission for a foreign job for a foreign client, it is possible that, in the event of a dispute, he will have considerable difficulty in collecting his compensation. The normal recourse in such situations, to sue for recovery in the courts, may be inordinately expensive, or even impossible. It is quite possible that the foreign client will not abide by the decision of a United States court, and for the architect or engineer to sue in his client's country would involve considerable expense and inconvenience. The architect should realize that if the client is a foreign government, it may not permit itself to be sued in its own courts.

Such refusal to pay his fee or even the fear of it may be avoided by inserting a provision in the agreement that the foreign government—the client—shall deposit with a bank in a city in the United States, dollars sufficient to cover the amount of the total estimated fee of the architect or engineer, and that upon the professional's certification to the bank that money is due under the contract, the bank must make payment. To minimize any fear on the part of the client, the agreement also should stipulate that any payments made by the bank shall not prejudice the right of the client to sue the professional (in the United States) for overpayment or wrongful payment. Such a clause will be found on page 253.

1.12 *Payment for Extra Work.* It is usually taken for granted by everyone concerned with construction that if an architect is required to perform extra services, or a builder to do extra work, he will be equitably paid for these efforts which were not contemplated in the original agreement. Disputes sometimes arise, however, in the course of deciding just what is equitable recompense. One area in which this is particularly true is that of prolonged contract administration services performed by the architect.

1.12.1 *Prolonged Contract Administration.* The slow and leisurely construction of a municipal library prolonged the architect's services beyond his endurance. Finally, almost two years beyond the estimated fifteen months for construction, when the building was still unfinished, and he was still being required to make inspection visits, the long-suffering architect commenced proceedings against his client for extra compensation for prolonged administration of the job. The contract between owner and architect stipulated that:

If the Architect is caused extra drafting or other expense due to changes ordered by the Owner, or due to the delinquency or insolvency of the Owner or Contractor, or as a result of damages by fire, he shall be *equitably* paid for such extra expense and the services involved.

The architect based his claim on the contention that, although the building contract did not state an anticipated time of completion of construction, the contractor's prolongation of the work constituted delinquency. His contention was upheld, and although a substantial award was rendered in favor of the architect, the amount was considerably less than the sum which the architect claimed. Since the controlling provision did not define the word "equitably" in terms of any specific standard of admeasurement (such as 2½ times technical personnel expense), the reasonable value of the extra services was debatable and undoubtedly accounted for the disparity between the amount of the claim and the sum finally awarded.

1.12.2 *How Is Extra Compensation Computed?* The present Standard Form of Agreement between owner and architect is much more definite. It fixes a standard of admeasurement for additional services, providing for these additional services to be computed as principal's time at a fixed rate, a multiple of direct personnel expense, and a multiple of the amount billed to the architect for additional services of his consultants. It also defines additional services as in part embracing administration services after the construction contract time has been exceeded by more than 20 percent. The inference seems clear that prolongation of the job by 20 percent is not considered abnormal, and that the architect should continue his duties during this additional time without additional compensation. However, two questions remain unresolved by the language quoted above.

First, if the job continues beyond the grace period of 20 percent and the architect is entitled to extra compensation, is his extra compensation to be computed from the original proposed date of completion, or from a date commencing with the end of the grace period? This point can be clarified by an additional clause as follows:

If the construction contract time is exceeded by more than the said percentage, the architect's extra expense for his extra services shall be computed from the date originally fixed for completion of the construction work.

If the architect's extra compensation does not cover the grace period, a second question arises: at which specific time during construction shall the architect give the free time? Presume that the presently used Standard Form of Agreement had applied to the library building. The actual elapsed time on a fifteen-month contract was fifteen plus twenty-five months. Of the additional twenty-five months, the architect donated three months (20 percent of 15) and was paid for twenty-two months. However, if he donated the first three months of extra work, he probably donated greater effort (and expense) than if he donated the last three months of extra work. Therefore, whenever appropriate, it would seem advisable for the contract to specifically allocate the period for which the architect expects extra compensation. Also, because the *construction contract time* may be extended by mutual agreement of the owner and the contractor, by reason of owner's changes or additions to the work, it would not seem unreasonable to provide for extra compensation, "should the *originally agreed upon construction contract time* be exceeded by more than 20 percent due to no fault of the Architect." A suggested provision is referred to on page 250.

1.13 *Amount of Compensation if Client Abandons the Work.* One of the troublesome problems which arises in the experience of many practitioners is that of computing compensation in the case of abandonment of the work designed or specified by them. In the case of every contract there is an implied undertaking on the part of each party that he will not intentionally and purposely do anything to prevent the other party from carrying out the agreement on his part. An owner ordinarily may not employ an architect to perform service for him at a price and then by abandoning the work deliberately prevent the architect from performing, without incurring liability. Good faith forbids such action on the owner's part. Under such circumstances, the architect, in the absence of any provision in the contract to the contrary, would be entitled to recover not only that portion of his fee which he has actually earned up to the date of abandonment by the owner, but also damages for the loss of the opportunity of which the architect is deprived as a result of being prevented by the owner from completing his services. The proper measure of such damages would be the loss of profits which the architect would have earned in the future under the contract.

In the preparation of the Standard Form of Agreement between owner and architect which fixed the architect's compensation at a percentage of cost of construction, it was deemed appropriate to provide that payments to the architect on account of his fee shall be made in certain installments and that if any work designed or specified by the architect was abandoned, he would be paid for the services performed.

Some time ago, the true legal significance of the clause referred to† was ruled upon by the Supreme Court of Wisconsin. The court held that the fundamental intent of the clause was to permit the owner to abandon the work; that his reasons for doing so were wholly immaterial; that it mattered not whether the owner was acting in good faith or bad faith and that such abandonment did not constitute a breach of contract on the owner's part rendering him liable to the architect for damages in the form of loss of profits which the architect might otherwise recover. Accordingly, the Wisconsin court limited the architect's recovery to that portion of his fee which he had actually earned and which had accrued up to the date of the abandonment of the project.[17]

In brief, to illustrate further, if the architect is to receive a percentage of the building cost and the abandonment takes place immediately upon completion of the schematic design phase, the architect under the Standard Form would be entitled to receive only 15 percent of the basic rate computed upon a reasonable estimated cost, or 35 percent upon completion of design development phase, or, if the abandonment takes place upon completion of specifications and general working drawings (exclusive of details), the architect's compensation would be limited to 75 percent of the basic

† The Standard Form, insofar as pertinent, now contains a clause substantially similar.

rate computed upon a reasonable estimated cost; or if bids have been received, then 80 percent computed upon the lowest bona fide bid.

If the abandonment takes place during the performance of any phase of the architect's services, it is expected that he will be compensated for his services rendered during such phase on a pro rata basis.

It must be remembered that the architect or engineer cannot compel his client to proceed with the completion of work which he has determined he no longer cares to undertake, and that the professional cannot persist in the rendition of services after the client has abandoned the work. Any services rendered after such abandonment would be considered voluntary, gratuitous, and not compensable.

1.13.1 *If Professional Agrees to Deferment of Payment.* As previously stated, under the Standard Form of Agreement between owner and architect, the owner has the absolute right, with or without reason, to abandon the work at any time. In such a situation, the architect is entitled to be paid for services rendered to the date of abandonment. Therefore, it is important that the agreement contain a special clause safeguarding the architect or engineer, in case of abandonment of the work, in those instances where the interim payments to the professional, on account of his basic fee, are reduced below those customarily provided for. An architect or engineer sometimes is asked to accept less than the amount he normally would earn at a particular point in his work, in order to assist the owner who must raise funds. Anticipating that the project will be completed and that he will not be injured financially—merely being required to wait a little longer for his full fee—the architect or engineer agrees. Then, if the project is abandoned, the owner may insist that the professional is not entitled to more than the agreed reduced amount which was to be paid at the date of abandonment. Consequently, it seems advisable under such circumstances to provide in the agreement that in case of abandonment the architect or engineer will be deemed to have earned the percentages normally earned—rather than the agreed reduced percentages, even though payment of the normal percentages is deferred. A typical provision that has been used to cover such a contingency is referred to on page 249.

1.13.2 *Other Remedies.* If the client abandons the architect, rather than the work, some architects or engineers are reluctant to sue their clients for breach of contract. Their reluctance may be due to a fear of adverse publicity or a variety of other reasons. Some professionals include in their agreements a schedule of payments which is to serve as a basis for payment of that portion of the fee already earned up to the date of the termination of their services and are satisfied to accept the amount actually earned and to consider the contract canceled by mutual consent in such a situation. However, in the absence of a provision thus limiting their rights, there are other remedies accorded to them.

In one instance, an architect designed and prepared plans and specifications which were accepted by the board of education for a school building which was to be built in stages when the needs required and the circumstances permitted. The school board proceeded with the erection of two units of the building, one soon after the contract was made and one three years later. These two units were constructed under the supervision of the architect, who was paid for his supervision in accordance with the agreement. Thereafter, the completion of the remainder of the building was delayed on account of war conditions.

After the war, and about ten years after the building had been designed, the school board announced its decision to complete the remaining unit of the building without the assistance of the architect; whereupon the architect claimed damages for breach of contract.

Despite contentions by the school board that the resolution of the former board was not authorized by referendum to construct this final unit, and the board had not been voted funds to do so, further that it could not contract with the architect for services reaching beyond the period of time for which the members had been elected, and could not bind their successors in office, the court ruled in favor of the architect, reversing a trial court decision.

The court said that where a party repudiates a contract made with an architect for his services, and refuses to be bound by its terms, the architect may exercise one of three remedies:

He may treat the contract as rescinded, and recover upon *quantum meruit* [reasonable value] so far as he has performed; . . . or he may keep the contract alive for the benefit of both parties, being at all times himself ready and able to perform, and at the end of the time specified in the contract for performance, sue and recover under the contract; or . . . he may treat the repudiation as putting an end to the contract for all purposes of performance, and sue for the profits he would have realized if he had not been prevented from performing.

The court said the testimony indicated that the board breached its contract and that the architect was entitled to recover the agreed-upon fee for supervising the third unit of the building, less the costs he would have incurred in said supervision had he not been prevented from fulfilling his contract.[18]

1.14   Right to Compensation if Professional Firm Membership Changes.
An agreement between an architect and his client is a contract for personal services, involving the element of personal confidence. Therefore, a change in the personnel of a partnership may permit the owner to terminate the agreement. In one instance, an architectural partnership consisting of A and B contracted to design and superintend the construction of a high school building. After the making of the contract, considerable time elapsed before the school bond referendum was held and before satisfactory terms for the sale of the school bonds were secured. In the meantime, A and B had

prepared and presented preliminary plans for the building. Then architect B retired, and architect A, who succeeded to the business, took in a new partner, C. The school board decided to have no further dealings with the firm as reconstituted, and employed another firm of architects, whereupon A and C sued for damages for breach of contract.

In upholding the school board, the court said:

> The business of an architect has the dignity of a learned profession. A competent architect is a person of peculiar skill and taste. He must be a man of culture, of disciplined mind, artistic eye, and trained hand; he must be able to visualize the possibilities of beauty and harmony in proportionate arrangement and construction of brick and stone and cement and steel; and he must have the art of deftness to set down his ideas with such precision in specifications and blueprints that contractors and workmen can readily follow them with fidelity. Moreover, he must be a man of the highest probity, zealous to see that his designs are fashioned of good materials and good workmanship, so that the finished edifice will endure and be worth its cost to his employer. All these qualifications of a personal nature are involved in any prudent contract for the services of an architect. And so it seems that when the school board employed [A and B] they contracted for the special knowledge, skill and taste, the professional pride of achievement, the wisdom of the counsel, and the personal probity of both [A and B].

The court therefore decided that the board was not bound to accept the services of any others than those with whom it had made the contract.[18] Recognizing the necessity for providing that the death or retirement of a partner should not provide legal cause for the termination of the owner-architect agreement, legal experts have included in the agreement a special provision, such as is referred to on page 252.

1.15 *Competition by Professionals.* The selection of an architect or engineer involves a process of relative evaluation on the part of a prospective client. The objective may be to procure the professional who will furnish the most comprehensive range of services, or who will provide the most innovative and imaginative answer to a problem, or who will perform the necessary services at the lowest cost. As in other aspects of our economic system, this evaluative process on the part of the clientele engenders competition.

1.15.1 *Bidding for Contract.* Until recently, commissions for architectural or engineering services were not usually awarded on the basis of competitive bidding. In some jurisdictions, registration laws specifically prohibit such practices. Statutes which require competitive bidding in the awarding of contracts for public works have been held generally, in the past, not to apply to contracts for architectural or engineering services. The fulfillment of such professional contracts requires a high degree of skill and knowledge, and the exercise of care to use these in the best interests of the client. It was felt that requiring competitive bidding by design professionals, and the compulsion to award a contract to the lowest bidder, could result in situations in which the lowest bid would be so low as to preclude the professional's devoting sufficient attention and care to the work except at a financial loss to himself, and that therefore the best interests of the public would not be served.

However, the U.S. Department of Justice has ruled that professional associations may not prohibit their members from submitting fee quotations for professional services, and may not establish recommended minimum fees. Such practices to avoid competition are now held to be violations of antitrust laws.

1.15.2   *Plans Submitted in Formal Design Competitions.* Many governmental bodies and some private concerns have chosen design professionals for proposed construction projects through the device of a design competition. The owner may advertise for submissions from all interested professionals, or may invite a selected number to submit designs for relative evaluation by a jury. For the owner, a competition may result in a great diversity of design solutions. For the professional, winning a competition may result in desirable publicity.

1.15.3   *Unlicensed Competitor.* In most states, professionals are licensed at the time they enter competitions. However, in a national competition, it is probable that all competitors will not be licensed in the state of the competition at the time of submitting their entries. State laws vary in the manner in which they define the practice of architecture. Some states define a practitioner as one who "holds himself out as able to perform or who does perform any professional service."

It is interesting to note further that the conditions and rules of specific competitions frequently stipulate that "each competitor in submitting his entry undertakes the obligation to accept a contract on the terms stated . . . if such winning competitor is not licensed for architectural practice in this State he shall become so licensed as soon as possible." Therefore, it is possible that where these two conditions apply to the same competition, an unlicensed competitor, by entering the competition, is holding himself out as able to perform professional services contrary to the licensing statute.

1.15.4   *Check before Entering.* Rules for competitions vary materially, and before a prospective competitor invests valuable time and energy in preparing a submission, he would be well advised to examine carefully the terms and conditions pertaining to the competition he contemplates entering. In reviewing the rules, answers to a number of questions should be sought, including the following:

1. Must a winner be selected? If the right is reserved to reject all plans submitted, or if there is no statement that a winner will be selected, it is possible that the jury may decide that no entry warrants a prize.

2. Must the winner be employed to design and administer the construction of an actual building project in addition to receiving a prize? If so, a contract exists which is binding on the winner as well as on the owner.

3. What is the amount of the professional's fee for these subsequent services? Will the amount of the prize be over and above the agreed fee for subsequent architectural and engineering services, or merged therein?

4. Who is the owner of drawings submitted by the winner? In the absence of a provision to the contrary, the drawings become the property of the competition owner instead of the competitor.

5. Must the winner's design as submitted in competition be considered the basis for constructing the proposed project, or may the owner, having selected a professional by competition, then require him to produce a different design for the actual building? If so, in what manner will the professional be compensated?

6. Must the winner associate with a local architect (to advise on the effects of local conditions, the requirements of local regulatory agencies, etc.)? If so, how will this associate be paid?

1.16   Conclusions. There is, then, a variety of shapes to the pitfalls in the path leading to an initiation of professional relationship. In establishing an association with his client, the prudent architect or engineer should safeguard against as many contingencies as may be foreseen, because each crisis arising in this relationship, even though it may not result in a lawsuit or legal proceeding, or even in monetary loss, will weaken the position of the architect as a trusted adviser of his client. The moral of the tale is as follows:

1. Don't neglect to have a written agreement signed by the client before beginning work or undertaking additional or extra work.

2. Don't fail to state in the agreement the amount of the professional's compensation, or the method of computing it.

3. Don't enter into a contract with a private corporation, or a public body, without verifying its right to make the contract and the authority of the signing officer to represent it.

4. Don't use unqualified contract words or phrases to which your client may attribute a meaning other than the one you intend.

5. Don't permit a cost limitation to be established in your agreement, either expressly or by implication, unless you are willing to accept the responsibilities involved.

6. Don't fail to restrict your obligation when it is necessary to include in the contract a reference to cost limitation, but it is recognized that you are not to suffer any penalties if actual cost exceeds the limitation.

7. Don't guarantee construction costs or permit a guarantee to be implied.

8. Don't overlook the importance of neutralizing unfair contract stipulations making your compensation subject to conditions beyond your control.

9. Don't select a basis for the professional's compensation which is inappropriate to the project at hand.

10. Don't fail to include specific rights and remedies to safeguard you against possible default in payment of compensation, especially in contracting with a foreign client.

11. Don't fail to be definite regarding compensation for prolonged contract administration.

12. Don't neglect to provide for appropriate payments to the professional in the event of abandonment of the project.

13. Don't fail to exercise the most advantageous remedy in case the client repudiates the agreement.

14. Don't forget that, unless specifically anticipated, a change in the membership of a professional partnership may dissolve an existing agreement with a client.

CHAPTER **2**

Legal Pitfalls in the Owner-Architect (Engineer) Relationship: Professional Services

When a prospective building owner engages an architect or engineer, it is not only because he believes that the professional has greater skill and knowledge in a specialized field, but also because he trusts the professional's honesty and good judgment; and he expects care and diligence to be exercised in applying these qualifications to the jobs at hand. And legal decisions have repeatedly certified to the validity of these beliefs and expectations.

2.1 Asserted Defects in Design. The client has been upheld by the court in his expectation that the architect or engineer will protect him from his own lack of technical knowledge, so that he may be provided with a building that will be suitable to its purpose, designed in the light of current legal restrictions, and reasonably well conceived in terms of today's technological knowledge. If there are defects in design, the courts frequently hold the professional responsible. Some courts rule that he impliedly warrants his design to be adequate for his client's purposes.

2.1.1 Responsibility re Purchase of Standard Building for Heavy Buses. Even if the professional does not, himself, "father the plan," but merely advises his client regarding the purchase of a standard building, his negligence may create responsibility on his part because of its unsuitability. For example, assume that an omnibus company, through the services of an architect, purchases from a nationally known supplier a standard building for the storage of buses. Actually, it is intended by the owner that heavy buses are to be stored in this building; however, due to the architect's failure to furnish proper information to the supplier, the building as furnished, although adequate for light buses, cannot support the buses belonging to the owner.

The fact that the design of the standard building is prepared by the supplier should not release the architect from responsibility for its adequacy, since, in this instance, it is his obligation to his client to exercise due care in providing a design which will meet his client's specific requirements. He should know that the storage of heavy buses is intended and must so advise the supplier. If he does not know and fails to make inquiry, it could hardly be urged by him that he exercised due care and that his failure did not constitute negligence. As an architect, he impliedly represents himself as possessed of such knowledge as is necessary for him to perform his duties. He does not have the legal prerogative to profess ignorance. It is incumbent upon him to take affirmative steps that are reasonably necessary in order to ascertain the facts. Despite the fact that the supplier prepares the plans for its standard building, the architect's contention that he relied upon the supplier's superior knowledge will be no defense to the owner's claim against him as an architect.

2.1.2   Use of Obsolete Site Survey. The necessity for the architect to check every layman's statement of his client concerning requirements and conditions is illustrated by an instance occurring in New York City several years ago. In accordance with the architect's request for a survey, his client furnished him with a survey which had been made twenty years previously. The architect used this survey as a basis for locating the new building. It was not until an exterior wall had been erected that it was discovered that, subsequent to the preparation of the old survey but prior to the design of the new building, the city had filed a map widening the street from 60 feet to 90 feet, so that the wall encroached substantially.

The city insisted on the removal of the encroaching portion of the building, and although the case was settled out of court, the architect wisely assumed the expense of this alteration. Although by agreement the furnishing of the survey was the responsibility of the client, it should not be assumed that in this instance the architect should have relied on its accuracy. Because of his technical knowledge and experience, he should not have used a survey made as much as twenty years before without questioning its accuracy.

2.1.3   Need to Verify Propriety of Using Particular Code. It is obvious that the architect is presumed to have a detailed knowledge of the building codes governing design and construction, and that he is duty-bound to his client as well as to the general public to prepare his plans and specifications in accordance with building code requirements. He would rightly be deemed negligent and responsible for injury or damage should he prepare contract documents in violation of the building code. Building codes vary from place to place, and even in the same place are revised from time to time as experience indicates the wisdom of amendments.

The importance of insuring that designs are prepared under the current statutory restrictions is exemplified by a case in a municipality which had formally adopted as its own building code the National Building Code recommended by the National Board of Fire Underwriters. Some time after a new building had been occupied by its owner, portions of the brick wall developed cracks. The owner alleged that this failure was a structural defect, and charged his architect with having designed a wall too weak for the loads it would have to carry, and further charged that the wall was so thin as to be in violation of the building code.

It developed that, subsequent to the city's adoption of the National Building Code, this code had been amended by the National Board of Fire Underwriters to permit thinner walls than the earlier code had specified. The architect's engineer had designed the allegedly offending wall in accordance with the latest edition of the code, but the city had never adopted the amendment to the code. Therefore, although the design had been prepared in good faith, the owner's allegation, that it was in violation of the code, technically was true.

It is hoped that all architects and engineers not only will ascertain whether the municipalities, in which their projects are located and which have adopted the National Building Code, also have adopted current amendments thereto, but in addition will urge the adoption by such municipalities of such amendments as may be lacking.

The influence that building codes exert upon professional practice is enormous, and legal hazards of the architect or engineer are multiplied because of the diversity of standards set by different local codes and because of the rapidity with which codes become obsolete owing to technological progress. Every architect and engineer owes it to the community and to his profession to work vigorously, through his professional societies, to focus public attention upon these problems, so that legal regulations may be better founded in current knowledge and practice.

2.1.4   *How Hot Is Hot?* One of the purposes of a building is normally that it provide a comfortable environment for the occupants. Although some clients establish specific standards of temperature and humidity which must be met in design, more usually the client expects the architect to create a comfortable environment. However, individual criteria of comfort vary, and a client may seek to charge an architect with negligence or incompetence if, upon moving into his new building, he is dissatisfied with the degree of comfort provided by the design.

A few years ago, a well-known firm of architects found itself defending an arbitration proceeding commenced by its client, a board of education, which claimed that the architects had created an uncomfortable school building and demanded damages of almost 2 million dollars. The architects had designed a complex of seventeen school buildings, comprising a senior and a junior high school, costing over 10 million dollars. In the year in which the school was first opened, September was very warm. Students, many of whom undoubtedly came from air-conditioned homes, complained to their parents that the new classrooms were too hot. Some of the parents could not understand why a 10 million dollar school did not have air conditioning. As dissatisfaction grew, the parent-teacher association became involved, thermal-environment committees were formed, and the controversy received widespread attention through the newspapers. Embarrassed by this adverse publicity, the architects attempted to pacify the trustees of the school, but to no avail. The trustees continued to assert that the school was hot, but no one defined "How hot is hot?"

The board of education finally employed an engineering firm to investigate conditions and to make recommendations for overcoming the alleged excessive heat. After detailed studies, the engineering firm reported that, in its opinion, an air-conditioning plant should be installed, at an estimated cost of $1,700,000. At last, four years after the school had been completed, an arbitration proceeding was instituted, in which the board of education demanded damages from the architects in the amount of $1,700,000.

An expert, testifying for the board, contended that there was inordinate heat gain in the classrooms because the buildings, of light construction with large expanses of glass walls, had been arranged so that a great many of these glass walls faced southerly and thus admitted solar heat. The architects' counsel countered that, at the insistence of the board, the senior high school and the junior high school had been separated, and linked together by a central cafeteria and boiler room designed to serve both schools. Because of this central building, and because of the shape of the site, a more desirable solar orientation of the classrooms could not be achieved.

The classrooms were equipped with unit ventilators at the exterior walls, to draw in outside air (and heat it during the winter months) and distribute it throughout the classrooms. The board contended that the units were inadequate for the purposes intended and that they contributed to malodorous conditions, variously described by teachers as being reminiscent of a body odor, chemicals, or cigar smoke. Architects' counsel suggested in his interrogation that these odors could be more reasonably ascribed to other causes—children returning to class after physical activities, chemicals used in cleaning the rooms, cigar-smoking groundskeepers working immediately outside the unit ventilators. The contention that the unit ventilators were inadequate was countered by evidence that the children had turned off the units—even though special locks had been installed—and had opened the sash, contrary to the intent of the design.

The design contemplated that used air would leave the classrooms through louvered corridor doors and would be exhausted through the roof by a central mechanical exhaust system. The board's expert expressed the opinion that this system was inadequate and that the architects should have specified a positive mechanical exhaust from each classroom. However, the defense showed that the system recommended by this expert was prohibited under the circumstances by regulations of the commissioner of education.

Finally, this case was resolved in favor of the architects after it was demonstrated among other things: (1) that under the State Education Law the architects were required to submit plans to the state commissioner for approval; (2) that the commissioner had in fact approved the plans in this instance; and (3) that under the law, the commissioner may not approve plans or specifications for a school building unless such documents adequately provide not only for the health and safety of the pupils, but also for "comfortable conditions in the school building."

Although in this instance the architects, in effect, were able to fix responsibility for deciding "How hot is hot?" upon the state commissioner, it is obvious that they received considerable unwarranted and undesirable publicity as a result of the question being raised.

2.2 Contract Documents. The documents forming the basis for a contract between his client and a building contractor are usually prepared by the architect. Through long usage, these documents have assumed a general organizational pattern, being subdivided into the agreement, the general conditions of the contract (general, supplementary, and other conditions), the drawings, and the specifications. Conventionally, the agreement recites the promise of the contractor to erect a building in accordance with the contract documents, and the promise of the owner to pay the contractor certain monies for so doing. The general conditions amplify the business and legal relationships of the contracting parties, while the drawings and the specifications describe the physical project. The drawings describe the quantities and locations of materials, while the specifications describe the quality of materials and the method of assembling them. This disposition of information is conventional but not obligatory, and varies in minor detail for reasons of convenience.

In case of a conflict between the several contract documents, court decisions have given the specifications precedence over the drawings and the agreement over either. However, the documents are intended to be complementary, and in the absence of conflict, what is called for by any one is as binding as if called for by all. Therefore, there is no advantage in adding to the agreement many stipulations which might be placed in the specifications instead.

In the preparation of the general conditions of the contract, it is strongly recommended that the Standard Form of the American Institute of Architects be used. Even in cases where the Standard Form is not sufficiently comprehensive, or does not represent in all details the intent of the contracting parties, it is advantageous to include the Standard Form and to modify it where necessary by supplementary general conditions. The Standard General Conditions promulgated by the American Institute of Architects have received the approval of many contractors' associations, and most contractors are familiar with them and reassured by their inclusion in the contract.

Despite the fact that court records are replete with decisions establishing the legal force and advantage of provisions of this document, one may not maintain that no legal difficulty can ensue in any instance where the Standard Form is used. The architect is not relieved from the duty to exercise his technical knowledge and judgment merely because he uses the Standard Form.

It is impossible as a practical matter to cover every contingency in the standard general conditions. Supplementary general conditions are almost inevitable if the document is to meet accurately all the requirements peculiar to a particular project. In the writing of supplementary general conditions, one must be careful not to contradict the standard general conditions which they are to supplement. Where an ambiguity occurs through a conflict between the general conditions and the supplementary conditions written especially for the specific contract, it is presumed that these supplementary conditions more accurately reflect the understanding of the parties than do the printed standard general conditions. Suggested supplementary general conditions which are considered to be of value will be found on page 294.

2.2.1 *Danger in Not Identifying All Documents.* Because of the binding nature of the contract documents, it is desirable to have both parties identify each page of all these documents by initialing them at the time of signing the contract. Every drawing and every page of the specifications should be so initialed, in order to preclude a charge that a different page has been substituted, or a plea of ignorance, in the event of a disagreement between owner and contractor or between owner and architect.

A case in point involved the glazing of a synagogue. The architect had specified both clear and colored glass in a large glazed wall—clear glass above, to illuminate a canopy which the congregation intended to suspend from the ceiling and colored glass below. Later, it was decided not to install the canopy, and when the building was completed, the congregation was dissatisfied with the strong light and accompanying glare in the sanctuary.

The contention was made at the trial that the architect had specified clear glass without the knowledge and consent of the owner.

Fortunately for the architect, however, he had insisted, at the time of signing the contract, that the president of the congregation initial every page, including an elevation drawing clearly showing colored glass below and clear glass above.

In another instance involving an apartment building in New York City, it appeared that a plastering contractor agreed to plaster a seven-story building "according to the plans furnished." The plasterer testified that he had received all plans except those for the basement and bulkhead, and since he was to plaster the building according to the plans furnished, he contended that he was not obliged to plaster the basement and bulkhead. The owner claimed that a complete set of plans had been delivered, and that in any event, since reference to a seven-story building was made in the contract, it was the plasterer's obligation to plaster the seven-story building completely.

In this case, there was no written proof as to what plans had actually been the basis for the contract. The court accepted the plasterer's version of the facts, and ruled that under the law the contract was not to plaster a seven-story building, but was to plaster a seven-story building "according to the plans furnished," and since the plans for the basement and bulkhead were never furnished, the plasterer was not required to do this work.[19] Such misunderstandings could result in serious injustices unless the contract documents are clearly and unmistakably identified.

2.2.2   General Imperfections in Specification Writing. In the writing of the specifications, which constitute an order for materials and labor, completeness and clarity are of prime importance. Unlike other types of literary effort, specifications are not improved by the use of terms which are more or less synonymous in order to avoid repetition and to achieve euphony. In specifications, which are contract documents, the word expressing the exact intention should be repeated as often as is necessary to make the meaning clear. Among the causes of ambiguity are the imperfection of language and the variant modes of expression in use by different individuals. Therefore, definitions of certain terms should be included in the supplementary general conditions—not always the dictionary definitions, but the meaning of the words as used in the contract. In practice, some words are susceptible of numerous interpretations. If a unit price on excavation is mentioned, what is the definition of "per cubic yard of earth"? Is it measured in its original situation, in transit, or placed as fill in a new location? What is the exact distinction between the words "earth" and "rock"?

Completeness does not imply verbosity. Unnecessary repetition, long sentences, and the use of obscure terms contribute to misunderstandings and tend to create legal problems. Despite an unquestioned desire to communicate their instructions, drafters of specifications do not always use the most apt words to express their intent, and superfluous words are often used—perhaps owing to an unnecessary abundance of caution on the part of the writer.

Streamlining, the deletion of language having no force, when employed judiciously, is a major contribution to the improvement of specifications.

Through this method words having no legal significance can be omitted from a specification without changing its meaning, and only those words will be inserted which appear essential upon mature consideration. The use of fewer words will prevent the work from seeming more difficult than it actually is, and provided these fewer words are clear and of specific import, it will simplify the document and thereby avoid confusion. However, the deletions must be done with extreme care, in order to avoid ambiguity.

2.2.3 The Intent That Was "Concealed." The omission of a single word, at first glance appearing repetitious, resulted in an action tried some years ago. A subcontractor sued a general contractor to recover a balance claimed to be due under a contract which provided, among other things, for the furnishing of insulation around heating pipes. The general contractor resisted payment, claiming that the subcontractor had failed to complete the work by omitting to cover approximately 25,000 feet of radiator connections. The radiator connections which the subcontractor had failed to cover were exposed connections. The specifications provided that "all concealed heating risers and radiator connections shall be covered." The subcontractor claimed that the word "concealed" related not only to the heating risers but also to the radiator connections, and therefore he was obliged to cover radiator connections only if they were concealed. On the other hand, the general contractor claimed that the word "concealed" was limited to heating risers, and therefore the subcontractor was bound to cover all radiator connections whether they were concealed or exposed. Under a contract provision that in any dispute the architect's decision was to be final, the architect ruled for the subcontractor, and the court refused to interfere with the architect's decision.[20]

2.2.4 Specifying Methods as Well as Results. A fundamental principle of specification writing is that a specific way of doing a job or of producing material may not be described or specified if a guaranteed result is to be demanded. It has been established by court decisions, and reasonably so, that if one must guarantee the result of his work, and assume the responsibility implied in a guarantee, he must have latitude to accomplish the work in a manner which he is confident will achieve the desired result.

A leading case on this aspect of the specification writer's obligations involved the erection of a courthouse and prison. The plaintiff contracted to furnish all the necessary materials and labor to make watertight a boiler room, in accordance with the specifications. The specifications were most precise as to all details of materials and construction. However, the boiler room did not remain waterproof; immediately after completion of the job a considerable amount of water and dampness became evident—notwithstanding that every requirement of the plans and specifications had been complied with literally. The contractor was forced to sue to recover the contract price. The case eventually reached the highest tribunal of the state. In holding for the contractor (plaintiff), the court stated:

The promise is not to make water tight, but to make water tight by following the plans and specifications prepared by the defendant, from which the plaintiff [contractor] had no right to depart, even if the departure would have produced a waterproof cellar. . . . There was no discretion as to the materials used or the manner in which the work should be done. The plaintiff had no alternative except to follow the plan under the direction of the defendant's officers in charge. The defendant [owner] relied upon the skill of its engineer in preparing the plan, with the most minute specifications, and bound the plaintiff to absolute conformity therewith.

. . .If the plan and specifications were defective it was not the fault of the plaintiff, but of the defendant, for it caused them to be made and it alone had the power to alter them. . . . If there was an implied warranty of sufficiency, it was made by the party who prepared the plan and specifications, because they were its work, and in calling for proposals to produce a specified result by following them, it may fairly be said to have warranted them adequate to produce that result. . . . The responsibility rests upon the party who fathers the plan and specifications and presents it to the other with the implied representation that it is adequate for the purpose to be accomplished.[21]

In another case the specification provided that a subcontractor was to furnish a cellar floor of concrete with cement topping, and that it was to be made perfectly watertight. The plans showed the floor to be 6 inches thick. However, neither the plans nor the specifications provided in detail for the method by which the contractor was to build the floor. Immediately after the floor was finished, water burst through and flowed in to a depth of 9 inches. In the ensuing lawsuit the court held that the contractor had agreed to furnish an absolutely watertight floor, and that since the details of construction were not incorporated in the contract documents, the contractor had the option to build in any way he pleased, of the materials named, so long as he made the floor waterproof. This he failed to accomplish, and therefore the court held in favor of the owner.[22]

In the first of these two cases, where the contractor was not bound on his guarantee to attain the intended result, the method of construction was specified in detail. In the second case he also guaranteed a result, but as the details were not specified, he was required to exercise his own judgment and discretion and to produce a watertight floor.

If the results expressly guaranteed or impliedly warranted by the contractor are not attained, the owner does not necessarily waive his rights against the latter by requiring him to adopt measures protecting the owner's property. In one case in point, no architect had been employed, and the contractor drew the contract, plans, and specifications for a residence in New York. The contract required the foundation wall to have a firm footing of concrete of a certain size.

Although somewhat larger footings were actually provided, the filled ground was not strong enough to support the building, and during progress of the work the house began to settle, until the front was about 6 inches lower than the rear.

Such a spectacular defect, of course, did not escape the notice of the owner, who then required the contractor to underpin the foundation and jack up the building, and refused to make any payment until this work had been done.

The result, however, was unsatisfactory, and the owner refused final payment to the contractor, claiming that the contract was not performed in a good and workmanlike manner. The court, in an action to foreclose a mechanic's lien for the unpaid balance, said that if the plans and specifications had provided detailed instructions as to placing the footings and the character of the underlying soil, the risk would lie with the owner. However, in this case the plans were silent as to the method of contructing the foundation. In such case, normally it would be the duty of the contractor to construct it upon solid ground, so as to produce a level structure, even though it might be necessary to make greater excavation or to provide more substantial fill. Nevertheless, the lower court found that in this instance, by requiring the contractor to underpin the foundation and jack up the building, the owner had waived the defective construction and thereafter could not hold the contractor to an implied obligation to build a level structure. The appellate court, however, held that the evidence did not justify a finding that the substantial defect had been waived by the owner.[23]

2.2.5   *When Is a Tower "Knocked Down"?* The necessity for exact definitions of words used in the contract is exemplified by a court case arising out of the exact meaning of the words "knocked down." Plaintiff, a steel erector, had contracted with a general contractor to assemble and erect a four-legged self-supporting steel television tower, 760 feet in height. The specifications stated that the tower was to be shipped "knocked down," and that the steel erector was not to perform any fabrication. The contract drawings showed the tower to be comprised of trusses, each truss made up of complete members of two angles back to back, as well as single members. The drawings further depicted the bolts to be inserted at the end connections, but did not indicate the intermediate stitch bolts necessary to attach gusset plates to the composite members at secondary connections.

The erector, in bidding on the job, therefore assumed that when the specifications stated that the tower would be shipped "knocked down," the specifications did not mean completely knocked down, but rather partially knocked down, to the extent that the composite members would have been formed in the steel fabricator's plant and shipped with gusset plates inserted between the component parts of each composite member, and that his own work with respect to such members would be confined to the assembling of those end connections therefor, for which bolts were shown on the drawings. Several weeks after the contract had been signed, the general contractor furnished the steel erector with detailed erection drawings, as promised in the contract. These erection drawings showed stitch bolts to form composite members and bolts to attach gusset plates, none of these bolts having appeared on the original contract drawings. Shortly thereafter the tower was shipped to the job completely disassembled, necessitating the insertion of approximately 50,000 bolts instead of an estimated 12,000 bolts called for by the contract drawings.

At the trial the steel erector contended that the erection drawings altered the scope of the work, and that it was never contemplated that the tower would be shipped completely knocked down, but rather knocked down to the extent previously indicated. He urged further that in this instance there was no conflict between the drawings and specifications; on the contrary they could be reconciled so that the usual rule, which gives precedence to specifications over drawings, in case of a conflict, did not apply. The general contractor claimed that the term "knocked down" as used in the specifications was an absolute term that meant the tower would be shipped completely disassembled.

The court charged the jury that the drawings and specifications were inseparable; that they must be read and considered together. The court further charged that the contractor by its invitation to bid represented that the drawings and specifications were adequate for bidding purposes and that the steel erector was entitled to rely thereon. The jury returned a verdict in favor of the steel erector. In order to have avoided this dispute, the general contractor should have defined the term "knocked down"; or he could have conveyed his intent more clearly by a provision in the specifications such as: "Make all connections, whether or not shown on the drawings." Curiously enough, such a provision was embodied in the specifications which formed part of the contract documents between the general contractor and the owner, but for some reason, never revealed, it was not incorporated in the specifications submitted to the steel erector when he was invited to bid on the job.

2.2.6 *Confusion in Describing Scope of Work.* Although plans and specifications are considered to be inseparable parts of the same instructions, confusion may result if the scope of the work is described in part in the specifications and in part in the drawings, but not completely shown in either document alone.

Heating specifications for a hospital required some ducts to be stainless steel and others to be of galvanized steel, as follows:

47. Stainless steel vent ducts are required for Kitchen, Serving Rooms, Hoods, and elsewhere where indicated on the drawings as stainless steel.
48. Galvanized sheet steel: All ducts not otherwise noted on the drawings or specified shall be constructed of galvanized sheet steel.

A ninth-floor drawing was the only drawing specifically indicating stainless steel ducts. The heating contractor urged that stainless steel was required on that floor only. Under protest, he installed stainless steel ducts in the kitchen, serving rooms, and hoods, on all floors. He sued for the difference in cost between stainless steel and galvanized steel ducts installed by him at all areas, other than the ninth floor. The court interpreted the above provisions as contemplating two categories of locations where stainless steel was to be used: (1) where "specified" and (2) where shown on drawings. Consequently the claim was dismissed.[24]

2.2.7   The Detestable "Ditto" in Finish Schedule. Another instance of confusion, not so readily resolved, centered about a single small "ditto" in a finish schedule. Plaintiff, a plastering subcontractor, sued to recover for extra work and materials which he claimed was due under a contract in which he agreed to do all the plastering work for a building in accordance with certain plans and specifications which contained a "Finish Schedule," as follows:

Finish number	Concrete walls and columns	Hollow tile or brick walls
1	Cement plaster	Cement plaster
2	Gypsum plaster	Gypsum plaster
3	Cement plaster	Cement plaster
4	Concrete plywood forms	Cement plaster
5	Concrete plywood forms	ditto

Plaintiff, the plasterer, testified that in preparing his bid on the job he had failed to include the finishing work designated as number 5 on this schedule. This came about, as he contended, because the use of the word "ditto" was misleading and ambiguous. He had read item number 5 horizontally, as though the word "ditto" referred to the second column where the words "concrete plywood forms" appear and not to the words "cement plaster" above the word "ditto." The general contractor insisted that the plasterer was compelled to do finish number 5. The plasterer did the work under protest, and subsequently demanded payment for it as extra work. The litigation that followed was protracted and endured for several years. Ultimately an appellate court decided for the general contractor in a 3 to 2 decision. It is interesting to note that the two judges in the minority believed the schedule should be read horizontally; that if intended to be read vertically, the word "ditto" should have appeared also in item number 4, which was the same as item number 3 above.[25]

2.2.8   *Unsound Utilization of Subsurface Data.* In issuing plans and specifications for bidding purposes, it is impliedly represented that these documents are adequate for bidding and that the bidder is entitled to rely thereon. Although in most bidding or contractual forms, including standard forms, the bidder signs a statement or otherwise acknowledges that he has visited the site and examined all conditions affecting the work, it is not expected that each bidder will make his own subsurface exploration. It is more economical, and hence more usual, to furnish all bidders with the results of test borings made at the owner's expense. These preliminary borings are too few in number to guarantee all subsurface conditions, but are sufficiently frequent to permit a more realistic bid than could be made without them. A high groundwater table increases the cost of performing the work and is one of the items usually recorded during those preliminary site explorations.

These tests are useful to the bidders, however, only if the complete results are furnished to them. In one instance, a boring company had been employed to examine the site, and the boring company furnished the architect with a site plan showing the location of tests and the type of bearing found at different levels at each location. For the information of bidders, the architect traced this information and issued it as one drawing of the set bearing his own title block. Included on the original drawings were small triangles, one at each test location, some triangles filled and some open. The symbol legend did not explain their significance. This drawing was accurately traced in the architect's office, showing the triangles on the plan but not identifying them. Unfortunately, the architect did not question the boring company and the successful bidder did not question the architect, for these triangles, properly interpreted, indicated a very high water table.

The proposal form contained the usual stipulation that the bidder was to visit the site and examine all conditions affecting the work. The successful bidder had in fact visited the site, but did not discern the presence of groundwater.

When construction started and the contractor discovered a serious water condition, he made claim against the owner for additional expenses incurred in dewatering the site, asserting that he was misled by the factual representation. In essence, he contended that his bid had contemplated a dry site and that since no water level had been recorded on the architect's drawings, although water must have been found in the original borings, he was prejudiced financially. Ultimately, the dispute was resolved by a substantial award in favor of the contractor.

Three lessons can be learned from this unfortunate dispute. First, before using a boring sheet, or tracing it into his own set, an architect should exercise every reasonable effort to make certain that the boring sheet is clear, unambiguous, and understandable. Second, if a review by the architect of a boring sheet indicates any ambiguity, or need for further clarification, he should communicate promptly with the testing company and make every effort to eliminate any possible doubt. Finally, in the absence of a compelling reason to the contrary, it is advisable to exclude the boring drawings from the contract documents, and merely make them available at the architect's office for inspection by the contractor, while at the same time disclaiming any representation or guarantee as to their completeness or accuracy; making it clear in a cautionary provision that the bidders must visit the site and make their own independent investigations, in a manner similar to the following:

SITE INVESTIGATION

The Contractor acknowledges that he has satisfied himself as to the nature and location of the work, the general and local conditions, particularly those bearing upon transportation, disposal, handling and storage of materials, availability of labor, water, electric power, roads and uncertainties of weather, groundwater table or similar physical conditions at the site, the conformation and condition of the ground, the character, quality and quantity of surface and sub-surface materials to be encountered, the character of equipment and facilities needed prior to and during the prosecution of the work and all other matters which can in any way affect the work or the cost thereof under this Contract. Any failure by the Contractor to acquaint himself with all the available information concerning these conditions will not relieve him from responsibility for estimating properly the difficulty or cost of successfully performing the work.

BORINGS AND SUB-SURFACE DATA

The Contractor may examine the logs of soundings, borings, rock cores and other sub-surface data, if available, by making a request therefor to the Architect. Such data is offered in good faith solely for the purpose of placing the Contractor in receipt of all information available, and in no event is to be considered a part of the Contract Documents. The Contractor must interpret such data according to his own judgment and acknowledges that he is not relying upon the same as accurately describing the sub-surface conditions which may be found to exist. The Contractor further acknowledges that he assumes all risks contingent upon the nature of the sub-surface conditions to be actually encountered by him in performing the work covered by the Contract, even though such actual conditions may result in the Contractor performing more or less work than he originally anticipated.

2.2.9 *Delay Compounded by Inadequate Information.* No subsurface investigations whatever were made in connection with a building project, and the actual foundation work differed so materially from that contemplated by the contract drawings that the completion of the building was delayed by almost a year. The unfortunate owner not only was denied use of the building for this period, but also was made defendant in a lawsuit by the contractor for the superstructure, who had nothing to do with the foundations except that his contract read: "The work of this contract is contingent upon the execution of the foregoing work by the Foundation Contractor, and shall follow said work in orderly sequence."

The plans and specifications for the foundation had been submitted to the contractor for the superstructure before bidding for information pertaining to work included in the foundation contract. A date was specified in the contract relating to the construction of the superstructure, for the completion of the foundation work, and the superstructure contractor assumed that he would start his own work on or about this date, particularly as the simple foundation work shown on the drawings could have been completed well before this date.

The foundation plans which had been furnished to the contractor for the superstructure showed only the existence of two small brick buildings on the site. In excavating to set footings, the foundation contractor uncovered a veritable maze of old walls and masonry footings, in part on wood piles driven into the bottom of a former pond. The owner's representative then directed borings to be made and, based upon conditions disclosed thereby, amended the foundation contract to include removal of old foundations and to fit actual site conditions.

As a result of the additional work required of the foundation contractor, the superstructure contractor was delayed in completing his work for nine months beyond the expected completion date, causing him to incur additional expense in the performance of his work. The superstructure contractor sued to recover from the owner these additional expenses which consisted of the following items:

1. The amount by which the salaries of mechanics and laborers had increased during the period of delay.

2. The increased cost of workmen's compensation.

3. The partial erection of the building in two sections (as was required to be done) increased the cost thereof.

4. Some of the subcontractors had their products and materials ready for delivery before the site was ready to receive them and were obliged to store them.

5. The work of erecting steel, setting granite, constructing floor and roof arches, laying of concrete, and setting of gypsum block was each more expensive to perform in winter than in warm weather.

6. And the cost of bronze increased during the period of delay.

The court, in upholding a recovery by the superstructure contractor, held that the latter had a contract to erect the superstructure as soon as the foundations were completed and that it entered into its contract upon the representations of the owner and upon plans and specifications submitted by it indicating that the foundation work could be done within three weeks—

rather than nine months later. The superstructure contractor had a right to rely on these plans and specifications for bidding purposes. Although the information to bidders required the superstructure contractor to visit the site and familiarize himself with the conditions under which the work was to be executed, the court ruled that he was not obliged to make soundings and borings to discover whether the plans and specifications regarding the foundations were true or false—since the work of the superstructure contractor was to commence only when the foundations were finished.[26]

2.3   *Administration of Construction Contracts (On-site Inspections).* On-site inspection services by the architect are presently referred to as a part of "Administration of the Construction Contract" by framers of standard forms of agreement between owner and architect. These forms properly and clearly emphasize that such services do not contemplate continuous and exhaustive on-site investigations, which, if desired by the owner, may be secured by the engagement of a project representative.

For many years, such inspections by the architect were called "supervision." Because owners sometimes mistakenly assumed from this word that the architect was bound to oversee everything that the contractor did in erecting the building, the standard forms later were changed to read "general and periodic supervision." However, even when the unqualified word "supervision" was used, courts interpreted it to mean general and periodic supervision as distinguished from continuous personal superintendence. In recognizing that the supervising architect is not bound to spend all of his time at a building being constructed under his professional care so that no negligence or fraud will be committed by any contractor or by anyone else, one court, in a leading case, aptly described the responsibility of the supervising architect in the following language:

The counsel would not contend that the architect is an insurer of the perfection of the mason work, the carpenter work, plumbing, etc. He is bound only to exercise reasonable care, and to use reasonable powers of observation and detection, in the supervision of the structure. When, therefore, it appears that the architect has made frequent visits to the building, and in a general way has performed the duties called for by the custom of his profession, the mere fact, for instance, that inferior brick have been used in places, does not establish, as a matter of law, that he has not entirely performed his contract. He might have directed at one of his visits that portions of the plumbing work be packed in wool; upon his next return to the building the pipes in question might have been covered with brick in the progress of the building. If he had inquired whether the wool-packing had been attended to, and had received an affirmative answer from the plumber and the bricklayer, I am of the opinion that his duty as an architect, in the matter of the required protection of said pipes from the weather, would have been ended. Yet, under these very circumstances, the packing might have been intentionally or carelessly omitted in fraud upon both architect and owner, and could it still be claimed that the architect had not fully performed his work? . . . An architect is no more a mere overseer or foreman or watchman than he is a guarantor of a flawless building, and the only question that can arise in a case where general performance of duty is shown is whether, considering all the circumstances and peculiar facts involved, he has or has not been guilty of negligence. This is a question of fact, and not of law. [27]

However, it must be borne in mind that when an owner employs an architect to oversee the erection of a building, he has the right to, and undoubtedly does, rely on the architect to exercise vigilance. In a New York case, the owner engaged a competent architect to draw plans for the construction of a seven-story building and to supervise its erection. The contractor's foreman made the mistake of placing a central column which supported the upper part of the building upon an insecure foundation which did not rest on solid ground, but upon backfilled earth. As a result of this defect, the building collapsed and fifteen people lost their lives.

There was evidence that the architect did not make a careful inspection of this detail of the work; had he done so, he might have discovered that the concrete was being laid on disturbed ground outside an old cistern wall. Though the suit was brought against the owner and not against the architect or contractor, the court in relieving the owner from any liability made the following significant observations:

In this case the owner was not competent himself to plan the building which he desired to erect. . . . He was not competent to construct or superintend the construction. . . . It was his duty to devolve these things upon persons possessing sufficient knowledge and skill to accomplish the result intended, with safety to the workmen and the public. . . . In other words, he committed the whole matter to a competent expert. . . . If the architect, who had general supervision, had insisted upon a careful inspection of every detail of the work and had been present when the concrete was about to be laid upon the disturbed ground outside the old cistern wall, he might have discovered a departure from the terms of the contract in that respect and prevented it. . . . He [the owner] omitted nothing that can be made the basis of a charge of personal negligence in going about the undertaking. He took all such measures to construct the building that any reasonably prudent man would under the same circumstances.

In concluding its opinion, the court stated:

No one could reasonably anticipate or guard against the unfortunate result, except the experts employed to plan and erect the building. [28]

2.4 Professional Negligence. Sometimes damage suits against architects are justified; not infrequently they have no valid legal basis. Experience has proved that clients will sometimes resort to extreme measures, including distorted, misleading, and false evidence, in an attempt to defeat the architect wishing to collect compensation justly earned. In one case, a well-known architect was charged by a client, for whom he had designed a large country house, with negligence supposedly indicated by various leaking parts which had caused damage. The client's butler testified that on a certain day during a rainstorm he was obliged to use 136 of his employer's $6.50 towels to absorb the water. The case finally exploded when it was established that on that same day other residents of the community, who did not have so many or such expensive towels, were obliged to use pumps to get the water out of their homes—for on this day a hurricane had occurred.

The preponderance of court decisions in a majority of the states indicates that the architect or engineer does not guarantee perfection in his plans and specifications, nor does he guarantee that a satisfactory building will result from his work. Although he may explicitly make such a guarantee—and if he does, the courts will hold him to his promise—such a promise will not be read into a contract by implication. A long history of precedent upholds the opinion that an architect or engineer is not ordinarily liable for defects, even if he has made a mistake, if he possesses the degree of skill and knowledge usually possessed by a member of his profession, and if he exercises reasonable care and diligence in applying his skill and knowledge to the situation in hand. However, if his skill and care fall below this standard, he may be adjudged liable for negligence.

The mere fact that an architect or engineer makes an error is not in itself evidence of negligence, so long as he has exercised reasonable care. This is illustrated by an instance in which the supervising architect failed to discover that a balcony and adjacent windows were constructed 2¾ inches higher than was shown on the drawings. The defect was caused by the mason's not having accurately followed the architect's plans. The court exonerated the architect, in substance, saying:

It was not his duty to do the work. The mason agreed to lay out his work himself. The architect was bound to put down on paper how every part was to be built, and the mason was to stake out, measure his lumber and make actual measurements in the construction work. It was not the duty of the architect to determine the elevations by actual measurements. The architect was diligent in his supervision and he had bestowed as much attention upon the building as was necessary. The fact that he did not discover this variation did not prove negligence on his part. It might have passed his observation, until the building was completed.[29]

In the final analysis, the question of negligence is one of fact, and the burden of proof rests upon the client. The standard of due care expected of an architect depends on the facts of each case. In general, it is recommended that the architect visit the job as frequently as is reasonably possible; that he keep detailed written records of his inspections, and wherever practical provide the owner with copies; and that written records be kept of conferences with the owner. Proof of frequent visits and the retention of detailed records of inspection are cogent evidence of care and vigilance and should persuade the triers of the facts that the architect has done everything that a reasonably prudent architect would do under similar circumstances. With evidence of such care before them, and considering that the architect is not a guarantor of a flawless building, it is reasonable to expect that, in the average case, the judge, jury, or arbitrators will exonerate an architect against whom a charge of negligence, arising out of supervision or on-site inspections, is made.

2.4.1 Unjustified Reliance on Manufacturer's Representations. A firm of architects was engaged to prepare plans and specifications for a weaving mill and to supervise its construction. The clients' industrial process required the building to be air-conditioned to maintain a temperature of 80°F and a humidity of 60 percent moisture. To prevent leakage and condensation, the architects specified foam glass insulation under a built-up roof, but because of a material shortage they changed the plans to fiber glass insulation, relying on the advertising of the manufacturer as to its adequacy, which the architects accepted without question. The architects did not specify a vapor seal, and the insulation soon became saturated, soggy, and inefficient, causing such high condensation on the ceiling of the buildings that a new roof had to be constructed so that the weaving process could be carried on. The mill owners sued the architects for damages.

Testimony brought forth the facts that the architects were aware of the intended use of the building, that they knew that the problem of proper insulation was of prime importance, and that they specified insulation which proved unsatisfactory, without making any tests to determine that moisture would not infiltrate, or making any investigation to determine whether the material had been used satisfactorily in similar buildings. Under such conditions the architects were held responsible.[30] A similar conclusion was reached by another court in the case referred to below.

2.4.2 Professional Liability Insurance—a Change in Coverage. When a client is sufficiently dissatisfied with his building, he may sue his architect or engineer. Even when such suits are successfully defended by the professional, he is put to considerable expense and worry, as well as mortification, by the action. Most professionals today carry professional liability insurance to protect themselves against loss arising out of damage or injury attributable to their errors or omissions. Policies of professional liability insurance should be carefully reviewed, because the scope of coverage varies from company to company, as do stipulations regarding the right of the company to select legal counsel and to defend claims or adjust settlements. Among the companies presently underwriting this type of insurance, there is no uniformity regarding coverage before or after the policy period. For instance, the policy written by company A covers claims made after expiration or cancellation of the policy, based on an error, a mistake, or an omission made during the policy period, but only if the insured gave notice thereof during the policy period. The policy written by company B covers mistakes, errors, or omissions occurring prior to the inception of the policy, provided further that the insured had no knowledge of them. In addition, some time limitation may be imposed in order to obtain retroactive coverage. The insurance company may not wish to insure against errors or omissions committed more than three years prior to the new coverage being obtained. Therefore, a professional who, while unaware of a prior error or any intimation of any such error, changes from company A to company B policy, maintaining at all times continuous errors or omissions coverage, would find that a claim asserted against him during the life of policy B, for an error made during the life of policy A, would be covered by policy B only if he had obtained retroactive coverage *and* the error or omission was not excluded in point of time.

The mere fact that one carries adequate insurance against liability for his errors and omissions is not necessarily proof against trouble, as can be seen from the following case in which an architectural firm was forced to sue an insurance company for money expended to settle a claim for alleged malpractice.

The architects had designed a hospital under the "Standard Form of Agreement between Owner and Architect" issued by the American Institute of Architects. Although the architects were ultimately responsible/to their client for the design of a heating system, they employed a firm of heating engineers to design the system which became the subject of dispute.

The system was a radiant heating system, designed to provide about 15 percent of the total required heat by hot water flowing through copper tubing embedded in the concrete floor, with the remainder supplied by copper tubing installed in the plaster ceiling. Although this is a commonly used and effective method of heating, it is obvious that a poor installation can be very costly to repair.

After the hospital was under construction, the Federal government prohibited the use of copper for such purposes, as a result of the Korean war. Unwilling to delay completion of the hospital, the client requested the architects to find a substitute for copper tubing. The architects found a tin-plated steel tubing, which the manufacturer represented to be an equivalent substitute suitable for use in place of copper. The engineers who had designed the original system thought the substitution would be suitable, and the hospital board agreed to the change. So the steel tubing was installed, without, however, any change being made in the design from that specified for copper.

When the heating installation was about one-half completed, the architects secured professional liability insurance, which required the insurance company:

To pay on behalf of the Insured all sums which the Insured shall become obligated to pay by reason of the liability imposed upon him by law for damages, including damages for care and loss of services, because of bodily injury, sickness or disease, including death at any time resulting therefrom, sustained by any person or persons; and because of injury to or destruction of property, including the loss of use thereof, all in direct consequence of any negligent act, error or omission of the Insured resulting in accident, in the performance of professional services for others in the Insured's profession as architect.

It was only a matter of months after completion when the hospital began to suffer a series of leaks in both the floor and ceiling systems. When notified of this situation, the architects called upon the contractor to make repairs. However, the number of leaks increased so rapidly that it soon became apparent that piecemeal repairs could not correct the difficulty. The hospital employed a heating engineer to investigate conditions and make recommendations. He reported that the ceiling system had broken down because of failure to install expansion joints and sufficient anchors necessitated by the less pliable steel in contrast to copper tubing. The pipes installed in the concrete floor had corroded away.

The hospital then made demand on the architects for the cost of correcting the situation, estimated at between $40,000 and $50,000. The architects submitted this demand to the insurance company, which denied coverage. The architects finally negotiated a settlement with the hospital in the amount of $956.66, but the insurance company refused to pay even this greatly reduced amount, and the architects instituted suit against the company.

In defending this suit, the insurance company contended that no negligence had been established in the performance of the architects' duty to the hospital; that the negligence, if any, was in design, and the design was made by someone other than the architects, and made prior to the policy period; and finally that even if the architects were negligent, their negligence did not occur during the policy period.

The court found, however, that the architects were negligent in their duty to the hospital, saying:

The evidence also discloses that plaintiffs [architects] knew nothing of the material or its use; they made no independent effort to ascertain the true suitability of the substitute material and if it could be safely installed in the precise manner originally prescribed for the copper tubing. . . . "It ill behooves a man professing professional skill to say I know nothing of an article which I am called upon to use in the practice of my profession."

The court also found no merit in the plea that the mistake had been made by others, saying:

We are told, however, that the failure, if any, was not the neglect of the plaintiffs [architects]; that plaintiffs had a right to rely on the representation of the manufacturer and of the approval of its use by the heating engineer employed by plaintiffs to design the heating system. . . . Here the heating engineer was acting solely under the direction of the plaintiffs and plaintiffs, by the contract with the hospital district, were directly responsible for the design and supervision of the installation of the heating system. A principal can be liable for the malpractice of his agent, assistant or employee.

The court further found that the architects' negligence had occurred during the policy period, because evidence was presented that during the installation of the steel piping, and during the policy period, the heating contractors' foreman had suggested to the architect that expansion joints be installed in the ceiling piping. The court said:

This testimony discloses that the precise failure which was a material causal factor in the subsequent damage was thereby called to the direct attention of plaintiffs and an opportunity afforded to correct the deficiency within the policy period.

The architects were awarded a judgment against the insurance company.[31]

Every architect and engineer should understand that a policy of insurance is a contract and that he is bound by his contract though he does not read or understand it. Does his policy state that it does not apply to claim arising out of:

(a) The making of boundary surveys, surveys of subsurface conditions, or ground testing, *unless covered by a specific endorsement?*

(b) The advising, or the requiring of, or any failure to advise or require, any form of insurance, suretyship, or bond?

(c) The liability of others assumed by the professional under a contract, *unless covered by specific endorsement?*

(d) Libel or slander though committed in the performance of his professional duties?

In all probability his policy does contain provisions such as stated above; if so, it behooves him to understand the limitations of coverage and to secure endorsements in the cases stated in (a) and (c) above. Moreover, his policy may provide that if he enters into a joint venture agreement, his liability as a joint venturer is not covered unless coverage is evidenced by a specific endorsement. If architects and engineers would only spend a little more time in reviewing their policies of insurance, they would be immeasurably more secure.

2.5   *Incompatible Professional Duties.* An architect or engineer owes undivided loyalty to his client, and may not, without the knowledge of his client, act also as a representative of furnishers and contractors, or receive from them any compensation, and a breach of duty in this respect destroys his right to compensation.

2.5.1   *Mechanical Engineer's Services Free if Successful Bidder.* An architect for a hotel in the South contracted with engineers, without the knowledge of the owner, whereby the engineers should prepare specifications covering the mechanical equipment for the building, with the understanding that, if they obtained the contract for the work, they would make no charge for their services in preparing the specifications; but if they failed to get the work, they should be paid by the architect 3 percent of the cost of the work as compensation for their services. These engineers were successful bidders for that branch of the work.

After the foundations had been put in, the owner announced that he had decided to abandon the project entirely, whereupon all work was stopped. The architect, whose contract included supervision of construction, then sued the owner for damages for breach of contract. During the taking of testimony at the trial, the matter of the agreement between the architect and the mechanical engineers was revealed. Although the verdict of the jury was in favor of the architect, the appellate court reversed the judgment, stating:

. . . it is well-settled that an architect employed to furnish the working plans and specifications and to superintend the construction of a building, is the agent of the owner, and in such relation his first duty is that of good faith and loyalty to his principal; and hence he should have no pecuniary interest in the performance of the contract for the work assigned by him, nor can he act as the agent or representative of furnishers and contractors or receive from them any pay, remuneration or compensation except with the full knowledge of his principal, and any breach of duty or good faith in this respect destroys his right to compensation and commission, not only on the grounds of actual damage or prejudice to the principal, but on the grounds of public policy.[13]

2.5.2   *Designer Agent of Owner and Contractor.* It has been held that an agent cannot assume incompatible duties, or represent adverse parties, and this applies regardless of good or bad faith. A designer was paid a fee by a community center to prepare plans for a swimming pool and to supervise the work as an architect would. The center employed a contractor to construct the pool, but on the day that work was to begin, the designer, having checked the contractor's organization, concluded that the latter did not have the experienced men needed to finish the construction on time, and arranged with the contractor to direct the job himself for a third of the contractor's profits.

The pool was finished on time and to the entire satisfaction of the center. However, the designer found it necessary to sue the contractor for one-third of the net profits. The court rejected his claim, saying:

The contract itself is void as against public policy and good morals, and both parties thereto being in pari delicto [equally guilty], the law will leave them as it finds them.

The court went on to say:

It is fundamental that an agent cannot take unto himself incompatible duties, or act in a transaction where he represents a person having an adverse interest. Where he does act for adverse interests he must necessarily be unfaithful to one or the other as the duties which he owes to his respective principals are conflicting and incapable of faithful performance by the same person. No man can serve two masters. . . . As agent for the center, plaintiff was duty bound to insure complete and satisfactory performance of the construction work. As an agent of the defendant and interested in receiving one-third of the net profits, plaintiff would always be under the temptation to minimize costs and cut corners.

The court found no merit in the designer's plea that his sole interest was to get the pool built properly and on time, that no fraud had been charged, and that the center was aware of the situation.[32]

2.6   Professional's Authority as Owner's Representative. The general concept of agency is much more readily understood than is the concept of responsibilities of the architect or engineer as agent of his client.

2.6.1   The Agency Relationship. In general, an agency relationship is one in which a principal authorizes an agent to represent him in dealing with third parties. The agent may be an employee of the principal, or he may be an independent party chosen by the principal for a specific limited purpose. The principal may be held liable for decisions made by his agent, or for commitments made by his agent to third parties where the third parties rely on the authority, or apparent authority, of the agent to act for his principal.

Such a relationship between principal and agent, implying that the principal consents to acts done on his behalf by his agent, is very different from an ordinary business relationship, where each party might be expected to be primarily concerned with protecting his own interests. The association between principal and agent is one based in trust and confidence, and consequently the agent has a duty of loyalty to his principal.

2.6.2   Design Professional as Owner's Agent. The architect or engineer, in the performance of his professional duties, is considered to be an agent with limited authority; limited not only to matters concerning the specific building project on hand, but further limited to those matters for which he is given specific authority in his agreement with his client. The client, usually unknowledgeable in building construction, places his trust in the integrity and competence of the professional, and the law demands that this trust be met with loyalty of the professional to his client's interests.

Nevertheless, the architect or engineer is commonly designated the arbitrator, at least in the first instance, of disputes arising between the owner and the contractor, and in this capacity he cannot be a partisan, but is required to act impartially and in good faith. The fact that he is employed by one of the parties does not, in itself, disqualify him from undertaking this essential function.

In the performance of his duties to provide administration of the construction contract, the scope of the professional's authority as agent is outlined by contract. Usually, his authority and duty are confined to determining in general if the work is done in accordance with the plans and specifications which have been made a part of the building contract. However, the owner can extend the authority of his agent by specific agreement. Because the duties of the professional are not the same in all cases, the contractor may not recognize the exact limits of this authority.

The fact that a building contract provides that all work shall be done to the satisfaction of the architect merely makes the architect the agent of the owner in deciding whether the work meets the requirements of the drawings and specifications. It does not give the architect the power to require, or to approve, materials or work different from what is stipulated in the contract. If the architect or engineer should exceed the limits of his authority, it has been held in several instances that the contractor had the right to rely on the professional's instructions issued. This is permitted under the theory of "apparent" authority. However, if a contractor is not sure of the extent of the professional's authority as agent, he should check with the owner.

If the professional exceeds his authority, the owner may subsequently ratify his agent's acts, either specifically, such as by signing a change order, or by implication, as by making payments to the contractor for work done in accordance with field orders of the professional. Although the contract may provide that change orders must be in writing, if the owner in the past has paid the contractor for extra work done in response to oral orders by the professional, he may be held to have waived this contract requirement. The owner who permits his architect to exceed his authority without objecting will be bound by his agent's acts if he has led the contractor to reasonably believe that the architect had authority to act as his agent.

2.6.2.1 *Limited scope of architect's authority as owner's representative.* During the construction of a building, the architect, while being the owner's designated representative, is usually expected to be an impartial interpreter of the contract documents and judge of their performance. By periodic visits to the site, he endeavors to safeguard the owner against defects and deficiencies in the work. He has authority to condemn work not conforming to the documents. He also is charged with the responsibility of certifying to the owner that the contractor is entitled to final payment or interim payments as established by the contract.

Though undoubtedly the architect will vigorously prosecute these duties, he may not overstep the boundaries of his rights. He has no power to approve a material departure from the contract documents, without his client's approval, and should he, during construction, fail to properly instruct the contractor, he may find that he is liable to the owner for defects in the final building.

2.6.2.2 *Improper approval of work.* A prospective homeowner employed an architect to prepare plans and specifications for a house to be built on a hillside lot in California. This contract, which excluded any supervision of construction, promised the architect 4 percent of the construction cost as his fee, and it was agreed that should the owner desire supervision he would pay the architect an additional 4 percent. The architect completed plans and specifications and was paid $490 for this service. Shortly after construction had started, the owner asked the architect to take over supervision of construction. Although the architect later insisted that he had not agreed to undertake supervision, and that additional payments of $441.10 to him by the owner were for "advice" and not for supervision, there is no doubt that he did supervise to some extent.

Within a day or two after having asked the architect to supervise, the owner reported to the architect that he had seen workmen placing foundation forms on loose earth fill. The architect said, "I can't believe it," but promised to straighten the matter out. A day or two later he informed the owner that everything had been fixed up.

The house was completed and, on the advice of the architect, accepted by the owner. Shortly after moving in, the owner noticed that rugs and furniture had a tendency to slide toward the front of the house. An inspection disclosed not only sloping floors, but cracks in plaster walls, and it was discovered that foundations had settled at least 2 inches.

The owner refused to make the final payment to the contractors, who then filed a mechanic's lien and later commenced an action to foreclose their lien. The owner filed an answer denying liability, and counterclaimed against the contractors for negligence. The owner also filed a suit for negligence against the architect. The action against the contractors was tried first. Testimony disclosed that, although the plans and specifications called for the front foundations to be a minimum of 6 inches below the original natural ground level, these foundations were in fact constructed on loose earth fill 18 to 20 inches above the natural ground level. The architect admitted that he had "told the men to go ahead and pour when the foundations were in fact 18 inches above . . . natural ground level."

The court found that the architect was the agent of the owner; that the contractors were entitled to rely on the architect's instructions; and when they did so, it constituted a waiver on the part of the owner of any failure by the contractors to follow the plans and specifications in that respect; that the depth of the front foundation trench was approved by the architect, and that such approval constituted a waiver by the owner of any defect existing therein. The court then found damages only for "that portion of the said defects for which . . . [the contractors] were and are responsible and which were not waived by . . . [the owner] by and through their architect," which damages were fixed in the sum of $2027.45.

Then the action involving the architect was tried before a jury, and although expert testimony disagreed substantially as to what had to be done to make the house conform to the plans and specifications, and the experts' estimates of the cost of repairs varied from $1846.50 to $17,354, the jury fixed the damages to the owner at $7000, deducted the amount of the judgment against the contractors, and brought in a verdict against the architect in the amount of $4972.55.

Judgment was entered, and the architect appealed, contending that the evidence established that the contractors and the architect were joint tort-feasors, and that consequently the satisfaction of the judgment against the contractor released the architect as a matter of law. The architect urged that, the subject matter of the action against him being the same as that involved in the action against the contractors, the first adjudication prevented the owner from securing any further recovery against the architect.

The appellate court, however, ruled that the architect and contractor were not joint tort-feasors but independent wrongdoers, as there was no unity of purpose nor concert of action between them. It ruled further that the judgment against the contractors and that against the architect did not result in the injured party recovering double compensation.[33]

2.6.2.3 Improper withholding of certificate of payment. In issuing or withholding a certificate for payment of a contractor's requisition, the architect, in the absence of express authority vested in him by the contract documents, may not consider other issues beyond determining if the contractor has in fact done the work covered by the requisition. In one instance, a heating contractor sued to recover a balance due him under a contract which provided that the installation of a heating plant was to "proceed as fast as the general construction will permit" and to be completed by a certain date, and that the payment therefor was to be "only upon certificates of the architects as follows: 85 percent of the work done and material furnished upon the premises at any time architects issue a certificate; the final payment to be made within 30 days after the completion of the work included within this contract, and all payments shall be due when certificates for same are issued."

The heating installation was not completed within the time specified in the contract, and the newly laid concrete floor of the basement was heaved up and ruined during the extreme cold weather immediately thereafter. Because of the breaking up of the floor, the architect withheld the last certificate of payment to the heating contractor. The court concluded that the architect had no right to do this, saying:

In the present case the architect clearly attemped to pass upon a matter not submitted to him by the contract, namely, the responsibility for injury to the cement floor. His powers were simply to issue certificates for "work done and materials furnished upon the premises" by the plaintiff. Manifestly that does not include power to determine that the plaintiff's delay caused the cement floor, which had been laid by another contractor, to heave up. A refusal to award a certificate because of matters entirely outside of the submission is necessarily a mistaken and arbitrary refusal and amounts in law to a fraudulent refusal, even though made in entire good faith. The architect, on the witness stand, stated that the breaking up of the floor was the only reason why the last certificate was withheld. This was in legal contemplation no reason. The plaintiff's work having been done and materials having been furnished, the certificate was due, and the question whether plaintiff's delay in installing the apparatus caused the breaking of the floor which another contractor had put in was a question to be fought out between the parties after the certificate was given. The architect mistook the scope of his duty and because of that misapprehension refused the certificate. This makes the refusal a mistaken refusal within the meaning of the law, and excuses the plaintiff from producing the certificate.[34]

This case illustrates the significance of vesting in the architect adequate authority. Such delegation is essential to permit him to act in safeguarding the owner's interests, particularly in the matter of withholding certificates of payment under appropriate conditions. The standard form confers such authority in specific contingencies, at least one of which, if it had been provided for, would have been applicable to the circumstances presented by this case. This is not to suggest that blind obedience to standard forms will serve as a panacea in all projects; content must vary to meet the exigencies of each occasion.

2.6.3 Contractor's Guilt Not Assignable to Engineer. In a case also involving inadequate soil conditions under building footings, the owner sued the contractor, claiming damages by reason of the contractor's failure to construct the building as required by the contract documents. In particular, it was alleged that the contractor failed to extend the footings a distance of 1 foot into virgin soil, and to furnish certain materials called for by the plans and specifications. Thereafter, the contractor commenced a third-party action against the engineer, claiming that "the damages alleged to have been a result of the contractor's workmanship were actually, in whole or in part, the result of defects in the plans and specifications prepared by the third-party defendants."

The court decided that the contractor, who breached his contract with the owner, could not recover damages from the engineer, even if the engineer had also breached his contract with the owner by preparing faulty plans and specifications. If the contractor had carefully followed the plans and specifications, even though a defective building resulted, the court found that he would not be liable to the owner at all, since he could not be held liable for damages caused by the engineer's breach of its obligations.

In finding that the contractor could not recover from the engineer either on the theory of implied indemnity or on the theory of apportionment of damages, the court said:

The damages plaintiff (owner) may recover in the action against V___ (contractor) are only those resulting directly, naturally and proximately from the breach of the

V___ construction contract and could not include damages arising from a breach of E___'s (engineer's) contractual or professional obligation to plaintiff (owner). If, as alleged in the specific denials in his answer and in his third party complaint V___ (contractor) has performed in a workmanlike manner, in accordance with the specific actions, he could not be liable to plaintiff (owner) at all—even though the building may be defective, and the plaintiff damaged as a result of E___'s (engineer's) improper plans and specifications. Since E___ was hired by and responsible to plaintiff and not to V___, it is not suggested that V___ could be vicariously liable to plaintiff on account of E___'s improper performance. Thus V___'s claim over may not rest on a common-law right of implied indemnity since he cannot, under any theory pleaded, be "compelled to pay for another's wrong."

. . . it seems evident that before there can be any apportionment of damages among wrongdoers it must be legally possible that they be held jointly or severally liable to the plaintiff for the same damages. When the wrongful conduct of each has contributed in some degree to the damages, the rule is that those damages should be apportioned among the wrongdoers in proportion to their respective degree of fault. Here, the alleged wrongful conduct of V___ and E___, although relating to the same building, would result, if established, in distinctly different and separable damages for which each must be held separately liable to plaintiff. There is no way that V___, who may be liable to plaintiff for breach of his construction contract, and E___, who may be responsible to plaintiff for breach of his contract or for malpractice or negligence because of the faulty plans and specifications, can be held jointly or severally responsible for the same damages. . . . [35]

2.7 Statute of Limitations. Many states have enacted statutes limiting the time within which litigation may be begun. The reason for such statutes is that over a period of time witnesses may have moved away or died, or may have forgotten details of the occurrence, and lack of evidence may lead to a miscarriage of justice.

The rules of the several states vary as to the time within which action must be started, and as to the point at which the prescribed time limit begins. In some instances the time period begins when the nonperformance or defective work occurs, and in others it begins when the injured party discovers or should discover the defect. While the latter is more common, in some cases the time period begins even later. Under the "continuous treatment" doctrine, the time period commences at the end of the professional relationship.

2.7.1 The "Continuous Treatment" Doctrine. This doctrine was first applied to medical malpractice, on the theory that the doctor-patient relationship

is basically one of trust and confidence and in most cases the patient has little or no knowledge of medicine. He, therefore, must depend exclusively on his physician and must have absolute trust in his judgment. Under such circumstances "little argument is needed to prove the proposition that the 'continuous treatment' theory is the fairer one. It would be absurd to require a wronged patient to interrupt corrective efforts by serving a summons on the physician" (citation). Moreover, under the contrary rule a physician, aware of his malpractice, might be encouraged to pursue useless corrective treatment until the Statute of Limitations on his original wrongful act or omission had expired.

This doctrine was later extended to apply to attorneys, accountants, and architects. In one case, an architect designed and supervised the construction of a library building at a community college. Immediately after construction had been completed and final payment had been made to the contractor, leaks began to appear in the newly completed roof. Upon being informed of this situation, the architect required the contractor to undertake corrective measures, and over a period of three years several remedial measures were attempted, but the leaks continued. During this time the architect communicated regularly with his client, expressing confidence in the effectiveness of the repair work being performed. Finally, however, the dissatisfied client sued the architect for professional malpractice. The architect countered that the statute of limitations had expired, as his professional relationship with his client had terminated with the issuance of the final certificate for payment, more than three years before the action was commenced.

In rejecting the architect's plea, the court said,

The architect creates and recommends plans to his client. These plans, conceived in his imagination, are proposed to his client as products of his education, experience and judgment. The client may offer suggestions to the architect, just as he might to his doctor, lawyer or accountant, but generally the client is required to rely almost totally on the professional advice of the architect. He must have confidence in the architect and place his full trust in him. Should problems or difficulties arise during the course of construction, the client, unknowledgeable as he is in matters of building design and construction, is forced to depend almost exclusively on the advice of the architect . . . it would be unfair and unreasonable to require the client in this situation to question the tactics of the architect or to interrupt corrective efforts by the service of a summons and complaint.

As with the doctor, lawyer, or accountant, acts of malpractice by an architect may not be readily apparent to the client. To apply the general rule that a claim for malpractice accrues upon the occasion of negligence may serve to encourage the architect to conceal his errors for a sufficient time so as to allow the Statute of Limitations to expire.

The court decided that the professional relationship between these parties continued through the entire period during which the architect acted on his client's behalf in the matter of the leaking roof.[36]

2.8   *Conclusions.* In providing design services and contract documents, and in supervising construction, the professional not only must guard against falling into pitfalls himself but, because of his professional position, must accept responsibility for guiding the owner and the contractor safely around such dangers as will arise. During these phases of the work, the following points should be borne in mind:

1. Don't forget that, because of the technical knowledge imputed to the professional, he should proceed upon the assumption that he is expected to:

    a. Provide a design which is suitable for its intended purpose.

    b. Question the validity of conditions reflected in basic documents such as surveys, when lapse of time dictates such need.

    c. Provide a design which conforms to the governing legal requirements.

2. Don't fail to check and recheck all contract documents to make absolutely certain that no conflicting instructions exist.

3. Don't neglect to have the contracting parties identify, by initialing each page, all contract documents, at the time of signing the contract.

4. Don't assume that the architect is relieved from the duty to exercise his technical knowledge and judgment merely because he makes use of standard contract forms.

5. Don't include in specifications language having no force, but don't delete language necessary to avoid confusion.

6. Don't specify methods of doing work if results are to be guaranteed by the contractor.

7. Don't fail to define all specifications terminology which may prove to be a pitfall for the unwary reader.

8. Don't assume, gratuitously, responsibility for the work of others by incorporating their findings in your own drawings; and when making them available for inspection, don't forget to disclaim responsibility as to their accuracy and completeness.

9. Don't forget that claims of contractors for extras may be successful if the architect's instructions by plans and specifications are incomplete or ambiguous.

10. Don't issue to the contractor instructions that are a material departure from the contract documents, without the owner's written approval.

11. Don't withhold a certificate of payment for any reason not specifically contemplated by the contract documents.

12. Don't neglect to visit the job site as frequently as may be necessary, and to prepare detailed records of these visits for the owner.

13. Don't rely solely on representations of manufacturers as to suitability of materials.

14. Don't serve two masters at the same time.

15. Don't change insurance companies without being assured of continuity of coverage for errors and omissions.

16. Don't fail to ascertain which risks are covered and which are excluded by your professional liability insurance policy.

CHAPTER 3

Legal Pitfalls in the Responsibility of the Professional to the Public

An old saw says, "The doctor buries his mistakes, while the architect covers his mistakes with ivy." The latter refers of course to aesthetic mistakes, but it is obvious that the architect's power to injure society is of a larger order than merely creating an offense against current visual taste. When we consider the possibility of an ineptly designed theater roof collapsing on hundreds of people, or of an ill-conceived street wall falling on passersby, it becomes apparent that the designer's capacity for mischief is so great as to require recognition by law. This recognition has manifested itself in the enactment of building codes and licensing laws, and more recently in court decisions holding the architect or engineer responsible for injury to the general public resulting from his negligence.

3.1 *State License to Practice.* Although the architectural student or the architect in training usually sees his goal quite clearly as the acquisition of a license to practice architecture, frequently neither the novice nor the established practitioner fully realizes the limitations of this license. There is no nationally recognized license, the sanctioning of professional practice being a jealously guarded state right under our laws. In each of the several states having statutes regulating architectural practice, the qualifications vary so that a man considered competent to practice in one state may not be so considered in another. Even an architect of world renown, with unquestioned superior ability, must secure a license to practice in each state in which one of his projects is to be built, or at the very minimum a temporary license, if sanctioned by the laws of the state. Failure to procure such a license may render the architect amenable to criminal penalties, such as a fine or imprisonment, or both. Such severe penalties, however, are not often invoked, as the authorities in many states do not appear to have the time, money, or inclination to prosecute violators.

But any such complacency on the part of governmental authorities does not indemnify the architect against all consequences of his illegal act. He is very likely to suffer a more painful blow in the discovery that the fruits of his labor may be enjoyed by his client without paying for them. It is a rule of law of almost universal application that the courts will not enforce a contract which is illegal or contrary to the public policy of the state; in consequence of which an architect, having competently performed his work, may find himself unable to collect an undisputed substantial balance due him merely because he omitted to secure an additional license in the state in which the project is located.

3.1.1   *Effect of One Partner's Lack of License in Foreign State.* In one instance, two New York architects, practicing as partners, entered into a contract to provide architectural services in connection with the proposed construction of a building in New Jersey. Both members of the firm were licensed in New York, but only one was licensed to practice in New Jersey. A court action to recover a balance due was dismissed—and the architects lost $35,000. The court ruled that since the client had entered into a contract with the architectural firm, the firm could not enforce the contract because one of the partners was not licensed in New Jersey, though licensed in New York and eminently qualified to practice architecture.

Therefore, if a firm of architects enters into a contract to perform professional services in a given state, all the members of the firm should be licensed in that state. When this is not possible or practicable, the contract sometimes is entered into only by and in the individual name of one or more of the partners who are licensed in the particular state.

3.1.2   *National Council of Architectural Registration Boards.* In order to accept engagements beyond the boundaries of the state of their professional birth, many architects record their professional qualifications in the files of the National Council of Architectural Registration Boards. Such recording does not in itself convey the privilege to practice everywhere in the country. The architect practicing in a foreign state is no more legally qualified by an NCARB certificate than he is by his home-state license. The NCARB has no legal status as a licensing agency. This organization collects and verifies information as to a candidate's educational and professional qualifications, and submits a summary of this data to state boards upon request of the applicant. As verification by this office is accepted by most state boards, licensing of the same architect in several states is a relatively simple procedure. However, it is necessary to make application to each state for a license to practice in that state.

Many professionals have suggested the possibility of a Federal licensing law, which would permit an architect or engineer who is duly licensed thereunder to practice in any state. But this suggestion overlooks the fact that the building codes and environmental requirements vary throughout the various states and the mere possession of a Federal license would not establish necessarily that the holder thereof is qualified to practice in each state. As a compromise suggestion, it seems to the authors that steps should be taken by the design professions to bring about a change in the governing registration statutes of the several states, or if possible to secure enactment of a Federal law which would permit an architect or engineer duly licensed in one state to undertake a project located in another state, provided he is associated with another member of his profession resident and practicing in such other state and who will contribute his knowledge of local conditions and requirements.

3.1.3   *Some Statutes Protect Only Use of Title "Architect."* It would be unwise for one to contract to perform architectural services in a state in which he is not licensed, even though the statute merely protects the title "Architect" and perhaps specifically authorizes the doing by others of things normally done by architects, providing a penalty only for the use of the title without a certificate. A firm of East Coast architects recently became involved in a lawsuit in a Midwestern state having such a statute. At the time the architects signed a contract to design a shopping center in that state, they were not registered there, although they obtained certificates of registration immediately thereafter. When the architects sued for their fee, the client pleaded the original lack of certificates of registration as a defense, and the trial court ruled that the contract was null and void, and awarded judgment dismissing the architect's action. On appeal, the higher court reversed this judgment, but significantly in a very close decision (5 to 4).[37] The chapter of the code entitled "Registered Architects" stated in part:

Any person wishing to practice architecture in the State of Iowa under the title "Architect" shall secure from the board a certificate under the title "Architect" as provided by this chapter. Each member of a firm or corporation practicing architecture must have a certificate of registration under the provisions of this chapter. . . .

And the following section provided:

Nothing contained in this chapter shall prevent any person from making plans and specifications or supervising the construction of any building or part thereof, for himself or others, provided he does not use any form of the word or title "Architect."

In a second case, in another state with a very similar statute protecting the title "Architect," designers were forced to resort to litigation to collect their fee. The firm consisted of a licensed professional engineer and his partner who was not licensed either as an architect or engineer, but had been an architect in Holland. They were engaged to design an addition to a nursing home, and did in fact carry the job through to construction of a scale model of the proposed addition and completion of working drawings and specifications, after which the client became dissatisfied and terminated their services. The partners then filed a lien for ". . . professional engineering services including consultation, investigation, evaluation, planning and design. . . ."

The client urged that the designers were not entitled to maintain an action to recover their fees, because neither partner was a licensed architect, and consequently the agreement was illegal and unenforceable. The court found that their services were primarily architectural rather than engineering, but since they had not represented themselves to be licensed architects, the court upheld their right to compensation, saying:

The language of the act, we believe, expresses the legislative intent that it is not the *performance of work* falling within the ambit of the statutory definition of the practice of architecture that is prohibited, but the *misrepresentation* to the public that the individual is an architect authorized and licensed by law to practice architecture.[38]

In both these cases, and in others on record as well, although the architects finally won their cases, they were obviously put to considerable trouble and expense to collect their fees.

3.1.4   What Constitutes the Practice of Architecture? There are as many definitions of the term "architectural practice" as there are states in the Union. Although, in general, any person is regarded as practicing architecture who charges or accepts a fee for the preparation of plans or specifications or for the supervision of the construction of a building, some states grant temporary certificates for a single project to architects licensed in another state, and some states exempt services rendered in connection with a building of limited scope, delimited by price or by physical size.

It must be realized also that the laws of many states not only prohibit the practice of architecture without a license, but in addition provide that no one may offer to practice without such a license. Consequently, it would seem the part of wisdom for the architect to secure his license in the foreign state before signing his agreement with the owner. Procurement of the license during the performance of services may not be sufficient to overcome a defense that the contract itself is illegal, because the architect, when he became a party thereto, "offered to practice architecture" without a license. Not only do the statutes of the several states vary considerably in detail, but the matter is further complicated by the overlapping of professional areas assigned to architects and to engineers, as well as those areas normally thought of as interior design or landscape architecture. In one state, the court has held that a licensed professional engineer was practicing engineering and not architecture (and therefore did not need to be licensed as an architect), in designing a single-family residence.[39] The confusion is compounded by the fact that many subcontractors or materialmen provide design services incidental to the proper specifying of their equipment.

3.1.5   Contractor's Designs Incidental to His Providing Equipment. During the construction of an office building, the owner decided to install electronic computing equipment on one of the upper floors. The great amount of heat generated by this equipment created a special problem in air-conditioning the space where it was to be installed. When the architect's proposed solution to this problem was submitted to an air-conditioning contractor, it was found that the cost exceeded the budget. The owner then asked the contractor to submit a design which would be within the budget. The contractor submitted a proposal, which was approved by the architect, and was told to start work. But before he bought any materials for the job, he was informed that the owner had employed a second air-conditioning contractor, who in fact did the work.

The original contractor sued for damages in the sum of $1500 for "work performed in designing and preparing drawings for said mechanical work," arising out of a breach of contract. The owner contended that the contract was for professional engineering services, and since the contractor was not licensed as an engineer, the contract was illegal so as to preclude recovery.

The state supreme court decided that the contract was not illegal under the licensing statute, because the plans, specifications, and estimates were furnished with the understanding that they were subject to approval by the owner's architect and engineer, and the installation was to be under their supervision, and the allegedly professional work was incidental to the air-conditioning contract.[40]

3.1.6   Sale by Owner of His Architect's Plans Not Considered Practice of Architecture. In 1955, a builder of more than a quarter of a century of experience conceived an idea for a convertible building. Not himself an architect, he had plans embodying his idea prepared by an architect. To construct the building, a corporation was formed with three shareholders. The builder owned the plans for the building, and his two associates owned the land on which it was to be built. The agreement between him and his associates was that he would be paid $4000 for the plans and $3000 for supervising the construction. After the building was completed, however, his associates refused to pay the builder, contending that in providing plans and supervision he was practicing architecture in violation of a state statute which read in part as follows:

DEFINITIONS: As used in this chapter . . . the "practice of architecture" is the rendering or offering to render of service to clients by consultation, investigation, evaluations, preliminary studies, plans, specifications and coordination of structural factors concerning the aesthetic or structural design and supervision of construction of buildings or any other service in connection with the designing or supervision of construction of buildings located within the boundaries of this state, regardless of whether such persons are performing one or all of these duties.

The court decided that the builder was not practicing architecture and was entitled to recover the agreed-upon amount, saying:

. . .The utilization, under an agreement that the plaintiff [builder] would be paid $4000 for them, of plans and specifications which were prepared for the plaintiff by an architect and were owned by the plaintiff did not involve the rendering of a service by him to a client, or the practice of architecture within the meaning of the statute.

What has already been said applies equally to the supervisory services rendered by the plaintiff. In performing these services, he was not engaged in the practice of architecture. . . . In addition the act concerning architects specifically exempts from its provisions "the superintendence by builders . . . of the construction or structural alteration of buildings or structures." . . . The relationship of the plaintiff to the project was that of a builder. . . . [41]

3.1.7 Does a Single Transaction Constitute Professional Practice? In some jurisdictions, the practice of architecture or engineering has been interpreted by the courts as implying continuity of activity. Such expressions as "pursue the practice of any professional business," "practicing architecture," "engaging in the practice of law," "engaging in business," usually contemplate a course of business or professional practice, and not single isolated acts arising from unusual circumstances.

A case in point involved a woman who, while staying at her summer house in New England, met a distinguished local architect. She asked him to prepare tentative sketches for a building to be erected in her home state. He did so, twice visiting her home to which she had returned. On the second visit she told him to go ahead with the work. He returned to his own office and prepared and completed the plans and specifications. The building was constructed according to them, and the architect visited the job frequently during progress of the work to supervise and to consult with the owner. When he was not paid and finally sued for payment, his client claimed that the contract, upon which the action was based, was illegal under the laws of her home state and on that account he was precluded from recovering. The court upheld a jury verdict for the architect, saying:

It does not appear that the plaintiff ever acted as an architect with reference to any other building in New Jersey, or that he ever in any manner solicited business in New Jersey; and we think the jury was warranted in finding that the facts submitted did not indicate that he had any intention in the future of "pursuing the practice of architecture in New Jersey." The preliminary conferences out of which the contract grew were all held in Massachusetts, and all the plans and specifications were drawn in the plaintiff's office in Boston. His only visits to New Jersey were for the purpose of submitting his plans and sketches to the defendant, and the necessary trips there to supervise the construction of the building, and the approving of the work and bills.[42]

It should be noted, however, that since this case was decided, the law has been changed in New Jersey, so that, like New York and several other states, a single act or transaction constitutes the practice of architecture. This was determined by the court in one state on the basis that the statute, requiring a person practicing architecture to be registered by the state board of architecture, is not a revenue measure but a police measure, enacted for protection of public safety and health. Hence, the statute applies to a person engaging in a single isolated architectural transaction as well as a person practicing architecture as a business or profession.[43]

3.1.8   Effect of Professional's Signing Drawings Prepared by a Nonlicensed Designer. An architect (engineer) may not legally associate himself in practice with a nonlicensed individual, unless this individual is his employee, working under his direction and supervision. Architects and engineers are sometimes requested to review, approve, and sign drawings and specifications which have been made by nonlicensed designers who have consulted with clients and prepared designs to meet their requirements, but who are prevented from filing these documents with an application for a building permit, owing to the fact that they are not licensed professionals. An architect or engineer acceding to such a request may be placing his own license to practice in jeopardy.

A state board of architecture revoked an architect's license on two counts, and he appealed the decision to the courts. The first charge was that he held himself out to the public as being in a professional partnership with one who, in fact, was neither a registered architect nor a registered engineer. The charge was based on a window sign and building directory at his office, which read, respectively:

C. M___ & R. E___, Architects and Engineers

and

M___, Charles & E___, Robert J., Architects & Consultants

Both men testified that the nonlicensed partner was in charge of the preparation of the sign and directory, and he had the wording approved by an attorney. As soon as the architect was notified that they were in violation of state statutes, he had the sign and directory corrected.

The second charge was that he allegedly placed his name and seal on architectural drawings which had been prepared by nonarchitects who were not operating under his "responsible supervisory control" in violation of state statutes. Evidence disclosed that clients initially contacted and engaged nonarchitects to prepare their plans. There was no contact or contract by them with the architect. Only after the plans were nearing completion did the draftsman take them to him for inspection and approval. The architect testified that at this time he would change anything in the drawings he felt was improper. The court stated that supervision at such a late stage did not satisfy the statute, but felt revocation of his license to be too severe a punishment on both charges. The case was remanded to the lower court, which modified the punishment to a sixty-day suspension of his license.[44]

3.2 Professional's Liability to Public. It already has been pointed out that an architect or engineer impliedly represents to his client that he possesses the requisite degree of learning, skill, and experience to qualify him to engage in his profession, that he will use reasonable care and diligence, and that he will honestly use his best judgment. It has been well established in the courts that if his client suffers damage through the architect's faulty design or through his negligent supervision, the architect is liable for this damage.

If, however, the architect's negligence results in injury to a member of the public—a third party with whom he has no contract, and to whom he has promised nothing—what are his responsibilities? There are two areas of the professional's activities in which a mistake may result in trouble: in the preparation of the plans and specifications, and in the supervision or administration of construction. If negligently prepared plans and specifications cause injury to a third party—either during construction to a contractor's employee, a sidewalk superintendent, or a passerby, or years later to a tenant in the building or the audience in a theater—the architect may be found liable. The mere passage of time does not necessarily grant immunity.

3.2.1 Defect in Design Evident—Not Concealed. For many years it was assumed that a building designer was not responsible for injuries caused to third parties, even though the injuries resulted from an act of negligence. Architects and engineers took comfort in the fact that no contractual relationship bound them to the general public.

More recently, however, on the basis of an important decision by the highest court in the State of New York, the picture has changed materially. It had been decided previously by that court that the manufacturer of an inherently dangerous chattel, defectively made, was liable for injuries to remote users, with whom there was no contractual relationship.[45] But until a few years ago, that court was never asked to determine if this doctrine of liability (called the MacPherson doctrine) would apply as well to those who plan structures on real property.

In 1957, the same court was asked to rule on the question of liability of an architect (engineer) to a third party, for faulty design. The case involved a child who was injured by a fall from a porch. It was contended that the architect, who had designed the building six years previously, was responsible for the accident, since through faulty design he had "created a hazardous and extremely dangerous condition." He was charged with negligence in having designed the porch, which was two risers above the ground, without a railing, although the step did not extend the full length of the porch. It also was charged that the door opened in such a manner that the user must back precariously close to the edge of the porch.

The court ruled that there was no discernible reason for distinction between the liability of one who supplies a chattel and one who designs or erects a structure, and that consequently the MacPherson doctrine did apply to architects and builders in their handiwork. However, it was inherent in the MacPherson doctrine that the manufacturer was liable only if the defect were not patent or discoverable by reasonable inspection. In this case, the condition was patent. The absence of a railing was visible to the naked eye; hence there was no hidden danger. Therefore, the court said that the MacPherson rule was not applicable, and the architect was exonerated.[46] This could lead one to the conclusion that if an architect or engineer is going to be careless, he shouldn't try to hide his mistakes.

3.2.2 Misfeasance versus Nonfeasance. When one considers the liability of an architect or engineer for injury resulting from negligent supervision, it is seen that here also he may be found responsible despite the absence of any contractual relationship. An additional question enters the picture here, however, and that is whether the architect or engineer has been guilty of misfeasance, or of nonfeasance, for these are not regarded by the courts to be the same in determining liability.

Generally, misfeasance is the improper doing of an act, whereas nonfeasance is the omission of an act. Where the professional produces faulty plans and specifications, he may be guilty of negligence (which, historically, was deemed to be affirmative negligence) or misfeasance. But negligent supervision is not necessarily affirmative, and may be nonfeasance. In general, if upon a site inspection, the professional discovers defective materials, but does not condemn them, he may be guilty of misfeasance. If, however, he fails to discover these defective materials, he may be guilty of nonfeasance. If misfeasance in supervision results in injury to a third party, the architect or engineer is liable. If nonfeasance is the cause, his liability is questionable. In New York, certain appellate courts have ruled that an architect or engineer has no liability to third parties for acts of nonfeasance. The highest court in the State of New York handed down a decision several years ago in an accident case which left this question open for further determination.[47]

However, the erosion of the distinction between affirmative and passive negligence may lead to a different result.

3.2.3 *Professional's Responsibility in Supervising Temporary Construction.* Another problem arose involving the architect's or engineer's responsibility for supervision of temporary construction, as distinguished from permanent construction.

About eleven o'clock on a rainy summer night during the construction of a tall office building, a construction worker employed by the foundation contractor removing old foundations was in the hole, two sublevels below the street. He had just finished hooking a piece of steel to the crane, and to reach a stair leading up, passed under a temporary platform made of planks laid on steel beams and old foundation walls. Between the edge of the platform and the wall was an opening 10 inches wide and 10 feet long, at the edge of which were piled thirty to seventy bull points, or steel drills, 30 inches long and weighing 20 pounds each. Also on the platform were seven air compressors, weighing 3 or 4 tons each, which vibrated while in use. This condition had existed for a month or two. The construction worker was struck by a bull point which fell through the opening.

During the ensuing legal action, it was brought out that the following contractual responsibilities existed:

1. The contract between the owner and the foundation contractor stipulated that the owner was to pay "all expenses and other items on the entire job," including purchasing and reshaping bull points and leasing the air compressors.

2. The contract between the owner and architect called for complete supervision of the work "in conformance with the drawings and specifications," but stated that the architect "cannot guarantee performance of the contracts for the work."

3. The contract between the architect and engineer required the engineer to insure that prosecution of the work be in accordance with the plans and specifications. The engineer had a resident inspector on the job at all times. Its supervision concededly included the manner of work, and safety and support of surrounding subways and buildings.

The jury rendered a verdict in favor of the defendant-owner. As to the architect and engineer, who also were defendants, the court said the evidence showed that their sole supervisory function was to insure performance of the construction work in accordance with the plans and specifications; to see that standards of safety were met in relation to permanent construction, adjacent buildings, structures, and subways, but not the safety of temporary platforms used in connection with the permanent work. And further:

There being no duty, we do not reach the question of liability to a third party by reason of non-feasance.[47]

During construction of an expressway, temporary formwork, which had been erected for concrete which was to constitute retaining walls bordering the roadway, collapsed causing the death of two carpenters and injury to a third. The supervising engineers were sued on the theory of negligence in that the contract between the engineers and the state imposed a duty toward employees engaged in construction. Furthermore, the engineers breached said duty in failing to insure that the forms were properly erected and the men working on the project properly safeguarded.

The jury rendered a verdict against the engineers in the aggregate amount of $400,000, but the judgment was unanimously reversed by an appellate court.

The injured parties pointed out that the engineers were required under their agreement to perform their work "in accordance with . . . the provisions of the contract documents." They referred to the agreement between the state and the contractor, which provided:

CONDUCT OF WORK: The Contractor shall, by working methods and orders of procedure subject to the approval of the Engineer, conduct the work in the most expeditious manner possible, having due regard for the safety of persons and property and safety for traffic, and for reducing to a minimum the encumbrance of the streets and site of the work with construction materials.

With regard to this the court said:

It is urged that this language creates a duty in favor of the workmen on the job. Even if we assume that this paragraph were a part of defendants' (engineers') obligations— and it is not clear that it is—it imposes no duty with respect to the contractor's employees. The language is such as to permit no interpretation other than it was designed to protect members of the public at large—not the workmen on the job. In any event and particularly since the defendants (engineers) were not parties to the agreement wherein this language is found, any duty intended to be created in favor of the workmen should have been clearly expressed. The language of the provision in question fails to meet this test.[48]

However, failure by the architect (engineer) to stop unsafe practices may be considered to be professional negligence. Courts have been unable with any uniformity to determine the extent of the architect's (engineer's) responsibility for construction safety. In a leading Illinois case, the majority opinion held that the architect's powers under the contract, which included authority to stop the work when necessary to insure the proper execution of the contract, were sufficient to make him responsible for safety on the job.

In this instance, three ironworkers were injured in the collapse of a building roof on which they were working, and they subsequently brought suit against the architect to recover for their injuries.

The architect had been retained by a school district to extend the gymnasium of a high school. His plans called for extending the building westerly, which necessitated the removal of the west wall of the gymnasium, the relocation of a proscenium truss from the original west wall to the new west wall, the removal of two steel columns in the old west wall (which together with the proscenium truss had originally supported the west ends of four east-west roof trusses), and the substitution of a new north-south, main bearing truss to carry the west ends of the existing roof trusses and the east ends of new trusses over the proposed extension.

The plans showed the reactions at each end of the new, main bearing truss under the loads imposed by the existing roof plus the new roof. The weight of the new roof could be computed from information shown on the plans, and by subtracting that figure from the total reaction, the weight of the old roof could be obtained.

The contractor decided to remove the original brick wall and shore up the west ends of the existing roof trusses by means of columns of tubular steel scaffolding placed approximately under the end of each truss so that the proscenium truss and its supporting columns could be removed.

The proscenium truss was moved safely to its new location. The north column was removed and the load of the roof was transferred to the shoring. During the removal of the south column, being supported by a crane while one man was cutting the column off at the bottom and a second was at the top knocking out the bolts connecting the truss to the column, the shoring proved inadequate and the roof collapsed.

The architect's contract with the school district provided for "the general administration of the construction contracts, and supervision of the work." and stated, "The Architect will endeavor to guard the Owner against defects and deficiencies in the work of the contractors, but he does not guarantee the performance of their contracts."

The construction contract provided:

PROTECTION OF WORK AND PROPERTY

The Contractor shall continuously maintain adequate protection of all his work from damage and shall protect the Owner's property from injury or loss arising in connection with this Contract. He shall make good any such damage, injury or loss, except such as may be directly due to errors in the Contract Documents or caused by agents or employees of the Owner, or due to causes beyond the Contractor's control and not to his fault or negligence. He shall adequately protect adjacent property as provided by law and the Contract Documents.

The Contractor shall take all necessary precautions for the safety of employees on the work, and shall comply with all applicable provisions of Federal, State, and Municipal safety laws and building codes to prevent accidents or injury to persons on, about or adjacent to the premises where the work is being performed. He shall erect and properly maintain at all times, as required by the conditions and progress of the work, all necessary safeguards for the protection of workmen and the public and shall post danger signs warning against the hazards created by such features of construction as protruding nails, hoists, well holes, elevator hatchways, scaffolding, window openings, stairways and falling materials; and he shall designate a responsible member of his organization on the work, whose duty shall be the prevention of accidents. The name and position of any person so designated shall be reported to the Architect by the Contractor. . . .

SUPERINTENDENCE: SUPERVISION

The Contractor shall keep in his work, during its progress, a competent superintendent and any necessary assistants, all satisfactory to the Architect. The superintendent shall not be changed except with the consent of the Architect, unless the superintendent proves to be unsatisfactory to the Contractor and ceases to be in his employ. . . .

The Contractor shall give efficient supervision to the work, using his best skill and attention. He shall carefully study and compare all drawings, specifications and other instructions and shall at once report to the Architect any error, inconsistency or omission which he may discover, but he shall not be held responsible for their existence or discovery. . . .

ARCHITECT'S STATUS

The Architect shall have general supervision and direction of the work. He is the agent of the Owner only to the extent provided in the Contract Documents and when in special instances he is authorized by the Owner so to act, and in such instances he shall, upon request, show the Contractor written authority. He has the authority to stop the work whenever such stoppage may be necessary to insure the proper execution of the Contract. . . .

PROTECTION

Bracing, Shoring and Sheeting: The Contractor shall provide all bracing, shoring and sheeting as required for safety and for the proper execution of the work, and have same removed when the work is completed.

In its opinion, the court stated:

Despite the argument of the architects that the shoring here was a method or technique of construction over which they had no control, we feel that under the terms of the contracts the architects had the right to interfere if the contractor began to shore in an obviously unsafe and hazardous manner. We agree with the architects that they had no duty to specify the method the contractor would use in shoring, but we believe that under the terms of these contracts the architects had the right to insist upon a safe and adequate use of that method.

From a careful examination of the record we conclude that if the architects knew or in the exercise of reasonable care should have known that the shoring was inadequate and unsafe, they had the right and corresponding duty to stop the work until the unsafe condition had been remedied. If the architects breached such a duty they would be liable to these plaintiffs who could foreseeably be injured by the breach.

Here it appears that the shoring and removal of part of the old gymnasium roof was a major part of the entire remodelling operation and one that involved obvious hazards. We think that the shoring operation was of such importance that the jury could find from the evidence that the architects were guilty of negligence in failing to inspect and watch over the shoring operation.[49]

3.2.4 *Professional's Responsibility in Approving Shop Drawings and Inspecting Equipment Installation.*

In another case involving safety of workmen on a construction site, the District Court's ruling, awarding damages against the architects, subsequently was reversed by the highest court in the State of Louisiana. In this case, it was alleged that the architects were negligent in approving inadequate shop drawings, and in failing to inspect equipment during installation. The pattern of facts and the decision of the Supreme Court were as follows:

Mrs. Cecelia LeBlanc Day instituted this suit on her own behalf and as natural tutrix of her minor children, Judy Dianne Day and Randall Joseph Day, to recover damages for the death of Willie Day, her husband and the father of her children. Day was fatally injured as a result of a boiler explosion which occurred while his employer, Vince Plumbing & Heating Company, a subcontractor, was installing a hot water system in a new building of the tuberculosis hospital at Greenwell Springs, Lousiana. Several persons, firms, and corporations, with their insurers, were named defendants. The district court gave judgment for plaintiff against Wilson and Coleman, the firm of architects on the building, and its insurer, and held the other defendants relieved of any liability. The Court of Appeals likewise gave judgment for plaintiff against the architects and their insurer. . . .

The Louisiana State Building Authority entered into a contract with defendant Wilson and Coleman, a firm of architects, to prepare plans and specifications for the construction of the New Patients' Building at the Greenwell Springs Tuberculosis Hospital. Upon completion of the plans and specifications by the architects, a contract was entered into with Charles Carter & Company, Inc., a general contractor, for construction of the building. The contractor in turn negotiated a subcontract with Vince Plumbing & Heating Company, in which the latter undertook to perform all mechanical work as per plans and specifications (which were made part of this subcontract), including heating, plumbing, etc., necessary to complete the central heating system and the domestic hot water system. The boiler which exploded was a part of the domestic hot water system. After installation the boiler was lighted by an employee of Vince to test its operation. The explosion occurred shortly afterwards, and Willie Day, plaintiff's husband, who was standing nearby, was scalded to death.

In their contract with the building authority the architects' services were to consist, among other things, of "supervision of the work" as indicated by a schedule set forth in the contract. According to this schedule they were to prepare "complete working drawings, and specifications for architectural, structural, plumbing, heating, electrical and other mechanical work." In this schedule they further bound themselves to exercise "adequate supervision of the execution of the work to reasonably insure strict conformity with the working drawings, specifications, and other contract documents," and this supervision was to include, among other things, " . . . (b) inspection of all samples, materials, and workmanship . . . (d) checking of all shop and setting drawings (e) frequent visits to the work site . . . "

Pursuant to the authority given them by this contract the architects employed a firm of consulting engineers, Chessen, Forrest & Holland, at a fee of 3 percent of the cost of mechanical and electrical work, to be paid from the proceeds of the 6 percent fee which the architects were to receive from the owner. Under their contract with the architects, the consulting engineers, among other things, prepared for the architects, plans and specifications for all mechanical and engineering equipment to be incorporated in the building. It was the duty of these engineers to consult with and advise the architects about the proper mechanical and electrical equipment for the building. They were to examine all shop drawings submitted by the contractor or the subcontractor and make a final inspection and report to the architects when the general contractor had completed the work. The architects admitted that they relied on the consulting engineers' technical ability for the installation of the mechanical and electrical equipment, of which the boiler that exploded was a part, because they themselves were without the specialized knowledge to determine whether the mechanical equipment was installed in a safe way.

The architects' specifications plainly stipulated that the hot water heater or boiler was to be provided with a thermostat, and that the contractor was to "equip hot water heaters with temperature and pressure relief valves."

The specifications further provided that in the installation of the domestic hot water system the contractor before proceeding with the work "shall make complete shop and working drawings of such apparatus or connections as directed by the Architects and/or hereinafter required. These drawings shall show construction details and dimensions of each piece of equipment so drawn." The provision quoted was found in that part of the specifications dealing with plumbing. In Section 1 of the general contract specifications under the heading "Shop Drawings" it was provided that four copies of shop drawings or data for all mechanical work should be submitted, and two corrected or approved copies returned to the contractor, and that no shop drawings should be submitted by any subcontractor directly to the architects or to the architects' consulting engineers. This section further specifically provided: "Shop drawings marked 'Approved as Noted,' are assumed to be approved for fabrication or placing orders."

. . .

After obtaining the subcontract, Sam Vince, sole owner of Vince Plumbing & Heating Company, furnished to the architects through the general contractor, as provided in the specifications, a brochure for their approval of certain equipment. The terms "brochure" and "shop drawing," as shown by this record, are interchangeable and mean the same thing. In other words, a brochure was considered by all as a shop drawing, as that term was used in the specifications. This brochure was submitted by the architects to the consulting engineers, who approved it with certain exceptions. This qualified approval, according to the evidence, was tantamount to rejection in toto. Vince then submitted a second brochure. This brochure also was referred to the architects' consulting engineers, and on the advice of the engineers was likewise disapproved by the architects. These two brochures were disapproved for causes which were in no way related to the subject of the boiler explosion. A third brochure was submitted to the architects, who, without submitting it to their consulting engineers, endorsed it "Approved as Noted" and returned it to Vince. All these brochures were prepared for Vince by Amstan Supply Division of American Radiator and Sanitary Corporation. The approved brochure did not specify or list a pressure relief valve for the hot water boiler which subsequently exploded.

After receiving the approved brochure or shop plan, Vince ordered the material and equipment shown in it, and proceeded with the installation of the domestic hot water system. In making the installation of the hot water heater a part of this system, Vince failed to follow the plain provision of the specifications that the hot water heater or boiler should be equipped with a thermostat and with a temperature and pressure relief valve. He installed the hot water boiler without a pressure relief valve, and instead of putting the thermostat and the temperature relief valve on the boiler he installed these safety devices on a hot water storage tank. After the installation of the hot water system Vince, to check his own work, caused the boiler to be lighted for a preliminary testing, and the explosion ensued which resulted in the death of Vince's employee Day.

At this point it may be well to note that Vince made this preliminary test without informing either the architects or the consulting engineers that the hot water system was ready for inspection, and did not request any of these persons to make an inspection at any time before the explosion.

It is clear from this record, as shown by the testimony of the experts, that because of the method of installation the explosion of the boiler was inevitable. Among other things, it was not equipped with a pressure relief valve as called for by the specifications, and further, if this boiler had been equipped with such a valve, the explosion could not have occurred. As stated by the Court of Appeals, the experts "all stated that, assuming all component parts performed their respective functions, the explosion could nevertheless have eventually occurred because of the absence of a pressure relief valve on the system."

Let us . . . consider the holding of the Court of Appeals that the terms and conditions of the architects' contract with the State Building Authority imposed upon the architects the obligation of supervising the installation of the domestic hot water system, that the architects breached this obligation because neither they nor their agents, the engineers, were aware that this system was being installed and neither they nor the engineers inspected the system during installation or after completion, and that all of this constituted negligence by the architects.

. . . (W)e should point out that we do not have here a case where the architects failed to provide in the specifications for a pressure relief valve on the boiler and for other safety devices; or a case where they inspected and approved the installation, or even where they had knowledge of the installation and stood by and permitted the boiler to be tested without having proper safety devices; or a case where they visited the site after the completion of the installation and, knowing that the boiler was to be tested, failed to observe that the boiler was not equipped with the safety devices stipulated in the specifications. Under such circumstances we should not hesitate to say that they breached a duty and that they reasonably should have foreseen that this breach would cause damage.

The narrow question here presented is whether the architects' contract with the owner imposed upon them the duty to be aware that the boiler was being installed by Vince, the plumbing subcontractor, and whether they were required by their contract to inspect the hot water system, of which the boiler was a part, during installation and before the boiler was tested by the subcontractor Vince.

In their contract with the owner the architects bound themselves to exercise "adequate supervision of the execution of the work to reasonably insure strict conformity with the working drawings, specifications, and other contract documents," and this supervision was to include "frequent visits to the work site." If this provision of the contract required the architects to know that the boiler was being installed and required them to inspect the installation while it was in progress and before the system was tested, then the decision of the Court of Appeals may be correct. We therefore must determine the meaning of the above quoted provision of the contract.

As we view the matter, the primary object of this provision was to impose the duty or obligation on the architects to insure to the owner that before final acceptance of the work the building would be completed in accordance with the plans and specifications; and to insure this result the architects were to make "frequent visits to the work site" during the progress of the work. Under the contract they as architects had no duty to supervise the contractor's method of doing the work. In fact, as architects they had no power or control over the contractor's method of performing his contract unless such power was provided for in the specifications. Their duty to the owner was to see that before final acceptance of the work the plans and specifications had been complied with, that proper materials had been used, and generally that the owner secured the building it had contracted for.

Thus we do not think that under the contract in the instant case the architects were charged with the duty or obligation to inspect the methods employed by the contractor or the subcontractor in fulfilling the contract or the subcontract. Consequently we do not agree with the Court of Appeals that the architects had a duty to the deceased Day, an employee of Vince, to inspect the hot water system during its installation, or that they were charged with the duty of knowing that the boiler was being installed.

We might add that the record discloses that as the work progressed over a period of some nine months before the explosion, the architects in performance of their duty to the owner made frequent visits to the work site in order to determine that the work in progress was being executed in conformity with the plans and specifications and other contract documents, all in accordance with what was considered by other architects who testified in the case as good and accepted architectural practice.

We finally consider the question of whether the architects were negligent in approving Vince's shop drawing or brochure which did not specify the pressure relief valve for the boiler and, if this was neligence, whether such negligence was a proximate cause of the accident.

. . .

It is to be noted that according to the specifications a shop plan "Approved as Noted" was assumed to be approved for fabrication or placing orders. The architects contend that the brochure approved by them was submitted by Vince to obtain their approval only for the purchase of the items listed and designated therein; that it was not approved for fabrication or as a detailed plan for the installation of the boiler.

Vince testified that these shop plans were made for him by Amstan to be presented to the architects and engineers for their approval, which had to be secured before the plumbing supply house would accept an order for the items listed. A representative of the plumbing supply house which prepared them stated that such documents are usually prepared for a contractor who wants to order from the company certain equipment, and do not necessarily list all items called for in the specifications because the supply house only furnishes the contractor that part of the equipment which he needs.

The plans and specifications require many items to be incorporated in the domestic hot water system and listed them in detail, whereas the brochure prepared by Amstan listed only a few of the items required by the specifications to be installed in the system. A comparison of the items listed in the brochure with those called for in the specifications shows beyond doubt that the brochure was not intended to include all of the equipment required for the installation of the boiler, a part of the domestic hot water system.

As we view the matter, the architects' approval of the brochure was only an approval for Vince to place the order with Amstan for the purchase of the items listed in it, and the brochure was not intended as a shop plan for fabrication or a plan showing construction details.

There is still another convincing reason why plaintiff cannot recover because of the architects' approval of the brochure. Let us assume a position most favorable to the plaintiff and concede that the brochure was in fact a shop plan submitted by Vince for installation of the boiler, purporting to show all construction details and all connections and safety devices to be installed thereon, but not listing or calling for a pressure relief valve, and that the architects were negligent in approving the shop plan for the installation of the boiler. Even if we should concede all this, however, it was established beyond any question by plaintiff's own witnesses that Vince, the subcontractor, did not use or rely on his brochure in his installation of the boiler. Accordingly its approval by the architects had no causal connection with, and was not a proximate cause of, the explosion. We therefore conclude that plaintiff's suit against the architects should be dismissed.

It is worthy of note that in this opinion the court outlined particular circumstances, which if present, would have led to a contrary decision that the architects had breached a professional duty. The court said that the architects would have been negligent:

1. If they had failed to specify a pressure relief valve;

2. If they inspected and approved the installation without proper safety devices;

3. If they had knowledge of the installation, and permitted the boiler to be tested without having proper safety devices;

4. If they visited the site after the installation, and knowing the boiler was to be tested, failed to notice the absence of the specified safety valve.

Although this case finally was dismissed by the Supreme Court of the State, both the District Court and the Court of Appeals found for the plaintiff against the architects. Therefore, it would seem wise to specify that no such operating tests be made until after inspection and approval by the architect or engineer.[50]

3.2.5   *Is Seller's Surveyor Liable to Purchaser for Mistakes?* A prospective purchaser of lots 36 and 37 in an unimproved subdivision informed the seller that before he purchased the lots he wanted a survey made and stakes driven, showing the boundaries of the lots; whereupon the seller engaged a registered engineer to make the survey and set the stakes. Later the seller and purchaser visited the site, and the seller pointed out the stakes, saying that they marked the boundaries of lots 36 and 37. They then visited the engineer, who said that his employees had made the survey and had placed the stakes, and that they marked the boundaries of lots 36 and 37.

The purchaser then bought the property and made improvements to the land enclosed by the boundary stakes, clearing off trees and brush, filling in a gully, building a retaining wall, and grading. After spending some $2672, he learned that the stakes were not correctly located, and that they enclosed portions of lots 33, 34, 35, and 36. The purchaser brought suit against the engineer for damages.

Noting the general rule:

The question of liability for negligence cannot arise at all until it is established that the man who has been negligent owed some duty to the person who seeks to make him liable for his negligence,

the court held that this duty can arise only in one of three ways: by contract, by statute, or under the common law. As the court found no contractual relationship, or any statute imposing liability, it ruled that, as there was no allegation of an attempt to deceive, and it could not reasonably be inferred that the engineer knew or should have known that the information would be used to grade, build walls, etc., there was no liability.[51] It therefore is apparent that the purchaser, and not the seller, should engage those who are to make the survey, the title search, and such matters as are of direct concern to his future use of the property.

However, in a later case decided by the Supreme Court of the State of Illinois, the court reached a different conclusion regarding the duty owed to third parties injured by the failure to perform contractual obligations. In this instance a homeowner extended a driveway and constructed a garage, relying on markers on the property which had been placed in accordance with an inaccurate survey. The survey had been made for a previous owner, and the face of the plat contained an "absolute guarantee for accuracy" by the surveyor. The survey error was such that portions of the driveway and garage encroached on an adjacent lot. In awarding damages to the homeowner against the surveyor, the court stated:

. . . the factors we consider relevant to our holding are:

(1) The express, unrestricted and wholly voluntary "absolute guarantee for accuracy" appearing on the face of the inaccurate plat;

(2) Defendant's knowledge that this plat would be used and relied on by others than the person ordering it, including plaintiffs;

(3) The fact that potential liability in this case is restricted to a comparatively small group, and that, ordinarily, only one member of that group will suffer loss;

(4) The absence of proof that copies of the corrected plat were delivered to anyone;

(5) The undesirability of requiring an innocent party to carry the burden of a surveyor's professional mistakes;

(6) That recovery here by a reliant user whose ultimate use was foreseeable will promote cautionary techniques among surveyors. [52]

The general trend of recent decisions indicates that the privity doctrine has less force as a defense than it used to have.

It is important to keep in mind that professional liability insurance policies usually provide that they do not cover liability arising out of the making or absence of "boundary surveys or surveys of subsurface conditions or ground testing unless specifically noted on the policy." It would be well for architects and engineers to consider the advisability of securing coverage against such contingencies through a suitable endorsement on their policies.

3.3 Conclusions. In order that the professional not be trapped through lack of knowledge of his responsibilities to the public at large, the following safeguards should be considered:

1. Don't perform professional services, or even offer to perform them, in a state in which you are not licensed, even if the statute merely protects the title "Architect."

2. Don't perform professional services as a partnership in any state, unless every partner is licensed in that state, unless you are positive that you are not violating the law by so doing.

3. Don't forget that the professional may be adjudged liable to anyone who is injured as a result of a hidden defect in his design.

4. Don't forget that an architect or engineer who prepares a faulty plan may be responsible to a third party for any injury caused thereby.

5. Don't forget that an architect or engineer who negligently supervises construction likewise may be liable to a third party who is injured as a result thereof.

6. Don't join forces with a partner or an associate who does not have a professional license to practice.

7. Don't place your name and seal on architectural drawings which had been prepared by one who is not licensed to practice.

8. Don't approve shop drawings for mechanical equipment designed by your engineer without the concurrence of the engineer.

9. Don't fail to insist that you be notified to inspect all important equipment before it is tested.

CHAPTER **4**

Legal Pitfalls in
Intraprofessional
Relationships

Today's building decisions are firmly grounded in the physical sciences, and the impact of technological advance and scientific discovery has revolutionized architectural practice. It has become so broad in scope, complex in function, and varied in structure, that no single individual, working alone, can competently make all the decisions in designing a building. The result is that the architect must surround himself with technical experts—the structural engineer, the mechanical engineer, the acoustician, etc.—each of whom contributes his specialized skill and knowledge to the problem at hand.

4.1 Architect's Responsibility for Mistakes of His Consultants. Normally, the architect assumes responsibility for the competency and correctness of the work of these experts. This total responsibility arises from the fact that, under usual circumstances, the owner has no direct contract with any of these experts. Because the architect ordinarily engages them, they become his subcontractors, and he must assume liability to the owner if the latter suffers injury or damage due to their negligence.

In order to avoid this legal responsibility, it would be essential for the architect to exclude specifically from the owner-architect agreement any reference to engineering services, and have the engineers enter into prime contracts with the owner. This is very seldom done, because it seems to place all members of the team on a parity, which could be disastrous in the event of differences of opinion; or if the architect does act as coordinator of the work of the others, his fee may not equitably reflect his time and effort. Finally, by tradition and custom the other experts have been engaged by the architect instead of by the owner precisely because this does place final responsibility in the hands of a captain of the team, who by training and experience is best equipped to combine into a harmonious whole the efforts of this multitude of advisers.

The architect accepts this position in hope and trust that all will go well; but occasionally he is rudely shocked into awareness of the responsibility he has assumed. When the owner makes a claim against the architect for errors of his engineers, the result may be costly to the architect—perhaps even jeopardizing his financial future. This is not to imply that those architects who have complete faith in the competence and moral responsibility of their engineers are unjustified. But if the owner is awarded a judgment against the architect due to the fault of the engineer, then, from a practical viewpoint, the architect may actually recover from the engineer only if the latter has sufficient funds or if he carries adequate insurance.

4.1.1   *Consultant's Professional Liability Insurance.* It is fair and desirable for the architect to insist, in his architect-engineer contracts, that his engineers agree to maintain and keep in force errors-and-omissions insurance in a stipulated amount, the amount varying according to circumstances. Such insistence would benefit the engineers also, who are as likely as the architects to disregard the importance of insurance until after an error has occurred, by which time it may be too late to procure insurance. The contract should provide that within a specified number of days after its execution, or in the alternative, prior to the commencement of any services by the engineer, he shall deliver to the architect certificates of insurance acceptable to the latter. The contract should state further that these certificates will embody a provision that the coverage under the errors-and-omissions insurance policy will not be canceled until a specified number (fifteen) days have elapsed after written notice of intended cancellation has been given to the architect. As an additional precaution, it would be advantageous to provide in the architect-engineer contract that if the engineer (1) shall fail to deliver to the architect the said certificate of insurance within the time specified, or (2) within fifteen days after notice of cancellation of coverage shall have been given to the architect shall fail to deliver to him a new certificate evidencing replacement of such coverage, the architect may terminate the contract without prejudice to any other right or remedy he may have.

4.1.2   *Consolidating Arbitration Proceedings.* Even in cases where there is adequate professional insurance or sufficient personal responsibility, there is still apt to be a further problem. If the owner demands arbitration, and secures an award against the architect, then the architect will demand arbitration against the engineer. Furthermore, there may be instances in which an engineer may assert a claim—such as one for extra compensation— against the architect, who in turn has a possible basis for a claim over against the owner predicated entirely or partly upon the same state of facts. Any such situation normally would result in two separate arbitration proceedings before different arbitrators, whose judgments may differ—though the same questions of law or fact may be presented for determination. The best wisdom would be to consolidate all these claims into a single arbitration proceeding, in which the same arbitrators could define, delineate, and apportion the responsibilities.

4.1.3 Special Provision Consolidating Proceedings and Effect Thereof. Standard forms of contracts do not appear to make any provision covering consolidation of two or more arbitration proceedings involving common questions. It is hoped that architects and engineers will recognize this serious problem and find a suitable contractual method to answer it. It would seem prudent to provide (in addition to the usual arbitration clause) in both the owner-architect agreement and the architect-engineer agreement:

If any dispute arises beween the owner and the architect, in which either party claims that the work of any engineer engaged by the architect is involved, in whole or in part, any dispute between the architect and the engineer arising out of or in connection therewith, shall be determined in the same arbitration proceeding, which shall be conducted under the Construction Industry Rules of the American Arbitration Association. If any dispute arises between the architect and the engineer, in which the engineer seeks to recover compensation from the architect, any claim by the architect against the owner arising, in whole or in part, out of or in connection with the engineer's claim, shall be determined in the same arbitration proceeding which shall be conducted under said rules.

It cannot be overlooked that there are problems inherent in determining in a single proceeding two or more separate disputes, such as the selection of the arbitrators and requiring agreement of all parties to the dispute; but if the arbitration is conducted under the Construction Industry Rules of the American Arbitration Association, no difficulty should arise in the selection of a single panel of arbitrators.

Under the said rules of the association, a proposed list of arbitrators is sent to each party. If none of the parties strikes out the name of any individual whose name appears on the list as a proposed arbitrator, the said individual, if able to serve, will be selected as an arbitrator. Sometimes the association finds it necessary or advisable to send more than one list in an effort to secure arbitrators to whom none of the parties has any objection. But in any matter, under the rules of the association, its administrator may designate the arbitrators, so that in case there are more than two parties to the dispute, thereby making it more difficult and perhaps impossible for the parties to select the same arbitrators, the administrator may exercise his choice and provide a fair and impartial panel of arbitrators which will determine the several disputes at the same time.

4.2 *Partnerships and Joint Ventures.* There exist today many partnerships among professionals—architects, engineers, planners, landscape architects, or combinations of these categories. These partnerships were designed to carry on all the professional activities of the firm—each partner contributing his skill in furtherance of a common effort. When professionals unite to undertake a specific project or series of projects, the association is not called a "partnership," but is called a "joint venture," and the participants are referred to as "associated architects," "associated engineers," or "associated architects and engineers," or otherwise appropriately designated. The fundamental practical distinction arises out of the scope of the undertaking, members of a partnership agreeing to a joint performance of all their professional activities.

Although there is a distinction in scope, similar legal principles are applied generally to both partnerships and joint ventures. Each contemplates a uniting of skill and labor, and usually property in the form of capital contributed by the participants. In partnerships, both profits and losses are shared; but although there is a sharing of profits in joint ventures, there is not always a sharing of losses. However, in any case, the rights and obligations of the parties are determined by law in the light of their specific agreement.

Partnership agreements among professionals should cover, as a minimum, the following points:

1. The name of the firm and its purpose must be stated.

2. The term of the copartnership should be agreed upon; shall it continue for a specific time, or shall it continue indefinitely until terminated by the election of any one party or the mutual agreement of all the parties? Shall the partnership continue until the happening of a specified contingency, viz.: death or retirement of a partner? Or shall the partnership practice continue among the surviving or remaining partners notwithstanding the death or retirement of one or more of the partners?

3. The location of the principal office of the firm should appear, and perhaps subsidiary offices should be located.

4. Contributions to capital should be determined.

a. Provision may be made for contributions in the form of cash, or in the form of jobs in work (the value of which may be determined and agreed upon in advance), or in the form of property, such as furniture, fixtures, etc. Provision may be made for a minimum capital, and a minimum contribution to such capital by the several members of the firm. Should the capital contribution of a partner fall below the required minimum, it may be provided that he is required to restore his deficiency within a specified period of time.

b. The possible need for future contributions should not be overlooked.

c. Whether a partner shall receive interest on his capital account should be considered. This may be important, because it may become desirable for a partner to make further contributions to capital in order to enable the firm to undertake larger projects. It is not uncommon to provide that an increase in the capital contribution of a partner shall not increase his share in the net income of the firm.

5. It is not unusual to expect each partner, at the outset, to bring to the new firm his personal clientele and prospects, insofar as they relate to the practice of the profession. Any exceptions should be defined clearly to avoid dissension at a later date.

6. The fiscal year of the copartnership must be agreed upon—not only for calculation of the firm's net income, but also for distribution of such income among the partners.

7. Authority to sign checks, drafts, or other similar instruments must be designated.

a. Sometimes it is provided that such instruments must be signed by two authorized partners. And considering the possibility that one may not be available, a substitute representative should be designated.

b. In signing contracts, the signature of one partner is sufficient from a legal viewpoint. However, to protect the other partners, each partner may be required by the copartnership agreement to secure the approval of one or more other copartners.

8. Provision for personal income of the partners must be considered carefully.

a. Partners may receive salary allowances—not necessarily equal in amount—and these salary allowances may be treated as an expense in computing the net income of the firm to be distributed. Or partners may receive fixed drawings, representing merely payments on account of their respective shares of the firm's net income.

b. Each partner may be reimbursed for expenses reasonably incurred by him personally on behalf of the firm.

c. Provision may be made to review annually (or more frequently) salary allowances or withdrawals in order to consider whether they should be changed. Questions reflecting inequities in this regard are worthy of early resolution.

d. Ratios in which profits and losses, arising out of the conduct of the practice of the firm, are to be shared or borne, should be established. It may be provided quite simply that all profits and losses shall be shared or borne in fixed ratios, or the ratios may vary; for example, the first $100,000 of profit or loss may be shared or borne equally among the partners, while any profit or loss in excess thereof may be allocated:

To Partner A: 50%
To Partner B: 25%
To Partner C: 25%

e. It is important to understand that under income tax regulations, each partner is taxed for his proportionate share of the firm's income whether distributed or not. All earnings and profits of a partnership are taxable to the individual partners, unaffected by the fact that they may be retained and accumulated by the firm. However, once so taxed, any later distribution of these undistributed earnings is tax exempt.

9. What bookkeeping system shall be used in keeping the firm's accounts and in computing the partners' respective shares of net income? Most professional firms use the cash receipts and disbursements system, sometimes referred to as the cash basis. This is the simplest form of accounting, recording cash income and cash expenditures, from which the cash profit or loss can be computed for any period. This, however, may not reflect the actual financial condition of a firm in the present world of credit buying. A more accurate method of keeping accounts is on the accrual basis, wherein the books record income earned but not collected, expenses incurred but not paid, and also prepaid income and "expense" as well as cash transactions.

10. Agreement should be reached regarding admission of a new partner. Must he be approved by all other partners, or will an approval less than unanimous be acceptable? How will his participation in net income be fixed? Will his participating share be borne automatically by the other partners on a pro rata basis?

11. A subject of grave importance deals with the withdrawal of a partner or partners from the firm, pursuant to an agreement which contemplates the continuance of the practice by the remaining partners.

a. If a partner should decide to withdraw, voluntarily, he should give reasonable notice of his intention (for example, ninety days), and it would be most desirable to have his withdrawal become effective only at the end of a fiscal year, in order to avoid complications in computing his share of the firm's annual net income.

b. Since it is conceivable that any one partner may prove to be less than satisfactory to the others, the partnership agreement could provide for the right to compel his withdrawal. Fairness requires that a firm basis be established for such an action—more than a bare majority vote of the other partners.

12. One of the most troublesome problems arising in partnerships is that of payment to a withdrawing partner or to the estate of a deceased

partner of his share or interest in a partnership, in lieu of an actual liquidation of the firm.

4.2.1   *Extent of Share in Firm Due Withdrawing Partner.* In one case, apparently because of the decline in an architectural firm's business, one of several partners was required to withdraw by the other partners, voting in accordance with the terms of the partnership agreement. To what share in the business of the firm is the involuntarily retired partner entitled in such a case? Ordinarily, in the absence of an agreement to the contrary, upon the retirement (voluntary or involuntary) of a partner, the firm would have to be dissolved and all uncollected fees, work in progress, as well as all other assets of the firm not reduced to cash at the time of such retirement would be for the benefit of all members of the firm in liquidation. However, this partnership agreement specifically contemplated the continuance of the firm despite the involuntary withdrawal of a partner, and provided that:

he shall be entitled to receive the book value of his capital account as of the effective date of his withdrawal, together with any accumulated earnings of the firm then due him, but nothing more.

The agreement also provided that:

Books of account of the transactions of the copartnership shall be maintained in accordance with generally accepted principles of accounting on the cash basis.

The involuntarily retired partner was paid only his share of the earnings of the firm actually received to the date of his retirement. He sued the firm to recover his share of monies earned by the firm while he was an active partner, but not collected by the firm at the time of his withdrawal, contending that "accumulated earnings" included "fees receivable," and "unbilled work in process," as well as the firm's interest in certain joint ventures that had not been reduced to cash, and that he was entitled to what he would have received on dissolution of the firm under the Partnership Law.

Counsel for the defendant firm pointed out that the normal rights of a withdrawing partner under the law could be altered by contractual agreement, and that the Partnership Law contained no requirement or guide as to the accounting methods to be employed in valuing a partner's interest. Therefore, the agreement to maintain books on a cash basis, whether wise or not, effectively delimited the rights of a withdrawing partner to participate only in those earnings actually received to the date of his withdrawal. Hence, he could not participate in fees which had not been collected at the time of his withdrawal, in unbilled work in process, nor in interests of the firm in joint ventures which had not been reduced to cash at that time. The court accepted this reasoning, and ruled for the defendant.

This case illustrates the necessity for an exact understanding of all terms and phrases used in a formal contract by all parties thereto. In this instance, both the withdrawing partner and the remaining members agreed that the term "capital account" as used in this provision of the contract included both the original contribution of the withdrawing partner as subsequently increased or decreased and his share of the annual net cash income not previously withdrawn. However, the court decided that both plaintiff and defendants were mistaken in their definition of "capital account," and that the term as used referred only to a partner's required capital contribution— the agreement having provided (in Article IV, referred to below in the court's opinion) that each partner was required to maintain his capital account at a specified amount and that if it fell below such level he was required to restore the deficiency.

As the decision of the court revolved about the definition of "capital account," it is interesting to follow the argument in some detail. Several points disclosed here are worthy of keeping in mind:

1. A word used by the parties in one sense is to be interpreted as employed in the same sense throughout the writing, in the absence of countervailing reasons.

2. In interpreting a contract, particular words should not be considered as isolated from context.

3. A contract should not be so construed as to be inequitable where language permits more equitable construction.

4. The court may not rewrite an agreement between members of a partnership, and the language of their contract is controlling even when the wisdom of the contract is questionable. The court said:

Plaintiff argues that since the term "capital account" includes his share of annual net income, the words "together with any accumulated earnings of the firm then due him" must have reference to something other than annual net income, namely, accounts receivable, advances receivable from clients, unbilled work in process and interests in joint ventures which have not been reduced to cash at the time. Defendants contend on the other hand that the words "together with any accumulated earnings" refer only to annual net income not previously withdrawn and were inserted merely as a precaution in order to insure that the term "capital account" would be interpreted as including such income and to preclude any contention by the remaining partners that a withdrawing partner is entitled to receive only his required contribution. This reasoning is untenable. If "capital account" includes unwithdrawn net income, then the accumulated earnings which a withdrawing partner is entitled to receive "together with" such capital account can not refer to such unwithdrawn net income. The alternative, assuming the parties to be correct in their definition of "capital account," is the conclusion of plaintiff that a withdrawing partner is entitled to his proportionate share of all earnings in matters pending at the time of withdrawal whether billed or unbilled, received or not received. However, this conclusion is not warranted by the terms of the contract.

The Court is of the opinion therefore that both plaintiff and defendants are mistaken in their definition of "capital account," and that as used in Section D of

Article XIV that term refers only to the required capital contribution of the withdrawing partner. Capital or capital account has been defined by the Courts as consisting of "money required of the partners by the partnership agreement." . . . While the term may be used in a broader sense and appears to have been so used by the firm's accountants, the more limited definition would have the effect of resolving any ambiguity in Article XIV and is at the same time most consistent with all other provisions of the contract.

Thus in Article IV which establishes the total capital of the firm and imposes an obligation upon the partners to furnish and maintain such capital, the parties speak of a partner's "capital account" as referring only to the required sum initially contributed by him as depleted by any operating losses and as restored to its original level by any additional contributions. Article IV refers to Article XIV, D but not for the purpose of making any exception to the above definition of the term "capital account."

Again, in Article XVI which deals with the rights of the estate of a deceased partner, "accumulated earnings" (which in said Article can only be interpreted as referring to net cash income) are specifically excluded from the term "capital account." It follows that "capital account" is used therein to mean only the book value of the deceased partner's required contribution. "A word used by the parties in one sense is to be interpreted as employed in the same sense throughout the writing in the absence of countervailing reasons." . . . Plaintiff is then to receive the book value of his required contribution as of the date of his withdrawal, along with any "accumulated earnings of the firm then due him . . . but nothing more." In determining the intention of the parties it is important to note that the partnership agreement required the firm's books of account to be kept on a cash basis. The essence of the cash method of keeping accounts is that the actual receipt determines whether an account should be included in income. It is in contrast with the accrual method wherein income is based upon the acquisition of the right to receive it rather than upon what has actually been received. In interpreting a contract particular words should not be considered as isolated from the context. . . . "Earnings" therefore should be construed in the light of the accounting system contemplated by the parties and prescribed by the agreement. It follows that the words "accumulated earnings of the firm" must mean undistributed net income of the firm computed on the cash basis of accounting. That would exclude all fees receivable and other interests of the partnership not reduced to cash at the end of the fiscal year.

This conclusion is reinforced by the words "then due him" which immediately follow the words "earnings of the firm." These words could have been inserted for no other reason than to exclude earnings not yet realized on the date of withdrawal and to limit a withdrawing partner to his share of net cash income actually received by the firm during the fiscal year. The subsequent inclusion of the limiting words "but nothing more" makes this abundantly clear.

The Court is aware that to some extent its construction of the contract places a withdrawing partner at the mercy of the partners. It is possible that they might deprive a withdrawing partner of his share by merely delaying the billing or collecting of earned fees. A contract should not be so construed where the language permits a more equitable construction. . . . However, the court may not rewrite an agreement between members of a partnership. . . . The language of the contract is controlling even where the wisdom of the contract is questionable.[53]

4.2.2 Limited Extent of Surviving Joint Venturers' Duty to Account. In the absence of a special agreement to the contrary, what are the rights and obligations of the surviving parties to a joint venture, when one of them dies? It has been held that, although the death of a member terminates the joint venture, it is the duty of the survivors to take possession of the assets, perform the contract, extinguish the liabilities, and close its business for the benefit of all parties concerned, and the representatives of the deceased joint venturer are entitled to share in the profits of all unfinished business for which the joint venture has been commissioned, though subsequently completed.

Two firms of architects, which we shall designate A and B, entered into a joint venture to design a railroad terminal station and buildings connected therewith, agreeing to divide the compensation as firms and not as individuals. They also agreed that a partner of firm A should be the executive head of the work. The joint venturers' contract with the railroad company stipulated that in case of the death of said partner, the company reserved the right to terminate the employment of A and B at any time upon notice in writing. The associated architects opened a separate office for this work and planned and supervised the construction of numerous buildings for the railroad during the following eight years, at the end of which time the executive head of the work, the partner in firm A, died.

Immediately following his death, without any suggestion on the part of the railroad company and without the knowledge of firm A, firm B wrote to the railroad company, directing its attention to the clause as to the right of the railroad to terminate the contract, and suggested that the company terminate its contract with the joint venturers and execute a new contract with firm B to complete the work relating to the terminal station, already under said contract. Firm B also suggested that the new contract should include a large hotel, for which preliminary drawings had been prepared by the joint venturers, although not yet authorized by contract with the railroad company.

The company did cancel its contract with the associated architects, signed a new contract with firm B covering both projects, and all the work was carried forward by firm B. The surviving partner of firm A then sued firm B, pleading that firm B was under an obligation to assist in completing the unfinished business of the joint venture for the benefit of all parties, and that the new contract placed firm B in a position where its interests conflicted with its trust duties as surviving joint venturer.

The court was asked to answer several questions, which it did as follows:

1. Was the agreement between the associated architects terminated by the death of a member of one of the firms?

The court, in ruling that the joint venture agreement was terminated, said:

It is a general rule that a contract of partnership is dissolved by the death of one of the parties, whether entered into for a fixed time or not, and that after his death the former partner cannot bind the estate of the decedent by new contracts; and although the partnership be expressly extended to executors, they could not be compelled to carry it on, and would be entitled to a dissolution and an account of the assets, subject to the liabilities of the firm incurred up to the time of dissolution.

2. By reason of the death, was the obligation of the joint venturers to the railroad company, with respect to the terminal station, canceled?

Here the court answered in the negative, stating the general rule that upon the death of one of several joint contractors before complete performance of the contract, the survivors are bound by the obligations of the contract, and entitled to its benefits.

3. Is firm B accountable to firm A for the profits derived from the terminal station project, for which the joint venture had a contract prior to the death of the executive head?

The court decided that firm A was entitled to share in these profits, since the contract was an asset of the joint venture.

4. In view of the fact that the joint venturers had no contract with the client for the hotel project, prior to the death of the executive head, is firm B accountable to firm A for fees relating to the project?

The court ruled that a "reasonable expectation" of securing a contract for the hotel was not an asset of the joint venture and for that reason firm A was not entitled to participate in the profits of that project. However, testimony disclosed that the hotel as finally constructed conformed substantially to the preliminary plans prepared by the associated architects prior to the death of the executive head, in their effort to secure from the railroad company a contract for professional services relating to this project. Firm B was to receive a fee equal to 5 percent of the cost of the hotel, of which 1 percent was allocated to preliminary drawings. Therefore, the court ruled that one-half of 1 percent (a half share in the contract price of the preliminaries) be awarded to firm A.[54]

4.2.3 When May a Partner or Joint Venturer Act Unilaterally? It is becoming more and more usual for architects to join in temporary associations lasting only for the duration of a single commission. Often the design will be provided by an architect whose office is at a considerable distance from the project, while the supervision of construction will be undertaken by a local architect. Where the client's contract is made with the associated architects as "Architect," and the associated architects subsequently disagree, the rights of the several individual architects are not always clear-cut.

In one instance, in connection with the construction of school buildings, a board of education, as "Owner," contracted with an "Architect" consisting of two separate architectural organizations, one an individual (architect A) and the other a partnership (architects B and C). The contract between owner and architect contained a clause which provided: "All questions in dispute under this agreement shall be submitted to arbitration at the choice of either party." On the same day, architect A signed a contract of association with architects B and C which incorporated by reference the provisions of the owner-architect contract. The agreement between the associated architects made architect A responsible for the supervision of construction and the issuance to the contractor of certificates for interim payments.

During the course of construction, architect A required justification of a requisition for $81,000 before he would approve its payment. The contractor notified the board and architect A of his intention to terminate his contract, and thereupon ceased work.

The board then negotiated a settlement with the contractor without consulting architect A or considering the data supporting his opinion that payment of this requisition would make total payments exceed the contractor's costs up to that time, and might enable the contractor to avoid completion of the job within the contract price. The board also discharged architect A but not architects B and C.

When architect A's claim for payment of fees was rejected by the board, he asked architects B and C to join with him in demanding arbitration. When they failed to do so, he served a demand for arbitration in his own name.

The court held that architect A had a right to demand arbitration, even without the acquiescence of the partnership firm of architects (B and C).

Although the court did not decide whether one of three or more equal associates or partners may compel arbitration of such a dispute, it found that this association was composed of two members, one being architect A and the other being the firm B and C.

The court decided that architect A was within his rights in demanding arbitration, citing the Partnership Law, which states:

Every partner is an agent of the partnership for the purpose of its business, and the act of every partner, including the execution in the partnership name of any instrument, for apparently carrying on in the usual way the business of the partnership of which he is a member *binds the partnership*, unless the partner so acting has in fact no authority to act for the partnership in the particular matter, and the person with whom he is dealing has knowledge of the fact that he has no such authority.[55]

Therefore, it is well for the articles of agreement to define clearly whether, and under that circumstances, a joint venturer or partner may act unilaterally.

4.3   Conclusions. In his dealings with other architects or engineers, or with contractors, there are reciprocal obligations explicitly or implicitly assumed by the professional, some of which, if foreseen, can be provided for in a manner fair to all. In associations such as partnerships and joint ventures, and in consultative endeavors, it is particularly important to be precise in establishing contractual relationships. The following precautions should be observed:

1. Don't forget that the architect may be liable to his clients for the negligence of his consultants.

2. Don't neglect to carry professional liability insurance, and to require it of your consultants.

3. Don't overlook the advantages of including the consultant and owner in the same arbitration proceeding.

4. Don't be lax in providing for every foreseeable contingency in partnership and joint venture agreements (see also Chapter 17).

5. Don't fail to define the circumstances under which a joint venturer or partner may or may not act unilaterally.

CHAPTER 5

Legal Pitfalls in the Owner-Contractor Relationship: Contracts

Probably the protagonists most frequently appearing in the arena of disputes concerning building construction are the building owner and the contractor. The owner is a customer of the building business, rather than a performer, and may be concerned with building only once in a lifetime. The contractor, although he may have spent his lifetime in building, usually is not trained in law. Because of the very complexity of their contractual relationship, it is almost inevitable that misunderstandings will arise; and what to the layman may seem unquestionable justice may in fact be based on an untenable legal theory. A legally enforceable contract may impose obligations upon the owner or the contractor which neither anticipated.

5.1 What Constitutes Acceptance of an Offer? An offer and an acceptance are essential to an enforceable contract. But what, in the eyes of the law, constitutes a valid acceptance? One might imagine that to begin work on the job, even without formally notifying the owner that his offer is accepted, in itself would be evidence of acceptance, but this is not always so, as indicated in the following case.

A contractor was furnished with plans and specifications for fitting up a suite of offices, and was requested to make an estimate of the cost of doing the work, which he did. After he sent his estimate to the owners, he received the following note:

Upon an agreement to finish the fitting up of offices ———— Broadway in two weeks from date, you can begin at once.

The contractor did not make any reply to this note, but immediately purchased material and started to work on the project.

On the next day, the offer quoted above was countermanded by a second note to the contractor, and the latter brought an action for damages for a breach of contract. The trial court said that he had a right to act upon the first note, and to commence the job, and that there was a binding contract between the parties. The higher court, however, reversed this judgment, holding that before an offer can ripen into a contract, it must be accepted; also that the acceptance must be brought to the knowledge of the party making the offer. Here the contractor failed to communicate properly to the owner his acceptance of the offer which had been made. Thus the court stated:

We understand the rule to be, that where an offer is made by one party to another when they are not together, the acceptance of it by that other must be manifested by some appropriate act. It does not need that the acceptance shall come to the knowledge of the one making the offer before he shall be bound. But though the manifestation need not be brought to his knowledge before he becomes bound, he is not bound, if that manifestation is not put in a proper way to be in the usual course of events, in some reasonable time communicated to him. Thus a letter received by mail, containing a proposal, may be answered by letter by mail, containing the acceptance. . . .

Conceding that the testimony shows, that the plaintiff did resolve to accept this offer, he did no act which indicated an acceptance of it to the defendants. He, a carpenter and builder, purchased stuff for the work. But it was stuff as fit for any other like work. He began work upon the stuff, but as he would have done for any other like work. There was nothing in his thought formed but not uttered, nor in his acts that indicated or set in motion an indication to the defendants of his acceptance of their offer, or which could necessarily result therein.[56]

5.2 *Oral Understandings Not Expressed in Written Contract.* The language of contracts should be clear and unambiguous in order to avoid the necessity for the court to construe the intent of the parties; and, of course, the language should include all the agreed-upon stipulations, as a written contract usually may not be changed by a verbal understanding that preceded the writing but was not expressed therein.

In one instance a contractor whom the owner intended to employ did not operate a union shop. The contractor assured the owner that there would be no difficulties with the union; and the contractor was awarded the contract to do a portion of the job with the verbal understanding that the contractor guaranteed that no such difficulties would arise. The written contract, however, did not make any reference to this understanding.

The work had hardly commenced when the union served notice on the owner and architect that none of the other work on the job would be attended to, so long as the nonunion contractor was employed. The result was that the owner, in order to secure the erection of his house, was forced to make a new contract with a union contractor for the work which the original contractor was to have performed. The latter promptly sued the owner for breach of the written contract. The court refused to allow evidence of the oral understanding, and the contractor was awarded damages.

5.3 Liability for Delay. One of the most prevalent problems that an owner must face in a building construction project is the matter of claims by a contractor for delays. The general contractor and subcontractors encounter similar problems in their dealings with each other. Unlike other damage claims, such as those involving defective workmanship, the damages attributable to delays are not readily ascertainable, and frequently, from a practical viewpoint, the claimant's attitude may be "the sky is the limit." A failure to deliver and install materials costing only a few thousand dollars may be asserted to have caused damages for delay in the realm of hundreds of thousands of dollars. The general contractor's claim against the owner for damages for delay may even be based upon the acts or omissions of a separate contractor. The problem is so complex, and fraught with such danger, that every reasonable precaution should be provided in the contract documents to safeguard those against whom such claims may be asserted.

Building contracts are sometimes written to excuse nonperformance or to excuse delay on the part of the builder because of "conditions beyond his control, including labor, disputes, fire," etc. The word "including," as used here, has been construed by courts to be a word of limitation, whereby the specific language limits the prior general language, so that the only operative "conditions beyond his control" are those specifically enumerated. In order to avoid having to list each and every contemplated condition, the contract should state "including, without limitation," or "including, but not limited to," or, after enumerating the specific items, "or any similar or dissimilar causes beyond his control."

One manufacturer of building parts has been advised to incorporate the following sweeping provision in its standard contract, in order to avoid liability for contingencies beyond its control and to limit its liability for damages for delay which may be within its control:

The seller shall not be liable, in any case, for any delay in manufacture, shipment or delivery, due to fires, strikes, lockouts, differences with workmen, shortages of cars, delays in transportation, accidents at mills, demands or requirements of the Government of the United States, or of any other state or government, inability to procure supplies or raw materials, after the exercise of reasonable efforts, or other similar or dissimilar contingencies beyond its control.

In any event, the seller shall not be liable for damages for delays in manufacture, shipment or delivery, whether caused by the fault (including without limitation the negligence) of the seller, its agents, servants or employees, beyond the actual total loss sustained by the buyer, and occasioned wholly and directly as a result of any and all such delays, not exceeding, in the event of only one delay, or more than one delay, a sum or sums, as the case may be, equal, in the aggregate, to five per cent of the total price stipulated in this contract.

A comparable provision may be used to protect others, such as a building owner or general contractor, against unfair or exaggerated claims. Consideration also may be given to inclusion of a clause permitting the architect (engineer) to determine with finality who should bear the responsibility for delay, or a clause providing that, in case of a number of disputes involving alleged responsibility for delay, the several questions or claims shall be decided in a single arbitration proceeding.

It is important to bear in mind that since some courts will not uphold a provision excusing or limiting liability for damages resulting from delays, careful consideration must be given by local legal counsel before any such provision is incorporated into any contract.

5.4   *Contract Based on Mistaken Bid.* An acceptance of an offer is necessary before a contract comes into being. It is well known that a contractor's bid may be withdrawn at any time before its acceptance, if he finds he has made a mistake. But what happens if he does not discover his mistake until after his bid has been accepted and a contract has been signed?

A carpentry contractor in Connecticut found himself in such a situation, when a client visited his shop and urged him to complete an estimate he had not had time to complete the evening before. He sat down at his workbench and added up the items he had prepared. In his haste he made an error in addition, making the apparent cost $1450.40 instead of $2210.40, and later the same day he executed a written contract to do the work for $1450.40. When the owner secured the contractor's signature to the contract, he had good reason to believe that there must have been a substantial omission or error in the amount.

That evening the carpenter discovered his mistake, and offered to do the work for $2210.40, or for as low an amount as any other responsible contractor would do it. The owner refused, however, and insisted that the work be done for $1450.40, as written in the contract. When the contractor refused to proceed, the owner let the work to others at $2375, and sued the careless arithmetician for breach of contract. In rejecting the owner's claim, the court decided that although the mistake of only one party to a contract is not a ground for its reformation, it may afford a basis for its cancellation. It held:

1. That the mistake was so essential and fundamental that the minds of the parties had never met.

2. That since the agreement was unperformed and the owner had not been prejudiced in any way, he would not be permitted to gain an unfair

advantage over the carpenter, even though the mistake was unilateral; and that the carpenter was entitled to a cancellation of the contract.

3. That although the mistake involved some degree of negligence, it did not amount to a violation of a positive legal duty.[57]

5.5 Interim Payments. Where a contract makes no mention of interim payments, ordinarily the work must be completed before payment can be required.

A contract was executed between owner and general contractor for concrete work for a manufacturing building, in which nothing was said in writing about the time or manner of payment. After two months the work had progressed as far as the first floor, and the contractor sent a bill for work done up to that time. The owner refused to pay the bill, and the contractor stopped work.

A few days later, the owner wrote the contractor a letter containing the following:

Notwithstanding you promised to let us know on Monday whether you would complete the job or throw up the contract, you have not up to this time advised us of your intention. . . . Under the circumstances we are compelled to accept your action as being an abandonment of your contract and of every effort upon your part to complete your work on our building. As you know, the bill which you sent us and which we declined to pay is not correct, either in items or amount, nor is there anything due you under our contract as we understand it until you have completed your work on the building.

The contractor replied the following day by letter which stated:

There is nothing in our agreement which says that I shall wait until the job is completed before any payment is due, nor can this be reasonably implied. . . .

Finally, the contractor sued the owner for the amount of the bill presented, plus damages for breach of contract. The court held:

Where a contract is made to perform work and no agreement is made as to payment, the work must be substantially performed before payment can be demanded.[58]

5.6 Owner's Changes. It is not unusual for the architect to discover after the fact that his client unwittingly has amended a carefully drawn contract by issuing verbal instructions directly to the contractor. The owner often believes that he is the one to be satisfied as he is paying for the building; and sometimes he does not fully understand the rather formidable drawings and specifications which he approved prior to signing the contract. Thus, when he visits the job, and thinks of a seemingly minor improvement, he is likely to request informally that the contractor follow out this new idea. All too often this seemingly small matter affects other parts of the job in a series of chain reactions, which result in a less satisfying building at a greater cost than that originally planned.

5.6.1 *Work Not to Be Performed under Verbal Authorization.* In order to avoid the difficulties previously mentioned, or unnecessary controversies, building contracts are frequently found to contain provisions requiring that changes or alterations in the work must be based on a written order to the contractor. For instance, some variation of the following is commonly made a part of the contract:

The Contractor shall not vary from the drawings and specifications. Should the Owner at any time during the progress of the work request any alterations or additions to or deviations or omissions from the work included in the specifications, such request shall be acceded to by the Contractor and the same shall in no way affect or make void the Contract. No such alterations, additions, deviations or omissions which affect the price or the time of completion as agreed upon shall be done, however, without a written order signed by the Owner and the Architect.

5.6.2 *May Requirement for Written Change Orders Be Waived?* A provision requiring change orders to be in writing is some measure of protection. But where it appears that extras, changes, or alterations performed under verbal orders from the owner are expected by both parties to be paid for, the court may consider the provision requiring written orders to have been waived.

When difficulties arose between a general contractor and a subcontractor during the construction of a hangar for the Navy Department, the general contractor terminated the subcontract. The subcontractor brought suit for the balance due it under the contract, and for four items of extra labor and materials: (1) grading north side of hangar, $6140.75; (2) excavation north side of hangar, $1206.80; (3) thirty-one barrels of cement, $105.40; (4) 914 feet of sewer pipe, $1096.80.

The case was appealed because the trial court had permitted the jury to consider these items as extras, although they had not been authorized in writing by the contractor to the subcontractor as required by the contract. The general contractor contended that, lacking written orders, the subcontractor was not entitled to compensation for the work done or materials furnished. The subcontractor admitted that there was no written order, but said that there was a verbal agreement that the work be done, and that the written authorization thereby had been waived.

The court ruled that, under both New Jersey law and Federal decisions, a written contract may be waived by a verbal agreement if the evidence (1) is clear and of a satisfactory character; (2) shows a distinct agreement that the work be deemed extra work; (3) shows a definite agreement by the owner or contractor to pay for the extra work.

Referring to a prior decision, the court quoted as follows:

The next question concerns the right of the plaintiff to recover for extras not covered by the contract and for which the plaintiff produced no written order signed by the engineer and the township committee. In that regard the contract provided that the plaintiff should not be entitled "to receive payment for any extra work as extra work unless such bill for extras be accompanied by an order in writing from the engineer and said township committee, who shall fix the price for such work." The court admitted proof which tended to show that at regular meetings of the township committee and acting as such the committee, the engineer and the plaintiff fully discussed and considered such extra items and work, and the plaintiff was then directed to proceed with them; they saying, "their word was as good as their contract." That a contract requirement such as here provided may be subsequently waived by the parties is established by the authorities. . . . The court therefore was not in error in admitting testimony tending to show such waiver.[59]

But in a state such as New York, such testimony is not admissible in the trial of an action if the agreement not only provides that any order for extras, changes, or alterations must be in writing and signed by the owner or his architect, but also expressly provides that the agreement cannot be changed orally. These legal tools may be of great value to a lawyer defending a lawsuit against claims for extras, changes, or alterations based upon an alleged oral agreement. However, those experienced in the building field know that once a dispute is presented to a panel of arbitrators, since they have the right to determine questions of law, they may ignore completely such technical legal points and find the contractor is entitled to be paid despite the absence of any written promise, which absence would be cause for rejection of the claim in a court of law.

5.6.3   *Special Provision—Written Order a Condition Precedent to Enforcement of Claim.* Some courts have taken the position that it is up to the arbitrators to determine whether the owner, by his conduct, is prevented from insisting on the requirement of a writing covering the claim. Therefore it seems desirable, whenever legally possible in those instances where arbitration is stipulated, for each lawyer representing an owner to consider whether it would be appropriate to provide that, as a condition precedent to the contractor's right to arbitrate a claim for extras, changes, or alterations, he must base his claim upon a written order from the owner. A suggested provision reads as follows:

No action or proceeding shall be prosecuted or maintained by the Contractor against the Owner for any extras, alterations or changes unless the Contractor's claims therefor are based upon a written order from the Owner, signed or countersigned by the Architect, or a written order from the Architect stating that the Owner has authorized the extra work, alterations or changes.

5.6.4   *Distinction between "Extra Work" and "Additional Work."* Many people presume that the terms "extra work" and "additional work" are synonymous, and use them interchangeably. However, courts have made a clear distinction between these terms when they are used either in building contracts or architects' agreements. In a case which has illuminated the legal pathway for more than fifty years, the court drew a sharp distinction between these terms by defining "extra work" as:

Work arising outside of and entirely independent of the contract, and not required in its performance,

and defining "additional work" as:

Necessarily required in the performance of the contract, not intentionally omitted from the contract, and evidently necessary to the completion of the work.

In this case, even though the contract stated that "no *extra* work will be allowed or paid for unless the same is done upon a written order of the Inspector of Repairs and Supplies," the court held that, in order to entitle the contractor to recover for *additional* work ordered by the said inspector, it was not necessary that the orders should have been given in writing; and the court considered which items of the contractor's claim would, and which items thereof would not, come within the category of additional work.[60]

In a second case, a contractor, building several houses for an owner, sued to enforce a lien because he had not been paid for certain items installed under an oral agreement made subsequent to the original contract. The contract stated:

No *alterations* shall be made in the work except upon written order of the Architect; the amount to be paid by the Owner or allowed by the Contractor by virtue of such *alterations* to be stated in said order.

The court held that, despite the absence of a written order, the contractor should be paid for installing medicine cabinets, which the original plans did not call for, defining this as extra work—rather than an alteration. But it did not allow additional payment for roofs, the form of which had been changed from peak to mansard, defining this as an alteration within the terms of the contract provision quoted above, which required a written order covering alterations.[61]

5.6.5   Binding Effect of Unit Prices Submitted. When extra work as such is mentioned in the contract, and unit prices for the extra work are included, the contractor is held to have agreed to perform such work at that price if requested by the owner to do so.

In one instance, a foundation contractor was asked to submit unit prices for sidewalks as extra work, not included in the scope of work originally contemplated. Although he did submit unit prices, when he was later requested to provide sidewalks he refused, saying that the unit prices were to apply only if the two parties later agreed to contract for their installation. The court rejected this point of view, ruling that the inclusion of unit prices for extra work clearly implied an obligation to do such work at the stipulated price, when requested to do so.[62]

5.7   Contract Objective Not Clear. The precise nature of the obligations incurred by the parties to a contract may not always be completely understood, either because of ambiguity or misinterpretation. If the contract is not of uncertain meaning, the courts will not make a new one for the parties, but if uncertainty lurks in the words used by the parties, the courts must seek to ascertain their intention.

5.7.1   Inconsistency in Requirements for Pile Foundations. It has been held that where the contractor performed his contract according to only one of two inconsistent clauses in the contract he was entitled to payment.

In this case, pile foundations were to be constructed for the apron building at an airport in accordance with plans and specifications prepared by the owner's engineers. The contract included the following provision:

PILES I: All piles shall be steel encased cast in place concrete piles of a safe working load capacity of 20 tons . . .

DRIVING: . . . The safe value of piles shall be determined by the following formula:

$$P = \frac{2\ WH}{S + 0.1}$$

where P equals the safe load in pounds, W equals weight of the striking part of the hammer in pounds, H equals the fall in feet of the striking part of the hammer or stroke, S equals average penetration per blow in inches under the last five blows. The Engineers may modify the required value of S on the basis of the load tests.

This formula, said the court, "is recognized and accepted in the engineering world as a proper formula for determining the theoretical safe value of piles." As applied in this case, P was 40,000 pounds, W was 5000 pounds, H was 3 feet, and S was 0.65 inches. Thus a pile, driven with a penetration of 3.25 inches or less under the last five blows, would be driven in accordance with the formula.

As a condition precedent to the award of a contract, the contractor was to drive a number of test piles to determine for himself what lengths and gauge of pile casings would meet the foregoing requirements. Such test piles, if satisfactory, were to be accepted by the owner as piles in place for payment. The owner reserved the right, before awarding the contract, to require load tests in accordance with its specifications, and would pay for these tests at the rate of $750 each. It was further stated that "The bid will be rejected if the piles fail to comply with the test load requirements. . . of the specifications."

These preliminary load tests were made on three piles driven by the contractor in the presence of the engineers to a point where the total penetration under the last five blows was less than 3.25 inches. The load tests, however, showed that one of the three piles subsided more than the specified maximum when loaded with 20 tons. The results of these tests were examined by the contractor, the engineers, and the owner, and the engineers recommended that the contract be awarded "on the basis of this data." The contract was formally executed without any further changes regarding developing of the desired load-bearing capacity.

During the next six months, 4325 piles were driven under the observation of the engineers. Each pile was driven until the engineers ordered the driving to stop, when the penetration under a series of five blows was less than 3.25 inches. Except for the three load tests, made prior to awarding the contract, no further load tests had been ordered by the engineers until this time.

Then a load test made on a single designated pile showed that, although it had been driven to a total penetration of less than 3.25 inches under the last five blows, when tested under an actual load the subsidence was greater than the maximum specified. The owner wrote to the contractor that this pile was not acceptable, and asked the contractor to furnish his plans for fulfilling the contract. All further pile driving was suspended until this question was determined.

The contractor took the position that all piles had been driven in accordance with the specifications (that is, the formula), and that he was not responsible if the pile failed under the load test.

Finally, after tests on two more piles indicated that they could not carry 20 tons, and after several conferences between the parties, the contractor was required to drive extra piles under an order for extra work which provided that the owner did not waive its right to deduct the cost of such work from final payments to the contractor, until the owner's contention, that the piles previously driven were not in accordance with the specifications, was judicially determined.

Upon completion of the job the owner deducted $69,843.70, the cost of such work, from the final payment to the contractor. Thereupon the contractor entered suit, claiming that these additional piles were not called for in the original contract, and should be paid for as an extra. The owner contended that this was merely furnishing work and materials in satisfaction of the contractor's obligations under the original contract and should not be paid for as an extra. It was the owner's position that the primary objective of the contract was the achievement of a safe working load of 20 tons, the formula being used merely to furnish a working guide to accomplish this objective.

The contractor contended that the two requirements were intended to be cooperative, and that until the value of S in the formula was changed by the engineers on the basis of load tests, the piles should be driven according to the formula as originally written.

The court decided for the contractor, stating that although the objective of the agreement was the installation of piles which would support a load of 20 tons, it was not feasible to test every pile. The cost of such tests would have been prohibitive, as it would have amounted to $3,265,500, or more than six times the entire contract price of $512,000. Therefore, the contractor was entitled to rely on the formula as a workable method of achieving the desired result.[63]

5.7.2 *Contradiction in Requiring both Waterproof Results and Pumps.* Where a contract is not absolutely clear as to its objective, it is left to the court to determine what had been contemplated. Because the majority of owners have no technical knowledge of what effort must be expended to accomplish an expected result, what may seem "reasonable" to the owner is not necessarily the same as what may seem "reasonable" to the contractor— or to the court.

A case in point involved the meaning of the term "waterproof" in a contract to overcome a water problem in a residential basement. The contract provided for the "basement area to be waterproofed, as shown in sketch, all labor, materials, including cost of pump or other materials, in order to resolve water problem in basement of home in accordance with our engineer's decisions to waterproof area shown in sketch including walls and floor."

When the job was finished—and, in fact, two pumps were installed— the owner contended that it could not be determined whether or not the basement was waterproof until the end of the approaching winter season.

The court, however, decided that the contractor had fulfilled his contract by installing two pumps, reasoning as follows:

From the fact that the contract required the installation of a pump, and actually two pumps were installed, it seems to me to be obvious that the floor, at least, was not intended to be so treated that it would become absolutely impervious to water. The expert . . . testified that to make this cellar literally impervious to water, which was his definition of the word "waterproof" as used in the contract, would require that the building be jacked up and a new floor and foundation be built. This clearly was not within the contemplation of the parties.[64]

5.7.3 *Unilateral Misunderstanding of Clear Language.* If a contract is ambiguous, the court or a jury may consider the resulting actions of the parties as a basis for determining what they really intended. However, if a contract is free from ambiguity, and is so clear that it is capable of only one reasonable meaning, the mere fact that one party misinterpreted it will not relieve him from its terms and conditions.

In one case, a dispute arose as to the meaning of an "escalation clause" in a subcontract to furnish and erect the structural steel for a multistory office building. This clause provided:

The price or prices herein stated are based on prices for component materials, labor rates applicable to the fabrication and erection thereof and freight rates, in effect as of the date of this proposal. If, at any time prior to completion of performance of the work to be performed hereunder, any of said material prices, labor rates and/or freight rates shall be increased or decreased, then in respect of any of said work performed thereafter there shall be a corresponding increase or decrease in the prices herein stated.

The steel subcontractor was also a steel manufacturer, and subsequent to the signing of the contract it raised its regular prices to all purchasers of steel products from its mills, including its own fabrication division. Pursuant to the escalation clause, it accordingly increased its contract price for the fabrication and erection of the steel for the office building.

The general contractor refused to pay the increase, claiming that the term "prices for component materials" as used in the contract had reference only to prices paid by the steel company to obtain iron ore, steel scrap, limestone, etc., in order to produce steel.

The steel subcontractor, having refused to accept such an interpretation, filed a mechanic's lien against the building and instituted an action for its foreclosure.

It was argued that an escalation clause is not intended to enable one party to make the bargain more profitable for himself, and that it was not intended in this case to give the steel subcontractor an arbitrary unilateral power to change the contract price.

However, the court held that the term "prices for component materials" was not ambiguous, and that the subcontractor was entitled to adjust the contract price to cover the increase in the cost of the steel. The court said:

Mere assertion by one that contract language means something to him, where it is otherwise clear, unequivocal and understandable when read in connection with the whole contract, is not in and of itself enough to raise a triable issue of fact. It has long been the rule that when a contract is clear in and of itself, circumstances extrinsic to the document may not be considered, . . . and that where the intention of the parties may be gathered from the four corners of the instrument, interpretation of the contract is a question of law, and no trial is necessary to determine the legal effect of the contract.[65]

5.8 *Terms of Relet Contract Following Default.* If a contractor should default on his contract, and it then becomes necessary to relet the contract to another in order to get the work accomplished, it is important that the terms of the relet contract be identical with the terms of the original contract except for any differences involving (1) the time for completion of the work and (2) the amount to be paid for the work. Only in this way can the owner properly determine the excess cost of the relet contract, which he may seek to recover from the defaulting original contractor. This matter of identical terms and conditions became the vital, basic, and decisive point in an interesting case.

In this case, which occurred during wartime, the original contractor had agreed to furnish and deliver certain materials to the government. As he could not deliver them on the agreed date, the government declared him to be in default, and relet the contract to a second supplier. This relet contract contained a "liquidated damage" clause, and its price exceeded the original contract price by $21,000. The original contract did not contain a "liquidated damage" clause.

The second contractor also delayed in performance, and he was charged $9000 under the liquidated damage clause contained in his contract with the government. To secure reimbursement for the excess cost of $21,000, the government withheld from the original contractor an equivalent amount, which incidentally was owed to him under another contract.

The original contractor then commenced an action against the government, claiming that he could not be held liable for the excess cost of $21,000. His theory was that although he had agreed to reimburse the government for any excess cost incurred by it in reletting the contract as a result of his default, the government had relieved him of this responsibility by reletting the contract in a form materially different from that originally specified.

The original contractor contended that the inclusion of a liquidated damage clause in the relet contract—a clause that did not appear in the original contract—affected, as a matter of law, the price bid by the second contractor. More specifically he argued that the second contractor must have recognized that the added clause increased its risk, should it delay in making delivery; therefore it must be conclusively presumed to have included in its bid a contingency of at least $21,000 for assuming that risk.

The court, in an opinion containing as many philosophical as legal implications, rejected this argument, saying:

That argument rests on the axiom that businessmen invariably recognize the risks they take and always nicely calculate them in dollars and cents. Doubtless at one time many economists, believing it to be self-evidently true that every man is solely a fanatically rational "economic man," accepted that axiom as virtually a law of nature; but, as the result of accurate observation of human behavior, that axiom is now generally treated as an assumption to be used most cautiously with full awareness that it is a "neglective fiction." J. M. Clark, employing what he calls "non-Euclidean economics," suggests as an axiom or postulate that most businessmen do not act with rational foresight, and that a competitive system is possible only because most of them do not intelligently pursue their own self-interest. He refers to the "fanatically economic man," and says, "The consistent economic man has long been known to be a sheer abstraction, though not everyone has realized the importance of the elements left out. . . ." Courts use such (and other) fictions; but this particular fiction should surely not be the basis of a "conclusive presumption" or otherwise serve as a substitute for evidence.

The court held that if the inclusion of the liquidated damage clause increased the price bid by the second contractor, then to that extent only the original contractor would be released from liability for excess cost. The court ruled further that under no circumstances would the original contractor be entitled to a credit for the $9000 liquidated damages which the government had charged against the second contractor, since the defaults of the two contractors were separate and unrelated.[66]

From the standpoint of architects and engineers, this case appears to be of great significance. It illustrates the necessity for reletting a contract after a default in exactly the same terms as originally specified—except, of course, as to price and time for performance. Otherwise there is an ever-present danger that the original contractor who has defaulted may be relieved from liability for excess cost, in whole or in part.

By way of further illustration, in another case a defaulting dredging contractor was relieved completely of such responsibility because the owner, in reletting the defaulted contract, changed the place specified for dumping the spoil, even though this change lessened the cost of the work as relet.[67]

Once a contract has been relet, and the excess cost thereby ascertained, the relet contract may be altered as desired, by adding a bathroom or changing other work—particularly if the original contract documents as well as the relet contract documents contain the usual provision reserving to the owner the right to order extra work or make changes.

5.9   Conclusions. An incomplete understanding of the legal obligations of the owner and the contractor, implied as well as expressed, may lead to disputes during performance of the contract. Even if those disputes result in nothing more than ill feeling, they are impediments to the successful completion of the work. Therefore, at the time of preparing or signing contracts, it would be well to keep in mind the following points:

1. Don't start work without a contract, in the belief that the starting constitutes the necessary acceptance of an offer.

2. Don't fail to include in the written agreement every oral understanding.

3. Don't fail to consider the need for protection against claims resulting from delays.

4. Don't forget that "including" is a word of limitation unless followed by such words as "but not limited to . . ." or "without limitation."

5. Don't rely on a mistake by the other party to a contract to give you an advantage.

6. Don't depend upon custom to establish your right to interim payments; if the contract does not contemplate interim payments, the work must be completed before payment can be required.

7. Don't forget to stipulate that orders for extras, changes, or alterations must be in writing and signed by the proper party.

8. Don't confuse "extra work" (not contemplated in the original contract) and "additional work" (necessary for the completion of the original contract).

9. Don't forget that a contract performed according to only one of two inconsistent or contradictory conditions may be said to have been performed.

10. Don't provide for a guarantee of results and then contradict the intent of the guarantee by other words and phrases.

11. Don't rely upon your own interpretation of a contract to establish your intent, if the contract language clearly establishes a contrary one.

12. Don't change the terms of the original contract until after the relet contract is entered into, if excess cost is to be collected from the original defaulting contractor.

13. Don't forget that the submission of unit prices requires the contractor to do the work for those prices.

CHAPTER **6**

Legal Pitfalls in the Owner-Contractor Relationship: Performance

6.1 *When May One Be Relieved from a Contract?* May one ever be relieved from a contract duly executed? Under what circumstances? A contract is a promise to which the law attaches a legal obligation. In the event of breach of a contract to buy or sell real estate, the injured party may sue to compel specific performance; that is, the court may compel the seller to convey title, or the buyer to accept title, according to the contract they had signed. However, if a builder were to fail to carry out his building contract, or one of its stipulations, the law would not take him by the scruff of the neck and compel him to finish the building. In such a case the remedy of the owner would be to sue the delinquent builder for damages.

6.1.1 *Impossibility of Performance.* Contracts may be terminated before fulfillment by mutual consent; but if this is not done, normally one must meet his contractual obligations, unless the contract becomes impossible of completion. Contracts may be impossible of completion as a result of a change in law; a new zoning law may prohibit the erection of a contemplated building. Another possible valid excuse is destruction of the subject matter; one cannot enforce a contract to add a second story to a building if the building burns to the ground. The impossibility may be existing or subsequent. It must, however, be more than exceedingly expensive, inconvenient, or even absurd. To excuse nonperformance, it must be shown that the thing cannot by any reasonable means be effected.

During World War II a builder contracted with a lumber supply company for the purchase and delivery of several hundred thousand board feet of lumber. Although the supply company in turn contracted to purchase the material from a large mill in North Carolina, the contract that had been entered into between the supply company and the builder did not specify the source from which the lumber was to be procured. Subsequently, the War Production Board, under its powers to allocate priorities, commandeered the entire output of the North Carolina mill. The supply company sought to excuse nonperformance of its contract with the builder by pleading that under the terms of the contract it was excused if conditions beyond its control made performance impossible, and that since the lumber could not be obtained from the mill which had contracted to provide it, this was a condition beyond its control.

The court held, however, that since the procurement of the lumber from this particular mill was not an express or implied condition of the supply company's contract with the builder, the inability of the supply company to secure the lumber from such source was not a condition beyond its control. In ruling that the supply company was obliged to search elsewhere for the lumber, the court stated:

If conditions beyond the control of the plaintiff [the lumber supply company] have made it impossible for plaintiff to procure the required lumber, performance of the contract has been frustrated, and plaintiff would not be liable for its default. If Rules and Regulations of the War Production Board made it impossible for plaintiff to procure the lumber, the Rules and Regulations would be a bona fide excuse. But the reply does not allege impossibility, and in failing to do so is insufficient as a defense. . . .

The term "impossible" does not mean an absolute impossibility. If it did, impossibility of performance could be negatived merely by showing that the required lumber was available at some backwoods source not known to anyone but the inhabitants of the surrounding area. "Impossible" must be given reasonable and practical construction . . . but it is not satisfied by the allegation employed herein that plaintiff sought to procure the lumber "from its usual and regular channels as well as elsewhere." . . . Under the contract as it is presently written, plaintiff is under obligation to furnish the lumber if it can be obtained. To be excused from this obligation, plaintiff must allege "impossibility" of obtaining that lumber. Only then would the defense have merit.[68]

6.1.2 Special Provisions for Termination without Liability when Performance Becomes Impossible. Had it wished to do so, the supply company, in the case last mentioned, could have made its performance of the contract contingent upon procuring lumber from a particular mill by stipulating that the contract may be terminated without liability:

In case of the inability of the seller to procure from _____ (its source of supply) the materials contracted to be sold and delivered hereunder.

Or, if it did not wish to reveal the name of its source, it could have stipulated that the contract may be terminated without liability:

In case of the inability of the seller to procure from its usual sources of supply, after the exercise of reasonable efforts, the materials contracted to be sold and delivered hereunder.

6.1.3   *Contract Requirements Incapable of Execution.* In one case, a contractor signed a contract to remodel a mill building and undertook to take down and rearrange a sprinkler system which protected four floors of the original building, so that it would serve an enlarged building of three additional stories. The pipes in the original building were sufficient in length for the renovation and appeared to be in good condition in their original location. The contractor contended that it was not until he had taken down the system that he discovered that the pipes had become so rusted and weakened by scale on the interior that they could not withstand the necessary pressure or deliver the required volume of water. The contract stated that the "system shall be installed in accordance with the underwriter's rules." The underwriter refused to approve the remodelled system if these pipes were used. The owner did not offer to supply new pipes which the contractor felt he was under no obligation to furnish. Therefore, the contractor sued for recovery for partial performance.

The court ruled that if a defect in the quality of the original pipes made it impossible for the contractor to install them so as to obtain underwriter's approval, and if this defect was unknown to owner and contractor when they entered into the construction contract, then the contractor was entitled to receive payment in full for the construction of the building, less such amount as it would have cost the contractor to install the old sprinkler system.[69]

6.1.4   *Contractor Not Relieved from Guarantee by Owner's Changes.* Should a contractor protect his interests by assuring himself that the contract as described in the contract documents is actually possible of performance? In some jurisdictions, if he were to contract to do the impossible, he could be held to his undertaking.

A contract for alterations to a public school contained the following provisions:

Contractor to guarantee to heat the building to 70 degrees F. when outside temperature drops to 10 degrees below zero. Contractor to submit drawings and details covering the installation of this system for the approval of the architect. This work to be completed on or before _____. This Heating and Ventilating system is to conform to all States Rules and Regulations. The Town of _____ may make any changes by altering, adding to or deducting from the work without invalidating the contract, and the Contractor shall perform any work, not otherwise provided for, that may be required, and shall accept payment therefor on the basis of the cost as submitted by the Contractor in writing and accepted by the Building Committee in writing and approved by the Architect. . . . No changes shall be made until a written order has been issued and approved by the Architect and signed by the Building Committee. *Any additions, changes or alterations of this contract, or of the work, shall be performed subject to, and in all respects in accordance with, the terms of this contract.*

A sub-bid, which was accepted by the building committee and became a part of the contract, provided for the installation of a particular heating unit by manufacturer A. Two weeks after the contract had been signed, the architect wrote to the contractor:

I have been instructed by the Building Committee for the _____ School to have you submit the cost of substituting a Number _____ Heavy Duty Warm Air Furnace with casing, blower, motor, filters and humidifier, instead of the type on which you based your proposal. All to be in accordance with the other terms of the plans and specifications.

The contractor's price for this substitution of manufacturer B's unit instead of manufacturer A's was accepted by the building committee. Thereupon the contractor installed a B furnace of the size, and with the attachments ordered, which, however, did not heat the building to 70°F when the outside temperature dropped to 10° below zero.

The building committee refused to pay the contractor because the heating plant did not heat according to the guarantee, although it was admitted that the installation had been done in a workmanlike manner and had been approved by the architect. The contractor sued for payment, claiming that with the committee's substitution of B's heater the guarantee clause was eliminated, because the contractor had no choice in the selection of the heater.

The court decided, however, that it was more reasonable to conclude that the guarantee clause continued unaffected. It stated: "It does not appear that the plaintiff contracted to do the impossible. But if he had, he could be held to his undertaking."[70]

6.2   *Measures of Damage for Breach of Construction Contract.* When one party to a contract breaches it, the court usually compensates the other party who has been injured by awarding him a sum approximating as far as possible his actual loss. The measure of damage which will be applied by the court in a given case will vary depending upon who is guilty of the breach (owner or contractor), the point of progress of the work when the breach occurs, and other factors.

6.2.1   *Owner's Breach.* If the owner breaches a construction contract before the contractor commences construction, the contractor is entitled to recover the profit he would have made if performance had not been prevented by the owner.

If the owner's breach occurs after the contractor has performed his work in part, the contractor is entitled to recover not only the value of the labor performed and materials furnished, but, in addition, the profit he would have earned if the contract had been completed.

6.2.2   *Contractor's Breach.* If the contractor breaches a construction contract before he receives final payment, he may not be permitted to recover any balance if his performance is not substantial. On the other hand, if his omissions or deviations are slight and unintentional, usually he will be permitted to recover for the work completed, but his recovery will be diminished by allowing the owner damages to compensate him for the deficiencies.

The measure of damage recoverable by the owner usually is the market price of completing or correcting the contractor's performance. However, when it would be unfair to apply this general rule, the courts apply another rule known as the "difference in value" rule, as illustrated by the following case.

A contractor who had built a country residence sued to recover a balance remaining unpaid. There was no complaint of defective performance until about nine months after the owner occupied the dwelling. One of the specifications for the plumbing work provided that "all wrought iron pipe must be well-galvanized, lap-welded pipe of the grade known as 'standard pipe' of Reading manufacture." The owner learned that some of the pipe, instead of being made by Reading, was the product of other factories. The contractor was accordingly directed by the architect to do the work anew, although most of the plumbing by that time had been encased within the walls. Obedience to the architect's direction meant more than the substitution of other pipe. It meant the demolition at great expense of substantial parts of the completed structure. The contractor left the work untouched, and asked for a certificate that the final payment was due. The architect's refusal of the certificate was followed by court action. After noting that the omission of the prescribed brand of pipe was neither fraudulent nor willful and that the pipe as furnished was substantially the same in quality, weight, market price, serviceability, and appearance as the pipe called for in the specifications, the court refused to apply the general rule that the measure of damage is the cost of correcting the defect. Instead, the court applied the "difference in value" rule, saying:

In the circumstances of this case, we think the measure of the allowance is not the cost of replacement, which would be great, but the difference in value, which would be either nominal or nothing. Some of the exposed sections might perhaps have been replaced at moderate expense. The defendant did not limit his demand to them, but treated the plumbing as a unit to be corrected from cellar to roof. In point of fact, the plaintiff never reached the stage at which evidence of the extent of the allowance became necessary. The trial court had excluded evidence that the defect was unsubstantial, and in view of that ruling there was no occasion for the plaintiff to go farther with an offer of proof. We think, however, that the offer, if it had been made, would not of necessity have been defective because directed to difference in value. It is true that in most cases the cost of replacement is the measure. . . . The owner is entitled to the money which will permit him to complete, unless the cost of completion is grossly and unfairly out of proportion to the good to be attained. When that is true, the measure is the difference in value. Specifications call, let us say, for a foundation built of granite quarried in Vermont. On the completion of the building, the owner learns that through the blunder of a subcontractor part of the foundation has been built of granite of the same quality quarried in New Hampshire. The measure of allowance is not the cost of reconstruction. "There may be omissions of that which could not afterwards be supplied exactly as called for by the contract without taking down the building to its foundations, and at the same time the omission may not affect the value of the building for use or otherwise except so slightly as to be hardly appreciable." . . . The rule that gives a remedy in cases of substantial performance with compensation for defects of trivial or inappreciable importance, has been developed by the courts as an instrument of justice. The measure of the allowance must be shaped to the same end.[71]

Even where a contractor who breaches his contract has received final payment, the owner, nevertheless, may recover damages, unless he has waived his rights. The measure of his damage normally is the market price of completing or correcting the performance.

For instance, a developer agreed to construct a house for a purchaser in accord with a demonstration model house. Although the demonstration model had an attached garage substantially at street level, in building the new house the developer encountered rock close to the surface, and instead of excavating it, placed the house so high above the street that the driveway had to be installed at a 22½ percent grade, almost twice what is considered to be a reasonable maximum. Although the plans were silent as to the grade of the driveway, when the owner protested at the time, he was put off by the developer with assurances not to worry, that when finished the grade would not exceed 10 percent and that the owner would be happy when he got into his new home.

The owner, however, was not happy, and sued the developer for damages for breach of the construction contract. Although the developer contended that the measure of damages should be the difference between the value of the premises as built and the value as it should have been built, the court said:

In a case such as the present when the variance is so substantial as to render the finished building partially unusable and unsafe, the measure of damage is "the market price of completing or correcting the performance."[72]

If it had not been possible to remedy the defect in the driveway, the damages would have been measured by the difference between the value of the defective structure and that of the structure if it had been completed properly.

6.2.3 Liquidated Damages for Delay. Where a construction contract specifies a date of completion, it is often because the owner will suffer loss or damage if he is unable to occupy his building at a certain time. Unless delay in completing the building is caused by the owner, the contractor may be considered to have breached his contract if he does not meet the completion date, without justifiable excuse.

Often, instead of specifying a date of completion, the contract will require the builder to complete the work in a designated number of days from the date he is given access to the site, in order that the owner not be liable for delaying the job if the site is not immediately available. In order to avoid misunderstanding, the word "days" should be qualified: . . . is it to mean "working days" or "calendar days"?

The amount of actual damages which will be suffered by the owner in the event of delay is not always easy to ascertain at the time of making the contract. Consequently, it is not uncommon to stipulate a dollar amount as liquidated damages. If the amount is not a genuine estimate of actual damages expected, the court may be suspicious that it is a penalty for delay, and in many jurisdictions it will not be enforced unless it is coupled with a provision for a bonus for completion ahead of schedule.

However, a contract provision stipulating liquidated damages for delay in the completion of a construction contract may be enforced, even though no actual damages were sustained owing to the delay. A contractor was late in completing each of four construction jobs for the U.S. Government. After extensions of time were granted by the government due to delays occasioned by causes beyond the control and without the fault or negligence of the contractor, the government withheld $8300 as liquidated damages for delay in performance. The parties stipulated that the government suffered no actual damages, and because of this the contractor contended that the provision for liquidated damages "is clearly a penalty and not enforceable where the party seeking to enforce it formally admits he sustained no actual damage."

The court said:

Two requirements must be considered to determine whether the provision included in the contract fixing the amount payable on breach will be interpreted as an enforceable liquidated damage clause rather than an unenforceable penalty clause: First, the amount so fixed must be a reasonable forecast of just compensation for the harm that is caused by the breach, and second, the harm that is caused by the breach must be one that is incapable or very difficult of actual estimation. . . .

Whether these requirements have been complied with must be viewed as of the time the contract was executed rather than when the contract was breached or at some other subsequent time. . . .

. . . If in the course of subsequent developments, damages prove to be greater than those stipulated, the party entitled to damages is bound by the liquidated damage agreement. It is not unfair to hold the contractor performing the work to such agreement if by reason of later developments damages prove to be less or nonexistent. . . .[73]

6.3   Who Bears Loss for Destruction—by Inevitable Accident—of Building Being Built, Remodelled, or Repaired? This question is not always readily answered. Although general rules have been established, the courts will not insert in a contract, by construction, stipulations regarding unexpected contingencies.

The importance of including definite provisions in a contract to safeguard one against an act of Providence is pointed up by an enlightened opinion. A violent storm almost destroyed a house which was being worked on by a builder under a contract which provided that he would erect and complete a new building to correspond with plans submitted.

After the storm the builder began to reconstruct the house according to the plans, "having in mind that the work of placing the house in the condition it was before the storm would be charged to the defendant" (owner); but the owner told the builder that his services were dispensed with, and that he could not go on with the work.

The builder filed a bill for foreclosing a statutory lien for labor and materials furnished, but not paid for. He claimed that there remained owing to him a balance of $4805.50 under the contract which promised him $12,800 to be paid one-third upon completion of the frame, one-third when the building was entirely enclosed, and the remaining one-third upon final completion. He agreed to complete the building to the owner's entire satisfaction within a period of nine weeks. The building was not completed in nine weeks, nor was it completed three months thereafter, when the storm almost destroyed it.

The court decided that although the contract was an entire one, since payment was to be made in installments as the work progressed, each installment becomes a debt due to the builder, as the particular portion of the work specified is completed. And if the house is destroyed by an enevitable accident, the owner is bound to pay the installments then due upon the completion of a particular stage. But the owner would not be responsible for that part of the work which had been performed during the next succeeding stage which was not fully completed at the time of the accident. As to such work, the loss would fall upon the contractor. Thus the court said:

An inevitable accident will not excuse the performance of a contract where its essential purposes are still capable of substantial performance though literal performance is impossible. . . .

The loss caused by the destruction by storm of a building partly finished falls upon the one who has undertaken to complete and deliver it to the owner for a stipulated price. . . . As to the last one-third of the construction named in the contract, it appears . . . that it had not been completed. Therefore the law will leave both parties where the storm found them. . . .

In pointing out that the liability for damage resulting from inevitable accident falls upon an owner if he agrees to furnish any part of the material or labor, or if the construction contract involves the repairing or remodelling of an existing building, the court said:

The general rule also seems to be that where the contract provides for furnishing by the owner a part or all of the material or labor, upon the destruction of a building in the course of construction by storm or other unforeseen calamity, the loss must fall upon the owner. . . . The rule is somewhat different where the contract is to repair and remodel an old building. . . . The continued existence of the old building is an implied condition of the contract, and the destruction of such part [which is to be remodelled] may relieve the contractor from liability for any damage . . . and place it upon the owner.[74]

In the contract under consideration, the contractor did not guard against the unexpected contingency which had occurred, and since the contract made no provision for a dispensation, the law gave him none.

Therefore, it would be wise for the parties to stipulate specifically: (1)Whether the contract is entire or divisible; (2) who must bear the loss, under a contract for the construction, repair, or remodelling of a building, in the event of a calamity.

6.4   *Contractor's Assumption of Increase in Cost Resulting from a Change in Building Department Requirements.* Where requirements of the building department are changed after a building contract has been signed, who must bear the additional costs arising out of more expensive requirements? It may be the owner or the contractor, depending upon the terms of the contract.

An acoustical ceiling was installed in a bowling alley under a contract which specified:

1. That the contractor was to furnish, without extra charge, any work or materials "required to conform the building to all Laws, and the Rules and Regulations of all Municipal Departments and the Board of Fire Underwriters."

2. That if there was any conflict between drawings and specifications and the law, "the law is to be followed."

3. That the contractor would perform without additional cost all work necessary to obtain approval from all municipal authorities having jurisdiction.

The town building department insisted upon a two-hour fire rating, and a rider to the contract contained two clauses, one that the contractor would install a certain ceiling as per plans and specifications prepared by the architects, and the other as follows:

It is understood that a two-hour fire rating is now required on all areas and Contractor assumes responsibility for putting in ceiling, curtain walls, etc., which shall meet the Town of _____ building requirements and any other governing codes.

The contractor complied with the building inspector's requirements, and submitted a bill for payment over and above the contract price for the "extra and/or additional work" done in this regard. He claimed that a specific set of plans and specifications was incorporated into the contract, and that the ceiling which finally had to be installed differed from the original plans and specifications, and that two clauses in the rider were repugnant to each other; one called for a specific ceiling per plans and specifications, and the other for a ceiling which would meet a two-hour fire rating requirement of the town.

The court, however, found the clauses reconcilable, and held that the contractor was obligated to put in a ceiling meeting the requirements of the town despite additional expense. The court said:

. . . The plaintiff specifically assumed the obligation of erecting a ceiling with a two-hour fire rating. The provision of the rider in itself was sufficient to obligate the plaintiff to put in a ceiling meeting the requirements of the Town of _____ despite additional expense. . . .

. . . The mere fact that the performance of a contract becomes economically unprofitable is insufficient to relieve a party from his contractual obligations. . . . This is so even though the increased cost and expense result from the interference of law or government regulation.[75]

It is a settled principle of law that one who contracts absolutely and unqualifiedly to do something possible to be done must make his promise good unless its performance be rendered actually impossible by an act of God, the law, or the other party of the contract.

6.5 *Contractor Relieved by Assumption by Owner of Joint Responsibility.*
Whether or not a contract is considered to be completed may be an important element in fixing responsibilities. One court held that a contractor was not liable for damage done to his work by others, even though his own contract called for further work to be done, because this further work was

the joint responsibility of contractor and owner. After a fire had partially destroyed a building, the owner contracted with a glass company for the replacement of several large plate glass windows. The contract provided for washing the windows, the expense of washing to be divided between the contractor and the owner. Later, upon washing the windows, it was discovered that since their installation another contractor, who had the job of washing the soot and smoke of the fire from the building walls, used an acid which spilled upon the glass and etched it so that washing could not obliterate the indentations.

The owner refused to pay the glass contractor, urging that as a matter of law the contract was not fully completed—because the glass was not washed at the time it was damaged—and that, therefore, the glass contractor was responsible until the full performance of every provision of the contract. The court held, however, that the contract was completed with respect to the item of the installation of the glass, which was in no way connected with its subsequent washing. The court stated:

If there was not a full and final performance as to the installation of the glass, then it might be said that the contract was not complete, and the glass was not delivered . . . in the condition, that under the contract it was to be, but the glass windows were installed, the installation was complete, and there was nothing else to do concerning the windows excepting to wash the same and this operation was the joint enterprise . . . of the parties to this litigation, and this circumstance in our judgment, destroys the claim that the contract was not completed in the substantial and legal sense from which the glass company would retain responsibility for the delivery and installation of the glass itself.[76]

6.6   Is Subcontractor Liable for Defective Materials? Generally, there is implied in every contract for work, labor, and services a duty to perform same skillfully, carefully, diligently, and in a workmanlike manner. However, it has long been an established rule that a builder is not responsible for insufficiencies resulting from latent defects in materials where he had no knowledge of the defect, acted in good faith, and exercised reasonable care and skill.

While current opinions lean toward supporting the idea of an implied warranty of fitness in the sale of new houses by builder-vendors (see Chapter 11), ordinarily a contractor who is not negligent may not be held liable for latent defects in materials specified by the owner (or the owner's agent) and purchased from a reputable dealer.

In a recent case, a masonry subcontractor agreed to furnish all necessary labor, material, and equipment to install and clean all masonry work in a building. The contract specified, "Face brick shall be $24'' \times 2\,\frac{1}{4}'' \times 3''$ and shall be used for all brick exposed in the finished work. Face brick shall be M— Stone, color as selected by the Architect."

The subcontractor purchased the specified face brick from its only manufacturer, and properly installed it in strict accordance with the plans and specifications. It was only when his work was substantially completed that it was discovered that water leakage had occurred due to the failure of the mortar to adhere to the brick. Expert testimony indicated that acid present on the brick surface, possibly resulting from the manufacturer's failure to clean off a mold-releasing compound, reacted with the alkaline mortar to prevent a tight bond between the mortar and the brick.

The general contractor, upon discovery of the condition caused by the latent defect in the brick, called upon the subcontractor to correct the condition by waterproofing the exterior walls of the building. Upon the subcontractor's refusal to accede to this demand, the general contractor had the condition corrected at a cost of $12,255 and withheld this amount from the final payment due the subcontractor, who sued for the balance due.

The contract contained the following provisions:

Unless otherwise specified all materials shall be new and both workmanship and materials shall be of good quality. The Contractor shall, if required, furnish satisfactory evidence as to the kind and quality of materials.

The Contractor shall remedy any defects due to the faulty materials or workmanship and pay for any damage to other work resulting therefrom, which shall appear within a period of one year from the date of final payment, or from the date of the Owner's substantial usage or occupancy of the Project, whichever is earlier . . .

The court held that if either the general contractor or the owner had a claim for damages caused by the latent defect present in the brick purchased from the manufacturer, it did not lie against the subcontractor. The court said:

It is our view that the covenant to furnish materials "of good quality" is qualified by the "unless otherwise specified" phrase of this provision by virtue of the specification which requires appellee (subcontractor) to purchase only M— Stone which the owner knew was manufactured by and could be procured only from one manufacturer, to wit, M—. By requiring appellee to furnish only brick of a certain distinctive type produced by a single manufacturer, appellee was relieved and held harmless from its covenant to furnish only brick "of good quality." Under the terms of the contract appellee had no freedom of choice either as to the selection of the type of brick it would furnish or the manufacturer from whom such material could be procured. Having released appellee from the covenant to furnish brick "of good quality" by having otherwise specified that only M— Stone be used in the performance of the masonry subcontract, the fact that the brick used by appellee contained a latent defect unknown to it cannot be said to constitute a breach of express warranty.[77]

6.7 *Contracts with Government Agencies.* When one contracts to do work or perform services for a governmental agency, he must exercise extreme care to insure that he does not extinguish inadvertently his right to compensation. Government contracts almost always contain provisions answering the government's need for finality and certainty in winding up its contracts. In virtually all cases, the government does not voluntarily choose the parties with whom it does business; the jobs are usually advertised and awarded to the lowest responsible bidder. In view of the tremendous number of contracts and contractors involved, there is a real necessity for clauses establishing finality in respect of the subject matter of each contract and the government's responsibility.

The courts have held that a contracting party ought to be chargeable with knowledge of the provisions contained in an agreement into which he has entered and therefore, one should double-check the exact procedures required in order to protect his rights.

6.7.1 *Acceptance of Final Payment May or May Not Constitute Release.*
If a contract clause recites that acceptance by the contractor of final payment shall release the government from further liability, courts have upheld its validity.

In a case involving a $350,000 contract for heating, ventilating, and air-conditioning work in a municipal power plant, the contractor sued to recover approximately $20,000 for extra work which the city required it to perform. The contract stipulated:

The acceptance by the Contractor or any person claiming under the Contractor of the final payment aforesaid, as audited by the Comptroller, whether such payment be made pursuant to any judgment or order of any Court or otherwise, shall be and shall operate as a release to the City from all claim and liability to the Contractor for anything theretofore done or furnished for, or relating to, the Works, or for any prior act, neglect, fault or default of the Board, the City or of any person relating to, or affecting the Works.

Despite this provision, the contractor claimed that his acceptance of final payment did not constitute a release to the city of his claims for extra work, because some six months earlier he had submitted a general release which stated that he was reserving the claims in question. The court refused to uphold this view, however, saying that:

. . . when plaintiff contracting company accepted the final payment under the contract, it could not thereafter assert claims for additional sums which it had attempted to reserve by a wholly unnecessary and ineffective general release which was not provided for or required by the contract.[78]

Under other circumstances, where the evidence indicated that the intent of *both* parties was contrary to a provision releasing the owner upon acceptance of final payment by the contractor, the same court previously had upheld a contractor's claim for extras. The court distinguished between these cases as follows:

... / plaintiff contractor performed extra work under a contract similar to the present one, and at the very time it accepted final payment it executed a release reserving a claim for the extras. In accepting such payment, despite the further claim, the plaintiff acted upon the advice of the Brooklyn Borough President, by whom the original contract had been executed on behalf of the city. In addition, it was alleged that the release had been prepared in the Comptroller's office, that only through an error had the warrant not been corrected to conform to the release and that neither party had intended the payment in question to be accepted as the final payment.[79]

6.7.2   Contracting Officer Judge as Well as Representative of Disputant. In contracts with the Federal government, decisions of the contracting officer may be made final and conclusive under certain circumstances, thus making one party to the contract the judge as well as a disputant. Although this situation was modified somewhat in 1954 by the Wunderlich Act (Public Law 356), the contracting officer's decisions may still be final unless certain procedures are carefully followed by the contractor.

The statute is so named because it was intended to overcome the effect of the decision of the United States Supreme Court in the case of *United States v. Wunderlich,*[80] which held that although the decision of the contracting officer was arbitrary and capricious, the unsuccessful contractor who did not assent to the decision had no recourse because there was no proof that the decision was fraudulent or made in bad faith.

The statute provides (1) for judicial review of the decision of any governmental department or agency on a question of law; and (2) a decision concerning a question of fact shall be subject to judicial review if the decision is claimed to be fraudulent, capricious, arbitrary, or so grossly erroneous as necessarily to imply bad faith, or is not supported by substantial evidence.

6.7.3   Contractor Must Exercise His Remedies Strictly in Accordance with Contract. Although some measure of protection is afforded parties contracting with the government through judicial review, the contractor's right to such review will be lost by not following required procedures. A contractor lost his right to review simply because he failed to first exhaust his administrative remedies which were required in the contract. The contract contained a "disputes" clause as follows:

Except as otherwise provided in this contract, any dispute concerning a question of fact arising under this contract which is not disposed of by agreement shall be decided by the Contracting Officer, who shall reduce his decision to writing and mail or otherwise furnish a copy thereof to the Contractor. Within 30 days from the date of receipt of such copy, the Contractor may appeal by mailing or otherwise furnishing to the Contracting Officer a written appeal addressed to the head of the department, and the decision of the head of the department or his duly authorized representative for the hearings of such appeals shall, unless determined by a court of competent jurisdiction to have been fraudulent, arbitrary, capricious, or so grossly erroneous as necessarily to imply bad faith, be final and conclusive; Provided, That if no such appeal to the head of the department is taken, the decision of the Contracting Officer shall be final and conclusive. In connection with any appeal proceeding under this clause, the Contractor shall be afforded an opportunity to be heard and to offer evidence in support of its appeal. Pending final decision of a dispute hereunder, the Contractor shall proceed diligently with the performance of the contract and in accordance with the Contracting Officer's decision.

At the end of a lengthy correspondence, the contracting officer for the government wrote to the contractor:

You are advised that this office does not concur in your opinion that the work under your contract has been satisfactorily fulfilled. . . .

Demand therefore is again made that you immediately proceed to bring all the work under your contract into compliance with your contract requirements. No further notice will be furnished to you regarding this matter.

In the event that this corrective work is not started on or before May 1, 1956 this office intends to authorize the Station to complete this work. The full cost of the work will then be charged to your account. Our present estimate indicates that a cost of approximately $5,000 is involved.

The government had the corrective work done, and sent the contractor a bill for $4545.32. The contractor failed to pay, and court action was started. Because the correspondence clearly indicated that the contractor must have understood that this letter contained the contracting officer's final decision, and the contractor did not appeal to the head of the department, the court decided in favor of the government holding that the contractor "chose not to follow the only avenue for relief," that is, to appeal within thirty days to the department head from the contracting officer's decision.[81]

6.8   *Liability of Contractor for His Design Decisions.* Where the contractor both plans and executes the work, negligence in either endeavor makes him liable for damages resulting from his negligence. A householder, whose home was in need of alteration work, contracted with a home improvement company to remedy the defects of the twenty-five-year-old house. One of the principal defects was a substantial hump in the floor of the living room and dining room. The builder agreed to try to lower the posts under the dining room, and to shorten the studding in the basement partition under the living room. In the specification he commented: "This should lower the floor to some extent, possibly level out to where the floor belongs, but not completely." Instead, however, he attempted to lower the hump by cutting six or seven joists where they were intended to rest on the main girder which ran the entire length of the house and left these joists "just hanging in midair," and removing support from the first floor and the partition walls it carried.

Shortly afterwards the owner noticed cracks in the walls, and complained to the builder, who went to the house with an assistant to make an inspection. The assistant said he believed the cracks to be caused by settlement of the house or vibration of passing streetcars. The builder consequently disclaimed responsibility for the damage. As time went on, the cracks ran all along the wall from the front to the rear of the house. In some places they were 2 inches wide.

The owner eventually employed a second home improvement company, which estimated the cost of remedying the damage to be about $830. When it had completed the work, over a year after the cracks first had been noticed, it rendered a bill for $1050. Subsequently, the original improvement company sued the homeowner to recover an alleged balance. The homeowner denied that this balance was due and counterclaimed against the original improvement company for the said sum of $1050 as damages. A judgment was rendered in favor of the homeowner.

The improvement company appealed. Its primary contention was that it had not been proved that its work was the proximate cause of the damage. It urged that defective ground was causing the house to settle, and that this condition was an independent factor which was the superseding cause of the damage. However, the court held:

We recognize that the active operation of an intervening force, which is a force which actively operates in producing injury to another after the actor's negligent act has been committed, may be a superseding cause which relieves the actor from all liability for another's injury occurring thereafter. But . . . the extraordinary operation of a force of nature, which merely increases or accelerates injury to another which would otherwise have resulted from the actor's negligent conduct, does not prevent the actor from being liable for such injury.

The builder further contended that, even if his work was not satisfactory, the owner saw its progress, and having made no objection, his silence constituted an acceptance of the work and a waiver of any defects. The owner admitted to being at the house when one of the carpenters was in the basement cutting the joists with a hatchet and saw. But he maintained that, not being a carpenter, he did not understand the nature of the work. In this regard, the court said:

. . . The mere fact that an owner of a building takes possession of it after it has been erected or repaired does not in itself constitute an acceptance of the contractor's workmanship. . . . Nor is the failure of an owner to take charge of the prosecution of the work, when he finds that the contractor is not complying strictly with the conditions of the contract, a waiver of his right to damages for defective work.

The builder finally contended that the owner was dilatory in correcting the damage, and that this resulted in the second builder charging $1050 instead of $830. But the court said:

There is no question that where one party commits a breach of contract, it is the duty of the other party to make all reasonable efforts to minimize the loss sustained as a result of the breach. . . . It is common knowledge that a contractor's estimate of the cost of a job is often considerably less than the actual amount of the bill. There is no evidence to show that the delay prejudiced plaintiff.[82]

6.9   Contractor Not Liable for Damage Resulting from Owner's Directions. In another instance involving a small house, an owner unwisely undertook to act as his own architect and builder. After excavating for a cellar, pouring footings and setting building-block foundation walls, and laying first-floor joists and subflooring, he suspended work for about a year. After this interval he employed a contractor with a bulldozer to backfill around the foundation walls and to grade the lot. The work was done on the basis of verbal instructions issued by the owner, who returned to the site later to find that the backfill had been completed and the rear foundation wall was cracked. The wall had been pushed out of plumb, leaning inward below grade level, and outward above grade level. There was a long horizontal crack.

The owner sued the contractor for damages, contending that the work was not performed with ordinary skill and care, and that the contractor was liable either for breach of an implied undertaking to exercise reasonable care, or for negligence in failing to exercise such care. There was no evidence that the bulldozer had struck the wall. It appeared that the crack was caused by the pressure of the bulldozer and the earth, exerted against the unsupported base of the wall in the muddy trench. An engineer, called by the owner as an expert, testified that it was not a safe practice to backfill before the house is erected unless the wall is supported by shoring or propping.

The contractor contended that he had performed the work according to the directions of the owner. Neither party was an engineer, and neither was conscious of the danger explained by the expert. In upholding a judgment in favor of the defendant contractor, the appellate court said:

If a building contractor does his work in accordance with the plans and specifications and without negligence, he will not be liable to the owner where the building is subsequently damaged by reason of some defect in the building or some fault in the soil, in the absence of an express warranty that the plans and specifications are sufficient, inasmuch as he does not warrant their sufficiency but only the skill and care with which he performs his work and the soundness of the materials used therein.[83]

6.10   Acceptance by FHA Does Not Necessarily Prove Conformance to FHA Specifications. Where a developer contracts to furnish a house conforming to FHA specifications, the acceptance of the completed house by the FHA does not necessarily establish performance of the contract.

A developer was engaged in building and selling houses in a subdivision. He sold some of the houses after they were built, some while in the course of construction, and in other instances only vacant lots. The construction of these houses was being financed by a private title company, with the FHA insuring or guaranteeing the loans.

In May _____ a prospective homeowner and his wife purchased a house in the course of construction for $5675, of which $5100 was to be obtained from an "FHA Loan." When this contract was made, only the excavation for the basement had been completed, and the contract stipulated that the house was "to be finished in detail as per plans and specifications."

The developer proceeded to build the house. Representatives of the FHA inspected the construction from time to time. The loan was made and insured, and the howeowners took possession in the summer.

During the following two winters the basement was flooded seven or eight times when there were only ordinary rainfalls. On several occasions the water was so deep the owner could not reach the furnace except by wading. The water came over the top of the basement walls, through holes and cracks in the walls, and up through the floor. It came under the basement door like "a shower bath going full tilt." In some places the water coming through or over the wall gushed out a distance of 3 feet.

The homeowners sued the developer for breach of contract, claiming that the unqualified words "plans and specifications" mentioned in the contract referred to those prescribed by the FHA. The trial court refused to allow this oral testimony as evidence, and decided for the developer, ruling that the homeowners had not proved that the FHA specifications were part of the contract. The homeowners then appealed.

The appellate court ruled that although oral evidence is not admissible to vary a writpen contract, it is admissible to make definite what is indefinitely expressed in the contract. Therefore, the trial court should have admitted in evidence an FHA pamphlet entitled "Minimum Construction Requirements for New Dwellings" which specified:

1. Where water conditions necessitate dampproofing basements or cellars, the enclosing foundation walls, unless dampproofed in some other manner, shall be parged on the exterior with at least one-half inch of cement plaster. The cement plaster shall be carried down to cove at the bottom, extending to the outside edge of the footings.

2. If water conditions exist and additional precautions are necessary, the exterior walls below finished grade shall be waterproofed and a sump pump shall be installed, located at the low point of the floor. In cases where the water exists under pressure, basement floors shall be waterproofed and reinforced.

3. A dry basement shall be provided, and where dampness or water conditions exist, walls and floors shall be made watertight before final acceptance.

The appellate court held that item 3 required that a dry basement shall be provided, that the owners' evidence of water entering proved lack of substantial performance of the contract, and that although item 3 required walls and floors to be made watertight "before final acceptance," the owners had not forfeited their claim by failure to discover the defects before accepting the building.[84]

6.11   Claims against Owner, Engineer, Contractor, Subcontractor, and Surety Arising from Collapse of Parapet Wall. It is possible for a contractor, perhaps unknowingly, but surely unwisely, to contract to accept liability for damage or injury arising out of acts of someone else—acts over which he has no control or even of which he has no knowledge. In such a case, though he may be protected by ordinary public liability insurance covering any liability imposed upon him "by law," he may be jeopardizing his entire resources if he does not secure contractual liability insurance to safeguard him against any liability assumed "by contract."

During construction of a two-story steel frame building, the entire parapet along the street wall of the building for 100 feet collapsed. The brick and block parapet wall rested upon 12 WF 27 spandrel beams, supported every 20 feet by steel columns. During construction the spandrel beams were braced by wood shoring posts, and it was thé removal of these temporary posts that precipitated the collapse. According to the contractor, the steel spandrel beams, under the load of a 5-foot-high parapet placed eccentrically, had rotated, the top flange advancing outward, throwing the entire masonry parapet into the street.

The owner claimed the cause to be improper workmanship by the contractor and demanded that the contractor rebuild the wall at his own expense. The contractor refused to comply with the owner's demand, but nevertheless rebuilt the wall, without prejudice to his rights.

The owner had protected himself by an indemnification provision in the construction contract. By the terms of this provision, the contractor assumed:

. . . entire responsibility and liability in and for any and all damage or injury of any kind or nature whatever to all persons, whether employees or otherwise, and to all property growing out of or resulting from the execution of the work provided for in this contract or occurring in connection therewith, and agrees to indemnify and save harmless, the Owner, its agents, servants and employees from and against any and all loss, expense, damages or injury growing out of or resulting from or occurring in connection with the execution of the work herein provided for or occurring in connection with or resulting from the use by the Contractor, its agents, or employees, of any materials, tools, implements, appliances, scaffolding, ways, hoists, elevators, works or machinery or other property of the Owner, whether the same arise under the common law or the so-called Workmen's Compensation Law (which may be in effect in the locality in which the work is situated) or otherwise. In the event of any such loss, expense, damage or injury, or if any claim or demand for such damages is made against the Owner, its agents, servants or employees, the Owner may withhold from any payment due or hereafter to become due to the Contractor under the terms of this contract, an amount sufficient in its judgment to protect and indemnify it from any and all such claims, expenses, loss, damage or injury, or the Owner, in its discretion, may require the Contractor to furnish a Surety bond satisfactory to the Owner guaranteeing such protection, which bond shall be furnished by the Contractor within five days after written demand has been made therefor.

The owner and contractor submitted the question of responsibility for the cost of rebuilding the wall to a panel of arbitrators. The owner, who contended that the collapse of the wall was caused by defective materials and workmanship provided by the contractor, also urged that wherever the fault lay, the contractor had agreed specifically in the provision noted above to indemnify the owner against any and all damage to property and injury to person, even though arising out of negligence on the part of the owner or its agents.

The contractor contended that the above indemnity clause did not apply, asserting that the accident did not arise out of the execution of the work, but instead, out of faulty plans prepared by the owner's engineer, and that the contractor, in agreeing to construct a building "according to plans, drawings and specifications and layouts, prepared by" the engineer, was entitled to rely upon the sufficiency of these documents. Therefore, as the owner had impliedly warranted their sufficiency, he was liable to the contractor for breach of warranty because they were defective, and the owner should assume the cost of rebuilding the wall.

The hearings were complicated by contradictory opinions expressed by experts appearing for the owner and for the contractor as to the contributory effect of several alleged instances of faulty workmanship, and of alleged defects in the plans and specifications.

It was argued by the owner that:

1. Single angles were used to connect the spandrels to girders, instead of two angles as required by plans;
2. In two instances bolt-holes in these connections were double-punched;
3. Masonry anchors were insufficient in number and improperly installed;
4. The masonry parapet walls projected 8" beyond the center-line of spandrels instead of 7", as shown on plans;
5. Temporary wood supports were installed contrary to standard practice, and then suddenly removed;
6. A loose bolt had been installed.

The contractor rebutted these arguments, and countered that:

1. Faulty design was the sole cause of collapse; and that the wall was subsequently rebuilt to a different and stronger design prepared by the owner's engineer.
2. The engineer misinterpreted the effect of the initial angle of twist of the spandrel, occasioned by the contemplated eccentric loading. The angle of twist caused increased eccentricity of load, in turn causing a greater rotation of the angle of twist, until finally the parapet wall slid off the beams.

3. It was unwarranted to assume that the owner, who had a right to rely upon its engineer to provide adequate plans, should nevertheless require the contractor to safeguard it against any possible deficiency in the plans, particularly as many courts have taken the position that:

Where one party furnishes specifications and plans for a contractor to follow in a construction job, he thereby impliedly warrants their sufficiency for the purpose.[85]

4. In order for the contractor to be liable it would have been necessary for the catastrophic occurrence to have grown out of the execution of the work (not the preparation of the plans), or to have "resulted from the use by the Contractor of any materials, tools, implements, appliances, . . . or other property of the Owner," which clause was excerpted with minor editorial changes from a contract already construed by the courts, but which was not relevant here, because no materials, tools, etc., of the owner were contemplated for use in the construction of this building.

5. Because he was directed to rebuild the wall in accordance with a new design different from that specified by the contract, the contractor, who rebuilt the wall under protest, was required to perform extra work, and therefore was entitled to extra compensation.

In due course an award was rendered in favor of the contractor, who naturally was pleased with the result; but little did he realize that his troubles were far from over. As a result of the collapse of the wall, an employee of a subcontractor who had been working on the wall was thrown to the street below and injured. After the arbitration award had been rendered, the injured employee died. His estate commenced an action to recover $600,000 damages against the owner, the contractor, and the subcontractor who had erected the steel spandrel beams. Later the engineer who had designed the wall was added as a party defendant. At first the contractor was not at all concerned, since he had taken the precaution to secure public liability insurance in a very substantial amount, but to his dismay, he soon discovered that he was in serious legal difficulty. The owner served a cross claim against the contractor, alleging that if the owner was liable to the estate of the deceased employee for his injuries or death, then the contractor was required to indemnify the owner under the indemnification provision, quoted previously. The contractor's insurance company notified the contractor that although he was insured for any liability imposed upon him "by law," his policy did not provide coverage for any liability imposed upon him "by contract," such as the indemnification provision. The insurance company, while disclaiming any liability for any judgment that might be recovered by the owner against the contractor, under the indemnification provision, nevertheless undertook to defend the contractor, but only under a full reservation of the company's rights based on the said disclaimer.

Although the contractor was disturbed by the disclaimer, he found some comfort in the fact that the insurance company had agreed to defend him without expense, and he hoped that all would turn out well. But soon his troubles multiplied. At the time the contractor had signed the construction contract, he had furnished the owner with a performance bond in the sum of approximately $175,000, issued by a recognized surety company. Following the accident, in order to secure payments from the owner, he was required to furnish the owner with additional bonds totaling $50,000, in accordance with the terms and conditions set forth in the last sentence of the said indemnification provision. In order to secure the performance bond, as well as the additional bonds, the contractor had agreed to indemnify the surety company for any liability assumed by it under the said three bonds. The owner, who had already served a cross claim against the contractor, also started a third-party action against the surety company. In his third-party action, the owner maintained that since the indemnification provision was part of the construction contract, the surety company, by furnishing the performance bond, was required to indemnify the owner thereunder for any claim established against it by the estate of the deceased employee. Also, since the surety company had guaranteed, through the medium of the two additional bonds aggregating $50,000, that the contractor would discharge his obligations to the owner under the indemnification provision, the surety company also was required to indemnify the owner under said additional bonds.

Following the commencement of the third-party action, the surety company directed the contractor's attention to the fact that he had agreed to indemnify it for any liability that the surety company might have assumed under all three bonds, and called upon him to engage counsel, at his own expense, to defend the company, in accordance with his agreement. Thereupon the contractor engaged counsel to defend the surety company. Weeks turned into months, and months into years. Finally the day of trial arrived. The estate of the deceased employee was not concerned with the conflicting claims and contentions of the several defendants, each of whom attempted to shift the burden over to the other, or with the question of responsibility, if any, of the surety company under the said bonds. The only interest of the estate was to recover as much as possible from any one or more of the party defendants. After days of protracted negotiations, a settlement figure was suggested which was satisfactory to the estate. But who would pay and how much? The problem was not a simple one. Realizing that the case would take weeks to try, that great expense would be incurred in the defense of the action, and no one being absolutely certain of success—there was only one remaining alternative. The hat was passed around and each of the original defendants, as well as the engineer who had been added as a defendant, made a contribution. The total was sufficient to satisfy the minimum settlement demand of the estate. Thus the trials and tribulations of a complicated lawsuit came to an end, and the unfortunate contractor finally found peace and serenity.

6.12   *Conclusions.* In order to avoid some of the legal pitfalls inherent in the complex task of assembling a building and the consequent responsibilities of the owner and the contractor, consideration should be given to the following:

1. Don't think that performance of a contract becomes impossible simply because it becomes exceedingly expensive, inconvenient, or even absurd.

2. Don't omit to define adequately those conditions beyond your control which would excuse delay or nonperformance.

3. Don't forget that a contractor may recover for partial performance if contract requirements prevent full performance.

4. Don't overlook the fact that a contractor will not necessarily be relieved from his guarantee by owner's changes, and that if the contractor contracts to do the impossible he may be held to his promise.

5. Don't fail to be definite regarding whether the contract is entire or severable.

6. Don't fail to arrive at an understanding regarding who shall bear the loss in the event of a calamity resulting in damage to or destruction of a building being built, remodelled, or repaired.

7. Don't fail to arrive at an understanding regarding who shall pay the additional cost arising from a subsequent change in building department requirements.

8. Don't forget that assumption by owner of joint responsibility with contractor involves risks.

9. Don't neglect in disputes under contracts with the government to follow specifically and carefully the avenue for relief stipulated in the contract.

10. Don't rely upon the owner's taking possession as a waiver of his right to damages for defective work.

11. Don't forget that the injured party must make all reasonable efforts to minimize the loss resulting from a breach of contract.

12. Don't blame the contractor for defects arising out of faulty instructions given to him.

13. Don't rely upon acceptance by FHA as proof that the building necessarily conforms to FHA specifications.

CHAPTER 7

Legal Pitfalls in the Responsibility of the Contractor and the Owner to the Public at Large

Just as the professional man now finds himself more and more frequently held liable for injury to the general public, so does the contractor, and also the owner. The tendency today is for the injured party to institute damage suits against everyone who might have some color of responsibility, however remote, in the hope that at least one of this multiplicity of defendants will be found liable. This results in complex pleadings and interpleadings, in which, not infrequently, the owner will be held jointly liable with the contractor for the latter's mistakes, or the contractor will be held jointly liable with his subcontractor for the mistakes of the latter.

The standard general conditions of the contract between the owner and the contractor make it mandatory for the contractor to maintain liability insurance to protect himself from claims for damages resulting from injury to persons—whether his employees or others—or damage to property; claims which may arise out of or result from his operations under the contract. This provision is included for the protection of the owner, so that he will not find himself with a partially completed building and a contractor in such financial straits that he cannot complete his contract.

It would seem reasonable for the contractor to insist that the owner, also, maintain liability insurance in order that the contractor not find himself creditor of an insolvent owner. However, the standard general conditions do not require this, but permit the owner at his option to maintain, or not to maintain, liability insurance to protect himself. There is no doubt that, in fact, not only owners, but architects, engineers, and contractors as well, are more and more often made codefendants or third-party defendants in the same action as are actual malfeasors in building operations, and they are frequently found liable in the courts.

7.1   *Liability of the Owner—General.* It is true that, as a general rule, an owner who undertakes to erect a building, and employs a competent architect and a competent contractor, is not responsible for an accident caused by the failure of the contractor to follow adequate plans or the failure of the architect to properly plan or supervise the work. This is so because generally speaking the architect and the contractor are not agents or servants of the owner, but are engaged in the exercise of independent callings; hence, the negligence of either architect or contractor cannot be imputed to the owner. However, this general rule is subject to so many exceptions that it would be sheer delusion to assume, without the slightest reservation, that the owner cannot be held liable.

In those instances where the general contractor is engaged on a "cost-plus basis," instead of a "lump-sum basis," he has been regarded in the eyes of the law as an agent of the owner, so that if the general contractor is negligent, his negligence renders the owner liable.

The owner also may be liable under certain circumstances where he maintains supervision of the work, to a greater degree than merely inspecting—or even changing—the work to the extent necessary to produce the result intended by the contract, but rather retaining the right to control the workmen, in the sense that he can direct them in detail as to how the work is to be performed and who should do it. He is not liable merely because he is authorized to prescribe what is to be done, but he is liable when he is authorized to prescribe how it is to be done.

7.1.1   *When Inherently Dangerous Activities Are Involved.* The rule that an employer of an independent contractor is generally not liable for the negligence of the independent contractor is subject to exceptions where the work involves inherently dangerous activities. This exception was set forth in a case where a housing commission, during the construction of a low-rent housing project, instructed its contractor to erect a retaining wall on the adjacent property. Rock blasting was necessary in the construction of the wall. The commission had made an agreement with the adjacent landowner, which contained the following recital:

. . . and as between first parties and second party said F___-L___ Inc. (the independent contractor) is to be held harmless from any damages resulting to first parties or anyone else from the construction and maintenance of said retaining wall . . . .

During the necessary blasting of rock for the construction of the wall, the property owner's house was damaged, and he instituted suit against the commission and its contractor. A directed verdict was granted in favor of the contractor because of the above release, but a judgment against the commission was granted and upheld on appeal. The court stated that the exculpatory clause quoted above did not change the liability of the commission because there was no specific language to the effect that it should be absolved of responsibility. Also, the court said that the rule by which the release of the agent operates to release his principal did not apply here since the contractor constructing the wall was an independent contractor.[86]

7.1.2   Owner Acting as General Contractor Must Maintain Safe Place to Work. Where an owner lets separate contracts for portions of the work to various contractors, and in substance is acting as a general contractor maintaining general supervision of the work, he has the duty to use reasonable care in providing a safe place to work, and safe access thereto.

In one case, a servant of a subcontractor was injured while installing an elevator in a building under construction. Beside the elevator well was a shaft for a stairway. The shaft was not visible on the ground floor where he was at work, except by lifting one's eyes and looking directly upward. Far up the shaft, masons working on a scaffold were laying brick. One of the bricks fell from the scaffold and struck him on the head while he stood beneath the shaft, intent upon his work. He sued the owner of the building, who was in substance a general contractor maintaining general supervision through a superintendent on the job. In speaking of the liability of the owner, the court said:

We think the owner of the building, acting as a general contractor, was under a duty to the plaintiff to use reasonable care in maintaining the approaches to the elevator in a condition of reasonable safety, and is answerable in damages if the duty was ignored. Liability is not defeated by the fact that the plaintiff was a servant of a subcontractor and not a servant of the owner. He [plaintiff] had come into the building in furtherance of the owner's business, and was using ways and approaches necessary or suitable to enable him to go forward with his work. In such circumstances, the duty of protection is independent of the relation of servant and employer.[87]

7.1.3   When Owner Assumes Direction of the Work. Another instance where the owner may be held liable, despite the fact that he engaged a general contractor, is one in which he assumes a measure of direction of the work in a particular instance, and as a result of his carelessness someone is injured. A case in point involved a plaintiff who was employed by a contractor erecting floor arches. He was injured while temporarily within a hoist shaft, operated by another contractor constructing the brick walls of the building. There was testimony that the foreman in charge of the plaintiff's work had been directed by the owner's superintendent to carry on the floor work, and that the owner's superintendent had said he would notify the engineer operating the hoist not to operate it above the eighth floor, which would be the danger zone where men might be working on the floor arches. The owner's superintendent failed to act in accordance with that assurance, as a result of which the plaintiff was injured. The court held that when the owner, through his superintendent, assumed some measure of direction of the work, he was negligent in not acting in accordance with that assurance.[88]

7.1.4   *Liability for Violation of Nondelegable Duty.* There are certain duties imposed by statute upon the owner of a building under construction, which duties may not be delegated to others. If an owner fails to perform such a duty, he is responsible and liable for the consequences of such failure, even though he has engaged an independent contractor to carry out the work. For instance, a state labor law placed upon "*all contractors and owners*, when constructing . . . buildings" direct and positive duties for the protection of the employees on building construction work, including the duty thoroughly to plank over floor beams of iron and steel, and the duty to enclose and fence in by barriers the sides of a shaft or opening in the floor of a building under construction.

In the contract between owner and contractor for construction of a building in that state, it was provided that the contractor agreed to "erect and maintain all such temporary work as may be required for the protection of the public and those employed in or about the building, including guards and barriers around openings." Nevertheless, when a construction worker fell through an unprotected opening and was injured, the court ruled that this provision in the contract conferred no immunity upon the owner for damages. The court reasoned that since the state labor law imposed upon an owner and contractor the duty of providing barriers, such duty could not be delegated by the owner to the contractor, nor by a contractor to a subcontractor.[89]

Another exception to the general rule exonerating an owner from liability for injury or damage occurring during the construction of a building is one created in favor of persons on a public thoroughfare who are injured while passing a construction site. In one case, a passerby was struck by a plank falling from the temporary shed over the sidewalk. He sued both the owner and the general contractor to recover damages for personal injuries he sustained. There was evidence that the plank had been leaning over the parapet of the sidewalk shed since the previous day, and that on prior occasions debris and wood had been thrown from the windows of the building under construction and haphazardly piled on top of the sidewalk shed.

The proof in the case disclosed that the owner had at least constructive notice (through lapse of time) of the existence of the dangerous conditions. The court ruled that, as to persons on the highway, the owner was charged with the duty of excercising reasonable care in the performance of the work which the owner had initiated, and this common-law duty was nondelegable. The owner therefore may not be heard to say that his duty to safeguard persons on the highway was delegated to others, so that the fact that the general contractor had contracted to perform the task of carrying out the construction work did not relieve the owner of responsibility to the injured person.[90]

7.2   How May Owner Protect Himself? Under such circumstances as the foregoing, how might an owner have been protected against the consequences of his legal responsibility? One possible way would have been through the purchase of adequate liability insurance. The amounts awarded under judgments in such cases have recently increased materially; and it is wise that a substantial amount of insurance covering liability for personal injuries, including death, and for property damage, be secured by every owner. This insurance may be maintained by the owner separately, or may be included under a policy issued to the contractor. The cost of the insurance covering the owner's interest will be borne by him.

7.2.1   Owner's Right to Be Indemnified by Contractor—General. The right to indemnity springs from a contract, expressed or implied. Where several tort-feasors are involved, an implied contract of indemnity may arise in favor of one wrongdoer as against another wrongdoer. While previously there had been an important distinction in legal precedents between active and passive negligence, there now is a general rule of law that indemnity, or apportionment of liability, rests upon those causing the damage, and the responsibility must be determined by the facts in each particular case. No longer will one who claims he was guilty of passive negligence be able to avoid liability on the theory that his failure was a fault of omission as distinguished from affirmative negligence where the fact was that of commission.

7.2.2   Contractor's Agreement to Indemnify Owner against the Latter's Own Negligence. A contractor for a municipal power plant specifically assumed responsibility not only for his own negligence, but, also, for that of the city under a contract which provided that:

The Contractor shall be *solely responsible* and liable for and shall fully protect and indemnify the City against all claims for injuries to person or damage to property occasioned by or resulting from methods or processes in the performance of the Works *whether such damages or injuries be attributable to negligence of the Contractor or his employees or otherwise.*

and further that:

The liability of the Contractor under this contract is absolute and is not dependent upon any question of negligence on his part or on the part of his agents, servants or employees, and neither the approval by the Engineers or the Chief Engineer of the methods of doing the work nor the failure of the Engineers or the Chief Engineer to call attention to improper or inadequate methods or to require a change in methods, nor the neglect of the Engineers or the Chief Engineer to direct the Contractor to take any particular precautions or to refrain from doing any particular thing shall excuse the Contractor in case of any such injury or damage to property.

During the job a workman was killed by a fall into an unguarded turbine pit. The city was adjudged liable for failure to comply with a section of the state labor law requiring the owner and the contractor to protect by standard railings any opening into which a workman might fall. Although the city, as owner, was guilty of active negligence in violating a statute, it was permitted to recover against the contractor. The court held that the intent of the contract to indemnify the city against the city's own negligence was unequivocally expressed. [92]

7.2.3 Special Provision: Contractor Indemnifies Owner Irrespective of Owner's Negligence. If it is the intent of the parties that the liability of the contractor shall be absolute, irrespective of any question of negligence on the part of the owner, the agreement should clearly so stipulate as indicated previously. Another clause worthy of consideration by the legal draftsman reads as follows:

The Contractor shall be solely responsible for all injuries to person or damage to property occurring on account of or in connection with the work hereunder and shall indemnify and save harmless the Owner from and against liability, loss and expense (including, but not limited to, loss and expense because of liability for the payment of Workmen's Compensation under the Workmen's Compensation Law of any state) arising out of injuries (including death) to persons (including, but not limited to, respective employees of the Owner and Contractor) or damage to property (including, but not limited to, property of Owner) occurring on account of or in connection with the work hereunder, irrespective of the actual cause of the accident and irrespective of whether it shall have been due, in whole or in part, to negligence of the Contractor or the Owner, their respective agents, servants or employees. The liability of the Contractor under the foregoing provisions is absolute, and is not dependent upon any question of negligence on the part of the Contractor or the Owner of their respective agents, employees, servants or contractors.

7.2.4 Statutory Prohibition against Exempting Owners and Contractors from Liability for Their Own Negligence. In many cases, including some of those heretofore discussed, an owner has sought to avoid liability by inserting an indemnification provision in an agreement with its contractor whereby the contractor has assumed total liability irrespective of fault. The New York Legislature enacted a new statute in 1975 prohibiting one wrongdoer from assuming responsibility for the negligence of another, as follows:

A covenant, promise, agreement or understanding in, or in connection with or collateral to a contract or agreement relative to the construction, alteration, repair or maintenance of a building structure, appurtenances and appliances including moving, demolition and excavating connected therewith, purporting to indemnify or hold harmless the promisee against liability for damage arising out of bodily injury to persons or damage to property caused by or resulting from the sole negligence of the promisee, his agents or employees, or indemnitee, is against public policy and is void and unenforceable; provided that this section shall not affect the validity of any insurance contract, workmen's compensation agreement or other agreement issued by an admitted insurer.[91]

Under the above statute, one may not be indemnified against his own negligence.

7.2.5   Need for Contractual Liability Insurance Applicable to Contractor's Indemnity. Any provision for indemnity, if the contractor should be insolvent, is of value only if the owner can look to the company which issued the liability insurance policy in favor of the contractor. As previously emphasized under the usual terms of such a policy, the insurance company agrees to indemnify its assured against "a liability imposed by law." Ordinarily, it would not cover any liability imposed upon the contractor under an indemnification provision unless contractual liability insurance applicable to such an obligation on the contractor's part is secured. Therefore, it is imperative that a contractor, who becomes an indemnitor, secure such contractual liability insurance. Otherwise, when sued upon the indemnity agreement, his carrier may disclaim responsibility. It is equally important for the owner and his representative to verify that such insurance has been obtained in every instance where an express agreement to indemnify has been exacted from the contractor; otherwise the owner may not be able to look to the contractor's insurance carrier for reimbursement of any loss.

7.2.6   Special Provision: Contractor Indemnifies Architect as Well as Owner. In an attempt to safeguard the architect's interest as well as that of the owner, through use of an express indemnity agreement, the following form has been used:

The Contractor shall be solely responsible for all injuries to persons or damage to property occurring on account of or in connection with the work hereunder, and shall indemnify and save harmless the Owner and the Architect (jointly and severally) from and against liability, loss and expense (including, but not limited to, loss and expense because of liability for the payment of Workmen's Compensation under the Workmen's Compensation Law of any state) arising out of injuries (including death) to persons (including, but not limited to, respective employees of the Owner, Architect and Contractor) or damage to property (including, but not limited to, property of the Owner or the Architect) occurring on account of or in connection with the work hereunder, irrespective of the actual cause of the accident, and irrespective of whether it shall have been due, in whole or in part, to negligence of the Contractor, or the Owner or the Architect, their respective agents, servants or employees. The liability of the Contractor under the foregoing provisions is absolute, and is not dependent upon any question of negligence on the part of the Contractor, or the Owner or the Architect, or their respective agents, employees, servants or contractors. The approval by the Architect of the methods of doing the work, or the failure of the Architect to call attention to improper or inadequate methods, or to require a change in methods, or to direct the Contractor to take any particular precautions, or to refrain from doing any particular thing shall not excuse the Contractor in case of any such injury to person or damage to property. The foregoing provisions are for the benefit of the Owner and Architect, respectively, each of whom shall have a separate, independent and direct right of action, thereon, and for the enforcement thereof.

What has been said regarding the need for contractual liability insurance when an owner is indemnified applies equally to a contractual obligation indemnifying the architect.

7.2.7   *Statutory Prohibition against Indemnity in Favor of Professional.* In some areas it may be illegal for a professional man to evade responsibility in this manner for faulty designs or specifications prepared or used by him. In New York State a statute passed in 1965 specifically prohibits architects, engineers, and surveyors from securing this kind of indemnity against liability, as being against public policy, as follows:

Agreements by owners, contractors, subcontractors or suppliers to indemnify architects, engineers and surveyors from liability caused by or arising out of defects in maps, plans, designs and specifications void and unenforceable.

Every covenant, agreement or understanding, in, or in connection with any contract or agreement made and entered into by owners, contractors, subcontractors or suppliers whereby an architect, engineer, surveyor or their agents, servants or employees are indemnified for damages arising from liability for bodily injury to persons or damage to property caused by or arising out of defects in maps, plans, designs or specifications, prepared, acquired or used by such architect, engineer, surveyor, or their agents, servants or employees shall be deemed void as against public policy and wholly unenforceable.[93]

It will be observed that the statutory provision quoted above does not render illegal an agreement on the part of the contractor to indemnify a professional from liability caused by faulty construction (as distinguished from faulty design documents) for which the professional may be held responsible due to negligent supervision.

7.3   *Liability of Contractor—General.* The liability of a general contractor for the negligent acts of his subcontractors is similar to that of the owner for the acts of his contractor; that is, the general contractor ordinarily is not responsible for the negligence of an independent subcontractor. However, this general rule is subject to exceptions quite similar to those exceptions which cast an owner liable in damages. Thus, the general contractor may not evade a nondelegable statutory duty; for example, where a statute provides that the general contractor shall furnish temporary planking, he would not be relieved of responsibility merely because he subcontracted all or any part of this work. Also, the general contractor would be responsible where he reserves control of the equipment to be used by his subcontractor in the construction work or the manner or method of performing such work. Mere reservation by the general contractor of supervision for the purpose of seeing that the contract work is done by his subcontractor in compliance with the plans and specifications is not in control of the work or the manner of doing it so as to render him liable for the negligence of the subcontractor.

7.3.1 *Who Is in Charge of the Work?* When a safety code makes the duty to provide safety equipment that of a person *"in charge"* of construction work, the question arises as to who is in charge of the work which a general contractor sublets to a subcontractor. This question arose in an action by the legal representative of a deceased ironworker to recover damages against a general contractor. The decedent died from injuries suffered when he fell from the 150-foot level of an openwork structural steel television and radio tower being erected by his employer (a steel erector) under a subcontract with the defendant, the general contractor. The decedent was stooped over on a narrow foot walk and lost his balance when struck by heavy bolts which dropped from the 210-foot level, where two other employees of the steel erector were bolting sections. The decedent had not been provided with a safety belt or lifeline at any time during the period of more than one month that he had worked on the job. The state safety code imposed the duty to provide lifelines and safety belts upon "any manager, superintendent, owner, foreman or other person *in charge* of any building construction *or other place* . . ." Plaintiff contended that a finding of negligence might be rested upon the general contractor for having violated his alleged duty to provide the subcontractor's employees with safety belts and lifelines. The court ruled that since the general contractor had contracted away to the steel erector the direction and control of the work of erecting the tower and the manner of its performance, the general contractor was not a "person in charge" of the work. Therefore, he was not obliged in the circumstances to comply with the provisions of the state safety code. Thus the court said:

A duty created by the Safety Code becomes an obligation of the construction general contractor only if he is a "person in charge of" "any . . . place" where performance of the particular duty is requisite. We find nothing here to support an inference that defendant was "in charge" of the "place" at which the decedent was working at the time of his fall; therefore defendant was not obliged to provide him with a safety belt and life line as required by the Code. The "place" was the very work itself. Mere reservation of supervision for the purpose of seeing that the contract work is done in compliance with the plans and specifications is not control of the work or of the manner of doing it and did not operate to put defendant "in charge" of that "place" nor impose upon defendant any statutory duty to the deceased so long as the supervision related only to the results and not to the method of doing the work.

. . .

The decisions are in accord that there is no reason why in the interests of justice the statute should apply to a case where the general contractor, as in the present case, has contracted away the direction and control of the details of the work and the manner of its performance at the place where the violation occurs. "That authority precedes responsibility, or control is a prerequisite of liability, is a well-recognized principle of law as well as of ethics."[94]

7.3.2   When General Contractor Assumes Control and Gives Instructions Involving Safety of Subcontractor's Employees. A general contractor is not obliged to protect employees of a subcontractor against the negligence of their employer or that of a fellow servant; nor does the mere retention by the general contractor of the power of general supervision to see that the overall work proceeds properly and to coordinate the actions of several subcontractors on the site ordinarily cast him in damages for the negligence of any of the latter. These rules, as is often the case, yield under the circumstances of a given case (1) where the situation is governed by statute, or (2) where the general contractor, by his act or conduct assumes control and gives specific instructions which necessarily involve the safety of the subcontractor's men. Two examples will serve to clarify the latter point.

In one instance, a subcontractor erecting formwork for concrete floors in a hospital under construction used a certain method for support of the retaining platform in each bay. A carpenter employed by this subcontractor noticed that this method of support was lacking in the bay in which he was about to work. When he could not find his superior to obtain instructions, he called to the general contractor's superintendent, who told him to "go ahead, it's all right." When he moved onto the deck, it broke, throwing him to the ground and injuring him. In the ensuing litigation, it was held that the carpenter's conversation with the general contractor's superintendent raised the question that the superintendent had assumed such a degree of control over the work as to render the general contractor responsible for the injury.[95]

Another example illustrating how a general contractor may incur liability for the death of his subcontractor's employee by giving specific instructions involving the safety of such employee appears in the case involving the death of the ironworker who fell from the tower while erecting steel sections. It will be recalled that the deceased ironworker had not been provided with a safety belt or lifeline while he worked on the job and that the court had ruled that the duty of providing such equipment was not imposed upon the general contractor. Nevertheless, the court ruled that there was evidence independent of a failure of any statutory duty, which, if believed, would justify a jury in finding that the general contractor was liable, since his representative actually interfered with the matter of supplying safety belts and lifelines by the steel erector, and participated in the latter's failure to do so. Specifically, there was evidence that about a month before the date of the accident, fellow workers of the decedent asked their foreman if they had to get safety belts and lifelines. When the foreman said, "We haven't got any, but we will have to get them," the representative of the general contractor said that the workers did without them before, that they could do without them now, and that these safety devices would hold up the job.[94]

7.3.3 Duty to Provide a Safe Place to Work. A general contractor owes the duty of making safe, by reasonable care, the places of work provided for by him, and the ways and the approaches thereto. Workmen coming onto the premises to perform construction work are in effect invitees, no matter whose employees they may be, so that the common stairways used by such employees to get from one floor to the next floor must be made safe by the general contractor. This duty also extends to the other common areas. However, the duty to make and keep the premises safe does not extend to the very work on which the subcontractor and his employees are engaged.

In one case, it appeared that the workmen were injured when a floor, from which some of the concrete subcontractor's employees had removed the bracing, collapsed while fellow employees were pouring concrete upon it. The floor on which the injured employees of the subcontractor were working was in the course of construction. Under such circumstances, the court held that the duty of the general contractor to supply a safe place to work did not extend to this situation.[96]

7.3.4 Duty of a General Contractor to Protect Public from Injury Resulting from Negligence of Subcontractor. The general contractor has a duty to protect members of the public such as passersby from injury which they may sustain as a result of a subcontractor's negligence. In a case involving a multiplicity of defendants, a pedestrian was injured when struck by a bag of terrazzo pebbles—one of a pile of such bags on the sidewalk in front of a building being renovated for a bank. The general contractor had subcontracted certain tiling, terrazzo, and other work to subcontractor A, who, in turn, subcontracted the terrazzo floor work to subcontractor B. In an action to recover damages for personal injuries, the general contractor as well as the owner and both subcontractors were held liable.

There was evidence that the bags were piled negligently and in violation of permits obtained from the city. Subcontractor B was held liable because it had ordered the terrazzo pebbles for its own use on the job and the bags were left negligently piled on the sidewalk for a week. The general contractor had a duty of general superintendence, and was held liable because he too knew of the existence of the dangerous condition on the sidewalk. Since subcontractor A had subcontracted the terrazzo work, he, on his part, assumed the position of general contractor of the terrazzo work and was held responsible in that he also knew of the dangerous condition.[97]

7.3.5 Liability to Third Party after Acceptance of Building by Owner, for Concealed Dangerous Condition Created by Subcontractor. Until quite recent years, it was the prevailing rule that the contractor would be liable for any injury resulting from his negligence before his work was completed, but that his responsibility was terminated and he was not liable to any third person once the structure was completed and accepted by the owner. Several recent decisions have placed building contractors on the same footing as sellers of goods, and have held them to the general standard of reasonable care for the protection of anyone who may foreseeably be endangered by their negligence, even after acceptance of the work by the owner. In demolishing the legal doctrine (formerly adhered to by most courts) which insulated builders from liability to ultimate users after completion of the work, many courts now fasten liability upon such contractors for concealed dangers created by their subcontractors. Such liability may arise as a result of the general contractor's failure to discover and to insist upon the removal of a hidden dangerous condition created by the subcontractor.

The present trend is illustrated in the following situation in which the plaintiff's husband was the third owner of a house which had been completed more than two years prior to the time of a tragic occurrence. Returning home with her son from a two-week visit in the Middle West, she found the doors and windows closed, the hall gas heater on, and her husband and two other children dead from asphyxiation.

An action for damages for wrongful death was brought against the contractor by the widow and another surviving member of the family. Evidence disclosed that the general contractor engaged a licensed plumbing contractor to install the heaters; that the hall gas heater had been modified to accommodate a secondary heat exchanger mounted over it in the wall, and the orifices admitting the gas were too large in size. The effect of installing the secondary heat exchanger was such that the heater would be vented only partially, and a substantial amount of carbon monoxide would spill into the house. Despite the fact that the building had been completed and accepted by the owner long prior to the accident, the court rejected the general contractor's argument that he could not be held responsible for the death of third persons with whom there was no privity of contract. Turning to the question of the general contractor's liability for the negligent installation of the defective heater by his subcontractor, the court ruled that the contractor was responsible for the death of plaintiff's husband and children, saying:

... The contractor ... has supervision over the entire building and its construction, including the work performed by a subcontractor, and where he negligently creates a condition, either by himself or through a subcontractor, he is primarily responsible for that condition and the consequences that may follow from it. He is in full control of the construction, and knows or should know what is being placed in the building. Indeed, what is placed there is peculiarly within his knowledge, and where, as here, it involves a defective appliance which is covered and hidden by the walls in the course of construction, the responsibility for such defect should rest upon him as well as on the subcontractor.[98]

In another action, a member of the public who sustained injuries as a result of the fall of a heating duct, long after its installation had been accepted by the owner, was awarded damages against a general contractor, his subcontractor, and an engineering firm. The injured person, an employee of a racing association, was in a building familiarly known as the "Club House." While walking through the Club House, the employee was struck when the heating duct fell. The general contractor had contracted with the racing association, the owner, to erect and install the heating, ventilating, and air-conditioning systems. It had engaged a subcontractor to install the heating ducts. The engineers who prepared the plans and specifications for the equipment had agreed to "supervise the contractor's work throughout the job." The general contractor was obligated to keep a "competent superintendent" on the job to provide "efficient supervision."

The duct which fell was approximately 20 feet long and weighed approximately 500 pounds. It had been suspended by hangers from the $\frac{7}{8}$-inch ceiling sheathing, and was not in any way affixed directly to the joists; and to secure the hangers, nails—rather than lag screws—were used.

The specifications required the subcontractor to perform his work in a first-class and workmanlike manner and to securely support the ducts from the building construction in an approved manner. The court was satisfied that the securing of a duct of the weight involved to the ceiling by the means employed was not in accordance with generally accepted practice and that it was not installed in a first-class or workmanlike manner. The court also was satisfied that the general contractor did not exercise ordinary care in superintending the installation of the duct. The court concluded that the general contractor should reasonably have foreseen that persons in the Club House would be exposed to grave risk of injury if the duct was not properly and securely installed; that the subcontractor was negligent in the installation of the work, and the general contractor was negligent in the supervision and inspection of the subcontractor's work.

With respect to the engineers, the court recognized that although they undertook to exercise only general supervision over the installation of the duct work, they retained the ultimate control to approve or reject any work done by the general contractor and the subcontractors. The evidence revealed that the engineers made no attempt to ascertain whether the ducts were secured to the joists; that they made no visits to the job site at a time when they could ascertain how the ducts were being installed. In other words, they failed to see that they were properly installed and took no steps after their installation to ascertain how and by what means they were secured. The court concluded that the engineers failed to use due care in carrying out their undertaking of general supervision.

Having determined that each of the defendants was negligent, the court ruled that despite the absence of privity of contract between the plaintiff and the defendants the action was not barred. Unlike the situation previously discussed on page 70 involving the absence of a railing that constituted an obvious defect, here the dangerous condition that had been created was hidden. Adverting to the MacPherson doctrine, which rendered a manufacturer of an automobile liable to a third party because of a latent defect, despite the absence of privity of contract, the court applied the same doctrine in this case, saying:

The attempt to differentiate between chattels and real structures, in this regard is in my judgment without support either in reason or logic.[99]

7.3.6 Liability without Negligence—Inherently Dangerous Activities.
Such activities as blasting during excavation can sometimes cause damage to nearby property, owing to the passage of shock waves, either through the air or through the ground, even though the blasting contractor has used all proper care. The current trend of legal opinion is to hold the contractor liable for such damage, whether or not he has been negligent in his operation.

A case illustrating this attitude involved damage to a building, which damage was attributed by its owner to blasting in the neighborhood. Although the blasting contractor countered that the condition of the building was caused by lack of proper maintenance, testimony indicated that the building had been undamaged before the blast, and an insurance adjuster stated his opinion that damage to an automobile housed in the building was the result of a concussion.

In this case the court said:

The principal question posed on this appeal is whether a person who has sustained property damage caused by blasting on nearby property can maintain an action for damages without a showing that the blaster was negligent. Since 1893, when this court decided the case of Booth v. Rome, W. & O.T.R.R. Co. (140 N. Y. 267) it has been the law of this State that proof of negligence was required unless the blast was accompanied by an actual physical invasion of the damaged property—for example, by rocks or other material being cast upon the premises. We are now asked to reconsider that rule . . . .

Since blasting involves a substantial risk of harm no matter the degree of care exercised, we perceive no reason for ever permitting a person who engages in such an activity to impose this risk upon nearby persons or property without assuming responsibility therefor.[100]

7.4 When Is a Building Complete?
The question,"When is a building complete?" often elicits different answers, when asked of the owner or asked of the contractor. Generally, this question would center upon whether the building had been completed in accordance with the plans and specifications. But in the following case, involving the construction of a cooperative

apartment house, a specific definition of the word was included in the contract for purchase of apartments.

Because shares were sold to ninety-four purchasers of apartments while the building was still under construction, the contract contained a clause whereby the promoters agreed to complete the building. The cooperative plan was not to take effect until completion of the building; and in the event that it were not completed, then the million dollars deposited in escrow by the purchasers was to be returned to them by the escrow holder.

In order to avoid a multiplicity of controversies with the purchasers concerning whether the building in fact had been completed, the contract provided that the building should be deemed completed when three specific conditions had been met: (1) when the city issued a certificate of occupancy, (2) when the lending institution made final payment on the building loan, and (3) when a specified insurance company accepted a permanent mortgage.

The contract stated:

When the three events above mentioned have occurred, the same shall be deemed and considered by all parties hereto as conclusive proof that the building has been fully completed in accordance with the provisions of this agreement.

The three events specified in the contract occurred. The contract provided that no change in its terms should be binding unless in writing and signed by one of the promoters in behalf of all of them.

Despite the occurrence of the three events mentioned above, the apartment purchasers brought suit for damages for alleged failure of the promoters to complete the building according to a verbal agreement, made after the cooperative plan took effect and the apartment owners had acquired their stock. This agreement was asserted to declare that the promoters "would do everything necessary to fully and properly complete the building and furnish the necessary equipment . . . in accordance with the plan of organization." The chairman of plaintiff's board of directors called this alleged oral agreement "the heart of the plaintiff's complaint."

The court held that the conditions stated in the written contract were truly objective tests because the certificate of occupancy certified that the "structure conforms substantially to the approved plans and specification." Such certificate could be issued only on an affidavit of completion by a "licensed architect, licensed professional engineer or superintendent of construction who supervised the construction," and only after the city department of housing and buildings had verified such facts.

The court also concluded that the lending institution would not make final payment on the building loan until its architect or engineer was satisfied that the building was completed; and the insurance company to which the mortgage was to be assigned could normally be relied upon to insist on a completed building for collateral.

With regard to the contract clause stating that "no change or modification of the terms and conditions of this agreement shall be binding upon the Sellers unless the same shall be in writing, signed by . . . the Sellers," the court stated:

The purpose of inserting this provision . . . is clear. If it were possible to eliminate the objective test of completion contained in the contract by providing an oral promise to finish what the contract stated must conclusively be presumed to have been finished, there would have been little purpose in incorporating such a test in the contract.[101]

7.5 Public Works; Lowest Responsible Bidder. In many jurisdictions it is provided that a contract for public construction must be awarded to the "lowest responsible bidder . . . after advertisement for sealed bids." Such stipulations are of long standing, and, as stated by one court, are based "upon motives of public economy, and originated, perhaps, in some degree of distrust of the officers to whom the duty of making contracts for the public service was committed. If executed according to its intention, it will preclude favoritism and jobbing, and such was its obvious purpose. It does not require any argument to show that a contract made in violation of its requirements is null and void."[102]

It generally is held that such statutes are for the benefit of the taxpayers, and not for the protection of an aggrieved bidder. If a contract for public construction is made without such competitive bidding, a taxpayer is entitled to have the contract set aside, even though no actual injury was suffered, but merely because the public has been deprived of the protection intended by the law.

In declaring illegal a contract awarded without competitive bidding, contrary to the governing statute, one court stated:

If the Board of Education had violated subdivision 8 of Section 875 as above quoted, by awarding a contract for school furniture in excess of $1,000 without advertising for estimates, the contract would be illegal. If it had accomplished the same result by indirection, that is, had so fixed or manipulated the specifications as to shut out competitive bidding or permit unfair advantage or favoritism, the contract would likewise be illegal. . . . The principle underlying the law relating to the public letting of contracts through advertisement is stated . . . as follows: "When by charter or statute a municipality can only let its contracts to the lowest bidder after advertisement, an implied condition and restriction is placed upon the proceedings of the municipality that the various steps adopted by it to let a contract shall be of such a nature and taken in such form as in good faith to invite competition. . . . The plan and specifications are essential to competitive bidding because it is only through their agency that there is a reasonable assurance that all bidders are competing upon the same basis and without favoritism and that no fraud enters into the award."[103]

7.5.1 *Specifications Precluding Competitive Bidding.* Another case affirms the principle that specifications for public work must be written without any equivocation that might preclude competitive bidding. A village advertised for bids to furnish and install a new 3500-kilowatt generator to supplement its existing power plant. The specifications called for the engine, of no particular design, to be tested at the factory.

Two bids were submitted, differing in design. Bidder A proposed a four-cycle "V" engine with a factory test for $615,685, while bidder B offered a two-cycle "in line" engine for $673,840, but without a factory test. The village water and light commission, after considering both bids, and consulting its engineer, recommended that the board of trustees accept A's lower bid.

This recommendation was made close to election time, and the new incoming mayor requested that action on the bids be deferred so that he and the two newly elected trustees could act on the matter; and this was done. However, the reconstituted board of trustees dismissed and replaced the members of the water and light commission, and voted to award the contract for the generator to bidder B. Bidder A then brought suit on the ground that the contract did not conform to the specifications.

The court set the contract aside and directed the board of trustees "to award the contract as required by law." However, the trustees declined to take any action on the bids in hand, but instead requested the new chairman of the water and light commission to prepare different specifications for the generator.

The chairman, with the assistance of bidder B, prepared new specifications for the generator, calling for a design identical to that proposed by B in his first, now invalid, bid. The specifications required that a successful bidder must have constructed at least three similar units showing satisfactory operating experience.

Although by this time a majority of the water and light commissioners had decided that expansion of the present power plant was not the most economical answer to the problem, the trustees nevertheless accepted the new specifications and advertised for bids. B was the only bidder and was again awarded the contract.

There ensued a taxpayer's action to annul the resolution awarding this contract, brought on the ground that the specifications precluded competitive bidding. The trial court decided that the evidence showed only that "other manufacturers are not at the present time constructing the equipment required by the specifications. There is no showing that they could not do so if they felt so inclined."

However, on appeal, the higher court held that the specifications did indeed stifle competition. It said:

We do not mean to suggest that specifications for public projects are illegal merely because they tend to favor one manufacturer over another. More must appear in order to render the specifications and the contract based thereon illegal . . . since a particular product, that is, one marketed by only one manufacturer, may be required in the public interest. However, an objectionable and invalidating element is introduced when the specifications are drawn to the advantage of one manufacturer not for any reason in the public interest, but rather, to ensure the award of the contract to that particular manufacturer. . . . The record fails to explain or justify inclusion in the specifications of a distinctive design customarily employed by but one prospective bidder. Other manufacturers could, of course, construct the machine but only at a prohibitive cost, and, hence, not at a competitive price. In a very real sense, and for all practical purposes, the competitive bidding required by the statute was effectively eliminated. . . . Such a scheme or plan is illegal in the absence of a clear showing that it is essential to the public interest.[104]

7.5.2 Who Is a "Responsible Bidder"? Where a statute requires the award of the contract to the "lowest responsible bidder," how may a public agency determine whether or not a bidder is "responsible"? The agency, after deliberation upon the facts in hand, may legally decide that the lowest bidder is not responsible. The courts usually will not question the wisdom of such a decision, so long as it had a reasonable and plausible basis, and so long as there was no fraud on the part of the agency.

The lowest bidder for the construction of a municipal incinerator appealed to the court to set aside the award of a contract to a competitor who had submitted a higher bid. Testimony disclosed that at a meeting of the board of trustees of the village, held after the bids were opened, the consulting engineer and the superintendent of public works both advised against accepting the lowest bid because:

1. The bidder did not give the required answer to the questionnaire in that in each instance his answer containing the name of the company manufacturing a particular piece of equipment stated "or equal"; that this was contrary to the purpose of the questionnaire, making it difficult for the village to check, and permitting the bidder to substitute equipment by a different manufacturer.

2. The bidder did not have a regular permanent engineering staff, as required in the specifications.

3. The bidder did not show that he had previously built five plants of comparative size, as required by the specifications.

The board also listened to others who spoke in behalf of the bidder, and considered an extensive report made by the consulting engineer. After conferring, the board rejected the lowest bidder. Having noted that the board came to its decision after hearing witnesses, and after considering the engineer's report, the court said:

The board used a common-sense approach and method in making its determination, and this court cannot say that it was wrong in the method chosen; nor will it define or limit the standards the board should have used as guides so long as the method chosen was reasonable.

The burden of proof was on the petitioner [the lowest bidder] to show that it was a responsible bidder. It cannot be said that the board abused its discretion in determining that the petitioner was not a responsible bidder . . . so long as there was a reasonable and plausible basis for its determination. . . . The issue is not whether the determination of the town board was wise, but whether there was a reasonable and plausible basis for such determination . . . In the absence of any finding of fraud on the part of the members of the town board, it is to be presumed that they honestly determined that there was risk in letting the contract to the petitioner.[105]

In a somewhat comparable situation, but in which the views of the consulting engineer were adopted without question, and the board heard no witnesses and did not exercise its own judgment, the court, in annulling the resolution awarding a contract to a higher bidder, said that the board should have made a more extensive inquiry.[106]

7.6   Conclusions. In order to protect themselves against liability for the negligent acts of others during construction of a building, the owner and contractor should adopt the following precautions:

Owner:

1. Don't assume that you will be immune from responsibility for damages because you have engaged an independent contractor. It is the part of wisdom to make a contrary assumption.

2. Don't assume that the contractor's liability insurance will protect you from liability unless his policy so states.

3. Don't fail to purchase your own liability insurance when you are not covered by the contractor's policy.

4. Don't forget that it is wiser to be overinsured than to be underinsured.

5. Don't treat an agreement by a contractor to indemnify you as a substitute for your own liability insurance.

6. Don't forget to verify that the contractor has secured contractual liability insurance which is specifically applicable to any obligations assumed by him under an indemnity agreement written in your favor.

7. Don't forget that when competitive bidding is required, specifications may not be drawn to the advantage of one manufacturer, except when justified by the public interest.

8. Don't determine that a low bidder is not "responsible" without a reasonable basis for such a determination.

Contractor:

1. Don't forget that by engaging a subcontractor, the general contractor may not avoid duties imposed upon him by statute.

2. Don't hesitate to exercise such general superintendence as is necessary to see that the subcontractor performs his contract. However, in exercising such superintendence, don't control and direct the manner in which the work shall be done.

3. Don't give instructions involving the safety of subcontractor's employees.

4. Don't forget that it is the duty of a general contractor to provide a safe place to work for all workmen, no matter whose employees they may be.

5. Don't assume that engaging a subcontractor relieves you from your responsibility to protect the public from injury.

6. Don't forget that you may be held liable for injury sustained long after completion and acceptance of the work.

7. Don't fail to consider the need for products liability—completed operations insurance, to protect you from liability for damage or injury occurring after completion of your operations.

8. Don't agree to indemnify anyone unless you fully understand the scope of your undertaking and are prepared to assume all of the risks involved.

9. Don't overlook the fact that an indemnity agreement may be so broad in scope as to make you an insurer for the negligence of others.

10. Don't forget to secure contractual liability insurance to protect you in case of liability to the owner under an indemnity agreement.

11. Don't neglect to read the Don'ts directed above to the owner.

CHAPTER 8

Legal Pitfalls Arising out of the Relationships of the Several Contractors

Essentially, the relationship between a contractor and his subcontractor is no different than the relationship between owner and contractor. When a subcontract is let, the general contractor, to all intents and purposes, stands in the shoes of the owner, so that many of the pitfalls discussed in Chapters 5 and 6 are equally applicable to the relationships between the several contractors. Therefore, those pitfalls should be borne in mind in connection with the additional material in this chapter.

8.1 Contract Conditions

8.1.1 Consequences of Variance between Conditions in Subcontract and Prime Contract. In writing subcontracts the general contractor would be wise to include all of the material terms and conditions to which his own contract with the owner are subject. Otherwise, those terms and conditions may not apply to the subcontract.

A contract with the _____ Transit Commission for the construction of a street tunnel stipulated that the commission could cancel the contract upon the engineer certifying that the work was so slow as to indicate that it would not be completed within the time fixed. The contractor let part of the work under a subcontract which provided that the work should be subject to the direction and to the satisfaction of the commission or its engineer, without referring to the original contract, and without stipulating that the subcontract should be dependent upon the continued existence of the general contract.

The general contract was canceled for lack of progress before the subcontractor had completed his work, although there was no criticism of the subcontractor's progress. The court held that where the subcontractor was prevented from performing his contract by the termination of the contract of the general contractor, who had not protected himself against such a contingency, the subcontractor could recover the benefit of his contract, less the reasonable cost of completing his work.[107]

8.1.2 *Temporary Heat—for How Long?* Where it is necessary for the court to construe a contract, it tries to do so in a reasonable manner, rather than so as to place one party at the mercy of the other. On October 3, 1930, a contractor signed a contract to provide the heating plant for several new buildings at a state hospital and to complete his work by October 1, 1931. The contract contained the following provision:

Temporary heat shall be provided by the heating contractor for each building or a portion of a building after the same is temporarily enclosed, between October 15 and May 1 unless otherwise directed by the State, until final certificate is issued, in general by the following method:

The heating contractor shall install his apparatus, piping and radiation within the buildings and shall operate the systems (within the buildings) during the periods of temporary heat.

Although the completion date for general construction was the same as for the heating work, the general construction contractor had financial difficulties; and in December 1931, its contract was canceled for failure to progress. The state then relet the unfinished portion of the general construction, and fixed a new completion date in August 1932.

The second general construction contractor also had financial difficulties; and its contract was canceled in June 1933, at which time—twenty months after the original completion date—the heating contractor received his final payment. He sued to recover the cost of furnishing temporary heat beyond the original completion date.

The state contended that the heating contractor was required to furnish temporary heat until the completion of the general construction contract regardless of any delay or the cause thereof. However, the court decided that it was not within the contemplation of the parties that the heating contractor should furnish temporary heat indefinitely, saying:

Our guide is the reasonable expectation and purpose of the ordinary businessman when making an ordinary business contract. It is his intention expressed or fairly to be inferred, that counts.[108]

8.1.3   *Contract Price—Adjustable Downward but Not Upward.* Where a contract is not ambiguous, courts will not attempt to judge what might be considered the reasonable expectation of the parties. A disadvantageous stipulation in the contract may be quite apparent, or may be abstruse, to one party, if not to both; and one is not relieved from an agreement because he is ignorant of the meaning of definite and unambiguous conditions therein.

A lump-sum contract between a general contractor and an unlettered subcontractor contained the following provision regarding a change in the amount of work:

This price is based on an estimated _____ cubic yards of concrete. In case the quantity is less than this, there shall be a reduction in the lump sum price, computed at a unit price of _____ dollars per cubic yard.

The contract made no provision for an adjustment in price if the quantity of concrete exceeded the estimate. Actually, a greater quantity was used; and the subcontractor depended upon the above provision in demanding extra compensation. This case was settled out of court; but if it had gone to trial, it is quite possible that the subcontractor would have been unsuccessful. It would seem from the language that it was the true intent of the parties to protect the general contractor in the event of a change from the estimate, without giving a corresponding protection to the subcontractor. This ambiguity could have been avoided by the subcontractor, if he had carefully read and fully understood the agreement, and insisted before signing upon measures to protect his own interest.

8.1.4   *Neutralizing Unfair Contract Conditions.* Not infrequently the contract made by a general contractor with his subcontractors will state that the sums payable to the subcontractor will be paid when, as, and if the general contractor receives payment from the owner. The subcontractor agrees to this stipulation as an accommodation to the general contractor, so that the latter need not be pinched for funds. What the subcontractor does not always realize, however, is that by accepting this inclusion, he is agreeing that if the general contractor never is paid by the owner, the subcontractor need never be paid at all.

In order to avoid doing work without compensation, it would be well, while still being accommodating, to insist upon the inclusion of a second sentence to neutralize this limitation. The intent of the substance of the following provision applies to professional consultants of the architect, as well as to other subcontractors:

The sums payable by the Prime Contractor to the Subcontractor hereunder shall be paid when, as, and if the Prime Contractor receives payment from the Owner on account of the Subcontractor's work.

It is understood, however, that if the Prime Contractor fails to receive such payment from the Owner for any reason other than the fault of the Subcontractor, such failure shall not prejudice the Subcontractor's right to recover from the Prime Contractor any sum payable hereunder.

8.2   Performance

8.2.1   Effect of Impairment of General Contractor's Credit.

Unless expressly permitted to do so by his contract, a contractor will not be excused from completing his work merely because the credit of the person to whom he contracted to furnish labor and material has become impaired. A flooring subcontractor agreed to furnish the labor and materials necessary to lay, scrape, and finish the floors for an apartment house, the price for which was to be paid in installments as the work progressed. After the contract had been signed the general contractor became insolvent, so that he no longer was a good credit risk. The flooring contractor was unable to collect a debt due him from the same general contractor under a separate contract for a different job.

Under those circumstances, the flooring contractor refused to extend further credit by performing the new job, and repudiated the contract. The court held, however, that mere belief that one party will be unable to pay when the time for payment comes will not excuse performance by the other party, stating:

The fact that the credit of a party to a contract (to whom by the terms of the contract labor and materials are to be furnished) has become impaired, so that he is no longer a good credit risk, and that he has failed to meet other independent obligations, does not relieve the other party from performance, and is no defense to an action for the breach of such contract, for it does not appear therefrom that he cannot and will not perform his part when the time for performance comes. [109]

8.2.2   Liquidated Damages Applicable to Delay—Not Abandonment.

Construction contracts frequently stipulated an allowance "by way of liquidated damages" arising out of delay in completion of the work. Such an allowance ordinarily is the limit of the injured party's recovery, and is an agreed-upon substitute for actual damages which he may sustain. However, this will not necessarily hold true, if the work is totally abandoned rather than merely delayed.

A general contractor contracted with a stone company for the furnishing by the latter of cut stone for a library. Because of the difficulties and added expense of winter work, the contract provided that all the stone should be delivered on or before the first of August, and that should the stone company fail to meet this deadline it would pay the general contractor a certain sum as liquidated damages "for each and every day thereafter the said work shall remain incomplete."

The stone company furnished a bond which provided:

Now, therefore the condition of the foregoing obligation is such that if the Principal [stone company] shall well and truly indemnify and save harmless the said obligee [general contractor] from any pecuniary loss resulting from the breach of any of the terms, covenants and conditions of the said contract on the part of the said Principal to be performed, then this obligation shall be void; otherwise to remain in full force and effect in law.

The bond also provided that the surety company should have the right to complete the contract, if the stone company should default in the performance thereof.

The job began according to schedule; but it soon became apparent that the stone would not be delivered by August 1; and, in fact, the stone company defaulted on that date; and at about the same time it made an assignment for the benefit of its creditors. The surety on the bond was notified of the default, but did not elect to undertake completion of the contract; and the general contractor relet to another stone company the contract for furnishing the stone. Despite vigorous efforts the work ran into the winter and increased costs were incurred.

The general contractor, instead of suing the surety for liquidated damages, sued for actual damages arising out of the default of the original stone company. The court upheld this claim, saying that no provision had been made to cover total abandonment; that liability for the stipulated liquidated damages did not accrue until the contractor had fulfilled his agreement, and that the per diem allowance was not to be in lieu of performance, but upon performance after the time fixed in the agreement.[110]

8.2.3 Time for Subcontractor's Performance Waived by General Contractor's Negligence and Failure to Prepare His Own Work. Where one party to a contract insists upon strict compliance with the provisions for time of completion, he, himself, must have performed his part of the agreement on time, and must not have contributed to the other party's delay. Where the work to be performed by a subcontractor cannot be performed until other work to be done by the general contractor is finished, failure of the latter to complete his work on time is a sufficient excuse for the subcontractor's delay beyond the agreed time for completion.

Also, where one party to a contract claims that he was put to additional expense owing to the negligence of the other party, his claim will not be supported if he, himself, has been guilty of contributory negligence.

The following case illustrates both these points.

A general contractor, bidding on the construction of a new highway bridge, invited proposals by subcontractors to furnish, fabricate, and erect the structural steel. He stated in his invitation that his acceptance of such a proposal should constitute a binding agreement subject to his being awarded the general contract, and that all agreements were contingent on strikes, fires, or other causes beyond the control of the subcontractor. The state awarded the contract, stipulating a date for completion by this general contractor; but there was no completion date specified in the steel subcontract.

The general contractor and the steel subcontractor prepared a progress schedule in the expectation that the steel arches would be delivered to the bridge site and would be erected in May or June. However, the subcontractor was delayed in fabrication not only by late deliveries of structural steel, but also by the fact that some of the steel delivered was laminated and had to be rejected. As a result of these delays, he did not deliver and install the steel bearing plates designed to support the arches until August; and the arches themselves were not floated to the bridge site until mid-September, and were not raised into place until the end of that month. When the arches were erected, it was found that the north and south halves did not meet, but were approximately 9 inches apart laterally; and considerable corrective work was performed by the subcontractor to bring the bridge into alignment. All of this caused additional delay, with the result that the structural steelwork was not completed until the middle of December.

Unable to complete his contract by December 31, and subjected to additional costs, the general contractor withheld final payment from the steel subcontractor. The subcontractor sued to recover this payment, plus compensation for the extra corrective work. The general contractor's principal defense was based upon his contention that he had relied upon the subcontractor's express representation that the bridge superstructure would be erected during the month of May, and that because this promise was not fulfilled, he had been unable to meet his completion date.

Testimony disclosed that the general contractor's own work of preparing concrete bearing surfaces for the steel bearing plates had not been completed prior to the arrival of the steel. In fact, one bearing plate was removed, and the concrete surface underneath was bushhammered by the general contractor as late as September 10.

The court found it was not established that the subcontract was awarded on any condition or representation in respect of time for performance; that the subcontractor had completed his work within a "reasonable time" after his late acquisition of the steel, due to causes beyond his control; and that the general contractor's preparatory work, necessary to be done before the steel could be erected, had not been finished until a few days before the steel arches were floated to the bridge site. The court said:

It is a well-settled rule that where one party demands strict performance as to time by another party, he must perform on his part all the conditions which are requisite in order to enable the other party to perform on his part, and a failure on the part of the party demanding performance to do the preliminary work required, in order to enable the other party to complete his work within the time limited operates as a waiver of the time provisions of the contract . . . Moreover, the evidence establishes, and I find, that the delay in the completion of the bridge, after the delivery and erection of the arches, was caused by the fact that the bearing surfaces of the abutments were not only defectively hammered, but also by the fact that these defects were never properly corrected by the defendant [general contractor] and that the extra expense that defendant incurred was caused by its own negligence in this respect; and may not properly be offset against plaintiff's [subcontractor's] claim. Plaintiff's work was done in accordance with the plans and specifications, as agreed, and plaintiff is consequently entitled to recover the balance due under its contract. . . .

With respect of the subcontractor's claim for compensation for extra corrective work to bring the bridge into alignment, the court found no merit in this claim, because the subcontractor as well as the general contractor had contributed to the necessity for this extra work. The court said:

Although it was defendant's obligation to prepare the concrete bearing surfaces, it was plaintiff's obligation also not to set the bearing shoes or plates on improperly finished or irregular bearing surfaces. Plaintiff knew on August 18, when the bearing shoes were erected, that the concrete abutments upon which the shoes were set had not been properly prepared and that it was necessary that this condition be corrected before the arches were erected. Nevertheless plaintiff erected the arches, in September, without further inspection of the bearing surfaces and without attempting to ascertain whether the necessary correction had been made, except by inquiring of defendant's superintendent. While the extra work performed was necessitated in part by the defendant's fault, it was also due to the plaintiff's failure to see that the correction had been made, as the general specifications and proper practice required. . . . [111]

8.2.4 Damages Caused by Other Contractors. It is well understood that when separate contractors are engaged for different portions of the work, each of them must prepare a progress plan covering his own work so that he may properly schedule the completion of his work within the time specified in his contract, and each contractor is expected to prosecute his work in a prompt and efficient manner and to furnish materials when needed. Lack of progress and coordination on the part of one contractor may cause another contractor to be delayed and compel him to perform parts of his operations in a segregated and piecemeal manner, not originally contemplated, thereby increasing his cost of performance.

When such delays occur, the contractor who has been delayed often makes claim against the owner and seeks to hold him responsible for the damages sustained. As a result, the question is posed whether the owner is liable for such delay.

Although the cases are not entirely harmonious, there are many decisions which appear to be sound and which hold that the owner is not automatically liable for such delay. To hold an owner responsible, more must be shown than the mere fact that one separate contractor delayed another. Though automatic liability on the owner's part does not follow as a general rule, there are numerous decisions which sustain recovery by a contractor against an owner, where there is evidence of active interference on his part. For example, in one case, the foundation contractor encountered serious difficulties, thus delaying the superstructure contractor. Although it was obvious that the delay would be prolonged, the state nevertheless ordered the claimant to proceed with the fabrication of its steel, which then had to be stored out-of-doors until it could be used. As a result, it had to be repainted at considerable additional expense to the claimant. The court allowed a claim for damages on the ground that the damages arose from active interference by the state, rather than merely from delay.[112]

In another case, the owner let a contract to one contractor for the construction of a powerhouse and concrete tunnels, and another contract to a separate contractor for the installation of the heating equipment, and a piping system therein, both to be completed on the same date. Installation of the piping system in an orderly and continuous manner was vital to the heating contractor's schedule, and he reasonably assumed that the tunnels would be constructed in a continuous fashion. Over the heating contractor's protest, the contractor for the construction of the powerhouse and tunnels was permitted by the owner to build them in disjointed sections which completely disrupted the heating contractor's schedule and subjected him to considerable water damage. There was considerable delay in the completion of all of the work. The court held that the owner was liable for the delay and extra expense on the ground that, by permitting the contractor for the construction of the powerhouse and tunnels to proceed in a disjointed manner and compelling the heating contractor to proceed in the same manner, it had actively interfered with the heating contractor's work and prevented him from using customary economical methods.[113]

In an effort to avoid liability on the part of the owner to one contractor for the acts or omissions of a separate contractor, a clause such as the following has been used in construction contracts:

Should the Contractor sustain any damage through any act or omission of any other Contractor having a contract with the Owner, the Contractor shall have no claim against the Owner for such damage, but shall have a right of action against the other Contractor to recover the damages sustained by reason of the acts or omissions of such Contractor.

It is open to serious doubt whether such a clause would protect an owner if active interference on his part contributes to the delay. However, it could be helpful to him in any jurisdiction where the courts might hold that an owner is automatically liable, despite absence of any interference on his part. In any case, the clause makes it clear that a contractor who has been delayed shall have a right of action against any other contractor whose acts or omissions caused him delay.

8.2.5   General Contractor Not Liable to Subcontractor because of Professional's Default. If the architect is dilatory in prosecuting some duty contemplated by the owner-builder contract—such as providing supplementary drawings to the builder—the builder must look to the owner for damages, as there is no obligation on the part of the architect to the builder. Where the damaged party is a subcontractor, his relationship to the architect is still further removed; and it has been held that the general contractor is not liable to a subcontractor because of the architect's default in providing supplementary drawings.

A decision of long standing concerned the claims of a subcontractor who had agreed to quarry, cut, and install stone facing for a city house "under the direction and to the satisfaction of the Messrs. _____, architects, acting for the purpose of this contract as agents of the owner," according to drawings and specifications prepared by the said architects. The contract further stated that "the Architects shall furnish . . . such further drawings or explanations as may be necessary to detail and illustrate the work to be done."

This subcontractor sued the general contractor (the only one with whom he had a direct contract) for damages resulting from delay of the architects in furnishing detailed plans required before the stone could be quarried. He claimed that, although he had constantly requested that plans be furnished him, they were unreasonably delayed, and that in consequence thereof he sustained losses. The elements of these losses were the carrying expenses of quarries reserved and equipped for operation, in order to execute the contract, and kept in idleness by the delays. The subcontractor argued that there was a positive and distinct covenant on the part of the general contractor that the architects would furnish such necessary details, that each party to a contract is under an implied obligation to do all that he reasonably can do to enable the other party to perform his contract, and that a party who fails to do so, either directly or indirectly, through the default of his agent, is liable for damages sustained by the other party.

The court, finding that the contract expressly described the architects as "acting for the purposes of this contract as agents of the owner," ruled that the subcontractor in effect agreed to do certain work for the defendant (general contractor) according to plans and specifications to be furnished by a third party, namely, the owner through his agents, the architects, and to look to that third-party's agents for such plans as he might from time to time require. If this left him in a position where he could not recover from anyone his damages by reason of the architect's delay in furnishing the plans, it was the result of the particular form of contract which he signed.[114]

8.3.   *Conclusions.* In executing subcontracts, and in performing work specified therein, it would be wise for contractors and subcontractors to keep these guideposts in sight:

1. Don't fail to incorporate into a subcontract all of the relevant and material terms and conditions of the prime contract.

2. Don't forget that a general contractor should make provision in his subcontracts to protect himself in case the prime contract is terminated.

3. Don't forget that the problems relating to temporary heat are such a frequent source of discord that extreme care should be exercised in specifying the rights of the parties under all circumstances.

4. Don't neglect to verify that provision is made for adjustments in the contract price to operate upward as well as downward.

5. Don't forget that the term "when, as, and if" ultimately may mean "never."

6. Don't abandon performance because the other party is no longer a good credit risk, unless your contract expressly permits you to do so.

7. Don't confuse "delay" and "abandonment," or fail to provide for both contingencies.

8. Don't expect to hold your subcontractor responsible for damages for delay if you, also, were at fault.

CHAPTER **9**

Legal Pitfalls in the Architect (Engineer)-Contractor Relationship

9.1 *Lack of Privity.* Ordinarily there is no direct contractual relationship between the architect (engineer) and the building contractor. Unless the professional is authorized by the owner to act as his agent in this regard, the professional has no power to make contracts or amend contracts with the builder. The primary duties of the design professional are to act as professional adviser to the owner, to give contract interpretations, and to judge performance by the contractor. Thus, there is said to be no "privity of contract" between the professional and the builder.

The traditional common-law rule in such a situation was to bar the right of direct legal action of one against the other, because of the absence of privity. The privity rule has gradually been eroded, and recently has fallen into general disrepute. The design professional may find himself sued by contractors or subcontractors who believe themselves injured by his actions or failure to act. Conversely, the contractor may be sued by the architect (engineer) if his negligence results in injury to the professional.

9.2 *Contractor's Claim against Professional for Alleged Damages.* In a recent Wisconsin case, a contractor brought action against an architect after steel roof joists in a building under construction collapsed. The cost of replacing and repairing the damaged work was $36,040, which had been borne by the contractor.

The architect had designed the building, specifying that the roof be supported by twenty-six steel joists, with a clear span of 100 feet. These joists were to be placed 4 feet apart, and were to be connected by eight lines of horizontal bridging. In erecting the joists, the contractor connected them with four lines of bridging, pending final alignment. During this alignment, which required loosening or removal of some of the bridging, and after eight of the joists had been welded in place, the remaining eighteen joists collapsed and fell to the gymnasium floor, displacing parts of the walls as they fell.

It was the contention of the contractor that the architect's specifying horizontal bridging instead of cross bridging was the cause of the collapse, or alternatively that if the contractor's construction procedures had caused the collapse, then the architect had violated a duty in not warning the contractor of the hazards of the erection procedure adopted by the contractor.

As a result of expert testimony that the design in this case complied with the *Manual of Steel Construction* of the American Institute of Steel Construction, Inc., and had not violated the Wisconsin Administrative Code, the court decided that the architect's design was not defective.

With regard to his alleged duty to warn the contractor about dangerous methods and procedures, there was expert testimony to the effect that the special precautions necessary when erecting long-span joists with horizontal bridging are generally known in the steel erection industry. It was also brought out that while the contractor had never built a building with so large a span, it had built fifty or sixty steel structures, some of which had floor or roof spans in excess of 50 feet. The court found that whatever danger existed was or should have been known to the contractor, and consequently the architect had no duty to warn as to the obvious hazard.

The court also examined the architect's contract with the owner, which provided in part:

He (the architect) will make periodic visits to the site to familiarize himself generally with the progress and quality of the work and to determine in general if the work is proceeding in accordance with the Contract Documents. He will not be required to make exhaustive or continuous on-site inspections to check the quality or quantity of the work and he will not be responsible for the Contractor's failure to carry out the construction work in accordance with the Contract Documents. During such visits and on the basis of his observations while at the site, he will keep the Owner informed of the progress of the work, will endeavor to guard the Owner against defects and deficiencies in the work of Contractors, and he may condemn work as failing to conform to the Contract Documents. . . .

The court said:

The contract does not make the defendant a supervisor of the project in the sense that he was responsible for the procedures adopted by the contractor. Defendant's obligations under the contract are primarily aimed at insuring the end product will comply with the plans and be of good workmanlike quality. This does not involve the safety of the procedures utilized.

. . . To hold otherwise would make the architect the general safety supervisor at the site, a job which would require his continuous presence in disregard of the express language of his contract. In addition, it would fundamentally alter the relationship between the owner, architect and contractor in a way not envisioned by the parties themselves. The mere fact that the defendant in this case was continuously represented on the site by Halverson cannot, as is suggested by plaintiff, alter the lack of a legal duty to interfere with the contractor's judgment as to procedure, absent a showing that the risks were so unusual as to be beyond the ability of the contractor to perceive, given his special knowledge and experience.[115]

9.3 Architect's Rights against Contractor in Case of Injury to Workmen. In some states, the professional being sued by injured workmen can bring a third-party action against the contractor, despite the fact that the workmen were employees of the contractor, were injured in the course of their employment, and were paid benefits under the Workmen's Compensation Act, and therefore could not bring action directly against their employer.

In the case quoted in Chapter 3,[†] in which the architect was judged negligent and therefore liable to three workmen injured in the collapse of a gymnasium roof which was being extended, the court decided that the architect had the right to initiate a third-party complaint against the contractor, although it was argued that this would make the contractor liable indirectly where it would not be liable directly. The court reasoned as follows in coming to its decision:

The contractor also insists that the original complaint and the third party complaint contain similar allegations of negligence, and that therefore there can be no indemnity over between two active wrongdoers. We do not agree with this conclusion. While the original complaint contained allegations of active wrongdoing, this does not constitute the sole basis for liability on the part of the architects. As we have suggested before, the jury could have based their verdict on the failure of the architects to stop work or prevent the contractor from performing its duties in an obviously unsafe manner. We believe that the evidence does not show that the architects were negligent in their primary duties, but could only show that they failed to sufficiently police the contractor's performance. When a jury could properly find that an injury was directly caused by improper construction methods and techniques used by a contractor, and that the architect was liable only by reason of a failure to stop work on the job, we think that the jury could find that the contractor was an active tortfeasor while the architect's fault was merely passive. We conclude that this is a proper case for a third party complaint and that the trial court erred in dismissing the architects' third party complaint on motion without presenting the issue to the jury.

9.4 Contractor's Responsibility for Professional's Extra Costs. It is not unusual for the owner-contractor agreement to stipulate that the contractor

† *Miller v. DeWitt,* 37 Ill. 2d 273, N.E.2d 630 (Ill. 1967).

shall pay certain costs incurred by the architect (engineer) in connection with the work; for example, reproduction cost of additional sets of drawings and specifications beyond a certain number; or professional services occasioned by the contractor's improper performance; or professional engineering services necessitated by controlled inspections. The agreement often makes the payment of such costs a responsibility of the contractor. It is well for the contract to state that, if the contractor fails to pay said costs, the architect (engineer) shall have a direct right of legal action against the contractor.

9.4.1 *Special Provision Requiring Contractor to Reimburse Professional for Cost of Reproductions.* When it is desired to require the contractor to reimburse the architect or engineer for the cost of reproduction of drawings and specifications, the inclusion of the following provision in the contract documents is worthy of consideration:

The Contractor for General Construction Work shall include in his estimate the sum of $ _____ dollars to cover reimbursement to the Architect (Engineer), as hereinafter provided, for the costs heretofore or hereafter incurred by the Architect (Engineer), for reproduction of all drawings, specifications, and details required for any purpose whatsoever in connection with the project, including, without limitation, the reproduction of all drawings and specifications for estimating and bidding of all trades, and the reproduction of details issued by the Architect's office for the use of all trades. The Contractor for General Construction Work shall reimburse the Architect (Engineer) for all such costs incurred by the Architect (Engineer) upon the latter's request. *The Architect (Engineer) shall have a direct right of action against the Contractor for General Construction Work in case the said Contractor shall fail to perform this provision in whole or in part.* Each Prime Contractor will be furnished sets of drawings and specifications in accordance with the following table. The cost of each set will be included in the "Reproduction Allowance" noted in the above paragraph. Additional sets of drawings and specifications, or any portions thereof, will be furnished at the cost of reproduction.

Contract			Heat., vent.	Plumbing	Elec.
General construction	15 dwg.	10 spec.	2	2	2
Heating, ventilation	3	6	6	2	2
Plumbing	2	2	2	2	2
Electrical	2	2	2	2	6

9.4.2 *Special Provision Requiring Contractor to Pay Professional's Fee for Field Inspections.* It is common practice for the owner-contractor agreement to require the contractor to pay for such items of service as:

1. Field inspection of poured-in-place concrete
2. Shop and field inspection of structural steel
3. Field inspection of pile foundations

In order to insure fair payment of professional fees for such inspections, it is well to include in the contract documents a statement definitely establishing the price of each such inspection and giving the professional a direct right of action against the contractor, as has been done in the following example requiring the contractor to pay for field inspection on concrete:

The mixing and placing of the concrete, inspection of footing bottoms, and the placing of the reinforcing steel will be inspected in the field by an Engineer selected by the Architect. The Contractor shall allow in his bid and pay out to the Engineer as directed by the Architect, the sum of _____ dollars per cubic yard of controlled concrete, based on an average of _____ cubic yards or more per day. Concrete rejected at the site for any reason shall be included in the quantity for inspection purposes. If the average daily yardage including all days when an inspector is required on the job, but concrete is not being placed, as for inspection of footing bottoms and checking of reinforcing, is less than _____ cubic yards as computed on completion of the work, the Contractor shall pay an increased price per cubic yard on a proportional basis between the actual yardage and the basic cubic yard average pour. *The Engineer shall have a direct right of action against the Contractor in case he shall fail to make payment to the Engineer as hereinabove provided.*

9.4.3 *Special Provision Requiring Payment of Professional's Costs Occasioned by Contractor's Improper Performance.* Frequently, the architect or engineer may be put to considerable unanticipated expense, arising in connection with the correction of work improperly performed by the contractor and consequently disapproved. Where it is expected that these expenses are to be paid by the contractor, a provision such as the following may be included in the contract documents:

When, in the opinion of the Architect (Engineer), work has not been performed in accordance with the Drawings and Specifications, such disapproved work shall be removed and replaced correctly. Should the Contractor wish to correct the work by methods other than removal and replacement as ordered, such corrective measures shall be taken as directed by the Architect (Engineer), with the Owner's written approval.

In any instance(s) provided for above, all costs arising therefrom shall be borne by the Contractor, including, without limitation, Architect's (Engineer's) expenses, computed at 2.5 times actual salary costs for time spent on investigations and making recommendations, plus all other incidental expenses incurred by the Architect and his Engineers in connection therewith. *The Architect (Engineer) shall have a direct right of action against the Contractor for payment of his said expenses in case the Contractor shall fail to make payment to the Architect (Engineer) as above provided.*

9.5 *Conclusions.* In order to avoid difficulties arising in the interrelationship between the architect or engineer and the builder, the following pitfalls should be kept in mind:

1. Don't presume that privity of contract is a requisite to establishing a liability assumed by contract.

2. Don't interfere with, and thereby assume responsibility for, the contractor's procedures, unless the design is so unusual as to require procedures different from those normally used.

3. Don't neglect to provide in the owner-builder contract for professional's direct right of action against the builder, should the builder default in his obligations to the professional.

CHAPTER 10

Legal Pitfalls in the Practice of Construction Management

Increased interest in the savings made possible by reducing construction time through phased, rather than sequential, design and construction has brought about the advent of a new profession—that of the construction manager. This new professional typically supplements the traditional activities of architects, engineers, and contractors by providing services in the areas of design review for construction feasibility and cost control, time scheduling of both design and construction, and on-site management in an effort to keep the construction work on schedule. His entry on the scene has complicated the legal status of the traditional performers because his activities sometimes extend into services which heretofore have been explicitly or implicitly assumed by the architect (engineer) or by the contractor.

10.1 *Responsibilities in General.* Many of the pitfalls ensnaring architects (engineers) and contractors which have been exposed elsewhere in this book also lie hidden in the path of the construction manager. The field of the latter is not so well defined as those of the other participants in a construction project, and consequently particular care should be taken to spell out his duties in each instance.

While in general it may be said that he acts as an agent of the owner, his relationship to the design professionals and to the contractors may vary considerably. He may serve as an intermediary between the owner and all of the other participants, or as an adviser separate from but equal to the architect (engineer), or perhaps as a joint venturer with him, or he may act as a consultant to the architect or engineer.

Because there is no traditional sphere of activities assigned by custom to the construction manager, it is even more important to him than to the architect (engineer) that there be a meeting of the minds between himself and his client regarding the scope of his services, his professional and legal relationship to the project, and the degree of responsibility to be assumed by him.

Some of the possible services of a construction manager are as follows:

Estimating construction costs and development of budget

Scheduling of design and construction and establishing a critical-path method network for phased construction

Design review for costs and construction feasibility

Bid packaging and contract awards

Coordinating the work of separate contractors

Monitoring the schedule as construction progresses

Processing shop drawings and samples

Review and processing change orders

Review certificates for payments

Reject work or stop work

Provide construction support activities such as:

Temporary facilities

Security force

Temporary utilities

Cleaning up

As this partial list indicates, the services of the construction manager are potentially so diverse that on each project, his particular contributions must be fully understood not only by the owner, but also by the architect (engineer) and the contractors.

10.1.1 *License to Practice.* The architect or engineer may expand his services to include construction management, but it is obvious that not all architects (engineers) are qualified to undertake these additional responsibilities. If the construction manager is not a licensed architect or engineer, he should check the definitions of professional practice in the laws of each state in which he intends to operate, before contracting to perform services which may be interpreted as being reserved to licensed professionals. It is possible that his activities, particularly during the design phase, may be deemed in violation of registration laws.

State statutes do not necessarily confine their restrictions to the principal architect of record, but include also the activities of consultants. A recent case involved an addition to a hospital in Vermont, in which the principal architect, at the direction of the client, engaged the services, as consultants, of an out-of-state firm specializing in hospital design. The consultant firm was not registered in Vermont, and this fact was instrumental in its inability to recover consultation fees when it sued the Vermont architect. The Supreme Court of Vermont, in overturning the judgment of the lower court, held that when the nonresident architect presumes to consult, advise, and service a Vermont client relative to Vermont construction, he puts himself within the scope of the Vermont architectural registration law. The court further stated that contracts entered into in violation of registration laws are held to be illegal, and by reason thereof, provisions for payment of fees are unenforceable.

10.2 Contracts. While the American Institute of Architects, the Associated General Contractors of America, and others have published forms for construction management contracts, it is impossible for any form to reflect accurately the special circumstances of any specific enterprise. It is urged that competent legal counsel should be sought by the parties to the agreements so that all of the desired terms and responsibilities of the parties are incorporated therein.

10.3 Responsibilities of the Construction Manager to Contractors. The contract between the construction manager and his client frequently contemplates a greater degree of control of construction operations than is normally assumed by an architect or engineer. The construction manager agrees not only to prepare a time schedule for construction but also to coordinate the work of several prime contractors in an effort to keep the work on schedule. This sometimes requires making modifications in scheduling an answer to unforeseen problems arising during the construction period.

While a contractor usually assumes the risks of delay in performance, as a general rule he is not responsible for delays caused by the owner. Therefore, a contractor who believes he has been damaged due to delays caused by the rescheduling of the construction manager (acting as the owner's agent), may make claim for damages against the construction manager as having acted negligently. This was the position taken by a contractor in a case involving the building of a power plant, in which time of completion was of the essence, because the owner's contracts for power from outside sources were nearing expiration.

10.3.1 When Rescheduling Causes Damage to Contractor. In the same case previously referred to above, the architect-engineer had contracted with the utility company (the owner) to provide services normally performed by a construction manager. In addition to design of the power plant and preparation of working drawings and specifications, it agreed to prepare a time schedule, obtain bids on certain equipment, develop bid packages for major prime contractors, and coordinate and expedite the work.

The coordination and expediting of the work, in order to meet the required date of completion, proved to be a difficult task, as a multitude of unforeseen troubles required repeated rescheduling by Mr. H——, the architect-engineer's field man. Delays occurred owing to prolonged preparation of shop drawings, late arrival of steel, late delivery of the boiler because of a factory strike, and damage to structural steel during installation of the boiler, with consequent deferred pouring of concrete slabs in the boiler area. Local labor problems, and torrential rains which made the access road to the site impassable, added to H——'s headaches. Nonetheless, by judicious rescheduling, sometimes on a daily basis, he was able to see the work completed only a month beyond the originally stipulated date.

However, a prime contractor on the project filed a claim for extra costs in the amount of $327,579, and brought suit against the owner and the architect-engineer for breach of contract, negligence, equitable adjustment of the contract price, and recovery of final payment, thereby increasing his claim to $595,236.

In rejecting this claim, the court noted that the plaintiff's contract gave the architect-engineer broad discretionary powers in the planning and management of the project, subject to an implied duty of reasonableness and care commensurate with the standards of the profession. It was brought out that H—— had made his decisions on the basis of (1) the promised date of completion, (2) his previous experience in supervising construction of power plants, (3) the economic impact of his decisions on all of the various contractors. The plaintiff's own job superintendent testified that H——'s decisions were impartial.

The court found that there was nothing unlawful or negligent in what the architect-engineer did at the site, and that it had treated the plaintiff equitably and the same as all the other contractors, and the plaintiff was denied recovery from the owner or the architect-engineer.[117]

10.4   *Responsibilities to Third Parties.* An architect or engineer, faced with a charge of negligence, may assert that he has performed his duties in accordance with standards of due care customary in his profession. Because construction management is a relatively new field, no customary standards of practice have been established. Consequently, the courts, in adjudicating a case of alleged negligence, must look more closely at contract language in determining responsibilities and liabilities. Where a construction manager contracts to perform certain services, he is obliged to perform these services free of any negligence. If an injury results from a failure to perform, and the said failure arises out of his negligence, he may be found liable to the owner, a contractor, or even third parties, as was held in a recent case.

10.4.1   *Effect of Contract Provisions.* In this case, a workman on a construction site, employed by a subcontractor, was injured when he fell through a floor opening which had remained unguarded for three months. He brought an action for negligence against the owner and the architect-engineer.

In examining the responsibility of the owner, which had acted as its own general contractor and was legally in possession and control of the premises, the court said:

The possessor of land thus retaining control is subject to liability for personal injuries to business visitors caused by a natural or artificial condition if he knows, or by the exercise of reasonable care could discover the condition which, if known to him, he should realize as involving an unreasonable risk of harm to the invitee.

The architect-engineer had contracted with the owner to provide among other things the following services:

1. Overall planning and management of the construction work and building operations will be furnished in addition to coordinating, scheduling and expediting the work of the various contractors, handling incidental field engineering, and performing all managerial functions incident to the overall construction work as contrasted to the work of specific contracts.

2. Inspect field work performed by the various contractors to determine acceptability of the work. This service will include the necessary checking to insure compliance with the plans and specifications and to protect the District's (Owner's) interest in safety, housekeeping, fire prevention, and operation of the running plant.

The court, pointing to the architect-engineer's contractual duty "to protect the District's interest in safety," and noting that the architect-engineer's construction superintendent had made twice-daily safety inspections of the site, found no merit in the architect-engineer's plea that it had "no authority to stop the work; no authority to commandeer the employees of the various contractors and set them to work building or replacing covers for the holes; and that it had no obligation to build and guard the covers," and the jury verdict against both the owner and the architect-engineer was affirmed.[118]

10.5   *Conclusions.* The area of control, and consequent liability, of the construction manager has not yet been defined by custom. In some instances it penetrates areas traditionally associated with responsibilities that in the past have been assumed by the architect (engineer) or by the contractor. Therefore, one should become familiar with pitfalls disclosed in other chapters which have entrapped these others.

1. Don't perform professional services which could be interpreted as practicing architecture or engineering unless you are licensed to do so.

2. Don't fail to adequately define and delimit your contractual duties.

3. Don't assume responsibilities beyond those for which you have contracted.

4. Don't fail to select an appropriate basis for compensation, and state it in the agreement with your client.

5. Don't forget that a contractor's claims for extras may be successful if your decisions are negligent or unfair.

6. Don't forget that a contractor has a direct right of action against the construction manager as the owner's agent.

7. Don't forget that the language of your contract with a client may establish implied responsibilities to third parties.

CHAPTER **11**

Legal Pitfalls
When Professional
Is Developer

At present, there is a trend towards a blurring of the sharp distinction of the roles of designer, builder, and manufacturer. A manifestation of this trend has been the involvement of architectural firms as principals in land development projects. The architect, in joining forces with other specialists to form a development team, ordinarily makes his primary contribution in the field of planning and design, utilizing the same talents and experience which he would exercise in a project for a client.

11.1 Does the Architect-Developer Place His Professional License in Jeopardy? The American Institute of Architects does not find architect-developers in violation of its standards of ethical practice. However, despite this recent permission granted by the professional society, some state laws are more restrictive, and before associating himself as a principal in a development project, the architect should consult his attorney regarding the laws of each state in which he wishes to practice. Every state has statutes regulating the practice of architecture, but these regulations vary materially from state to state, and the laws of each state are subject to periodic revision.

In some states, architects are prohibited from having a financial interest in the ownership of projects for which they are architects and sometimes are even prohibited from taking payment in stock in the owner's company in lieu of architectural fees. The regulations of one state read, in part:

No registered architect shall engage in, or participate in, any profits from building contracting or on any project for which he has been employed as an architect.[119]

Regulations may delimit the activities of professionals even where those activities are engaged in outside the jurisdiction of the state where the professional is licensed or registered. One state defines professional misconduct, in part, as follows:

Being convicted or committing an act constituting a crime under . . . *the law of another jurisdiction* and which, if committed within this state, would have constituted a crime . . .[120] (emphasis supplied).

Thus the fact that an architect would engage in development work outside of the state would have no effect as to his violating the regulations, and risking his registration or license in the state in question.

11.2 Implied Warranty of Fitness. Greater obligations are often placed by law upon the seller of a new house than are placed upon the seller of an old house. While it has long been the rule that the seller of personal property impliedly warrants that his merchandise is fit for its intended purpose, traditionally, this rule was not applied to sales of real property. Unless the seller fraudulently deceived the purchaser by making false representations, the rule which was applied to real property sales was *caveat emptor*, or let the buyer beware. While this still generally applies to sales of old houses, the current trend of court decisions is to hold that the seller of a new house impliedly warrants that it was built in a workmanlike manner and is suitable for habitation, particularly where the seller is a developer-builder.

The concept of implied warranty was first applied to transactions in which the building was not completed at the time of sale, on the theory that the buyer of a house under construction is entitled to rely on an implied warranty that it will be completed in a manner to make it suitable for habitation. One court reasoned as follows:

When a vendee buys a development house from an advertised model, as in a Levitt or in a comparable project, he clearly relies on the skill of the developer and upon its implied representation that the house will be erected in reasonably workmanlike manner and will be reasonably fit for habitation. He has no architect or other professional advisor of his own, he has no real competency to inspect on his own, his actual examination is, in the nature of things, largely superficial, and his opportunity for obtaining meaningful protective changes in the conveyancing documents prepared by the builder vendor is negligible. If there is improper construction such as a defective heating system or a defective ceiling, stairway and the like, the well-being of the vendee and others is seriously endangered and serious injury is foreseeable. The public interest dictates that if such injury does result from the defective construction, its cost should be borne by the responsible developer who created the danger and who is in the better economic position to bear the loss rather than by the injured party who justifiably relied on the developer's skill and implied representation.[121]

In a number of recent cases, the doctrine of implied warranty has been extended to include sales of new houses after completion. One such case involved leaking basement walls resulting in flooding and damage to appliances in the basement. The owner had bought the house from the builder after completion. The flooding first occurred within a few weeks after occupancy by the new owner, and the builder made extensive efforts to correct the situation. He dug drainage ditches, backfilled the ditches around the foundation with gravel, poured 2 inches of concrete in the basement, and attempted to seal the block foundation wall with hot tar and tar paper, although he was hampered by the existence of an attached garage which prevented waterproofing being applied to the complete length of the outside of that wall of the basement. Despite these repairs, which cost the builder $4000, the basement was again flooded with approximately 2 feet of water about eighteen months later, and upon still another occasion four months after that.

The homeowner sued the builder for damages. The court was asked to decide, among other things, whether there is an implied warranty of fitness in the case of houses completed prior to sale. The court found it incongruous that a different rule should apply to the purchaser of a house which is near completion than would apply to one who purchases a new house. The court said:

We agree that a completed house can be inspected, to a limited extent, for defects by a purchaser before he signs the contract to buy. However, looking at the situation in a practical way, we are of the opinion that most potential homeowners lack the competency to do their own inspections. Even if he were skilled, there is little he could uncover, because most litigation is over defects which are found in the home's foundation. This can only be checked effectively at a time when none of the building proper has been constructed. It would seem to us, therefore, that the purchaser of a completed house is relying much more heavily on the superior skill and knowledge of the builder than is the purchaser of a house under construction.

Another anomalous outcome is the situation where a developer is constructing more than one house in a subdivision. One who purchases one of the houses one day before it is completed gets the benefits of an implied warranty that the house is free from structural defects and fit for habitation. The one who buys the house next door two days later—one day after completion—buys without implied warranty.[122]

11.2.1 *Implied Warranty When Land Is "Manufactured."* The warranty doctrine may be applied to real property sales even when no building has been built. In a California case, a developer sold residential lots to individual purchasers. One of the purchasers built a house on his lot and sold it. Within the next five years the rear slope of the lot settled, and the owner sued the developer and his engineers.

Although the trial court upheld the defendants' contention that there was no doctrine of implied warranty in the sale of residential lots, this was reversed by the District Court of Appeals. The court stated:

Here we have allegations that defendants manufactured the lot by cutting, grading, filling and compacting for the purpose of sale to the public and the construction of a house thereon, knowing that if said work was defective, it would cause damage to any improvements thereon; that the manufacturing process was defective in that it had inadequate provision for drainage, which caused water to accumulate between the fill and bedrock, in that it had organic matter beneath the fill which decomposed, causing the lot pad to settle; and that it had not been sufficiently compacted, which also caused the lot pad to settle. The alleged defects were not visible or apparent to a purchaser; conceivably they were many feet beneath the surface of the lot pad. Information thereof could have been ascertained by subsurface soil tests and by inspections at the time of filling and grading. Is the purchaser of a manufactured lot under obligation to employ a soils engineer to make expensive and disruptive soil tests? . . .

We conclude that the manufacturer of a lot may be held strictly liable in tort for damages suffered by the owner as a proximate result of any defects in the manufacturing process. [123]

11.3 *Liability under Implied Warranty Extends to Third Parties.* In an important trend-setting case, the justices of the Supreme Court of New Jersey unanimously recognized the need for imposing on builder-vendors an implied obligation of reasonable workmanship and habitability which survives delivery of the deed.

In this case, the purchaser of a tract house leased it to a tenant two years after he bought it from the developer, who also was the designer and builder. Two days after the tenant took occupancy of the building, his sixteen-month-old son was severely scalded when he turned on the hot water faucet in the bathroom lavatory. As a result, he was hospitalized for seventy-four days, and later had to undergo two skin-grafting operations. His parents sued the developer on two grounds, namely, negligence and implied warranty of fitness.

Testimony disclosed that the domestic hot water was heated by a coil immersed in the boiler. Since the heating closet was only 6 feet away from the bathroom lavatory, the water coming from the faucet was approximately 190°F. The developer had not installed automatic controls to limit the water temperature, relying instead on a warning included in a printed homeowner's guide issued to the purchasers.

The court ruled that the fact that the purchaser and his lessee may have known of the dangerous condition would not, as a matter of law, preclude a finding of negligence on the part of the builder-vendor, and that excessive hot water flowing from hot water faucets was not so patent a defect as to preclude the builder-vendor's liability in negligence for injury to a child of the purchaser's lessee.

The developer contended that imposition of warranty or strict liability principles on developers would make them "virtual insurers of the safety of all who thereafter come upon the premises." The court failed to agree with this interpretation. The injured party would, in fact, have to establish that the house was defective when constructed and sold, and that the defect proximately caused the injury. The court said:

... We are satisfied that, in the particular situation here, the plaintiffs may rely not only on the principles of negligence set forth under their first point but also on the implied warranty or strict principles set forth under their second point. We note, however, as indicated earlier in this opinion, that even under implied warranty or strict liability principles, the plaintiff's burden still remains of establishing to the jury's satisfaction that the design was unreasonably dangerous and proximately caused the injury.[121]

11.4 Conclusions. In taking an equity position in development building, the architect or engineer becomes involved in a whole range of problems with which he has had little experience, and which are beyond the scope of this book. However, even when participating as a member of a team of experts, the following points should be borne in mind:

1. Don't undertake development work which may jeopardize a professional license you wish to retain.

2. Don't fail to remember that the concept of implied warranty may be applied to a completed house as well as to one under construction.

3. Don't forget that the concept of implied warranty may be extended to third parties.

CHAPTER **12**

Arbitration

Unless the parties to a contract are able to reach an amicable understanding, they must resort to a legal tribunal for the resolution of their disagreements. Normally, they take their disputes to a court of law for determination; but the parties have the right to substitute a different tribunal—that is, arbitration. In general, it may be provided in their contract that future disputes shall be submitted to arbitration, or they may agree to arbitrate an existing dispute after it arises.

12.1   *Introductory.* An arbitration hearing differs from a court trial in that it is a less formal proceeding. Arbitrators are not required to follow the strict legal rules of evidence as to form and admissibility. They may accept all evidence they believe to be relevant and material, even where such evidence might not be accepted in court.

The arbitrator is not necessarily a lawyer or an officer of the court, but may be any neutral person who may be agreed upon by the parties. He should, of course, have no bias or any personal or financial interest in the result of the arbitration, or any previous or present relationship with either of the parties, and is usually one who has had past experience with construction projects.

Unlike a court trial, an arbitration hearing is not open to the public, and undesirable publicity may be avoided. The parties may be represented by counsel. Generally, the complaining party first presents his claim and proofs and his witnesses, and then the defending party presents his defense and proofs and his witnesses. All witnesses may be questioned by opposing counsel or by the arbitrator. Documentary evidence may be submitted to the arbitrator. The arbitrator does not have the power given to a court to compel witnesses to appear or to present documents, except in states in which he is given this power specifically by state arbitration laws.

The arbitrator may grant any award which he deems to be just and equitable after having afforded each party full and equal opportunity for the presentation of his case. The decision need not be in writing, nor are reasons for the decision required. Arbitrators' decisions are usually final and conclusive; that is, ordinarily they will not be upset by a court upon appeal based on the merits of the case. This is in sharp distinction to the right of appeal in litigation, where if one is not satisfied with a court decision, he may appeal to a higher court. Generally, an arbitrator's decision will not be invalidated even if he has made a mistake resulting in an erroneous award. In reviewing an arbitrator's award, the court will not review the findings of law and fact, but only whether the proceedings were free from fraud, the decision was within the limits of the issues submitted for arbitration, and the proceedings were fairly conducted.

12.2 Selection of Arbitrators. A traditional method of selecting arbitrators has been for each party to choose one, and then for these two to agree upon an umpire. Realistically considered, this method has practical disadvantages, because the very method of selecting the arbitrators taints two of them with the suspicion of partiality; and, in fact, although each may be completely honest, he may lean subconciously to his sponsor's position, leaving the umpire alone to make decisions of considerable importance.

Therefore, more and more often disputants resort to arbitration under the Construction Industry Rules of the American Arbitration Association. The rules permit a very simple method of procedure. The party demanding arbitration must put his demand in writing, serve one copy on his adversary, and file two copies with the association. The respondent is permitted to answer within seven days after notice from the association; but if he does not do so he is not in default. On the contrary, he is deemed to have denied the claim asserted in the demand.

The association attempts to find arbitrators acceptable to both parties but if this is not possible, the administrator of the association designates the arbitrator(s). Hearings are then held, where the right to examine and cross-examine witnesses is preserved, and where each party may be represented by counsel; and, finally, an award is made by the arbitrators.

12.3 Selection of Locale of Proceedings. Unless it is agreed between the parties where the proceedings are to take place, the association fixes the locale. It is very desirable that the parties make this determination in their agreement. In one instance, an East Coast architect, who was suffering from heart trouble, was faced with the expense and discomfort of traveling to the West Coast to attend hearings. Consequently, he settled for a paltry sum in order to avoid the long trip. Even had he been in good health, the expense of transporting his engineers and other witnesses to the West Coast would have been too heavy a burden.

It must be remembered also that the several states have not all adopted the Uniform Arbitration Law. A disagreement arose between a New York architect and his client during the construction of an addition to a convent located in a foreign state. Their contract called for arbitration, but did not specify the locale where the hearings would be held. The architect requested hearings in New York City, not alone because of convenience, but also because his counsel, doubtful of the wording of the law of the foreign state, feared that an award rendered therein might be unenforceable. The American Arbitration Association, pursuant to its rules, determined on hearings in New York; and after hearings, an award was rendered in favor of the architect.

The client refused to honor the award. The architect then procured a judgment in a New York court, based upon the award. Upon the client's assertion that the New York court had no jurisdiction in the case, it was pointed out that the foreign state was required to enforce the judgment under Article IV of the United States Constitution, which provides that: "Full faith and credit shall be given in each state to the public acts, records and judicial proceedings of every other state." As a result, the matter was disposed of in a manner satisfactory to the architect. It can readily be seen that it is desirable that the contract specify the locale of the arbitration hearings. This can be accomplished by including in the arbitration provision, the following additional language:

The arbitration shall be held in the City of _____, State of _____.

However, even with the inclusion of such a provision in the contract and the further inclusion that the decision of the arbitrators shall be a condition precedent to the right of any legal action, it does not necessarily prevent the allegedly injured party from instituting a court action, because the court may not enforce the contractual requirement for arbitration.

A recent case in point involved a New York architect who designed a residence in Florida. The standard form of agreement between owner and architect had been amended by an addendum stipulating that arbitration of all questions in dispute "shall be held in New York City, New York." Upon the owner's instituting a court action in Florida, alleging that the architect had negligently prepared plans and specifications and negligently supervised construction, the architect requested the court to enter an order directing the parties to proceed with arbitration in accordance with the terms and provisions of the contract.

This the lower court refused to do, and said decision was upheld on appeal by the District Court of Appeals of the State of Florida. It was held that the contractual provision calling for arbitration to take place in New York constituted a stipulation that the Florida Arbitration Code should not apply, and that by reason thereof, the Florida courts have no statutory authority to compel arbitration in another jurisdiction. Without the required statutory authority of the Florida Arbitration Code to enforce the arbitration provision, this provision was held to be voidable and prohibited same from being used as a bar to a court action by either party.[124]

12.4   *Advantages of Arbitration.* Is arbitration a satisfactory way of settling disputes involving architects, engineers, and contractors? Of the advantages of arbitration, two stand out prominently. First, in comparison to court actions, arbitration has proved to be efficient, expeditious, and economical. Congested court calendars prevail today in many jurisdictions; and the resulting delays sometimes effectively defeat justice. Second, in a court action one litigant may insist on his right to a trial by jury. The result is that the determination of intensely technical disputes is left in the hands of laymen. The housewife or banker, no matter how intelligent, may misconstrue the implications of a building specification. In arbitration proceedings under the administration of the American Arbitration Association, it is probable that at least one of the arbitrators will be an expert in the technical field under consideration.

12.5   *Disadvantages of Arbitration.* There are those who oppose arbitration, stressing that courts permit arbitrators to decide matters of law as well as matters of fact; and, as the arbitrators are not always versed in the technical facets of law, legal principles may be swept aside. It is felt also, that by waiving formal rules of evidence, injustices may result.

However, as more and more disputants have resorted to arbitration, as a condition precedent to court action or as an alternative thereto, it has continued to grow in stature in the public eye. It is obviously more suited to some controversies than to others. Each transaction must be considered on its own merits. It would be wise to seek the advice of one's attorney.

12.6   *Contract Provisions for Arbitration.* An agreement to submit disputes to arbitration need not be couched in special language, so long as it is clearly the intent of the parties to avail themselves of this method of settling their disputes. The following stipulation has been used:

All disputes arising under or relating to, or arising in connection with this Agreement, its breach or termination, shall be determined by arbitration in accordance with the Construction Industry Rules of the American Arbitration Association.

Although no special language is necessary, it is essential that the scope of the arbitrators' authority be clearly defined, and that words limiting their power to act be avoided, unless it is really intended to circumscribe their authority. A case in point occurred on the West Coast, where a builder, who had contracted to do certain work for a municipality, terminated the contract and abandoned the work. The builder claimed that the city had breached the contract by not paying him for work performed. The contract provided that questions in dispute shall be submitted to arbitration before a designated board of arbitration prior to any action at law being brought by either party. The court held that since the builder had terminated the contract and had abandoned the work the city was not bound to arbitrate.[125]

12.7 Architect (Engineer) as Arbitrator. Standard General Conditions of the contract in current use state that the architect shall decide claims and disputes relating to the execution or progress of the work, or the interpretation of the contract documents. For at least three-quarters of a century, it has been appreciated that the responsibilities of the design professions are not necessarily limited to the design of a structure and the supervision of its erection. As early as 1889, one court recognized that the scope of an architect's or an engineer's activities might well be broader than those implicit in his duties as the professional adviser and representative of his client; and that he might be given the power to act in a quasi-judicial role. Such a delegation of power was respected by the court in a decision rendered during that year, where the contract between owner and contractor provided that the engineer would estimate the quantity of the various kinds of work done, and that his estimate should be "final and conclusive." The court stated:

The chief engineer had the general powers and duties of an arbitrator, except as they were expressly or impliedly restricted or increased by the contract of the parties. . . . No court has any general powers of supervision over the awards of the arbitrators.

The court restricted the grounds on which the award could be set aside, as follows:

We regard the estimate of the chief engineer as conclusive, and that in the absence of proof of corruption, bad faith or misconduct on his part, or palpable mistake appearing on the face of the estimate, neither party can be allowed to prove that he decided wrong as to the law or facts.[126]

A judgment of another court determined that an engineer's decision was conclusive and binding when the contract so provided. In this case, involving grading for an airport, the contractor commenced an action at law to recover, at a rate higher than that determined by the owner's engineer, for placing backfill in a different location from that originally contemplated. The contract contained a "Schedule of Unit Prices" for "Classified Work," and defined "Classified Work" as "the items of . . . work set forth in the . . . Schedule of Unit Prices . . . and shall include any . . . work hereafter required which in the opinion of the Engineer is of the same general character as that set forth in any of said items." The term "Extra Work" was defined as "Unclassified Work required by the Engineer." Under the Schedule of Prices for Classified Work, the price for "Disposal of material suitable for backfill on construction site" was $2.50 per cubic yard; and under another provision of the contract "extra work" was to be paid for on a "cost-plus" basis.

After the job had started, the owner issued a change order, requiring the remaining excavated materials to be deposited at a location other than that designated in the original contract. The engineer determined that work under the change order was not work of the same general character as the classified work, but was "extra work" to be paid for on a cost-plus basis. The court, noting that the terms of the contract were concededly free from ambiguity, and finding that a reasonable basis existed for the engineer's determination, held that in the absence of fraud, bad faith, or palpable mistake his decision was conclusive and binding upon the contractor.[127]

Until a contract has been executed between owner and contractor, the architect's primary duty is to his client, and during on-site inspections he is acting as a representative of his client. However, when disputes arise during construction with regard to the execution or progress of the work, or the interpretation of the contract documents, the architect's role, in effect, changes from that of owner's representative to that of one vested with power to make decisions, at least in the first instance, with respect to claims of owner or contractor.

Whether his decisions are final or subject to review by formal arbitration, it is obvious that they must be carefully objective and punctiliously impartial. The architect must constantly guard against even the appearance of bias in such instances, for the circumstances are such that his position may be suspect by owner or contractor, or both, out of a belief by the owner that self-interest would indicate partiality to the contractor, who as one in the building business is more likely than the owner to be working with the architect again; or out of a belief by the contractor that the architect may still consider himself the representative of the owner, which, in fact, he was such a short time before. Even the most equitable decision may be unacceptable to an owner who cannot understand why his architect, to whom he is still paying a fee, should not agree with him completely.

All the architect's decisions are subject to review unless otherwise expressly provided in the contract documents. Since the status of an architect is that of an arbitrator when the contract documents make his decisions final or conclusive, an intention to attach finality to his decision must be expressed clearly, and only with full awareness of its legal implication. As one court said:

The intent must be clear to render arbitration the exclusive remedy; parties are not to be led into arbitration unwittingly through subtlety.[128]

Where the contract provides that the architect's decision shall be final and conclusive, his determination, even if erroneous, is ordinarily not reviewable on the merits. This legal principle has been expressed as follows:

When parties agree to arbitrate, they agree to waive the rules of evidence and the inexorable application of substantive rules as well. . . . The fact is that an agreement to arbitrate, . . . is a contractual method for settling disputes in which the parties create their own forums, pick their own judges, waive all but limited rights of review or appeal, dispense with the rules of evidence, and leave the issue to be determined in accordance with the sense of justice and equity that they may believe reposes in the breasts and minds of their self-chosen judges.[129]

Although an architect or engineer may be made the final judge, the question remains, should he be the final judge? Though an architect or engineer undoubtedly is capable of making fair decisions, we urge that he avoid the role of final judge, because of the possible suspicions already mentioned. Discretion indicates that he should stipulate that all of his decisions are subject to arbitration, with the exception of matters relating to artistic effect or requiring the contractor to act in an emergency.

This is not to suggest that the contract documents should not render his decision final, in case a party to the contract fails to seek review of the decision within a stipulated period of time. Such a failure would make the architect the final judge, not through his own choosing, but instead through the failure of a party to exercise a prescribed remedy.

Thus, the Standard General Conditions reserves to owner or contractor the right to review an architect's decision, except in certain instances, through an appeal by arbitration under the Construction Industry Rules of the American Arbitration Association within thirty days after the date on which the party making the demand received the architect's decision. This short statute of limitations applies only if the architect's decision is in writing and states that it is final but subject to appeal. Therefore under the Standard General Conditions, in order to resolve the controversy at an early date and to prevent the unsuccessful party from demanding arbitration long after the architect makes his determination, the architect's written decision should include the following words:

This decision is final, but subject to appeal within thirty days after date of receipt of this decision.

Since the architect's decision may become final through failure of the unsuccessful party to appeal therefrom, within the allotted period, it would seem important for him to notify each party in writing of the date, time, and place where opportunity to present evidence will be afforded. To avoid any question as to his right to counsel, a party should not be denied the right to appear at any hearings with legal counsel. Unless specifically required by the law of a particular jurisdiction, the architect is not required to state the reasons for his decision. The architect, in his written decision, after stating in general terms the nature of the dispute, may preface his findings with such words as:

I decide and find as follows:

The architect's decision should be acknowledged before a notary public.

12.8 Consolidating Arbitration Proceedings—Owner-Contractor-Subcontractor. Though courts may have the power to order consolidation of two or more arbitration proceedings, parties should not be required to seek such relief from the courts. The problem may be simplified by an appropriate provision in the agreement. On page 84 reference was made to a provision for the consolidation in arbitration of claims involving owner-architect-engineer.

It is not difficult to imagine a situation in which a dispute may arise between owner and contractor, in a project let under separate contracts, where the responsibility for a defect does not clearly rest entirely with one of the separate contractors, or where there is doubt as to which separate contractor is fully responsible. To cover this contingency, a clause reading substantially as follows may be considered:

In the event that the Owner is of the opinion that any Separate Building Contractor having contractual relations with the Owner (herein referred to as "Impleaded Party") may in any manner whatsoever be involved in any claim either of the Contractor or Owner, which is the subject of arbitration under this Agreement, the Owner shall have the right to make such "Impleaded Party," a party to an arbitration proceeding between the Owner and Contractor, by mailing a written notice to such "Impleaded Party" requiring him to become a party thereto. All questions raised by the Owner, the Contractor and each "Impleaded Party," shall be determined in one arbitration proceeding and an award rendered in favor of or against any of the parties thereto. The arbitration proceedings shall be conducted in accordance with the Construction Industry Rules of the American Arbitration Association.

The above provisions shall be applicable only to the special conditions set forth above where an "Impleaded Party" is involved and shall not apply to any arbitration where only the Owner and Contractor are involved. The inclusion of a similar clause in any Agreement made by the Owner with any "Impleaded Party" in connection with this Project shall be sufficient to enable the Owner to compel the Separate Building Contractor to become a party to any arbitration proceeding between the Owner and the Contractor.

The terms "Separate Contractor" and "Impleaded Party" are each used above as if singular in number but are intended to include as Impleaded Parties all Separate Contractors.

Recognizing that third parties may become involved in disputes between contractor and subcontractor, the following provision, in substance, has been used to permit consolidation of two or more related controversies involving contractor, subcontractor, and other persons having contractual relations with the contractor:

In the event that the Contractor is of the opinion that any other parties having contractual relations with the Contractor (herein referred to as "Impleaded Parties") may in any manner whatsoever be involved in any claim either of the Contractor or the Subcontractor which is the subject of arbitration under this agreement, the Contractor shall have the right to make such "Impleaded Parties" party to an arbitration proceeding between the Contractor and Subcontractor by mailing a written notice to such "Impleaded Parties" requiring them to become parties thereto. All questions raised by the Contractor, the Subcontractor and "Impleaded Parties" shall be determined in one arbitration proceeding and an award rendered in favor of or against any of the parties thereto. The arbitration proceedings shall be conducted in accordance with the Construction Industry Rules of the American Arbitration Association.

The above provisions shall be applicable only to the special conditions set forth above where an "Impleaded Party or Parties" are involved and shall not apply to any arbitration where only the Contractor and Subcontractor are involved. The inclusion of a similar clause in any agreement made by the Contractor with any "Impleaded Party" in connection with this Project shall be sufficient to enable the Contractor to compel the "Impleaded Party" to become a party to any arbitration proceeding between the Contractor and the Subcontractor.

CHAPTER **13**

Professional Corporations

13.1 Introductory. One of the principal and usual advantages of doing business in corporate form is to limit the liability of an owner for business hazards to the extent of the owner's equity in the corporation. Thus, if a large judgment were obtained against the corporation, the creditor normally could not seek to collect from the personal assets of the owner (stockholder) which were not a part of the business. To the professional practitioner aware of the sharp increase in awards for damages against members of his profession, the idea of incorporating and thereby insulating his personal assets from liability, may seem an attractive one.

However, the prudence of granting permission to corporations to practice architecture and engineering has troubled legislators over a long period of time, and there is no unanimity in the laws of the several states in this regard. In most states, corporations have been banned from the practice of architecture or engineering by legislation passed in the 1920s and 1930s. Some states have permitted corporate professional practice, subject however to the condition that the officers, or those in responsible charge of the work, are licensed to practice. A few states permit only those corporations which were practicing when the prohibition against corporate practice was enacted, to continue to practice, provided the chief executive officer is a licensed professional.

A primary concern of legislators has been the desirability of limiting corporate professional practice to those individuals licensed as qualified practitioners. On the other hand, attention and scrutiny must be given to those situations where the management of a professional firm comes under the control of nonprofessionals, perhaps through transfer of ownership of shares. While some states have included a code of ethics in their rules and regulations for registrants, or have stipulated a good moral character as a requisite for registration, these have seemed inapplicable to corporations. Further, it has been felt to be inappropriate for a professional to evade personal responsibility for his conduct under the limited liability of a corporation.

In order to permit professionals to avail themselves of some of the advantages of incorporation, and in response to pressure brought to bear upon state legislators in the 1960s, primarily by physicians, many states have established a classification of "professional corporation," permitting architects and engineers as well as other professionals to incorporate and practice as corporate entities, rather than as sole practitioners or partners. The principal distinction of a professional corporation is that the limitation of liability is not available in respect of negligence, or wrongful acts or misconduct committed by the professional or by another under his direct supervision and control. Typically, the professional, who in most cases is also a shareholder, remains personally liable in the event of an error or omission.

13.2   Advantages of the Corporate Form. A corporation is a separate legal entity, unlike a partnership. The professional practicing as a corporation is not a principal, but a shareholder and employee of the corporation. Certain fringe benefits with tax advantages are available to the architect or engineer as employee of a corporation which would not be available to one who is a sole proprietor or partner. Although a self-employed person can set aside a portion of his income in a pension plan, and deduct this amount as a business expense, the amount thus set aside is limited by law. However, the professional service corporation offers the availability of pension and profit sharing plans similar to those enjoyed by other corporate businesses. The amounts to be set aside for shareholder-employees of a professional service corporation may be substantially in excess of the amounts now available to sole proprietors or partners. Corporate pension and profit sharing plans, as well as certain life insurance programs, also enable the shareholder to achieve estate planning benefits not available through sole proprietorships or partnerships.

In addition, there are other tax benefits available to corporations: for example, the ability to purchase life insurance and medical insurance or to create a medical reimbursement plan and to obtain a deduction for these items as a cost of doing business. A partner or sole proprietor who acquired similar forms of insurance must pay the premiums with after-tax earnings. Corporate employees are eligible to exclude a portion of their salaries which are paid to them under wage-continuation plans in the event they are away from work because of sickness or injury. Corporations may pay death benefits to beneficiaries of employees up to $5000 without any tax resulting to the beneficiary.

Although by incorporating, an architect or engineer may not limit his personal liability for his own errors or omissions in his professional work, it may be possible in some states for him to limit his liability where errors and omissions are committed by others who are shareholders as well. The one committing the error may be solely responsible. This limitation would not be available to other members of a partnership. In the event one partner commits an error, this will result in liability to all the members of the partnership.

Aside from "malpractice" items, the professional service corporation does offer the shareholders limited liability in other business relationships which would not be available in the case of a partnership or sole proprietorship. Thus, a default under an office lease, or a rental agreement for equipment or automobiles, or a contract with third parties for services to be performed (such as those rendered by a consulting engineer) would leave the damaged party with no recourse except to recover damages from the corporation. No personal liability attaches to the individual professional (shareholder) in the aforesaid instances.

13.3 *Disadvantages of the Corporate Form.* The creation of the corporation adds to one's legal and administrative expenses. Aside from the initial incorporation costs, there are numerous Federal, state, and local reports which must be filed periodically. Separate income tax returns have to be filed for the corporation and the individual shareholders; needless to say, additional record keeping is required.

The legal relationships between shareholders are very different from those relationships between partners. Absent a partnership agreement to the contrary, a partner may perform certain acts on behalf of the partnership, retire, cause a dissolution, and perform a myriad of other acts. On the other hand, a shareholder's ability to withdraw from the corporation and demand the return of his capital and share of accumulated profits is much more restricted by rules of law. The admission of new shareholders also may cause problems.

There are certain formalities which the corporate form, as a vehicle for doing business, must adhere to as required by the laws regulating corporations. If these formalities are not met, it is possible that in the event of a dispute regarding taxes or professional liability, the court will disregard the corporate form.

The architect or engineer practicing as a corporate entity should investigate the laws of the several states in which he wishes to practice. Should the statute of a given state stipulate that no corporation may be deemed licensed to practice architecture or engineering, it would be unlawful for a corporation to permit a representative or employee to seek professional work on its behalf or for it. The corporation could not accept a professional commission in that state.

13.4 Statutory Qualifications for Practice as a Professional Corporation. What are the statutory restrictions which are placed on professional corporations by state law? Each state establishes its own qualifications, and in each jurisdiction it is only by careful examination of the statutes currently in force that one's rights and duties can be determined. The following brief discussion of the regulations in New York State may serve to illustrate the problems that may arise.

13.4.1. Charter. A corporate charter must be filed listing the names and addresses of the shareholders, directors, and officers; attached thereto must be a certificate by the State Education Department certifying that each of the aforesaid individuals is duly licensed to practice architecture or engineering, as the case may be.

13.4.2 Rendering of Services. Each financial plan and report issued by a corporation practicing the profession of architecture or engineering shall bear the name and seal of one or more of the architects and engineers who are in responsible charge of the plan or report. The foregoing signature and seal requirements apply to all documents prepared by the corporation, which under applicable law or the custom of the profession is required to bear such signature.

13.4.3 Purposes. The professional service corporation shall not engage in any business other than the rendering of professional services for which it is incorporated. The corporation may, however, invest its funds in real property, securities, and other forms of investments.

13.4.4 Ownership. Only individuals licensed by law to practice the profession in the state of incorporation may own shares. Furthermore, no individual may be an officer or director unless he is similarly licensed to practice.

13.4.5 Disqualification. In the event any shareholder, director, officer, or employee of a professional service corporation becomes legally disqualified (for instance, by suspension of his license), he is required to sever all employment with and financial interests in the corporation. The effect of the foregoing, including the death of such individual, requires the corporation to purchase the shares of the disqualified or deceased shareholder, unless other shareholders have agreed to purchase said shares. Unless the parties have agreed to a price or a method of computing a price, the corporation is required to purchase the shares at the book value determined in accordance with the regular method of accounting of the corporation. Thus, absent an agreement to the contrary, a professional service corporation on a cash method type of accounting would not be required to pay for work in process. The failure to purchase said shares shall constitute a ground for forfeiture of the corporation's charter, and the disqualified or deceased shareholder, if successful in an action at law to recover the price, shall be awarded attorney's fees and costs.

13.4.6 *Corporate Name.* The name of the professional service corporation may contain any word which, at the time of incorporation, could be used in the name of a partnership. In effect, generally, this means that a professional service corporation must contain the name of one or more of the shareholders unless the corporation is succeeding to the business of a partnership and the name of the partnership consists of deceased partners. However, if such is the case, it is necessary that at least two-thirds of the partners of the existing partnership become shareholders of the corporation. The corporate name shall conclude with the words "Professional Corporation," or the abbreviation "P.C." Some states permit the use of the words "Professional Association," or the abbreviation "P.A." At least one state specifically prohibits a name containing the designation "P.C." or "P.A."

13.4.7 *Annual Report.* Each year the professional services corporation shall furnish a statement to the licensing department (in New York, the Education Department) regarding architects and engineers; listing the names and addresses of each shareholder, director, and officer; and certifying that all such individuals are authorized to practice their profession within the state.

CHAPTER **14**

Copyrights

14.1 *Introductory: Statutory Copyright.* Most forms of agreement between professionals and their clients contain a statement stipulating that the drawings and specifications, as instruments of service, are to remain the property of the professional. It was thought wise to include this stipulation in the contract because, in its absence, the client ordinarily will become the owner of these documents if he fulfills his part of the contract and makes full payment to the professional. It was felt by the drafters of the standard forms to be unfair to permit the client to use these plans and specifications for purposes other than the contemplated project without further payment to the professional.

Such a contract provision, however, is not effective in preventing the use of the architect's or engineer's work by third parties. While the protection of ideas is a difficult matter, protection against unauthorized copying of the plans and specifications arising out of these ideas may be given by copyright if the documents bear a copyright notice, and are properly deposited and registered.

If the client becomes the owner of the documents, he may reuse them without fear of successful intervention by the architect (engineer). The client, as owner of the documents, could also register them and become the copyright owner of record. If the design professional's plans are used without his permission for projects other than the one he intended, he not only may lose justifiable compensation, but he may also be a potential defendant in a lawsuit resulting from their reuse where it is alleged that the architect erred in his design. The professional may retain his rights in the documents he has prepared, as against his client, by stipulating in his contract that the drawings and specifications are only instruments of service, as is provided in the standard forms of both the American Institute of Architects and the National Society of Professional Engineers. The NSPE form also states that the owner shall indemnify the engineer from liability or losses resulting from any reuse of the documents by the client. Such an indemnity provision could be written into the contract even if the client were to become the owner of the documents on completion of the project. However, such an indemnity clause would be of little value if the client were financially unable to pay the indemnity in the event of a claim.

Also, such a contract provision would be of no protection against copying the plans by third parties, who may acquire the right to do so because the plans have been "published." Therefore, the architect (engineer), in addition to retaining ownership of the plans, may wish to resort to registering his work under the copyright law, and thus receive statutory copyright protection.

14.1.1. *What Can Be Protected?* Copyright law does not protect ideas, but protects against unauthorized copying of the tangible medium or form in which they are expressed. Public Law 94-553, an act for the general revision of the copyright law, which became effective January 1, 1978, states at Section 102:

(*a*) Copyright protection subsists, in accordance with this title, in original works of authorship fixed in any tangible medium of expression, now known or later developed, from which they can be perceived, reproduced, or otherwise communicated, either directly or with the aid of a machine or device. Works of authorship include the following categories:

(1) literary works;
(2) musical works, including any accompanying words;
(3) dramatic works, including any accompanying music;
(4) pantomimes and choreographic works;
(5) pictorial, graphic, and sculptural works;
(6) motion pictures and other audiovisual works; and
(7) sound recordings.

(*b*) In no case does copyright protection for an original work of authorship extend to any idea, procedure, process, system, method of operation, concept, principle, or discovery, regardless of the form in which it is described, explained, illustrated, or embodied in such work.

If the plans and specifications are produced by an employee of the architect (engineer), the employer has the right to the copyright absent an agreement giving the employee copyright ownership.

If the professional's client is the owner of the plans, it is he who has the right to the copyright.

14.1.2   How Is Statutory Copyright Secured? In order to obtain protection under the federal copyright act, it is required that the material to be copyrighted contain a copyright notice whenever it is published and, as a prerequisite to any legal action for infringement of the copyright, that the material to be copyrighted be deposited and registered at the Copyright Office.

14.1.2.1   Notice of copyright. Public Law 94-553 states, at Section 401:

(*a*) *General Requirement:* Whenever a work protected under this title is published in the United States or elsewhere by authority of the copyright owner, a notice of copyright as provided by this section shall be placed on all publicly distributed copies from which the work can be visually perceived, either directly or with the aid of a machine or device.

(*b*) *Form of Notice:* The notice appearing on the copies shall consist of the following three elements:

(1) the symbol © (the letter C in a circle), or the word "Copyright," or the abbreviation "Copr."; and

(2) the year of first publication of the work; in the case of compilations or derivative works incorporating previously published material, the year of the first publication of the compilation or derivative work is sufficient. The year date may be omitted where a pictorial, graphic, or sculptural work, with accompanying text matter, if any, is reproduced in or on greeting cards, postcards, stationery, jewelry, dolls, toys, or any useful articles; and

(3) the name of the owner of copyright in the work, or an abbreviation by which the name can be recognized, or a generally known alternative designation of the owner.

That is, a copyright notice, such as "Copyright 1978 John Doe," should be affixed to each drawing and to each page of the specifications, before the work is "published." If this is not done, the work is released to the public domain, and may then be copied without permission. Even limited distributions, such as issuance to bidders, may be considered to be publication.

14.1.2.2   Copyright deposit and registration. Registration of the copyright may be obtained by delivering to the Copyright Office the documents required to be deposited together with the necessary application and fee. While such registration is not a condition of copyright protection, registration must be made previous to the institution of a legal action for infringement of copyright under the act.

14.1.3   Rights in Works Copyrighted. The owner of copyright under Public Law 94-553 has exclusive rights to reproduce, distribute, and display the copyrighted work, subject to such fair use purposes as criticism, news reporting, teaching, and so forth, which are not considered infringements of copyright. As a general rule, copyright in a work created on or after January 1978 endures for a term consisting of the life of the author and fifty years after the author's death.

14.2 *Common-law Copyright.* Until Public Law 94-553, the general revision of the copyright law, became effective on January 1, 1978, the architect or engineer could obtain statutory copyright protection by properly depositing and registering the material to be copyrighted, or alternatively he could trust to common-law copyright. The latter was the more usual choice because, although statutory copyright was more effective than common-law copyright, its perfection required positive action on the part of the professional, while common-law copyright operated without the necessity for registering the work with the Register of Copyrights.

Public Law 94-553 supersedes and invalidates common-law copyright, stating at Section 301:

On and after January 1, 1978, all legal or equitable rights that are equivalent to any of the exclusive rights within the general scope of copyright as specified by section 106 in works of authorship that are fixed in a tangible medium of expression and come within the subject matter of copyright as specified by sections 102 and 103, whether created before or after that date and whether published or unpublished, are governed exclusively by this title. Thereafter, no person is entitled to any such right in any such work under the common law or statutes of any State.

However, this section also states:

Nothing in this title annuls or limits any rights or remedies under the common law or statutes of any State with respect to . . . any cause of action arising from undertakings commenced before January 1, 1978.

Consequently, in such cases, common-law copyright still affords protection, and although its application has been limited, it is not obsolete.

14.2.1. *General.* The ownership and sole use of models, drawings, and specifications prepared by architects and engineers are afforded them under common-law copyright. This right of ownership is protected until, by publication, they become the property of the general public. Unless there is a specific contractual provision to the contrary, ownership of plans and specifications—and ownership of copyright—is transferred to the client who commissioned the professional to prepare them. The owner of a common-law copyright may, within the limitations noted above, maintain a legal action against anyone using or copying the documents without his consent.

14.2.2. *Common-law Copyright Terminates upon Publication.* Most disputes involving an alleged infringement of common-law copyright are concerned with the question of whether or not the author has published the work. The word "publication" in this context does not have its usual book or periodical connotation, but has a special legal meaning relating to a general publication sufficient to extinguish common-law copyright.

Because common-law copyright is a protection given by state law, court decisions in various jurisdictions are in conflict as to what constitutes the difference between general publication and limited publication. The former releases documents into the public domain while the latter does not.

14.2.2.1   What constitutes general publication? A general publication is not always easy to distinguish from a limited publication. One court defined them as follows:

. . . Only a general publication terminates a common–law copyright. It is "such a disclosure, communication, circulation, exhibition, or distribution of the subject of copyright, tendered or given to one or more members of the general public, as implies an abandonment of the right of copyright or its dedication to the public" (citation). A limited publication is "one which communicates a knowledge of its contents under conditions expressly or impliedly precluding its dedication to the public" (citation). Further, to be general a publication must be such " . . . as to justify the belief that it took place with the intention of rendering . . . (the) work common property." . . . As more recently stated, "a . . . publication which communicates the contents of a manuscript to a definitely selected group and for a limited purpose, and without the right of diffusion, reproduction, distribution or sale, is considered a 'limited publication,' which does not result in loss of the author's common-law right to his manuscript, but . . . the circulation must be restricted both as to persons and purpose, or it cannot be called a private or limited publication." . . . While the test is properly one of intention, it is clear that the unexpressed, subjective intention of the creator cannot be allowed to govern . . . rather the implications of his outward acts to the reasonable outsider are controlling.[130]

In a legal action charging infringement of common-law copyright, the defendant usually claims that the plaintiff has made a general publication of the plans, and that therefore a right to use the plans has been conferred upon the public. Consequently, the court must decide in each case whether previous actions of the plaintiff had deprived him of his copyright.

In one case, the court upheld the defendant's contention that there had been a general publication of the floor plans before the defendant copied them, because the plaintiff, a developer of tract houses, had invited the public to visit model homes, distributed brochures containing the floor plans, and sold over 1400 homes. He had also submitted the plans to magazines which published pictures and floor plans of his houses.[131]

In a second case, floor plans for a house developed by the owner and his wife were copied by a subcontractor who worked on the job. Although the court found that the owners, by putting the house up for sale on a multiple listing, holding open house exhibitions, and inviting the public to view the floor plan, had evinced an intention to make their plans public, it was held that the subcontractor had infringed the common-law copyright in copying the plans before these events occurred, and that showing him the drawings for purposes of bidding and construction was a limited publication that did not terminate the copyright.[132]

In a third case, concerning the unauthorized copying of plans for a restaurant, bidders were required to make a deposit of $25 in order to obtain a copy of the drawings and specifications. This deposit was forfeited if they failed to return the drawings and specifications. The defendant claimed that this constituted a sale of the documents to the bidders for $25. The court rejected his contention.

. . . It appears to us that requiring a deposit of $25 to take a look-see at such plans evinces, not an intention to sell them, but an intention to have them returned to the architect to use in construction perhaps in an area far removed from the local area where competition would be of no factor, and in which distant area there would be no question as to using them in an unfair competition problem. The A.I.A. conditions plus the written specifications confirm us in this conclusion. We have no doubt that under the facts of this case, A (architect) required a deposit to insure the return of the plans, since if A himself used the same plans to supervise the construction of an identical drive-in next door to Allen's, in equity he might have to respond in damages to Allen. Nowhere in this record did A concede non-ownership of these plans, but contrariwise said otherwise. He admitted that if the contractors did not return them, the latter could keep them—but not once did he admit, nor does the record reflect anything to the effect *that they could use them* to construct an identical structure in the area. . . . [133]

14.2.2.2 *Does filing plans for a building permit extinguish common-law copyright?* Courts are divided in their opinions on this matter. Although courts in several jurisdictions have held that when a designer has filed his plans in a public office he has published his work and thus lost his exclusive right to them, a majority of the more recent decisions hold that such required filing constitutes only a limited publication.

In one case, an architect prepared plans and specifications for the construction of an apartment building under a contract whereby he retained all property rights in them. A copy of the plans and specifications was filed by the then property owner in the office of the village clerk as required by village ordinance, and construction of the building was begun. The following year when the building was over 60 percent completed, the owner defaulted in mortgage payments and the mortgagee took over the premises in a foreclosure action. A third party purchased the property and completed the building, without the services of an architect. Claiming that this party used his plans and specifications without his consent, the architect brought an action for the reasonable value of his work, labor, and services. The lower court dismissed the complaint, holding that the filing of the plans with the village clerk constituted a publication thereof, resulting in the loss of his common-law copyright. Upon appeal, the Appellate Court reversed this judgment, holding that such filing was a limited publication made for the definite purpose of securing a building permit and did not result in the surrender of any rights inconsistent with such limited purpose. [134]

In another state, in a case in which the owner-architect agreement recited that the architect retained property rights, title, and interest to the plans, these plans were filed with the building department as required to obtain a building permit. The plans were copied by a third party to construct other buildings identical in design and specifications. In the legal action which followed, an issue in dispute was whether the architect lost his common-law rights in the plans when they were filed with the building department. In a well-reasoned decision, the court said:

There is no basis for concluding that by filing with the Woburn officials, Wood (architect) made manifest any objective intention to publish the plans generally. . . . On the contrary, the protective clause in Wood's contract with Moylan (owner) indicates that the intention was to preserve Wood's common-law rights in them. The sole reason for the filing of the plans was to procure official approval of them. The filing was a publication to but a single entity for a limited purpose. To hold that, in filing, an architect makes a general publication would be to limit his ability to effect a sale of more than one set of plans.

As already pointed out, this view was recognized in Smith v. Paul, 174 Cal. App.2d 744, 345 P. 2d 546, 77 A.L.R. 2d 1036. That case held that a necessary filing of architectural plans was not a general publication, despite a general statutory right to inspect and secure copies of "any public writing" on the part of the general public. This Commonwealth has a similar statutory provision: "Every person having custody of any public records shall, at reasonable times, permit them to be examined by any person, under his supervision, and shall furnish copies thereof on payment of a reasonable fee . . ." G.L.c.66, 10. The filed plans are without question "public records." The argument is advanced that in G.L.c.66, 10, the Legislature has in effect decreed that a filing of plans with a building department shall constitute a general publication. The power to copy public records has been said to be not limited by the use sought to be made of the copies. . . . It must be clear, however, that the principal objective of Woburn in compelling a filing is to insure that the public will be protected from unsafe construction. . . . There is no indication that a second and unrelated objective, one to compel an architect to divest himself of the fruit of his labor as a condition precedent to obtaining a building permit, is within the purpose of the filing requirements of G.L.c.66, 10. . . .

In the light of what has been said, we hold that the filing requirement and G.L.c.66, 10, give the public the right to inspect and, if necessary, to copy the filing plans for purposes reasonably related to the objectives behind the filing requirement, for example, to determine whether a building constructed in accordance with plans will comply with zoning and safety laws. The right does not extend to making copies which will impair the architect's common-law copyright and property in the plans. It is not the purpose of the filing requirement to facilitate and permit architectural plagiarism, or enable one to obtain free of charge the benefit of another's work and thus "to reap where it has not sown.". . .

We conclude that the public filing of plans in the circumstances alleged is only a limited publication of them. No objective intention to make a general publication appears. [130]

14.2.2.3 Does completion of the building extinguish common-law copyright?
Early decisions held that the construction of a building from plans conferred upon the public a right to their use. In one case, an architect and

builder erected a porch "of a new and novel design and artistic beauty" on the front of his house, which stood bordering a highway. Later he sought to enjoin the construction of copies of his porch. The court held that the completion of the design and its exposure to public gaze for three years constituted a general publication of the work.[135]

However, more recent decisions show a trend toward the opposite view. In the *Wood v. Skene* case, discussed previously in this chapter, the Massachusetts Court stated:

Observation or measurement of the exterior and interior of a completed building can hardly be said to approach an accurate copy of a set of plans. We do not suggest that a common-law copyright in the plans is infringed by a drawing made from observation of the interior or exterior of buildings. . . . On the other hand, the right fully to reproduce plans is a far more substantial aid to a builder not willing to pay for architectural services than the right to make sketches or drawings of a completed structure.

We thus hold that the construction of a building from the plans constitutes no publication of them at all.[130]

14.2.3. Efficacy of Reserving Ownership Rights by Including Restrictions on Drawings. If the designer does not specifically retain his property rights to plans by imprinting or stamping on his drawings a notice to this effect, it is possible that even the distribution of drawings and specifications to the client and to bidders may be considered to be a general publication. This was the finding of a court of higher jurisdiction in a recent case.

In this instance, the carpentry subcontractor on an apartment project allegedly used the architect's plans a year later to build a similar project. In upholding the lower court's dismissal of the architect's complaint, for failure to state a claim, the court said:

The only publication by K (architect) alleged in the complaint is found in paragraph 4 thereof which states that "on or about March 8, 1968, K created, designed and drew a series of approximately forty-four (44) architectural drawings, which drawings describe and represent a number of views and details of certain twelve (12) unit apartment buildings. K permitted the Springdale Green Company (owner) . . . to use said plans in the construction of an apartment project.". . .

The complaint does not allege that the publication of the architectural plans to the Springdale Green Company was made with any express restrictions, reservations or other limitations by means of an agreement, annotation on the plans, or otherwise, concerning the use and dissemination of such plans. The complaint therefore alleges a general publication of the drawings and plans to the Springdale Green Company. The allegation of a general publication of the architectural material is fatal to K's cause of action. Such a publication releases K's common-law copyright in the plans and drawings prior to the alleged use thereof by P. . . .

The architect's common-law protection must necessarily be conditioned upon notice of the rights reserved in the architectural material produced. No such reservation is claimed by K.[136]

14.2.4   *Employee Breached Implied Duty Not to Disclose Confidential Information to a Competitor.* In a case involving alleged infringement of common-law copyright, former employees of the designing firm were charged with disclosing confidential information to a competitor. The plaintiff company, which was engaged in the manufacture of steel joists, had construction plans prepared by its employees for a new plant. The new plant was completed in 1968.

In 1971, W, the man who had supervised the construction of the plant and who was still employed by the firm, was asked by M (a former employee who had become president of a competing joist company) to have plans drawn for a plant of the competing company.

W requested an engineering firm to design a joist plant, presented the engineer with plans of the plaintiff's plant, and asked that these plans be used as a guide. This was done, and in January 1972, W resigned from the plaintiff company to become a consultant to the defendant competitor, and construction was begun on the defendant's new plant. Shortly thereafter, legal action was instituted by the plaintiff, who alleged that its common-law copyright in the construction plans had been infringed, and that W and M had breached their obligation as employees not to disclose their employer's trade secrets or other confidential information to competitors.

The court, in rejecting the decision of the lower court, held that the plaintiff had not lost its common-law copyright protection through general publication, saying:

First, a distribution of plans to potential contractors and subcontractors for bidding purposes does not constitute general publication. . . . This is true even though the plans are not marked confidential, are not required to be returned, and can be obtained without paying a deposit. . . .

Second, an owner does not lose his common-law copyright by permitting interested persons to view and inspect a building during and after construction. . . . We do not believe that displaying a building during or after construction, or publishing photographs of it, can be said to be the equivalent of publishing the plans. While the observation of the building in person or through photographs may provide the basis for designing a similar building through a trained observer's initiative, it cannot provide the excuse for copying from plans without permission.[137]

The court found an infringement of common-law copyright despite modifications, including the length and width of the plant, the dimensions of the bay areas, column sizes, truss design, and crane rail design. The court quoted from an earlier decision:

In order to constitute an infringement . . . it is not necessary that the whole or even a large portion of the book (plans) shall have been copied. It is sufficient if a material and substantial part shall have been copied, even though it be but a small part of the whole. . . .[138]

With regard to the duties of the employees, the court held that W breached an implied duty not to disclose his employer's confidential information to a competitor.

14.3 Conclusions. In attempting to retain his rights to the fruits of his labors, the professional should keep in mind the following points:

1. Don't forget that the amended federal copyright act abolishes common-law copyright.

2. Don't overlook the necessity for marking on the plans, in proper form, a stipulation reserving your rights to those documents.

3. Don't forget that the client becomes the owner of the drawings and specifications in the absence of a contract provision to the contrary.

4. Don't overlook the fact that the owner of the plans, be it a client, a magazine, etc., may invoke copyright protection.

5. Don't forget that an indemnity provision is valuable only if the indemnitor (or his insurance carrier) has the financial means to meet the claims.

6. Don't forget that common-law rights to drawings and specifications may be lost through publication.

7. Don't forget that copying only a portion of the plans may be a violation of copyright.

8. Don't fail to realize that an employee has an implied duty not to disclose his employer's confidential information.

CHAPTER 15

Liens and Bonds

15.1 Introductory. These two topics are so closely interrelated at times that it seems appropriate to discuss them together in a single chapter.

15.2 Liens—General The subject of liens is so vast in scope, and the lien statutes are worded so differently in various jurisdictions, that it would be an imposition on the reader to attempt in this modest book to analyze all the lien laws throughout the United States. It seems more appropriate to describe the subject of liens in a general way and in addition, to discuss somewhat in detail the lien laws of various states selected for the purpose of illustrating the problems that may arise. In this manner the professional, contractor, subcontractor, and materialman may be afforded a better understanding of the subject of liens and may be made more acutely aware of the need to protect his rights, when necessary, through consultation with his own legal counsel. Such consultation is indispensable, since it is common knowledge that statutes are amended from time to time, so that the accuracy of any statement included in this chapter must be verified and independently interpreted.

The word "lien" is a French word, of the same origin as the word "liable," and originally signified a string, a tie, a bind. In its broader sense the word "lien" is used to denote a claim or hold which one person has upon the property of another as security for some debt or charge.

The property may or may not be in the possession of the one to whom the debt or obligation is due. On the one hand, a shoemaker may have a lien on a pair of shoes in his possession, as security for his labor; and a hotelkeeper similarly may have a lien on the luggage of a guest to ensure payment of hotel charges. On the other hand, the laborer who performs work in the improvement of real property, and who is dependent for subsistence upon prompt payment for his labor, may have a mechanic's lien upon the real estate; and although he cannot take it into his physical possession, he may be entitled to have the realty sold to satisfy the debt.

A mechanic's lien is a creature of statute. Although many mechanics' lien laws originally were passed to protect manual laborers, gradually the underlying purpose of these laws has been extended to protect contractors, subcontractors, and materialmen who have increased the value of real estate by performing labor or furnishing materials. Today in some jurisdictions the architect, engineer, surveyor, and landscape architect are given a right of lien under certain conditions.

Broadly speaking, there are two kinds of liens: private liens and public liens. The former arises out of the construction, alteration, or repair of private projects, and the latter out of public projects. Private liens usually attach to the real estate which has been improved through a contribution of the claimant. Public liens usually are restricted to the fund appropriated for the project, for obvious reasons. It would be patently absurd to permit a highway or a city hall to be sold to satisfy a lien, even if a purchaser could be found.

15.2.1 Architect's Lien. In some jurisdictions an architect has a right of lien for the preparation of drawings, irrespective of supervision. Other jurisdictions are not so liberal in this respect. For example, some courts have adopted the attitude that since the professional is not properly a mechanic, he is not entitled to the benefits of the mechanic's lien statute, though he prepared plans and supervised construction. In other states an architect's right of mechanic's lien for the value of his services in the preparation of drawings and specifications was denied on the ground that such documents are not incorporated into the structure. In some jurisdictions an architect who did not direct and oversee the erection of a building was not allowed a lien. In some jurisdictions an architect was allowed a lien for drawings only, while in still other jurisdictions an architect was allowed a lien for supervision, but not for preparing plans and specifications. Very significantly, in several jurisdictions it has been decided that, if the owner-architect agreement is entire, as distinguished from divisible, so that the fee covers both classes of service without apportionment, no lien exists for either class of service.

Thus, it is obvious that conflicts exist between various jurisdictions—attributable in great measure to the varied wording of the different statutes. It is these conflicts which emphasize the need for alertness on the part of the professional, and the necessity for legal counsel to safeguard his rights.

15.2.2   *The Massachusetts Rule.* In the Commonwealth of Massachusetts, an architect is not entitled to a mechanic's lien for services rendered in the preparation of plans or specifications. The rule appears to lean heavily on the theory that one is entitled to a mechanic's lien only if his labor actually enters into the structure, so as to become part of its materials, and that the professional service of the architect in preparing plans are not labor performed or furnished and actually used in the erection of a building. The rule is based on an early concept of a mechanic's lien expressed in a case decided in 1856, in which the court said:

... the plan of a house, the model of a ship, the moulds by which its timbers are to be hewed, may be necessary and even indispensable, but they do not enter into any structure so as to be a part of its materials, and cannot be regarded as within the provison of the statute.

The preparation of plans and specifications is a preliminary to the construction of a building, and is often merely tentative. It may or may not be followed by a construction according to the plans. It is seldom that either the external or internal form of a building is determined upon, or that its identity is anything more than an indefinite mental conception until after the plans have been completed. We are of the opinion that this professional work of the architect, in bringing into existence the definite form and conception of a building which may be erected if the landowner adopts the plan, is not "labor performed or furnished . . . and actually used in the erection" of a building within the meaning of our statute.[139]

Though the architect or engineer in Massachusetts is denied a mechanic's lien for preparing plans and specifications, he has a lien for labor performed in the supervision of the erection of a building; but if he agrees to prepare the plans as well as supervise construction for a lump sum, without apportioning the total price between the two items of service, he is denied a lien even for supervision. This denial results from the inability of the court to determine what portion of the lump-sum contract price should be fairly allocated to plans and supervision, respectively. Therefore, in order to preserve a right of lien in Massachusetts for supervisory services, the professional must enter into a divisible contract with his client, allocating a specific portion of his fee to supervision.

15.2.3   *The New Jersey Rule.* In New Jersey an architect who draws plans and specifications for a building *and* supervises the erection of the building is entitled to a mechanic's lien for his professional services. If the contractor should default, preventing the architect from fully performing his agreement to prepare plans and specifications and supervise construction, the architect is still entitled to assert his right of lien.[140]

15.2.4   *The New York Rule.* New York permits a mechanic's lien to be filed for materials furnished or labor performed "for the improvement of

real property." The term "improvement" includes the drawing by any architect or engineer of any plans or specifications which are prepared for or used
in connection with such improvement. The architect or engineer may file a
mechanic's lien for plans or specifications prepared by him, even though he
does not supervise the work; conversely, he may file a mechanic's lien for
services rendered in the supervision of the work, even though he does not
prepare the plans or specifications.

The lien may be filed for the preparation of plans and specifications, even
though no building is erected on the property. Though buildings are not
erected on "preliminary" studies or "preliminary" plans, such "preliminary"
service may be the basis for the improvement of property, permitting a lien
to be filed for the architect's or engineer's charges. However, more than
mere rough sketches are required in order to render lienable an architect's or
engineer's charges; the documents must have progressed to the point where
they may be said to be sufficiently formal to be called "plans." The mere
fact that they have been prepared to assist the owner in deciding whether he
wants to have a building constructed according to such design or which leave
some ultimate details to be selected and added later does not prevent the
preliminary documents being called plans, within the intendment of the
New York statute.[141]

15.2.5   *The Pennsylvania Rule.* The Pennsylvania statute now expressly
gives to an architect or engineer a right of lien, provided the professional
contracts with the owner not only to prepare the drawings and specifications, but also to supervise the erection, construction, alteration, or repair of
the project. Long before the adoption of this statute, the architect or engineer in Pennsylvania had a right of lien for preparation of plans and drawings, provided he supervised the work because the courts in the Commonwealth of Pennsylvania reasoned that the plans and specifications were
incidental to and enhanced the professional's work in supervising actual
construction.[142]

15.3   *Waiver of Right of Lien.* The mechanics' lien laws were established
to protect the laborer for hire. Several states have enacted statutes which
make it difficult for one to waive these rights except by express agreement.

Prior to 1975, Section 34 of the Lien Law of the State of New York read
as follows:

A contractor, subcontractor, material man or laborer may not waive his lien, except
by an express agreement in writing specifically to that effect, signed by him or his
agents.

Notwithstanding the above statute, a New York court refused to bind a
subcontractor to a general contractor's promise that no liens would be filed
by a subcontractor. The subcontract in question provided:

All terms and conditions of the Owner's Standard Contract 2500 with the Contractor will become part of this agreement.

The contract between the owner and the general contractor provided:

The Contractor shall promptly pay all just claims for labor, material or otherwise in and about the performance of the Work and the Contractor expressly covenants and agrees that no liens shall be filed either by the Contractor or by any subcontractor, workman or material man. . . .

The Contractor further agrees that if, notwithstanding the foregoing covenant, any liens should be filed . . . the Contractor will promptly discharge by bond or otherwise such lien or attachment and indemnify and protect . . . [the Owner] against any loss or expense in connection therewith. . . .

Despite a recognition that the pertinent provisions of the prime contract were by reference incorporated into the subcontract, and despite a previous ruling by the same court that:

. . . when a party to a written contract accepts it as a contract he is bound by the stipulations and conditions expressed in it whether he reads them or not. Ignorance through negligence or inexcusable trustfulness will not relieve a party from his contract obligations. He who signs or accepts a written contract, in the absence of fraud or other wrongful act on the part of another contracting party, is conclusively presumed to know its contents and to assent to them and there can be no evidence for the jury as to his understanding of its terms,

the court held that in this case the intention to waive the right to file a lien was not clear and unequivocal. It stated that the prime contract established the duty of the general contractor as to the filing of liens, including its obligations in the event liens were filed by subcontractors; that the owner was looking to the general contractor for protection; and that this article, when incorporated into the subcontract, was not an express agreement to waive the right of lien.[143] From this decision, and the general recognition in the construction industry that in most instances, contractors, subcontractors, materialmen, and laborers were being required to sign contracts, in which they expressly gave up their rights to file mechanics' liens in advance of work or the furnishing of materials, Section 34 of the Lien Law of the State of New York was rewritten in 1975.

This statutory change rendered void and wholly unenforceable a written waiver of lien except at the time or subsequent to the receipt of payment. Section 34 presently reads as follows:

Notwithstanding the provisions of any other general, specific or local law, any contract, agreement or understanding whereby the right to file or enforce any lien created under article two is waived, shall be void as against public policy and wholly unenforceable. This section shall not preclude a requirement for a written waiver of the right to file a mechanic's lien executed and delivered by a contractor, subcontractor, material supplier or laborer simultaneously with or after payment for the labor performed or the materials furnished has been made to such contractor, subcontractor, material man or laborer.

As can readily be seen from the specific wording of this statute, the rights of a mechanic's lienor, such as a laborer, an architect, a contractor, a materialman, and all other persons similarly situated, have been advanced. An owner may no longer mandate a waiver of lien prior to the employment of someone who will perform labor or furnish materials in connection with the improvement of real property.

15.4 State Lien Laws. In each instance the rights of owner, architect, contractor, and others depend upon the special provisions of the particular statute involved. It is only by a careful examination of the statutes in force at the time and place a claim arises that the exact rights of the parties can be determined properly. It must be recognized that the lien laws usually make a clear distinction between the rights of those in the several categories entitled to mechanics' liens; and, also, a clear distinction between lienors' rights in public construction and private construction.

In reviewing the various lien statutes, answers to many questions must be sought, including the following: Who is entitled to a mechanic's lien in private construction? In public construction? How does he assert his right of lien, and when must he do so? To what extent is the lien collectible? How may the owner limit his liability? How long does a lien endure? The limited review of the laws of a few specific states, which follows, serves to partially answer these and other questions, as well as illustrate the general trends of the statutes and their individual peculiarities.

15.4.1 California. Architects, engineers, surveyors, contractors, subcontractors, builders, and all persons performing labor, or furnishing materials, appliances, or power contributing to the construction, alteration, addition to, or repair of any building, structure, or other work of improvement, other than a public improvement, have a right of lien upon the property. This right of lien exists whether the work is done or the materials furnished at the instance of the owner, or any person acting under his authority, or under him as a contractor or otherwise. Every contractor, subcontractor, architect, builder, or other person having charge of the work is held to be the agent of the owner.

The lien may be perfected by filing with the county recorder of the county in which the property is located a written claim which must contain certain details required by the statute. The claim must be verified by oath. If the owner files a notice of completion within ten days after completion of the work of improvement, the original contractor has sixty days from such filing to record his lien claim, whereas all other claimants have thirty days. However, if the owner does not file a notice of completion, the original contractor, as well as all other claimants, have ninety days from the completion of the work of improvement within which to file their claims. Completion may result when the owner occupies or uses the work of improvement and there is a cessation of labor, or when the owner accepts the work, or completion may occur in other ways specified in the statute.

Every person, except a prime contractor, or one performing actual labor for wages, is required to notify the owner and the prime contractor, in writing, in the manner and in detail as specified in the statute, of his claim, not later than fifteen days prior to filing a claim of lien, in order for his lien to be valid. The owner may not waive this requirement.

Although normally the lien binds the property only for ninety days, unless enforcement proceedings are commenced within said period of time, there are exceptions prescribed by the statute which extend the time for the commencement of such proceedings under specified conditions, where credit is given.

In private construction, if the owner files with the county recorder the original contract and records a payment bond (which must give a direct right of action thereon to laborers, materialmen, and other beneficiaries thereof) for 50 percent of the contract price, he may limit his liability to the amount due the contractor; otherwise, liens of claimants, such as subcontractors, laborers, and materialmen, cannot be limited by the contract price stipulated in a prime contract. In any case, no lien may exceed the reasonable value of labor or material furnished. The owner and contractor cannot, by their agreement, or otherwise, prevent a subcontractor, material man, or laborer from asserting a lien, except with his consent.

Mechanics' liens take precedence over mortgages, deeds of trust, and other encumbrances which may have attached to the property after the time the work was started or the materials were furnished.

Any person, except the original contractor, who may perform work or furnish materials upon any public improvement, may, prior to the expiration of the time within which a claim of lien is required to be filed, give the owner, that is to say, the agency for which the work is done, a verified notice setting forth therein, among other details, that he has performed his work or furnished his materials, and the value, thereof.

Assuming that such notice is duly and properly served and filed as prescribed by the statute, the party receiving the notice must withhold sufficient funds to cover the claim, unless the contractor by delivery of a proper affidavit disputes the claim, in which case the claimant must file a counteraffidavit to dispute the contractor's affidavit; otherwise the monies withheld must be released.

In a private improvement, where the stop notice is duly and properly served and filed, it is the duty of the owner to withhold sufficient funds due or to become due the contractor unless a payment bond in a sum equal to

1¼ times the amount stated in such notice is filed with the person upon whom such notice was served.

Public improvements are not subject to liens for materials or labor. The statute makes detailed provisions requiring the furnishing by the contractor of bonds in public construction and the right of materialmen and laborers to sue within six months after claim is filed, on payment bonds given to protect them against loss.

15.4.2 Connecticut. Any person who provides materials or services in the construction, razing, or removal, or repair of any building or its appurtenances, or in the improvement of any lot or on-the-site development or subdivision of any plot of land, has a right of lien upon the building and its land, provided the claim exceeds $10. The services of an architect or engineer in the preparation of plans, used in the construction of the building, are considered to be services rendered in its construction.[144] The claim must be based upon an agreement with, or consent of, the owner or some person having authority.

To perfect his lien, the claimant must file in the office of the town clerk of the town in which the property is located, within sixty days after ceasing to render services or furnish materials, a written certificate, setting forth certain details prescribed by the statute, and signed and sworn to by him; otherwise the lien is invalid. In addition, and within seven days of lodging such certificate, a true and attested copy of said certificate must be served upon the owner of said building, lot, or plot of land. If the claimant is not a prime contractor, or a subcontractor having a written contract with the prime contractor, he also must give written notice within the same sixty days to the owner, in the manner specified in the statute, that he intends to claim a lien.

No mechanic's lien may attach, in favor of subcontractors, materialmen, or laborers, to a greater amount than the amount which the owner agreed to pay the prime contractor. Moreover, if the prime contractor defaults, the total of such liens may not attach to a greater amount than the contract price stipulated in the prime contract, *less* (1) the reasonable cost to the owner of satisfactorily completing the contract, (2) bona fide payments made by the owner to the prime contractor, and (3) damages sustained by the owner as a result of such default.

In determining the amount to which liens of subcontractors, materialmen, and laborers may attach, payments made by the owner in accordance with the prime contract, before liens are filed, are allowed to the owner as a credit. But payments made by the owner to the prime contractor in advance of the time stipulated in the prime contract are not protected, unless the owner gives written notice to each person who has furnished materials or rendered services, at least five days before such advance payment is made. If the liens exceed the balance of the contract price, less the credits to the owner, the subcontractors, materialmen, and laborers share in the available balance on a pro rata basis.

If an encumbrance, other than a mechanic's lien, is filed during construction, it takes precedence over mechanics' liens originating subsequent to the filing of the encumberance, but not over mechanics' liens originating prior thereto.

An action to foreclose the lien must be commenced within one year after the written certificate perfecting the lien has been filed.

Further, in Connecticut, public improvements are not subject to liens. Persons contracting with the state or any subdivision thereof, for construction of a public improvement, must provide a performance bond and a payment bond, if the contract price equals or exceeds $1000. Any claimant who has not received payment within ninety days after the last work was performed or materials furnished may bring suit on the bond. But if the claimant has no direct contract with the contractor who furnished the bond, he must give written notice to the contractor by registered or certified mail of his claim within ninety days after he furnished labor or materials. The notice must state the amount claimed and the name of the party for whom the material was furnished or for whom the labor was performed. Suit must be brought on the bond not later than one year after the date of final settlement of the prime contract.

A contract for public work, which requires a payment bond, shall also require a general contractor within forty-five days of payment by the municipality or state to pay any amounts due a subcontractor, who is deemed to be a laborer or a materialman. If the subcontractor is not paid within said due date, the subcontractor shall serve a notice of claim by registered mail and within 10 days of receipt of said claim, the contractor shall be liable for interest. A subcontractor may also require the funds due and owing to be paid into an escrow account, and if the general contractor refuses to do so and it is later determined that the funds are due and owing the subcontractor, the contractor may be liable for legal fees as well.

15.4.3   Florida. Several types of lienors are described as persons who shall have the rights to a mechanic's lien. These types include:

(1) Architects, engineers, landscape architects or land surveyors. Each of these professionals have rights to a lien on the property improved, for his services in preparing plans, specifications or drawings used in connection with improving real property *or* for his services in supervising any portion of the work of improving the real property. Since the statute provides that if the professional has a direct contract with the owner, his lien attaches to the real property regardless of whether it is actually improved, the implication is clear that he has no lien on the real property if he has no such direct contract and the property is not actually improved.

(2) Persons who are in privity with an owner and who perform labor or furnish services constituting an improvement or a part thereof.

(3) Persons who are not in privity with an owner and who perform labor or services or furnish materials constituting a part of an improvement under the direct contract of another person.

In order to perfect his lien, every lienor must record in the office of the clerk of the county in which the real property is located a verified claim of lien in the form required by the statute, signed by the lienor, his agent or attorney, and containing the information specified therein. The claim of lien may be recorded at any time during the progress of the work or thereafter but not later than ninety days after the final performance of the labor or services or materials by the lienor. However, if the original contractor defaults or the contract is terminated as provided in the statute, no claim for a lien attaching prior to such default may be recorded after ninety days from the date of such default or ninety days after the final performance of labor or services or furnishing of materials, whichever occurs first. The claim of lien should be served as provided in the statute within ten days after recording. Otherwise, it may be determined to be void to the extent that a person entitled to rely thereon has been prejudiced.

In addition to the above, and as a prerequisite to perfecting a lien, all lienors not in privity with the owner except laborers and the professionals previously referred to, must serve a written notice on the owner setting forth the lienor's name and address, a description sufficient for identification of the real property, and the nature of the services or materials furnished or to be furnished. This notice must be served by the lienor before commencing or not later than forty-five days from commencing to furnish his services or materials but in any event (1) before the prime contractor gives to the owner an affidavit stating that all lienors not in privity with the owner have been paid in full or the names of those who have not been paid in full and the amount due or to become due to each of them, or (2) abandonment, whichever shall occur first. The prime contractor is required to execute and deliver said affidavit to the owner at least five days before he institutes suit to enforce his lien as a prerequisite to the commencement of such suit.

The validity of the lien and the right to record a claim therefor is not affected by the insolvency, bankruptcy, or death of the owner before the claim of lien is recorded.

No lien continues for a longer period than one year after the claim of lien has been recorded unless within that time an action to enforce the lien has been commenced. The owner may elect to shorten the time for the commencement of such action by recording in the clerk's office a written notice to the lienor requiring him to file suit within sixty days after service of the notice by the clerk. If suit is not filed within said time, the lien will be extinguished automatically.

In any direct contract the owner may require the contractor to furnish a payment bond in at least the amount of the original contract price conditioned that the contractor will pay all persons supplying him labor, materials, and supplies used directly or indirectly by such contractor, subcontractor, or sub-subcontractor, and upon receipt of such bond is exempt from lien claims upon the real property. A beneficiary of the bond who has not received payment must deliver written notice of performance to the contractor within ninety days after performance by him of labor or after complete delivery by him of materials and supplies as a condition precedent to suit on the bond. Suit on the bond must be brought within one year after such performance of the labor or completion of such delivery, but the time for commencement of the action may be shortened by the owner in a manner similar to that previously noted with respect to filing suit to enforce a lien.

Normally, the total amount for which all liens may be enforced may not exceed the amount of the contract price fixed by the direct contract between owner and contractor. But if the owner makes payments on account of the direct contract prior to his recording a notice of the actual commencement of the improvement and posting a copy thereof, as required by the statute, such payments will not be protected. Under other conditions specified in the statute the owner's normal maximum liability may be increased by reason of improperly making payments, and it would be wise for each owner to be advised by his attorney in detail of the many rigid requirements which should be satisfied.

Mechanics' liens take precedence over any other encumbrances recorded after they attach, but not over such encumbrances recorded prior to the time the lien attaches. The statute makes detailed provision for any other priorities.

Any person entering into a formal contract for the construction of any public building or the prosecution and completion of any public work or for repairs upon any such building or work is required to provide a payment bond to protect laborers, materialmen, and suppliers who may sue on the bond. As a condition precedent to suit on the bond, the claimant, within ninety days after the performance of the labor or complete delivery of the materials and supplies, must give written notice of performance to the contractor and the nonpayment therefor. Action on the bond must be brought within one year from the performance of the labor or completion of delivery of the materials and supplies.

15.4.4   *Illinois.* Any person who contracts (expressly or impliedly) with the owner of a lot or tract of land or with one whom such owner has authorized or knowingly permitted to contract for the improvement of, or to improve the same, or who furnishes material, fixtures, apparatus, or machinery, or certain formwork, in the building, altering, repairing, or ornamenting of any house or other building, walk, fence, or improvement, or who furnishes fill or sod, or who excavates the land or landscapes or raises, lowers, or removes any house is entitled to a lien. An architect, structural engineer, professional engineer, or any person who furnished or performs labor in the building, altering, repairing, or ornamenting of the same also is entitled to a lien.

The contractor is required to give the owner, and it is the duty of the owner to require of the contractor before the owner, agent, or architect makes any payment to the contractor, a written statement under oath or verified by affidavit, of the names of all parties (except merchants and dealers in materials only) furnishing materials and labor and of the amounts due or to become due each. Failure to secure such statement, before making payment to contractor, renders the owner liable if subcontractors are not paid.

Within five days after demand, a similar statement (under oath, if required) must be furnished by the subcontractor, as often as requested in writing by the owner or contractor. Until such statement is furnished, the subcontractor may not sue the owner or contractor and the subcontractor's lien is subject to the liens of all other creditors.

It is not necessary to fix in any contract a time for completion or a time for payment in order to obtain a lien, provided the work is done or material furnished within three years from the commencement of such work or the commencement of furnishing such material.

The contractor's lien, as to the owner, may be filed in the office of the recorder of deeds of the county where the project is located at any time after the contract is made and within two years after its completion or the completion of any extra work or the furnishing of any extra material thereunder. But no contractor may be allowed to enforce his lien against or to the prejudice of any other creditor or encumbrancer or purchaser unless he files his lien or sues to enforce it within four months after such completion or furnishing.

The statute defines subcontractors as mechanics, workmen, or other persons who furnish materials, apparatus, machinery, or fixtures, or furnish or perform services or labor for the contractor, or furnish any material to be employed in the process of construction as a means for assisting in the erection of the building or improvement in what is commonly termed form or formwork, where concrete, cement, or like material is used in whole or in part.

If the legal effect of any contract between the owner and contractor is that no lien or claim may be filed or maintained by anyone, the provision is binding between such parties, but it is not binding upon a subcontractor or materialman unless (1) he had actual notice thereof before any labor or material is furnished by him, or (2) a duly written and signed stipulation or agreement to that effect has been filed in the office of the recorder of deeds of the county where the improvement is situated, prior to the commencement of the work upon the improvement, or within ten days after the execution of the principal contract, or not less than ten days prior to the contract of the subcontractor or materialman. Such filing is deemed to be sufficient notice to the subcontractor or materialman.

Furthermore, a subcontractor or party furnishing labor or materials, except as otherwise stated below, must serve on the owner, his agent, or architect, or the superintendent having charge of the building or improvement, written notice of his claim and the amount due or to become due, within sixty days after completion of the subcontract, or if extra or additional work or material is delivered thereafter, within sixty days after the date of completion of such extra or additional work or final delivery of such extra or additional material. If any money due is not paid within ten days after service of the notice, then a claim of lien may be filed or suit may be commenced by him to enforce same within the same limits as to time and in the same manner, as is provided for the contractor. If the land is registered under the Torrens System, then instead of serving the notice it must be filed in the office of the registrar of titles of the county in which the land is situated. Furthermore, such a notice is not necessary when the sworn statement of either the contractor or subcontractor, previously referred to, gives the owner notice of the amount due and to whom due.

The owner cannot be compelled to pay to subcontractors a greater sum for or on account of the completion of the improvement than the price stipulated in the prime contract unless payment is made to the contractor or to his order, in violation of the rights and interests of the other persons intended to be benefited by the statute, or unless an unreasonably low price fraudulently is fixed in the original contract between owner and contractor, for the purpose of defrauding subcontractors.

No encumbrance upon the land, created before or after the making of a contract, will operate upon the building erected or materials furnished until the liens in favor of the persons who performed the work or furnished the materials have been satisfied. Upon questions arising between encumbrancers and lien creditors, all previous encumbrances are preferred to the extent of the value of the land at the time of the making of the contract, and the lien creditor is preferred to the value of the improvements erected on the premises.

Upon all questions arising between different contractors having liens, no preference is given to the one whose contract was made first, except that the claim of any person for wages for labor by him personally performed will be preferred.

An action to enforce a lien must be commenced within two years after the contract has been completed or within two years after completion of the extra or additional work or furnishing of extra or additional material thereunder.

In public improvements, a lien exists in favor of any person who furnishes to a contractor having a contract for public improvement with the state, any county, township, school district, or municipality, material, labor, fixtures, apparatus, or machinery. The lien attaches only to that portion of such money, bonds, or warrants against which no voucher or other evidence of indebtedness has been issued and delivered to the contractor.

The claimant must file with the appropriate governmental body a written statement of his claims, as specified in the statute. The person claiming the lien must commence proceedings for an accounting within sixty days after filing his notice and must, within the same period, deliver a copy of the complaint to the appropriate governmental body or officer as specified in the statute, except that if money appropriated by the general assembly is to be used in connection with an improvement by the state, suit must be commenced and a copy of the complaint must be served upon the director not less than fifteen days before the date when the appropriation from which such money is to be paid will lapse.

The contractor must furnish completion bonds on the construction of Federal aid highways; also in connection with other road construction or repairs, and for construction of bridges and roads on district lines.

A bond is required of contractors who do work for the state or a political subdivision thereof, securing payment for materials and labor. Persons performing labor or furnishing materials may sue on the bond, but the claimant must file with the appropriate officer a verified notice of claim, embodying the information prescribed by the statute, within 180 days after performance of the work or furnishing of the materials. Action on the bond must be brought within six months after the project or work has been accepted by the state, and except where final settlement has been made between the state and the contractor, not before the expiration of 120 days after the date of the last item of work or materials.

15.4.5 *Massachusetts.* A person whom a debt is due for *personal* labor performed in the erection, alteration, repair, or removal of a building or structure upon land, by virtue of an agreement with, or by consent of, the owner of the building or structure, or his authorized representative, has a lien upon the building or structure and upon the interest of the owner thereof in the land upon which it is situated, for work actually performed. The mechanic's lien is created as soon as the labor is performed. But to keep the lien alive and prevent its dissolution, the person performing the personal labor must file, in the registry of deeds in the county or district where the land lies, a statement signed and sworn to by him or some person in his behalf, giving the name of the owner of record at the time the work was performed or at the time of filing the statement. The lien for personal labor does not extend to more than eighteen days work actually performed during the forty days immediately preceding the filing of the statement.

Further, in Massachusetts, a person who enters into a written contract with the owner of land, for the whole, or any part of the erection, alteration, repair, or removal of a building or structure upon land, or for furnishing material therefor, also has a lien upon the building or structure and upon the interest of the owner in the land, as appears of record at the date when notice of the contract is filed or recorded in the registry of deeds for the county or district where the land lies. The notice may be filed or recorded by any person entitled to a lien under the statute. The lien is security for the payment of all labor and material which the contractor thereafter furnishes by virtue of his contract. The notice must state the completion date and other information required by the statute. If the completion date is extended, notice thereof must be filed or recorded prior to the completion date originally fixed. Special provision is made in respect of place of filing of the notice in the case of registered land affected by the contractor's lien. As previously indicated on page 206, the lien of an architect or engineer is limited in Massachusetts.

A subcontractor or any person who furnishes labor or material under a contract with any subcontractor is also entitled to enforce a lien on the premises for his labor performed or material furnished subsequent to the filing or recording of the notice referred to in the preceding paragraph. To enforce his lien, the subcontractor or the person contracting with a subcontractor must file, in the registry of deeds for the county or district where the land lies, a notice of his contract in the form required by the statute. Actual notice of such filing must be given to the owner. The lien will not in any event exceed the amount due or to become due under the prime contract when notice is given to the owner.

The time for performance of the subcontract may not be extended beyond the time for performance of the original contract and any extension thereof, if within five days after receiving notice of the filing of the contract by a subcontractor or a sub-subcontractor, the owner files an objection thereto.

Within thirty days after the date on which the principal contract is to be performed the contractor must file a statement signed and sworn to by him or his agent, giving a just and true account of the amount due him and other details. A subcontractor or a person claiming by, through, or under him must file such a statement within thirty days after the date on which the contract of the subcontractor is to be performed. Failure of any person to file any required statement will dissolve his lien. The lien also will be dissolved unless an action to enforce it is filed within sixty days after the filing of the required statement.

No lien will take precedence as against a mortgage registered or recorded prior to the filing or recording of the notice of contract or against a purchaser, other than the owner who, in fact, entered into the contract upon which the lien is based, provided further that the deed was registered or recorded prior to the filing of the said notice. The only exception to the foregoing rule is where personal labor is performed in connection with an improvement which actually commences prior to the recording of the mortgage.

Massachusetts, as did many other states, passed a law making void and unenforceable any agreement which barred the filing of a notice of contract or the enforcement of a lien.

In public improvement, no liens attach to any building or land that is owned by the commonwealth or any subdivision thereof. A payment bond is required when the amount of the contract exceeds $5000 in the case of the commonwealth or exceeds $2000 in any other instance.

To secure the benefit of the bond, a claimant must file with the proper person designated in the statute a sworn statement of his claim. The claim must be filed prior to the expiration of ninety days after the claimant ceased to perform labor or furnish labor or materials or transportation. The statute contains special provisions relating to claims for transportation and demurrage charges; also for claims based on payments due for fringe benefits or for specially fabricated materials. If a claim is not paid within one year after it is filed, a petition may be filed to enforce it.

15.4.6 *Michigan*. Every person who, in pursuance of any contract with an owner, part owner, or lessee of any interest in real estate, builds, alters, improves, repairs, erects, ornaments, surveys, or plats any land or a portion thereof, or who engineers or designs any sewers, water lines, roads, streets, highways, or sidewalks, or who, pursuant to any such contract, furnishes any survey, plat, plat of survey, or design or engineering plan for the improvement of land not exceeding one-quarter section, or who furnishes any labor or materials in or for building, altering, improving, repairing, erecting, ornamenting, or putting in any house, building, or structure, or who excavates or builds, in whole or in part, any foundation, cellar, or basement for any house, building, structure, or buildings, or repairs any sidewalks, sewers, sewage disposal equipment, water lines, and pumping equipment or furnishes material therefor, or rents or leases equipment in connection therewith, and every subcontractor, laborer, or materialman who performs any labor or furnishes materials or leases equipment to the original or principal contractor, or any subcontractor, in carrying forward or completing the principal contract, has a lien. Subject to limitations specified in the statute, the lien extends to the interest of the owner, part owner, or in the property which is subject to the lien. Unquestionably, the architect has a lien for supervision. And when the architect uses his plan during supervision they become, in effect, his tools in supervising construction, and a lien also is allowed for the preparation of the documents.[145] However, the question whether a lien will be allowed for plans not accompanied by supervision is still open to future decision. Except as otherwise expressly provided in the statute, the engineer's lien appears to be limited similarly.

Any person who has a right of lien under the statute is required, within ninety days after furnishing the first of the material, or performing the first of the labor, or engineering or surveying services, or renting or leasing equipment for any contractor or subcontractor, to serve on the owner, part owner, or lessee of the premises, or his agent, in the manner provided for in the statute, a written notice informing him of the nature of the materials being furnished or labor being performed, or to be performed, and a description of the premises where furnished. The notice also must state that the person giving same will claim a lien upon the premises for any amounts unpaid, and it must contain other information prescribed by the statute.

Special provision is made in the case of a notice solely as to labor. The owner, part owner, or lessee is not liable to subcontractors, materialmen, or laborers for a greater amount than he contracted to pay the original contractor, and is entitled to recoup any damages which he may sustain by reason of any failure or omission in the performance of the original contract. But the risk of all payments made to the original contractor after the owner shall have received the notice, mentioned previously, is upon him, until the expiration of ninety days within which claims for lien may be recorded, as hereinafter mentioned, and no payment made to any contractor before the expiration of said ninety days will defeat any lien of any subcontractor, materialman, or laborer, unless and only to the extent that the payment has been distributed among the subcontractors, materialmen, and laborers.

No person has a right to claim a lien under the Michigan statute unless and until he serves a notice, as stated above, and such notice, together with proof of service thereof, is attached to a verified statement or account recorded with the office of the register of deeds within ninety days from the date on which the last of the materials, labor, or services shall have been furnished or performed, or within ninety days from the last date of use of any rented or leased equipment. The lien is perfected by the said filing of the verified statement or account. A copy of the statement must be served on the owner, part owner, or lessee as provided in the statute.

Except as otherwise noted below, the prime contract may be verbal or in writing; it may be an express contract or an implied one. A request to perform followed by performance ordinarily creates an implied contract.

If title to the land upon which the improvement is made is held by husband and wife jointly, or in case the land upon which the improvement is made is held and occupied as a homestead, the lien attaches to the lands and improvement only if the improvement is made pursuant to a contract in writing signed by both the husband and wife.

The owner, part owner, or lessee may at any time retain from any monies due or to become due the original contractor, any amount sufficient to pay all demands owing or unpaid to any subcontractor, materialman, or laborer who has properly recorded and served the notice previously referred to. The original contractor is required to give to the person with whom he made the principal contract a statement under oath of the number and names of every subcontractor or laborer in his employ, and of any person furnishing materials, giving the amount which is due or to become due, and there may be retained out of any money then due or to become due the contractor, an amount sufficient to pay all demands, due or to become due to the subcontractors, laborers, or materialmen, as shown by the contractor's statement, which may be paid to them according to their respective rights, and all payments so made will be considered the same as if paid to the original contractor. Until the contractor furnishes the said statement (which he must furnish whenever a payment becomes due him or he desires to draw any money), he has no right of action or lien and any payments made by the owner, part owner, or lessee before such statement is made, or without retaining sufficient money to pay the subcontractors, laborers, or materialmen, as shown by any statement furnished, is considered illegal and in violation of the rights of subcontractors, laborers, and materialmen.

The statute provides that a lien will not continue for more than one year after recording unless enforcement proceedings are begun prior to the expiration of said year.

Bonds are required for public improvements. Subcontractors, within sixty days after furnishing the last material or supplies or performing the last work covered by the subcontract, must serve a written notice in duplicate upon the board of officers or agents contracting on behalf of the governmental body that they rely upon the security of the payment bond given by the principal contractor. All others, except laborers, must within sixty days after furnishing the last material or supplies serve a written notice in duplicate upon such board of officers or agents setting forth that the contractor or subcontractor is indebted to them for a specified amount for the furnishing of certain specified materials or supplies. The payment bond may be prosecuted and a recovery had at any time within one year after completion and acceptance of the project. A subcontractor must show he has made payment in full for labor, materials, or supplies contracted by him.

15.4.7 Minnesota. Whoever contributes to the improvement of real estate by performing labor, or furnishing skill, material, or machinery for the purposes defined in the statute, whether under contract with the owner, or at the instance of an agent, trustee, contractor, or subcontractor of the owner, has a lien upon the improvement and its land. The architect (engineer) who furnishes plans and specifications for, *and* supervises the construction of, a building is entitled to a lien thereon. It has been held that if the owner abandons the project, thereby preventing supervision by the architect, he does not lose his right of lien.[146]

If the contribution is made under a contract with the owner and for an agreed price, the lien as against him will be for the sum agreed upon; otherwise, and in all cases as against others than the owner, the lien will be for the reasonable value of the work done, and of the skill, material, and machinery furnished. The lien extends to the entire interest and title of the owner in the premises improved; not exceeding, however, 80 acres in area except in the case of agricultural land which is limited to 40 acres.

The lien will cease at the end of ninety days after the doing of the last of the work or furnishing the last item of skill, material, or machinery, unless within such period a statement of the claim therefor is filed for record. The claim must be filed with the register of deeds of the county in which the improved premises are situated. Or if the claim relates to a railway, subway, or a utility such as telegraph, telephone, or electric light line, it must be filed with the secretary of state. In any case, the statement must be verified by the oath of some person having knowledge of the facts and must contain the information required by the statute.

An action may be commenced to enforce a lien by any lienholder who has filed his lien statement for record, and all other lienholders must be made defendants in that action. The lien will not be enforced unless the holder of the lien asserts it within one year from the date of the last item of his claim, either in his complaint if he commences an action, or in his answer in any action in which he may be made a defendant. At the time of the commencement of an action, a copy of the statement filed must be served personally or sent by certified mail.

It has been held in this state that a person who furnishes a common article of merchandise to one who is not the owner or contractor or subcontractor does not have a lien, even though the article is purchased for the purpose of selling it to the owner and, thereafter, actually used in the building. However, a person who furnishes material to a subcontractor for the construction of the building is entitled to a lien.

The owner may withhold from his contractor so much of the contract price as may be necessary to meet the demands of all persons, other than such contractor, having a lien upon the premises, and for which the contractor is liable; and he may pay and discharge all such liens and deduct the cost thereof from the contract price. No owner shall be required to pay his contractor until the expiration of 90 days from the completion of the improvement, except to the extent that the contractor shall deliver to the owner waivers of claims for mechanics' liens signed by those persons furnishing labor, skills, or materials for the improvement of property and who have given notice required by the applicable statute. The owner, within fifteen days after the completion of the contract, may require any person having a lien, by written request therefor, to furnish to him an itemized and verified statement of his lien claim, the amount thereof, and his name and address;

and no action or proceeding may be commenced for the enforcement of the lien until ten days after the statement is furnished. The purpose of this provision is for the protection of owners against defaulting contractors.

The statute makes provision for priorities. For example, it provides that all liens as against the owner of the land attach and take effect from the time the first item of material or labor is furnished upon the premises for the beginning of the improvement and are preferred to any mortgage or other encumbrancer not then of record, unless the lienholder had actual notice thereof. The statute also contains a provision covering the rights of bona fide purchasers, mortgagees, or encumbrancers without notice.

Further, in Minnesota, every prime contractor on a public improvement must give bond to the state or other public body. Bond must be for not less than the contract price except that in contracts with the commissioner of administration, or with the department of highways, the commissioner may fix the amount of the bond, but at not less than three-quarters of the contract price. If such bond be not given, the corporation or body for which the work is done will be liable to the persons furnishing the labor, skill, or materials to the contractor for any resulting loss. It should be noted, further, that with the approval of the commissioner of administration, if a contract does not exceed $5000, a person making a contract with the state, in lieu of giving a bond, may deposit a certified check with the state treasurer.

Before commencing an action on the bond, the claimant must file a written notice of his claim with the proper authorities within ninety days after the completion of the prime contract and the acceptance thereof by the public authority. An action on the bond must be commenced within one year after the filing of the notice of claim.

15.4.8 Missouri. Every mechanic or other person who performs any work or labor upon, or furnishes any material, fixtures, engine, boiler, or machinery, for any building, erection, or improvements upon land, or for repairing the same, under or by virtue of any contract (which need not be in writing) with the owner of such land or his agent, trustee, contractor, or subcontractor has a lien upon the building, erection, or improvements and upon the land belonging to the owner on which the same are situated, to the extent of 3 acres. However, if the building, erection, or improvement is upon any lot or land in any town, city, or village, or is for manufacturing, industrial, or commercial purposes and not within any city, town, or village, the lien will not be subject to the said area restriction. Since 1971, an architect, engineer, or land surveyor is entitled to a mechanic's lien for professional services rendered, including the preparation of plans and specifications. Previously, the design professional was allowed a lien for supervision of construction only, provided that the contract was divisible, and a specific amount of the fee was allocated for supervision. Notwithstanding the statutory change, the decision of the highest court in this state (quoted, in part, on page 21), in which it was held that the standard form of owner-architect agreement is not divisible, has not been overruled or modified.

The prime contractor must file his lien within six months after the indebtedness accrues. Every journeyman or day laborer must file his lien within sixty days, and every other person within four months after the indebtedness accrues. The lien must be filed with the clerk of the circuit court of the proper county and must be in the form required by the statute.

In addition, every person except the original contractor who may wish to avail himself of the benefit of the lien law is required to give ten days notice before the filing of his lien, to the owner or his agent, that he holds a claim against the building or improvement, setting forth the amount and from whom the same is due. Such notice must be served by any officer authorized by law to serve process in civil actions or by a person who would be a competent witness. When served by an officer, his official return endorsed on the notice is sufficient proof of service, and when served by another person, the fact of such service must be verified by the affidavit of the person making service.

An action to enforce a lien must be commenced within six months after filing same; otherwise, the lien will be invalidated.

Where a lien is filed by any person other than a contractor, it is the latter's duty to defend any action brought to enforce the lien, at his own expense; and while the action is pending, the owner may withhold from the contractor the amount of money for which the lien has been filed. In case of judgment against the owner or his property upon the lien, he is entitled to deduct from any amount due from him to the contractor the amount of the judgment and costs, and if he previously settled with the contractor in full, the owner is entitled to recover back from the contractor any amount paid for which the contractor was originally the party liable.

The lien for work and materials is preferred over all other encumbrances which may attach to the buildings or other improvements, or the ground, subsequent to the commencement of the buildings or improvements.

The liens for work and labor are upon an equal footing without preference to date of filing; and where the proceeds received from the sale of the property are not sufficient to discharge in full all the liens, the proceeds are divided among the lienors on a pro rata basis.

In public construction, no lien may attach to the land, building, or improvement. Bonds are required for public improvements. Any bond furnished by the contractor, among other conditions, must be conditioned for the payment of materials consumed or used in connection with the construction work and for all labor performed whether by subcontractor or otherwise. Suit may be brought in the name of the state, or political subdivision, school or road district for the benefit and use of the persons furnishing labor or material.

15.4.9 *New Jersey.* In private construction, any person who performs labor or furnishes materials for the erection, construction, completion, alteration, or removal of any building or for the erection or filling-in of any dock, wharf, etc., or improvement of land through irrigation or for sinking or drilling a well or for repair of fixed machinery in mills or factories or for sodding, seeding, planting, or landscaping, is entitled to a lien. The statute does not apply to any person who is to be paid for his labor within two weeks from date of performance and whose claim is not in excess of $200. (For discussion of lien of architect or engineer, refer to page 206.)

In private construction, there are two kinds of liens. One is a lien on the realty; the other is a lien on the contract price. Since these liens differ in many respects, they must be considered separately.

As far as a prime contractor is concerned, his lien, if any, attaches to the realty. Other claimants, such as subcontractors, laborers, and materialmen, may or may not have liens attaching to the realty. If the owner files a written and signed contract, or a duplicate thereof, together with the specifications or copies thereof, with the county clerk, before work is performed or materials are furnished, then the prime contractor is the only one who is entitled to a lien on the realty. There is no need to file the plans, regardless of whether they are referred to in the building contract. The purpose of filing the contract and specifications is to give notice to all those who intend performing labor or furnishing materials of the provisions of the contract so that they may ascertain whether such provisions are sufficiently favorable to the contractor to justify a conclusion on their part that the job will be profitable to him and warrant extension of credit to him for the labor or material which they intend to perform or furnish.

If the contract and specifications are filed, as stated above, the remedy of a claimant, other than the prime contractor, is to file and serve a stop notice on the owner of the property, so that his lien, if any, will attach to the monies owing by the owner to the prime contractor. If the contract and specifications are not filed in the county clerk's office, the owner's land and building become liable for the materials furnished or labor performed, and the liability of the realty is not limited to the monies owed by the owner to the prime contractor.

In private construction, in order for a person to obtain a lien on the realty, in a proper case, he must first file in the office of the appropriate county clerk a written notice of his intention to perform labor or furnish materials. Thereafter, but not later than four months after performing his last item of labor or furnishing his last item of materials, he may file a mechanic's lien claim. The lien claim, among other things, must contain a description of the land and building sufficient to identify it, the name of the owner of the land or the estate therein, and the name of the person who contracted the debt and for whom and at whose request labor was performed or the materials were furnished. In addition, the lien claim must contain a bill of particulars stating the amount and kind of labor performed or materials furnished, the prices at which and the times when the labor was performed or materials furnished, and the balance owing from the owner to the contractor after giving credit for all payments made and making all proper deductions.

Furthermore, a lien claim may not be filed more than two years after the date of filing of the notice of intention unless within the said two-year period a second notice of intention is filed. The second notice must be in the same form as required by law for the first notice, and in addition it must state that it is filed in order to protect and preserve the right of lien which is based on the first notice. Copy of any mechanic's notice of intention must be served upon the owner personally or by registered mail, within five days after it has been filed.

An action to enforce a lien claim against the realty must be commenced within four months from the date of the last work done or materials furnished. However, the time for the commencement of the action may be extended for a further period, not exceeding four months, by a written agreement signed by the parties whose interest may be affected by the lien. Any such agreement must be attached to the lien claim on file before the expiration of four months from the date when the last item of labor or materials has been performed or furnished.

Assuming that the building contract and specifications have been duly filed, the remedy of a claimant, other than a prime contractor, is to impound the funds owing to the prime contractor and in the possession of the owner by filing and serving a stop notice on the owner. Such a notice, which must be in written form, may be filed with the clerk of the proper county when the prime contractor has refused to pay any subcontractor materialman, journeyman, or laborer the amount of wages or any monies due him. The notice must state, among other things, the amount due, the owner's name, the name of the claimant, and the location of the property. Following the filing of the notice, the owner is required to give the principal contractor and any subcontractor written notice of the stop notice and demand that was served upon him. The statute provides for the method of service. At any time after the stop notice has been filed, but not later than five days following notice thereof from the owner, the prime contractor or subcontractor may dispute the claim and request the claimant to establish the same by judgment. Notice of the fact that the claim is disputed must be given to the owner, who thereafter may not pay the claim until it has been established by means of a judgment; thereupon the claimant is required to bring an action to establish his claim within sixty days after receipt of notice that the claim has been disputed. The rights of a claimant who has filed and served a stop notice are subject to any credits to which the owner may be entitled as against the prime contractor.

Until stop notices are filed and served, as stated above, the owner is protected in his payments to the contractor. However, if the owner makes payments in advance on the prime contract for the purpose of avoiding the provisions of the statute and the amount remaining due the prime contractor is not sufficient to satisfy the amounts claimed by the stop notices filed, the owner remains liable to the same extent as if the advanced payments had not been made. The statute makes provision for priority of liens under certain conditions.

Any person who furnishes labor or materials in connection with the execution of a contract for a public improvement is entitled to a lien on the monies due or to become due under the contract for the public improvement. The lienor must file his claim with the appropriate representative, named in the statute, of the public agency not later than sixty days after the work is completed or accepted. Notice of claim must be verified by oath and must contain the information required by the statute. The public agency may then require the contractor to show cause within five days why the lien should not be paid. If no such cause is shown, the public agency has the right to pay the claim, and if it does so, it is entitled to credit as against the prime contractor for the amount so paid. The lien of a laborer has priority.

An action on the claim may be commenced within sixty days from the date when all the work is completed or accepted. If an action is started by one claimant, then any other claimant may protect his claim by asserting it in his answer in the action.

A bond of 100 percent of the contract price is required of the contractor on public works. The bond must contain an additional obligation by the contractor and all subcontractors to pay for labor, material, and supplies. The statute contains a number of conditions which must be satisfied before a claimant may recover on the bond for payment of labor, material, or supplies. These conditions are discussed on page 239.

15.4.10 New York. In private construction, a contractor, subcontractor, laborer, or materialman who performs labor or furnishes materials with the consent or at the request of the owner, or his agent, for the improvement of real property, has a right of mechanic's lien. As used in the statute, an owner is the owner in fee of a real property, a tenant for one or more years, or a person in possession of real estate under a contract to purchase same. In public construction, a person performing labor or furnishing materials to a contractor, or its subcontractor, for the construction of a public improvement, pursuant to a contract between the contractor and the state, or a public corporation, has a right of mechanic's lien. A public corporation is a municipal corporation or a district corporation, or a corporation engaged in the construction of a public improvement. In public construction, as distinguished from private construction, it is not essential that a subcontractor, laborer, or materialman obtain the owner's consent or request directly from the owner. It is sufficient if the party with whom he contracts has obtained the consent of the owner or the latter's request to do the work.

In private construction, an architect or engineer, but not their employees, has a lien not only for supervision but also for the preparation of drawings and specifications prepared for or used in connection with the improvement. In public construction, neither the architect nor the engineer has a lien. The word "improvement" means demolition, erection, alteration, or repair of property, and any labor performed or materials furnished for its permanent improvement. It also includes materials actually manufactured for a particular job, though not delivered. To illustrate: a manufacturer of hangar doors, produced for a particular job, may file a lien following the manufacture of the doors, though the doors have not been delivered to the job site. One manufacturer followed this procedure promptly upon receiving notice that his customer had filed a petition in bankruptcy.

In private construction, the lien attaches to the real estate and extends to the owner's right, title, or interest therein. If the lienor performed his labor or furnished materials to an owner who is not the owner in fee of the real estate, but a tenant for one or more years, the lien would attach to the lease, as distinguished from the real estate itself, unless, of course, the owner of the fee affirmatively consented to the improvement, in which case the lien would attach to the real estate as well. Just how valuable a lien attaching to a lease would be depends upon the value of the lease itself.

In public construction, considerations of public policy make it necessary to prevent the lien from attaching to the real estate. The alternative remedy which is given is to permit the lien to attach to the fund that has been set aside by the governmental body or public corporation for the contemplated public improvement.

In private construction, the lien may not exceed the agreed price or value of the labor performed or the materials furnished at the time of its filing. The rule is no different in public construction. In private construction, no lien is permitted for damages for breach of contract. In public construction, such damages may be recovered if awarded by a judgment of the court of claims.

The mere fact that the lienor may in his notice of lien claim the agreed price or value of his labor performed, or materials furnished to the time of his filing a notice of lien, does not mean that ultimately he will be able to collect out of the real property, in the case of private construction, or out of the appropriated fund, in the case of public construction, the full amount of his lien. On the contrary, in the absence of fraud, neither the owner, state, nor public corporation can be compelled to pay to lienors a greater sum than the amount which it has agreed to pay by its contract for the completion of the building, less the amount paid on account under that contract, and less, further, a credit, in case of the contractor's default, for the cost or estimated cost of completion by the owner, state, or public corporation.

The lien is created by the filing of a notice of lien, and until the notice is filed, there is no lien. The filing of a notice of lien does not constitute a waiver by the claimant of his right to arbitration, if arbitration is provided for in his contract. He may demand arbitration either before or after filing his notice of lien. But he may lose his right to arbitrate if he sues to foreclose his lien before initiating abritration.

In the case of private construction, the notice of lien must be filed in the office of the clerk of the county where the real estate is located, and if located in more than one county, it must be filed in all counties where the real estate is situated. In public construction, the notice of lien must be filed with the head of the department having charge of construction and with the comptroller of the state, or the financial officer of the public corporation, charged with the disbursement of the fund applicable to the contract under which the claim is made.

The notice of lien must be filed within the time specified in the statute; otherwise, it has no legal force or effect. A distinction is drawn in respect of time for filing, in the case of private, as distinguished from public, construction. In private construction, it may be filed at any time during the progress of the work and furnishing of materials, or within four months after the completion of the contract, or the final performance of the work, or the final furnishing of the materials. Here the four-month period is measured by the completion of the lienor's contract, or the final performance of his work, or the final furnishing by him of materials. In public construction, the notice of lien may be filed at any time before construction of the public improvement is completed and accepted by the state, or public corporation, or within thirty days after such completion is accepted. It will be noted that, in the case of public construction, the thirty-day period does not begin to run from the time the claimant's work is completed, and accepted, but rather from the time that the construction of the entire public improvement is completed and accepted, so that conceivably a subcontractor may file a public lien long after his contract or work is performed or his materials have been furnished, provided such filing is within thirty days after the completion and acceptance of the entire project.

Once the lien has been filed it continues, in private construction, for one year. It may be renewed, however, from year to year, by order of the court, or the necessity to renew may be obviated by the commencement within the year of an action to foreclose the lien. A notice of pendency of action must be filed.

In public construction, the lien continues in the first instance for only six months from time of filing. It may be renewed from year to year thereafter by order of the court, or if an action to foreclose the lien is commenced within the life of the lien, it need not be renewed. A notice of pendency of such action must be filed.

In both private and public construction, the lien is discharged by failure to commence the action within the period stipulated above, or by failure to continue the lien by order of the court. The lien also may be discharged by an order of the court which will be granted upon the filing of a bond or depositing adequate monies to secure the ultimate payment of the lien—if its validity ultimately is established, in whole or in part, in court. Another method of satisfying the lien is by a certificate of satisfaction which the lienor may execute and acknowledge. The certificate is then filed in the appropriate office where the notice of lien was filed originally; thereupon the lien will be extinguished.

There is no priority within any class of lienors, but laborers receiving daily or weekly wages have a preference over all other liens within the same class.

In private construction, if a person in filing a lien willfully exaggerates the amount owing to him, his lien becomes void and he may not recover thereon or file a further lien for the same claim. Furthermore, he may be held liable for damages.

If a person files a notice of lien, but fails to establish its validity, or is unable to enforce his lien for the full amount owing to him, he may, nevertheless, recover the amount owing to him from any person who personally may be indebted to him by reason of the claim which he asserts.

Finally, it should be borne in mind that the bankruptcy or death of an owner or the fact that the owner has been placed in receivership does not prevent the filing of a lien in a proper case.

15.4.11   *Ohio.* A person or corporation who does work or labor upon, or furnishes machinery, material, or fuel, for constructing, altering, or repairing watercraft, or for erecting, altering, repairing, or removing a house, mill, manufactory, or any furnace or furnace material therein, or other building, appurtenance, fixtures, bridge, or other structure, or gas pipeline, or well, except a well drilled or constructed for the production of oil or gas, or who furnishes tile for the drainage of any lot or land or who does work or labor or furnishes material for the improvement, enhancement, or embellishment of real property by seeding, sodding, or planting, or by grading, or filling to establish a grade by virtue of a contract (express or implied) with the owner, part owner, or lessee of any interest in real estate or his authorized agent, has a lien to secure the payment thereof. In addition, every person who, as a subcontractor, laborer, or materialman, performs any labor or furnishes machinery, material, or fuel to an original or principal contractor, or any subcontractor, in carrying forward, performing, or completing any such contract has a lien. A right of lien exists for supervision by an architect or engineer where his contract with the owner is divisible and allocates a specific portion of his compensation to supervision.[147]

Liens also are provided in favor of persons who perform labor or furnish materials, etc., for the construction, alteration, or repair of any street, road, sidewalk, ditch, or sewer by virtue of a private contract entered into with an owner, part owner, or lessee.

Whenever any payment of money becomes due from the owner, part owner, or lessee, or whenever the original contractor desires to draw any money from any such person, under their contract, or whenever any mortgagee makes a written demand, the original contractor is required to give to the owner, part owner, lessee, or mortgagee, or his agent, a statement under oath. The statement must show the name and address of every laborer in the original contractor's employ who has not been paid in full; also the name and address of every subcontractor in his employ, and of every person furnishing machinery, material, or fuel, and the amount which is due or to become due them. The statement must be accompanied by a certificate signed by every person furnishing the original contractor machinery, material, or fuel. The certificate must contain the name and address of the materialman, the nature of the items furnished, the amount due, and other information. In lieu of such certificate, there may be furnished a written waiver of lien, release, or receipt.

The original contractor also must deliver similar sworn statements from each subcontractor, accompanied by like certificates from every person furnishing machinery, material, or fuel to the subcontractor.

The owner, part owner, lessee, or his agent must retain out of any money then due or to become due to the principal contractor an amount sufficient to pay all demands that are due or to become due to the subcontractors, laborers, and materialmen, as shown by the contractors' and subcontractors' statements and the certificates of materialmen and is required to pay said money to them according to their respective rights. As between the owner, part owner, lessee, or mortgagee and the contractor, subcontractors, and persons performing labor or furnishing machinery, material, or fuel, all payments so made are considered the same as if paid to the original contractor. The person making payment is released from further liability to the extent of the payments so made and he is not liable for any greater amount than he contracted to pay the original contractor, less any damage he sustained by reason of any failure or omission in performance by the original contractor.

Until the statements under oath are made and furnished, the contractor has no right of action or lien against the owner, part owner, or lessee on account of the principal contract except that his claim against the owner is not barred if no liens are filed within the period prescribed by the statute. The subcontractor has no right of action or lien until he has furnished such statements. Any payments made by the owner, part owner, or lessee, before such statements are made and furnished or without retaining sufficient money, if that amount is due or it is to become due, to pay the subcontractors, laborers, or materialmen, as shown by the said statements and certificates, are illegal and made in violation of the rights of the persons intended to be benefited by the statute, in consequence of which the rights of subcontractors, laborers, and materialmen to a lien are not affected thereby. The risk of all payments made to the original contractor before the contractor has furnished the required statement is upon the owner, part owner, or lessee, until the time for filing liens has expired.

The statute makes provision permitting any person whose name has been omitted from the sworn statement or affidavit given by the contractor or subcontractor to serve on the owner, part owner, or lessee of the premises, before final payment or distribution has been made, a written notice informing him of the nature of his claim which has been omitted and the amount due or to become due. It also permits the owner, part owner, lessee, mortgagee, or contractor, during the progress of the work, to demand in writing of the contractor or subcontractor, as the case may be, the written statements referred to, which must be furnished within ten days after demand, and for failure to furnish same, the person upon whom demand is made is liable to a penalty of $100 and also for all damages occasioned by his neglect or refusal to furnish the information.

To perfect a mechanic's lein, the claimant must file in the county recorder's office an affidavit verified under oath of his claim within sixty days (except in the special cases noted below) from the date on which he last furnished machinery, materials, or fuel or last performed labor. The affidavit must state the name and address of the claimant, the sum due over and above all setoffs, a description of the property, the name and address of the person to or for whom the said items were furnished and labor performed, and the name of the owner, part owner, or lessee, if known. A copy of the affidavit must be served on the owner, part owner, or lessee of the premises or his agent within thirty days after filing, but if none of the persons can be found within the county where the premises are situated, then such copy may be served by posting same in a conspicuous place on the premises within ten days after the expiration of said thirty days.

The statute also provides for liens arising out of the construction, alteration, or repair of roads, sewers, streets, and sidewalks and contains special provisions relating to perfecting liens upon gas and oil wells.

The lien is effective from the date the first labor is performed or the first machinery, materials, or fuel is furnished by the contractor under the original contract. It continues for six years from the date the necessary affidavit is filed. If an action to enforce the lien is commenced within the said six-year period, the lien continues until the entry of final judgment. However, the owner may require the person owning the lien to commence suit within sixty days after he receives a notice to start action as provided in the statute. If suit is not commenced pursuant to the notice, the lien will be extinguished.

The lien extends to the work on which the improvement is being made and to the interest of the owner, part owner, or lessee in the land at the time the work was commenced or the materials were begun to be furnished by the contractor under the original contract. The lien also extends to any interest in the property subsequently acquired by the owner, part owner, or lessee. If a person furnishes labor, machinery, material, or fuel for the erection of a new building or structure upon land which is not owned by the person contracting therefor, the lien will attach, nevertheless, to the building or structure.

A subcontractor, materialman, laborer, or mechanic who performs labor or furnishes material, fuel, or machinery for the construction, alteration, removal, or repair of a public improvement or public building provided for in a contract between the owner or any board officer or public authority and a principal contractor, or under a contract between such subcontractor, materialman, laborer, or mechanic and the principal contractor or subcontractor, may file with the owner, board, officer, or an authorized clerk or agent, no later than four months from the performance of the labor or delivery of the machinery, fuel, or materials, a sworn and itemized statement of the amount and value of the labor performed and material, etc., furnished. The statement must contain other information required by the statute.

Within ten days after such statement has been filed with the board, etc., a copy must be filed with the proper county recorder. The effect of such last-mentioned filing is to create a preference, to the extent indicated in the statute, over fellow subcontractors, materialmen, mechanics, and laborers who fail to file with the board, officer, or public authority a statement, and a copy thereof, with the county recorder. When the notice is received, the person receiving the same must withhold from the principal contractor all subsequent payments as do not, in the aggregate, exceed the claims.

Anyone receiving a copy of the said statement may require the claimant to institute suit within thirty days. Failure to institute suit upon such demand and within the time prescribed thereby renders the lien void, and the funds which otherwise would be subject to the lien are discharged. If a contractor or subcontractor gives notice to commence suit and files a bond for double the amount of the lien claim, the claimant's remedy is to sue upon the bond, and his failure to commence suit within thirty days after such notice is given renders the bond void.

15.4.12 *Pennsylvania.* Contractors and subcontractors have a lien on every improvement and the estate or title of the owner in property for all debts due for labor or materials furnished in the erection or construction, or the alteration or repair of the improvement, provided the amount of the claim, other than amounts determined by apportionment—as stated below—exceeds $500.

Where a debt is incurred for labor or materials furnished by the same claimant for work upon several different improvements which do not form all or part of a single business or residential plant, the claimant is required to file separate claims, with respect to each such improvement, with the amount of each claim determined by apportionment of the total debt to the several improvements. But in such case the amount of each separate claim may be less than $500, provided the total debt exceeds $500. In no other case may the claim be apportioned. The term "contractor" includes an architect or engineer, but he is accorded a lien only under the conditions mentioned on page 207.

In certain cases, liens are not allowed: for example, where either labor or material is furnished for a purely public purpose, or if the property is conveyed in good faith and for a valuable consideration prior to the filing of a claim for alterations or repairs. Furthermore, no lien is allowed against the estate of an owner in fee by reason of any consent given by the owner to a tenant to improve the leased premises unless it appears in a writing signed by the owner that the erection, construction, alteration, or repair was in fact for the immediate use and benefit of the owner. Finally, no lien is allowed for any portion of a debt representing the contract price of any materials against which the claimant holds or claims a security interest under the Pennsylvania Uniform Commercial Code or to which he has reserved title or the right to reacquire title.

To perfect a lien, every claimant must file a claim with the prothonotary within four months after the completion of his work, and in addition must serve written notice of such filing upon the owner within one month thereafter, giving the court term and number and date of filing of the claim. An affidavit of service of notice, or the acceptance of service, must be filed within twenty days after service, setting forth the date and manner (as required by the statute) of service. Failure to serve the notice or to file the affidavit or acceptance of service within the times specified is sufficient ground for striking off the claim. The claim must contain the information required by the statute.

Moreover, no lien claim by a subcontractor whether for the erection or construction or for alterations or repairs is valid unless, at least thirty days before the same is filed, he has given to the owner a *formal* written notice (containing seven items of information specified in the statute) of his intention to file a claim, except, however, that such formal written notice is not required where the lien claim has been filed pursuant to a rule to do so filed by the owner. The statute provides that the owner or contractor may file a rule requiring a subcontractor to file his claim within thirty days after notice of the rule or be forever barred from so doing.

The statute also requires that no claim by a subcontractor for alterations or repairs is valid unless, in addition to the formal written notice hereinbefore referred to, he has given to the owner on or before the date of completion of his work a written preliminary notice of his intention to file a claim if the amount due or to become due is not paid. Such notice need set forth only the name of the subcontractor, the contractor, a general description of the property against which the claim is to be filed, the amount then due or to become due, and a statement of intention to file a claim therefor.

A written contract between owner and contractor or a separate written instrument signed by the contractor which provides that no lien shall be filed by anyone is binding as against a subcontractor only (1) if he is given actual notice thereof prior to furnishing any labor or materials, *or* (2) if the contract or separate written instrument is filed in the office of the prothonotary before the commencement of the work upon the ground, or within ten days after the execution of the principal contract, or not less than ten days prior to the contract with the claimant subcontractor.

Where there has been no waiver of liens and the claims of subcontractors exceed in the aggregate the unpaid balance of the contract price specified in the contract between the owner and the contractor, then if the subcontractor has actual notice of the total amount of the contract price and of its provisions for the time or times for payment thereof, before any labor or materials were furnished by him, or if the contract or pertinent provisions thereof were filed in the office of the prothonotary in the time and manner provided in the statute, each claim, upon application of the owner, will be limited to its pro rata share of the contract price remaining unpaid, or which should have remained unpaid, whichever is greatest in amount at the time notice of intention to file a claim was first given to the owner. Such notice inures to the benefit of all claimants.

Any provisions of the contract between owner and contractor which reduce or impair the rights and remedies of a subcontractor, or which postpone the time for payment by the owner to the contractor for a period exceeding four months after completion of the work, are grounds for rescission by the subcontractor of his contract with the contractor, unless the subcontractor was given actual notice of the pertinent provisions prior to the time he made his contract with the contractor or the contract or the pertinent provisions thereof was filed in the office of the prothonotary, as previously stated.

The lien of a claim filed takes effect, and has priority in the case of the erection or construction of an improvement, as of the date of the visible commencement upon the ground of the work of erecting or constructing the improvement; and in the case of the alteration or repair of an improvement, as of the date of the filing of the claim.

An action prosecuting a claim to verdict or judgment must be commenced within two years from the date of filing of a claim unless the time is extended by the owner. A verdict must be recovered or judgment entered within five years after the filing of the claim and final judgment must be entered on a verdict within five years. The time period may be extended under certain conditions.

As stated previously, no lien is permitted for labor or materials that are furnished purely for public purposes. Every person entering into a contract with the municipality for the construction, erection, installation, completion, alteration, repair of, or addition to any public work or improvement is required to execute and deliver, if the contract exceeds $1000 (in addition to any other bond required by law) a payment bond for not less than 50 percent or more than 100 percent, of the contract price, conditioned for payment of all materials furnished and labor supplied or performed whether or not the material or labor enter into the contemplated improvement. In the case of contracts with counties exceeding $1500, similar bonds are required. The statute also requires a performance bond, and a payment bond in the case of any other public improvements. Claimants may sue on any payment bond furnished by the prime contractor where such bond is required. Specific regulations are established by statute in each instance dealing with the time within which written notice is required to be given to the contractor or surety before suit on the bond may be instituted and the time within which action must be commenced.

15.5   Bonds—General. Although the general purpose of contract bonds is similar to insurance against accident or fire, bonds differ materially from insurance contracts. Considerable confusion exists in the minds of architects and engineers, as well as in those of owners and contractors, regarding rights and duties of sureties, principals, obligees, and beneficiaries. Not only do statutory provisions vary in different jurisdictions, but the language of the bond—unlike insurance policies—varies with the contractual obligations assumed by the contractor in each specific instance.

Contract bonds have been used since the earliest days of contract construction in this country. Their development and acceptance were given considerable impetus by the Federal government, the Heard Act in 1894 prescribing a combined performance and payment bond for Federal construction contracts, and the Miller Act in 1935 separating those responsibilities into two distinct bonds, one assuring performance of the contract and the other guaranteeing payment of labor and material bills. In private construction, in general, development has followed much the same path.

15.5.1   Combined Bond—Possible Inadequacy of Amount to Protect Owner and Other Claimants. Although separate as well as combined bonds have been written, combined bonds may create special problems that ordinarily do not exist in the case of separate bonds. Where a combined bond is used, there is a conflict between the owner's interest in having the job fully and properly completed, and the materialman's interest in having his bill paid. Conceivably, unpaid bills could aggregate or exceed the principal amount of the bond, leaving nothing for the owner to claim in the event of nonperformance, unless the bond stipulates two separate penal sums, one adequate to protect the owner and the other sufficient to safeguard the interests of materialmen and other claimants.

15.5.2 Claimant Denied Recovery on Combined Bond for Sums Owing. Another problem deals with the enforcement of the bond. The owner's purpose in requiring a combined bond, according to one court, is primarily to safeguard him against nonperformance, and only secondarily to safeguard payment for labor and materials, so that unless the bond expressly confers upon a claimant, such as a laborer or materialman, a direct right of action, only the owner can sue on the bond. Thus, where the bond contained a condition reading, insofar as pertinent, as follows:

Now, therefore, the condition of this obligation is such that if the said principal shall . . . perform the work in accordance with the terms of the contract and with the plans and specifications, and will . . . complete the work within the time prescribed . . . and shall protect the said State of New York against and pay any excess of cost . . . and all amounts, . . . which may be recovered against said State . . . or which the said State . . . may be called upon to pay to any person . . . by reason of any damages, . . . arising or growing out of the doing of said work, . . . or from any other cause, and if the above . . . principal, . . . shall and do well and truly pay or cause to be paid in full the wages stipulated and agreed to be paid to each and every laborer employed by the said principal or by his agents, then this obligation shall be null and void, otherwise to remain in full force and virtue,

the court dismissed an action by laborers against the surety to recover unpaid wages. The court, while recognizing that the bond had a twofold function, ruled that the dominant purpose of the bond was to protect the owner. Thus the court said:

The dominant purpose of this bond was protection to the state. That is plain alike from its terms and from those of the statute which required that security be given. . . . This dominant purpose will be defeated if laborers may ignore the People, and sue in their own right. They may then sue for wages as often as there is default, and exhausting the penalty of the bond, leave nothing for the state.[148]

15.5.3 Materialman Allowed Recovery against Surety under Separate Payment Bond. In another case, where separate payment and performance bonds were furnished, the court permitted a materialman to sue the surety directly under the payment bond.

The general contractor for a large housing project sublet the plumbing and heating work under a contract in which the subcontractor agreed to furnish labor and materials "free of the lien of any third party," and to "indemnify and save harmless the contractor, the owners . . . against loss, damages or expense," to secure which the subcontractor agreed "to furnish a 20% Payment and a 20% Performance Bond," both of which were to be paid for by the general contractor.

The plumbing and heating subcontractor failed to pay a material bill of $17,077.36 for plumbing supplies used on the job. After demanding payment from the subcontractor to whom the materials had been supplied, and then from the general contractor, without avail, the materialman finally sued to recover from the general contractor and the surety company. The court held that the surety company was obligated to pay, stating that an unpaid materialman may, as a third-party beneficiary, recover against a general contractor and a surety on the payment bond, although he might not have the right to maintain a separate suit as a third-party beneficiary when the obligations of the surety are combined in a single payment-performance bond of which performance is regarded as the primary purpose.[149]

Therefore, when a combined bond is furnished, it is important that the bond or the statute pursuant to which it is furnished confer upon materialmen and laborers the right to sue the surety directly, and it would be well for such beneficiaries to verify, before extending credit, that such a right exists.

15.5.4   Special Provision Conferring Direct Right of Action on Labor and Material Bond. A direct right of action has been conferred upon materialmen and laborers in a bond by the following language:

The Principal and Surety agree that this bond shall be for the benefit of any materialman or laborer having a just claim as well as the Owner itself. All persons who shall have performed labor, rendered services or furnished materials and supplies, shall have a direct right of action against the Principal and his, its or their successors and assigns, and the Surety, or against either or both of any of them and their successors and assigns. Such persons may sue in their own name and may prosecute the suit to judgment and execution, without the necessity of joining with any other person as party plaintiff.

15.5.5   Beneficiary's Right to Recover on Statutory Bond Restricted by Terms of Governing Statute. A performance bond or payment bond, or both, may be required by a private owner, or in the case of contracts made by municipalities or other units of government, such bonds may be mandatory by statute. Although in the case of a statutory bond, reference is usually made in general language to the particular governing statute, in all probability the person for whose benefit the bond is intended is not familiar with the precise terms of the statute and does not realize that his right to recover on the bond is limited by the conditions of the statute, to the same extent as though the provisions of the statute were fully incorporated into the bond.

Therefore, it is essential that he familiarize himself with the statutory requirements which are read into the bond. A failure to do so may jeopardize his rights.

To illustrate: under the New Jersey statute it is provided with respect to a payment bond furnished by a contractor in connection with a public improvement (1) that a materialman must furnish a statement to the surety of the amount due before the acceptance of the building work or other improvement, or within eighty days thereafter, and (2) suit on the bond must be brought within one year from date of acceptance, but not prior to the expiration of eighty days from such acceptance. Thus, the right to bring an action on such a bond exists only in an instance where the building is finally accepted, where a statement of the amount due has been furnished to the surety not later than eighty days after acceptance, and where eighty days have elapsed thereafter. The claimant who does not make it a point to ascertain what the requirements of the statute are may fail to give notice to the surety within the required time or otherwise may fail to comply with the statute, in consequence of which he may lose his rights under the bond.

15.5.6 Duties and Responsibilities of Owner and Architect to Surety. Since one of the purposes of a payment bond issued by a surety company is to safeguard the owner against the contingency that the contractor may not pay for labor or material, and the surety is paid a premium for assuming the risk involved, one would imagine that under no circumstances could an owner or an architect be held liable to the surety if the latter is required to make good under such a bond. But the fact is that from the surety's duty to protect the owner, there springs a corresponding duty on the part of owner and architect to protect the surety against an impairment of what is commonly referred to as a surety's equitable right of subrogation.

Such right of subrogation means that when a surety is obliged, under the terms of a payment bond, to satisfy the claims of unpaid laborers and materialmen, it stands in the shoes of these claimants and therefore is entitled to collect from the owner any sums which he is required to withhold from the contractor until the satisfaction of such claims. Hence, when retainage funds are released to a contractor in violation of the terms of the contract documents, the surety's right of subrogation under a payment bond may be impaired, and the owner or architect, or both, may be held liable to the surety for any damages sustained. Such a liability may be imposed upon the architect, even though there is a complete absence of contractual relationship between him and the surety. The following cases vividly illustrate the legal pitfalls involved.

In the first case, the surety on a payment bond brought suit against a school district (owner) to recover a substantial sum which it had been compelled to pay to unpaid laborers and materialmen.

The construction contract provided that 15 percent of the contract price should be retained until the final completion and acceptance of the work and that the final payment would become due ten days after substantial completion of the work, provided the work was then fully completed and the contract fully performed. The construction contract further provided that upon receipt of written notice the architect would inspect the building, and if he found the work acceptable and the contract fully performed, he would promptly issue a final certificate to that effect; also, that before issuance of the final certificate, the contractor would submit evidence satisfactory to the architect that all payrolls, material bills, and other indebtedness connected with the work had been paid.

The general conditions provided that the contractor would submit to the architect an application for each payment and, if required, receipts or other vouchers showing his payments for materials and labor, including payments to subcontractors. The school district released to the contractor the retainage funds before the completion of the work and without requiring the contractor to furnish receipts or affidavits showing the payment of all bills for labor or materials.

The court held that when a building contract stipulates that a percentage of the contract price is to be retained until the final completion and acceptance of the work, such a stipulation is as much for the benefit of the surety as for the protection of the owner. The court further held that when the surety paid the claims of laborers and materialmen, it became subrogated to their rights against the school district and that the latter, having diverted the retainage funds from the purpose to which they were dedicated by releasing them to the contractor contrary to the terms of the contract documents, became liable to the surety for the damages sustained by it.[150]

In the second case, the surety on a payment bond sued an architect to recover damages claimed to have been sustained through the wrongful and negligent release by the architect of retainage funds which the surety asserted resulted in depriving it of resort to those funds under the said doctrine of equitable subrogation.

The contract documents required the owner to retain 15 percent of the contract price until the work was fully completed and the contract fully performed. The architect was required to make a final inspection, and before the issuance of final certificate, the contractor was obliged to submit evidence satisfactory to the architect that all payrolls, material bills, and other indebtedness connected with the work had been paid. The architect negligently approved the release of the retainage funds without exercising due diligence to ascertain whether there were outstanding bills for labor and materials.

The architect contended that there was no privity of contract between him and the surety; that he owed no duty to the surety and therefore could not be held liable to it regardless of negligent conduct and resulting damage. In rejecting this argument, the court ruled that the architect's duty to require the contractor to submit satisfactory evidence that all indebtednesses connected with the work had been paid was owing not only to the owner, but the surety as well, and that the architect was responsible to the surety for his negligence in approving the release of the retainage funds, without exercising proper diligence to make certain that the outstanding bills had been paid.[151]

Under the terms of the Owner-Contractor Agreement, and the General Conditions made a part thereof, published by the American Institute of Architects in 1976, the architects' duties with respect to the contractor are clearly set forth. It is emphasized that under these General Conditions, before the architect may issue a final certificate of payment he is not only empowered, but required to secure from the contractor an affidavit stating that all payrolls, bills for materials and equipment, and other indebtedness connected with the work for which the owner or his property might in any way be responsible have been paid or otherwise satisfied. In addition, if required by the owner, the architect must obtain from the contractor receipts, releases, and waivers of liens or other data establishing that such obligations have been paid or satisfied.

Before final payment is made, consent thereto of the surety, if any, must be obtained. Under certain circumstances set forth in the General Conditions the surety's consent also is required if after the work is substantially completed, but not fully completed, the owner makes payment pursuant to the architect's certification of the balance due for any part of the work fully completed and accepted. The surety's consent may be noted on the certificate of payment before it is delivered by the architect to the owner and contractor. In requesting the surety to give its consent, the architect, whenever in doubt as to the sufficiency of the documents furnished by the contractor, may submit copies thereof to the surety and thereby seek its opinion as to their adequacy. It is suggested that compliance by the architect with any time limitation, within which he is required to issue any certificate, should be made conditional upon the surety's prior consent to the certificate—if such consent is required.

It is extremely important for every architect to comply literally with all provisions in the contract documents which are conditions precedent to a contractor's right to receive any payments—whether such conditions be in the form promulgated by the American Institute of Architects or in any other pertinent form. There is neither room nor area for noncompliance with any such conditions. Uncompromising rigid compliance is the only safe course to follow.

PART TWO
Special Forms

CHAPTER 16

Contract Provisions:
Owner-Architect Agreements

Standard forms of contracts for use between the architect and his client, between his client and the contractor, and between the contractor and subcontractors have been prepared by the American Institute of Architects. These forms are the result of cumulative experience and much study, and are of great value to the architect or engineer undertaking a professional commission.

It is obvious, however, that special circumstances surrounding a particular commission may make it desirable to modify the obligations of the contracting parties as set forth in the standard forms. Since the drafting of contracts is specifically the province of the lawyer, and since state laws are not uniform in their requirements, competent legal counsel should be obtained in modifying the standard forms or in adopting different forms.

The following special provisions have been found useful in specific instances, and are presented as a checklist to cover certain situations. They should be incorporated into a contract only after consulting a lawyer.

16.1 *Secrecy of Owner's Processes and Equipment—Nondisclosure of Confidential Information.* In the present age of rapidly expanding technology, it is not unusual for an architect or engineer to be commissioned to design a plant for a new product, or a plant including unique equipment or processing methods. In such case the owner quite naturally desires to keep his inventions secret from possible competitors and prevent the unauthorized disclosure of confidential information. He may wish to incorporate safeguards into the contract with his architects and engineers similar to the following:

SUBCONTRACTS

The Architect (Engineer) shall not sublet any part of the Work without the prior written permission of the Owner.

DRAWINGS AND SPECIFICATIONS: TITLE TO WORK

Each drawing and/or specification prepared hereunder shall be submitted to the Owner promptly upon completion thereof so that the Owner may determine whether such drawing and specification will satisfy the Owner's needs. If the Owner should request that any change be made in any of said drawings or specifications, the Architect (Engineer) shall promptly make such change. Any such change which is inconsistent with prior written directions of the Owner shall be paid for by the Owner in accordance with the provisions of Article _____; any other change shall be made at no additional cost and expense to the Owner. The foregoing shall not limit or alter the Architect's (Engineer's) responsibility for performance of the Work. All designs, diagrams, plans, drawings, models, prototype devices, specifications, studies, calculations, estimates and notes, memoranda and other writings of a technical nature (herein collectively referred to as the "Data") which are furnished to the Architect (Engineer) by the Owner or which are prepared or procured by the Architect (Engineer) or any of its subcontractors for the performance of the Work shall be and remain the property of the Owner. Promptly upon completion or termination of the Work, and at such time or times prior thereto as the Owner may request, the Architect (Engineer) (and his subcontractors) shall deliver to the Owner all original tracings and copies of all the Data. If requested by the Owner, designs, diagrams, plans and/or drawings shall be made on drafting sheets furnished by the Owner. All plans, drawings and specifications shall be sufficient in numbers and complete to the extent that no additional drawings, design details or specifications will be required for any purpose whatever. The Architect (Engineer) may, however, use existing drawings and standards at the discretion of the Owner.

    The Architect (Engineer) shall not deliver or permit to be delivered any item of the Data in its possession or control to anyone other than the Owner, and other than an employee or subcontractor who has signed a written agreement as may be sufficient in the opinion of Owner's attorney to effectuate the purposes of this Agreement and safeguard the rights of the Owner hereunder and then only to the extent necessary for performance of the Architect's (Engineer's) services under this Agreement.

SECRECY

    A. The Architect (Engineer) shall not disclose or permit the disclosure of any Confidential Information, except to its employees and subcontractors who need such Confidential Information in order to properly perform the Work and who have signed written agreements, as may be sufficient in the opinion of Owner's attorney to effectuate the purposes of this Agreement and safeguard the rights of the Owner hereunder, and shall not use or permit to be used any Confidential Information for anyone other than the Owner, except when, after, and to the extent that such Confidential Information is known to the public or was known to the Architect (Engineer) prior to its disclosure to the Architect (Engineer) by or on behalf of the Owner, or is disclosed to the Architect (Engineer) by a third party on a nonconfidential basis.

B. As used herein, the term "Confidential Information" shall mean any and all information, know-how and data, technical or nontechnical, in any way relating to the subject matter of this Agreement or to any process used or product or apparatus manufactured, used or sold by the Owner, which is disclosed to the Architect (Engineer) by or on behalf of the Owner before, during or after the term of this Agreement.

C. The Architect (Engineer) shall in no event disclose that any Confidential Information is or is not being utilized by the Owner.

EMPLOYEES AND SUBCONTRACTORS

The Architect (Engineer) shall procure all such written agreements with its employees and subcontractors as may be necessary to effectuate the purpose of this Agreement and protect the rights of the Owner hereunder.

PUBLICITY

No information relative to the work shall be released by the Architect (Engineer) for publication, advertising or any other purpose without prior written approval of the Owner.

16.2 Scope of Services

16.2.1 Major Changes Defined. It is almost inevitable that the owner will request some changes after the designer has accomplished considerable work on the basis of a previous decision. Sometimes these changes, taken individually, seem insignificant, but in the aggregate may be costly to the architect or engineer. In order to avoid controversy, a major change or changes requiring extra compensation may be defined as follows:

If the Architect (Engineer) is caused extra drafting or other expenses due to a major change ordered by the Owner after the preliminary studies have been approved or due to the delinquency of the Owner or Contractor or as a result of damage to the building by fire or any other cause during construction, he shall be compensated for such work in the amount of $2\frac{1}{2}$ times the actual and reasonable salaries expended by him for technical personnel engaged in doing this work. The term "major change" means a change (in any drawings, plans, specifications, documents or work hereunder) which necessitates expenditures by the Architect (Engineer) for salaries for technical personnel exceeding the sum of $100.00 in the case of any one change or exceeding in the aggregate the sum of $1,000.00 in the case of more than one change.

16.2.2 Maximum Number of Submissions. Generally, the owner-architect agreement provides for each succeeding phase of the architect's services to be undertaken only after the owner's approval of the preceding phase. If the owner continues to refuse approval of submission after submission at any stage of the work, the architect's costs become disproportionate to his fee. To avoid such a possible result, the owner-architect agreement may provide for additional compensation, as follows:

If any documents mentioned in Article _____ are not found satisfactory by the Owner, they shall be revised in such a manner as to be acceptable to the Owner, but if more than six submissions of schematic design studies or design development documents are required by the Owner, the Architect shall be compensated for those submissions in excess of such number in the amount of (2½) times the actual and reasonable salaries expended by him for technical personnel engaged in preparing the excess submissions.

16.2.3 *Reduction in Scope, or Termination.* One of the occasions when misunderstandings are likely to occur between a professional man and his client is at the time of a major change in scope, or perhaps total abandonment of the project, particularly when the fee is a percentage of construction cost. The client naturally will be reluctant to pay for services he does not intend to use, and yet the architect or engineer may already have performed a considerable amount of work for which he should be equitably paid. It is possible to permit the owner complete freedom to modify or abandon the project, and yet make it abundantly clear that the architect is to be paid at the originally contemplated rate for all work done prior to this decision. In this regard, the following provisions are worthy of consideration for inclusion in the owner-architect (engineer) agreement:

I. Payments to the Architect on account of his fee shall be made as follows:

A. Upon completion and delivery to the Owner of acceptable Schematic Design Studies of the entire proposed work, (_____)% of the basic rate, computed upon a reasonable estimated cost of the entire work designed by the Architect (Engineer).

B. Upon completion and delivery of Design Development Documents, a further sum equal to (_____)% of the basic rate computed upon a reasonable cost estimated on the work shown and called for in the Design Development Documents.

C. Upon completion and delivery of the Construction Documents (exclusive of details), a further sum equal to (_____)% of the basic rate, computed upon a reasonable cost estimated on the work shown and called for in the Construction Documents.

D. From time to time as construction actually proceeds with all or a portion of the work, payments shall be made on account of the fee for that portion of the work which is actually constructed, which payments shall be a sum equal to (_____)% of the actual cost of such portion of the work as is actually constructed by the Owner. It is understood that any payments made to the Architect under subparagraphs A, B or C hereof for preparing Schematic Design Studies, Design Development Documents and Construction Documents covering proposed work not actually constructed by the Owner shall be retained by the Architect absolutely and shall not be considered as a payment on account of any sum due under this subparagraph D.

E. Notwithstanding the fact that the foregoing payments are to be made to the Architect only as above provided, it is understood that for purposes of Paragraph II hereinafter set forth, proportions of the sums above payable under subparagraphs A, B and C of this Paragraph I shall be deemed to have been earned as progress on the studies and documents is made by the Architect and in proportion to the services rendered by him in the preparation thereof.

II. The Owner may at any time after the execution of this Agreement abandon the work in whole or in part upon giving to the Architect not less than five days notice in writing by registered or certified mail, return receipt requested, and thereupon this Agreement shall be reduced in scope in accordance with the written notice of the Owner, subject to the provisions of subparagraph D of this Paragraph II. The Owner may terminate this Agreement in its entirety at any time (with or without cause), upon giving to the Architect not less than five days notice in writing by registered or certified mail, return receipt requested. In the event that this Agreement is entirely terminated as aforesaid, or is reduced in scope, in accordance with the written notice of the Owner or in the event any work designed or specified by the Architect is suspended in whole or in part, the Architect shall be paid for the services rendered as follows:

A. In the event that this Agreement is entirely terminated or the work is abandoned or suspended in whole or in part, during the preparation of the Schematic Design Studies, the Architect shall be paid a portion of his fee which would be earned upon completion and delivery thereof, such portion to be an amount sufficient to fairly compensate the Architect for the work done by him in said stage, and in proportion to the services rendered by him, in connection therewith.

B. In the event that this Agreement is entirely terminated or the work is abandoned or suspended in whole or in part, after the completion and delivery of the Schematic Design Studies, the Architect shall be paid such part of his fee as shall have been earned under Paragraph IA of this Agreement, plus such portion of the next succeeding installment of his fee as shall fairly compensate the Architect for the work done by him, and in proportion to the services rendered by him, in connection with the next succeeding stage.

C. In the event that this Agreement is entirely terminated or the work is abandoned or suspended in whole or in part, after completion and delivery of the Design Development Documents, the Architect shall be paid such part of his fee as shall have been earned under Paragraphs IA and B of this Agreement, plus such portion of the next succeeding installment of his fee as shall fairly compensate the Architect for the work done by him, and in proportion to the services rendered by him, in connection with the next succeeding stage.

D. Provided, however:

1. That if there is a change in the scope of the project previously authorized by the Owner and as planned by the Architect and such change shall result in a reduction of the cost, such change shall affect only the fee for that portion of the Architect's work still to be done and shall in no way reduce or alter the fee due to the Architect or amounts paid to him for his work completed before such change; and

2. That such termination, complete abandonment, reduction in scope or suspension shall not give rise to any cause of action for damages or for extra remuneration against the Owner, the intent being that in any such event any claim for remuneration or compensation shall be made by the Architect solely under the provisions of this Agreement.

16.2.4   Owner's Option to Dispense with Contract Administration Services. It may be that the scope of the architect's or engineer's activities will not have been determined at the time the agreement is signed. The following provision makes the professional's services involving the administration of the construction contract optional with the owner:

Within _____ days after Architect (Engineer) shall notify Owner of completion of Construction Documents (exclusive of details) Owner may elect, by written notice to the Architect (Engineer), sent by registered or certified mail, to dispense with any services by the Architect (Engineer) involving the administration of the construction contract. Upon the giving of such notice, the Architect's basic rate of compensation shall be reduced by a sum equal to one-fifth ($\frac{1}{5}$) thereof.

16.2.5   A Single Construction Contract, though Work Performed in Sections. It is generally recognized that if construction work is done under separate contracts instead of under a single prime contract, the architect's or engineer's services in administering the construction contract will be increased. Ordinarily, the agreement between the professional man and his client contemplates a higher fee for services let under separate contracts. Where the work is to be performed in sections, it may be necessary to stipulate that such letting will not constitute separate contracts, as illustrated by the following provision:

The basic rate applies to work let under a single contract; provided, however, that for the purpose of this article, notwithstanding the fact that the construction work may be performed in sections and an interval of time may elapse between the construction of each section, all of the construction work let out to cover all sections until the entire work is completed, shall be deemed and construed as a single contract, regardless of the lapse of an interval of time, and regardless of the fact that the work for the respective sections may be awarded to different contractors. As to those portions of the work which are let under separate contracts, except as hereinabove provided, the rate shall be (_____)%.

16.3   Delay

16.3.1   Prolonged Contract Administration. In order to clarify the matter of extra payment to the architect for providing prolonged construction administration, as discussed on pages 22–23, the provision in the agreement between owner and architect may be couched in language as follows:

Providing Contract Administration and observation of construction, after the *originally agreed upon* construction Contract Time has been exceeded by more than 20%

through no fault of the Architect. Should the said Construction Contract Time be exceeded by more than the said percentage, the Architect's extra expense for his extra services shall be computed from the date originally fixed for completion of the construction work.

16.3.2 *Adjustment of Fee if Work Postponed.* If the owner should find it expedient to postpone a part of architect's or engineer's services for a considerable time, it may appear, when the work finally is resumed, that circumstances have changed to such an extent as to make it appropriate to renegotiate the professional fee. This may be contemplated by the owner-architect agreement, as follows:

The Owner reserves the right to postpone any services to be performed by the Architect upon giving the Architect two weeks written notice. If, by reason of postponement, either party should suffer hardship in regard to the Architect's fee, due to a subsequent change in the cost of construction, or due to a subsequent change in the rate of technical salaries of the employees of the Architect, his Engineers or other Consultants the fee shall be equitably adjusted.

16.3.3 *Assumption by Contractor of Architect's Additional Costs Due to Delay.* It is not unusual for a construction job to be delayed beyond the expected completion date because the contractor is unable to finish the work according to schedule. This prolongation of the work, although not the fault of the architect or engineer, may increase his costs. This contingency is usually foreseen in the owner-architect agreement by arranging that the owner shall pay the architect an extra amount for prolonged contract administration. If it is desired that the contractor, instead of the owner, carry this risk and reimburse the owner for the additional costs, it may be stipulated in the owner-contractor agreement as follows:

If the work embraced by this contract is not completed on or before the time specified in this contract, then, without prejudice to any other rights, claims, or remedies the Owner may have, the architectural (engineering) and inspection costs and expenses incurred by the Architect (Engineer) upon the work, from the originally agreed upon completion date to the final completion date of all the Work, shall be borne by the Contractor, and will be deducted by the Architect (Engineer) from the final amount of the Contract sum.

16.4 *Safeguarding Architect's Compensation*
16.4.1 *Against Contingency that Owner May Not Be Financially Responsible.* How may the practitioner guarantee his compensation when he suspects his client may not be financially responsible? It sometimes happens that he is asked to perform professional services for a corporation whose financial status is somewhat questionable. Although the personal fortunes of its officers might be very large, they may not be attached to satisfy debts of the corporation. If the corporation were to declare itself bankrupt, the corporate assets might be insufficient to satisfy in full the claims of the archi-

tect. If the architect or engineer wishes the signing officer to guarantee payment of compensation not only in his capacity as a corporate officer, but also as an individual, consideration should be given to the following provision:

The undersigned (officer's name) hereby absolutely and unconditionally guarantees to (architect's or engineer's name) his legal representatives, successors and assigns, the full and prompt payment of all compensation of other sums now or hereafter due and payable to said Architect (or Engineer) under the annexed Agreement, between _____, Architect (Engineer), and _____, Owner, dated the _____ day of _____, 19____, hereby waiving acceptance of this guarantee and notice of any default by Owner. This guarantee shall be binding upon the undersigned, his successors and legal representatives.

16.4.2 *In Case Owner Fails to Make Payment of Installment.* If his client should fail to make an installment payment to the professional when such payment becomes due, the architect or engineer may wish to cease providing further services. This recourse is not usually open to him unless the agreement with his client provides for it. If he wishes to make this option possible, a clause similar to that below may be included in the agreement.

In the event that the Owner shall fail or refuse to make payment to the Architect (Engineer) of any portion of his fee, payable hereunder, or any other sum payable to the Architect (Engineer) hereunder, within ten days after the invoice therefor is rendered to the Owner, the Architect (Engineer) may suspend at any time thereafter further performance of his services hereunder until such default is remedied.

If the client's default continues for an unreasonable length of time, the professional may wish to elect to terminate the agreement. Such a right of election may be reserved by continuing the preceding clause as follows:

If such default shall continue for a period of thirty days, the Architect (Engineer) may, at his option, to be exercised at any time thereafter, prior to the remedying of such default, terminate this Agreement without prejudice to his right to recover from the Owner, for the services theretofore rendered and for reimbursements and other sums payable to him by the Owner hereunder, and without prejudice to any other right or remedy that the Architect (Engineer) may have by reason of the Owner's breach of this Agreement.

16.4.3 *In Case Architectural Partner Dies or Retires.* What are the architect's rights to compensation if one of the partners in the architectural firm dies or retires before the work has been completed? To prevent the client from lawfully terminating the agreement under such circumstances, the inclusion of the following in the agreement should be considered:

The Architect shall have the right to join with him in the performance of this Agreement, any Architect or Architects with whom he may in good faith enter into partnership relationship. In case of the death or retirement of one or more partners, the rights, and duties of the Architect, if a firm, shall devolve upon the surviving or remaining partner or partners or upon such firm as may be established by him or by them, and he, they or it shall be recognized as the "successor" of the Architect, and so on until the services covered by this Agreement have been performed.

16.4.4 Abandonment by Owner—Agreed Reduced Percentages Not to Control Architect's Compensation.

In those instances where the architect, as an accommodation to his client, agrees to accept interim payments on account of his basic fee, less than the percentages recommended in the standard forms prepared by the American Institute of Architects—thereby deferring payment of part of the fee—the following provision may be used, in order to make it crystal clear that in case of any abandonment of the work, the percentages recommended by the Institute are controlling in determining the architect's compensation to the date of abandonment.

The parties hereto acknowledge:

(1) [Here the legal draftsman would insert a provision to the effect that the architect normally is entitled to receive payment on account of his basic fee in the installments recognized by standard practice and would refer to the customary percentages payable at the completion of each phase of the work. Then he would continue as below.]

(2) That notwithstanding the foregoing, the Architect has agreed, as an accommodation to the Owner, to accept payments on account of his basic fee, as follows: [Here he would make provision for the reduced percentages to be paid to the architect at the completion of each phase of the work. Then he would continue as below.]

The parties hereto agree:

(3) That notwithstanding the provisions of Subdivision (2) above, payment of the sums payable to the Architect on account of his basic fee, shall be deemed to have been earned, in proportion to the services performed by him, according to the customary percentages referred to in Subdivision (1) hereof. Accordingly, in case of an abandonment or suspension of the work (for more than _____ days) after written notice by the Owner to the Architect, the Architect shall be entitled to be paid for the services performed by him. In such event, the amount to be paid to the Architect, shall be calculated according to the percentages of the basic fee referred to in Subdivision (1) above, and in proportion to the services performed by him in respect of each phase of the work.

16.4.5 Compensation Payable by Foreign Client

The Owner agrees to pay the Architect (Engineer) for the services described in this Agreement, a total fee of $_____, payable as follows:

(1) Upon the signing of this Agreement, the Owner shall cause to be deposited in a bank located in the City of _____, State of _____, U.S.A., designated by the Architect (Engineer) the sum of $_____, which shall cover the portion of the fee allocable to Phase I (Schematic Design Phase).

(2) Upon approval of Phase I, and before Phase II (Design Development Phase) is started, the Owner shall cause to be deposited in the said designated bank, the further sum of $_____, which shall cover the portion of the fee allocable to Phase II.

(3) Upon approval of Phase II and before Phase III (Construction Documents Phase) is started, the Owner shall cause to be deposited in the said designated bank, the further sum of $_____, which shall cover the portion of the fee allocable to Phase III.

(4) The Owner shall issue written irrevocable instructions to the said designated bank to disburse the funds deposited with said bank as hereinabove provided to the Architect (Engineer) and to no one else, upon the presentation at such bank, on or about the 10th day of each month, of Architect's (Engineer's) detailed bill, in duplicate, describing the services performed during the preceding month, and the portion of the fee earned and payable by reason thereof. The Architect's (Engineer's) bill shall be certified as true and correct by a principal of his organization. The bill shall be accompanied by a full progress report. Copies of all documents presented to the bank shall be mailed by the Architect (Engineer) directly to the Owner.

(5) The said designated bank shall be further instructed by the Owner not to make any payment to the Architect (Engineer) with respect to Phase II of this Agreement until the bank has been advised by the Owner that payments to the Architect (Engineer) with respect to Phase I have been approved by the Owner.

(6) Said designated bank shall be further instructed not to make any payment to the Architect (Engineer) with respect to Phase III of this Agreement, until the bank has been advised by the Owner that payments to the Architect (Engineer) with respect to Phase II have been approved by the Owner. Upon receipt of Owner's approval to make payments to the Architect (Engineer) for Phase III, the said designated bank shall nevertheless reserve 10% of the fund deposited with such bank under Subsection (3) above, until advised by the Owner that the Architect (Engineer) has completed performance of Phase III.

(7) The Owner shall arrange for the Architect (Engineer) to receive:

(*a*) A validated duplicate original of the Owner's irrevocable instructions to the said designated bank;

(*b*) A written confirmation of the Owner's irrevocable instructions to the said designated bank on the bank's formal stationery, addressed to the Architect (Engineer) and signed by an authorized officer of the bank;

(*c*) Copies of all Owner's advices to the said designated bank, stating Owner's approval of payments made to the Architect (Engineer) by the said bank.

(8) Notwithstanding any payments made to the Architect (Engineer) under the foregoing provisions, the Owner shall not be deemed to be foreclosed from requesting or suing for reimbursement, for any sums determined to be erroneously paid to

the Architect (Engineer) based upon examination of the record of the Architect's (Engineer's) performance or based upon any other warranted circumstances.†

16.5   *Reimbursement to Architect for Overhead*

16.5.1   *Reimbursement on Basis of Actual Overhead Rate Determined at End of Each Year*

The Architect shall be entitled to be reimbursed for his overhead on the sum of the direct wages and salaries of the Architect's technical personnel, computed thereon at his actual overhead rate, to be determined at the end of each year, as hereinafter provided.

Pending the determination of the Architect's actual overhead rate for the current fiscal year ending Dec. 31, 19_____, such overhead rate is tentatively fixed at the rate of 35%, for which the Architect may bill the Owner, subject to adjustment thereof, as hereinafter provided.

At the close of each fiscal year ending Dec 31, the actual overhead rate shall be computed for the year then ended from books of account maintained by the Architect, in accordance with generally accepted accounting principles, consistently applied and in such manner that they may be audited readily. This computed overhead rate shall be prepared by the Architect's certified public accountant and shall be presented to the Owner in a formal overhead study, on the basis of which a final overhead rate for the year or portion of the year (if less than a full year) then ended, shall be determined and applied retroactively to all billings rendered by the Architect to the Owner hereunder during the ended fiscal year period. Such billings thereupon shall be adjusted upward or downward, as the case may be, in accordance with the overhead rate finally determined as aforesaid, and credit memoranda, or additional billing therefor shall be processed promptly. The overhead rate finally determined, as aforementioned, then shall become the tentative overhead rate to be tentatively applied on all billings rendered by the Architect to the Owner hereunder during the next succeeding fiscal year. At the close of each fiscal year thereafter, the process and procedure hereinabove described shall be repeated and appropriate adjustment shall be made in respect of all billings rendered by the Architect to the Owner during the year then ended.

16.5.2   *Items Included in Calculating Overhead Rate*

The indirect expenses of the Architect which comprise his general overhead and which are allocable to this Agreement, include, but are not limited to, the following items to the extent not directly chargeable to particular projects:

Technical Staff Salaries:
   (a) idle or office time
   (b) sick leave
   (c) vacation

† The above form, in substance, may be used in a contract between an architect (engineer) and his client, a foreign government, to secure payment of his fees for services through the Construction Documents Phase. It does not cover subsequent services, since as is frequently the case, payment therefor is made in foreign currency in the locale of the job site.

(d) holiday

(e) bonus in accordance with general office practice

(f) participation in firm net income in accordance with formal employment agreements

Drafting materials and supplies

Blueprints, photostats, etc.

Travel

Photographs, perspectives, models

Normal selling expenses, brochures, etc.

Rent

Amortization of leasehold improvements

Light

General office salaries

Stenographic fees

Stationery, postage, supplies

Telephone and telegraph

Registrations, licenses, dues

Books and periodicals

Insurance, general

Group life insurance (exclusive of insurance on lives of principals)

Legal and accounting

All taxes except income taxes

Depreciation of office furniture, fixtures and equipment

Depreciation of office autos

General expense

16.6 *Certificate of Completion Not a Guarantee.* In order that there should be no possibility of the owner construing the certificate of completion as being a guarantee by the architect that the contractor has fully complied with every condition in the contract, the certificate of completion could be worded as follows:

The undersigned Architect certifies that he has made periodic visits to the job site to familiarize himself generally with the progress and quality of the work and to determine, in general, if the work has proceeded in accordance with the Contract Documents, and on the basis of his observations, while at the site, he has determined, in general, that all work has been completed in accordance with the Contract Documents, including authorized changes thereto.

Nothing contained in this Certificate is intended to alter the responsibilities of the Contractor to complete all the work in accordance with the Contract Documents, including authorized changes thereto, insofar as the undersigned may not have discovered, on the basis of his general observations, that work was not completed in accordance with such documents, including authorized changes thereto.

16.7 *Public Recognition for Professional.* One of the frustrations of the design professions lies in the difficulty of obtaining public recognition for important projects. News releases regarding new buildings frequently inform the public of its size, its cost, even the number of miles of piping it contains, but usually make no mention of the designer. The inclusion of one or both of the following provisions in the owner-architect (engineer) agreement may help to alleviate this unfortunate condition:

Upon completion of all stages of this project, the name of the Architect, his Engineer and his Interior Non-Structural Designer shall be appropriately displayed at the main entrance, foyer or lobby, in stone or on a bronze plaque, as mutually agreed, as follows:

> John Doe, Architect, AIA
> Richard Roe, Engineer, ASCE
> Mary Doe, Interior Designer

In all publicity, news releases or public ceremonies involving design of this structure, the above-listed shall be credited by name and title.

CHAPTER 17

Contract Provisions: Professional Partnerships

The greater the number of partners in a firm, the greater is the necessity for formalizing all the details of their relationship to the firm and to one another. This is particularly important where all partners do not share equally in investments and profits, or in the conduct of the business.

Ordinarily, each stockholder in a corporation may exercise a voice in its management proportionate to the number of shares of stock he holds. However, a corporation is not always permitted to practice architecture or engineering, and therefore it is desirable for such professional firms to establish their own policies regarding the voice each partner has in management and the number of votes required for management action, and to provide for changes occasioned by the admission of a new partner or the withdrawal or death of an existing partner. The following examples illustrate some points which should not be forgotten in forming a partnership.

17.1 Voice in Management

A. Voice of Each Partner Measured by a Number of Votes.

Each partner shall have a voice in the management and conduct of the affairs of the copartnership, which shall be measured by the number of votes (sometimes herein called "Voice in Management Votes") allocated to him under the provisions of this Agreement.

B. Initial Allocation of Number of "Voice in Management Votes."

There is hereby allocated to each partner who is a signatory to this Agreement the number of "Voice in Management Votes" set opposite his name as follows:

Name	Number of "Voice in Management Votes"
A	25.01
B	25.01
C	8.33
D	8.33
E	8.33
F	8.33
G	8.33
H	8.33
	Total 100.00

C. Disposition of "Voice in Management Votes" of a Deceased or Withdrawing Partner

In the event of the death or withdrawal (voluntary or involuntary) of a partner, the number of "Voice in Management Votes" possessed by him shall thereupon be apportioned to and among the surviving or remaining partners (as the case may be), in the proportion that the "Voice in Management Votes" then possessed by each of them respectively shall bear to the aggregate of all of such votes then possessed by the surviving or remaining partners.

D. Allocation of "Voice in Management Votes" to a New Partner and Resultant Decrease in "Voice in Management Votes" of Other Partners.

In the event of the admission of a new partner, there shall be allocated to him such number of "Voice in Management Votes" as shall be prescribed by partners of the firm possessing not less than seventy-five (75%) percent of the total number of "Voice in Management Votes" possessed by all of the partners then entitled to vote thereon; thereupon the number of "Voice in Management Votes" possessed by each of the other partners shall be reduced proportionately and ratably.

E. Number of Votes Required for Management Action

All management action involving, arising out of or relating to the copartnership or its affairs, shall be taken only with the affirmative consent and approval of the partners of the firm possessing not less than fifty-one (51%) percent of the total "Voice in Management Votes" possessed by all of the partners then entitled to vote thereon, except, however, that in the eight (8) special cases mentioned in *F* below, no action shall be taken except by an affirmative vote, in favor of such action, of partners possessing not less than seventy-five (75%) percent of the total "Voice in Management Votes" possessed by all of the partners then entitled to vote thereon. No management action shall be inconsistent with the express terms and conditions of this Agreement.

F. Meeting of Partners.

Any number of partners may meet at any time in the principal office of the copartnership, and at any such meeting(s) may vote upon any action proposed thereat; but such action shall not be effective unless approved by not less than the applicable percentage of "Voice in Management Votes" prescribed in this Agreement. The failure to give prior notice of any such meeting to any partner(s) shall not invalidate such meeting or any action duly taken thereat; except, however, that not less than ten days' written notice delivered personally or sent by mail shall be given by at least one partner to each other partner of any meeting on which it is proposed to vote upon:

1. Change in the name of the copartnership;
2. Increase or decrease in capital contributions of partners;
3. Increase or decrease in cash withdrawals (or salaries) of partners;
4. Change in participation of any one or more of the partners in the profits or losses of the firm;
5. Admission of new partners;
6. Involuntary withdrawal of a partner;
7. Borrowing of money for and in the name of the copartnership;
8. Termination of the copartnership.

G. Vote in Person, in Writing or by Proxy

A person entitled to vote at any meeting of the partners may vote in any manner following:

1. In person; *or*
2. By delivering or causing to be delivered at any such meeting his written approval or disapproval to any proposition intended to be voted upon at said meeting; *or*
3. By proxy.

No partner shall issue a proxy to any person other than a partner of this copartnership firm. A proxy, in order to be valid, must be in writing signed by the partner issuing the same. The death or withdrawal of a partner shall automatically revoke any proxy issued by him, as of the date of his death or his withdrawal, whichever event shall first occur, but nothing contained herein shall be construed to prevent him from limiting the effective period of the proxy in any manner.

17.2   Definition of Income (General).   The fact that the partners, and sometimes associates, participate in the profits of an architectural or engineering firm, necessitates a careful definition of what constitutes profits or net income of the firm, for the purpose of computing payments to participants. Of the following definitions, definition I was prepared for the purpose of computing the share of the firm's net income of an associate who receives a regular salary and also participates in such net income; definition II was prepared for the purpose of computing the associate's share of net profits derived from a specific job which he secures for the firm; and definition III was prepared for the purpose of computing the share of an associate who, in addition to his salary, receives a share of the net income of the practice, as reported by the firm for income tax purposes, subject, however, to certain adjustments mentioned in the definition.

17.2.1   When Associate Receives Salary plus Share in Net Income (Definition I)

I. For the purpose of computing the firm's (employer's) annual net income, in order to determine the amount of the Associate's participation therein, it is understood:

(*a*) The firm's annual net income shall be the excess of fees and miscellaneous charges to its clients, and all other items of income relating to its professional activities as architects, actually received by it, over-and-above operating costs and general administrative expenses actually paid by it as a firm;

(*b*) Operating costs and general administrative expenses shall include all operating costs and expenses; including without limiting the same to:

(1) Fees paid by the firm to consulting architects, consulting engineers and other consultants, other than members, associates or employees of the firm.

(2) Basic weekly salary of $_____ to be paid to the Associate as set forth in this Agreement. It is understood, however, that the amount received by the Associate representing a share of the firm's annual net income, as distinguished from the amount, if any, paid to the Associate, as a share of net profits derived from any specific job which he secures (*Authors' note: See definition II*), shall not be considered as an expense for the foregoing purposes;

(3) Basic weekly salary paid by the firm to any other employee or associate, who may or may not participate in the firm's annual net income. It is understood, however, that the amount received by any such other person representing a share of the firm's annual net income (as distinguished from a sum paid for procuring jobs on behalf of the firm) shall not be considered an expense for the foregoing purposes;

(4) The amount, if any, paid by the firm to the Associate as a share of net profits derived from any specific job which he secures (*Authors' note: See definition II*);

(5) The amount, if any, paid by the firm to anyone else (whether or not regularly employed by the firm) as compensation for procuring any contract(s) on behalf of the firm, pursuant to which contract(s) the firm shall be employed to render architectural services or services as consulting architects, said compensation to be represented by a participation in the profits actually derived by the firm under any such contract(s);

(6) Sums withdrawn by the partners of the firm for actual expenses incurred or payable by them in their business as architects;

(7) All taxes now or hereafter imposed upon the firm as a partnership enterprise only. Such taxes shall be considered an element of expense for the fiscal year in which payment is made, or at the option of the firm, which may be varied at any time, for the fiscal year in which the same shall accrue for tax purposes; and

(8) When and if applicable, accrued depreciation of furniture, fixtures and equipment shall be deducted from the firm's gross annual income in determining its annual net income.

(c) For the purposes of this paragraph, no sum of any nature paid or payable to a partner or partners of the firm (other than for out of pocket expenses) shall be considered as a cost or expense, even though the same be considered as salaries of partners of basic salaries for partners, or in any other category for other purposes, under other provisions of this Agreement.

17.2.2.   When Associate Receives a Share of Net Profits Derived from Specific Job (Definition II)

II. For the purpose of determining the net profits derived by the firm from the full or partial performance of any contract which the Associate shall initiate and also procure on behalf of the firm as set forth in this Agreement, in order to determine the amount of the Associate's participation therein as set forth in this Agreement, it is understood that such net profits shall be the excess of fees actually received by the firm pursuant to any such contract(s) over and above the sum of any and all operating costs and expenses actually paid by the firm in connection with or arising out of the full or partial performance thereof by the firm. Costs and expenses shall include all operating costs and expenses, including without limiting the same to (a) salaries of partners and staff members' salaries directly chargeable to any such contract(s); (b) fees paid to consulting engineers, consulting architects, other consultants and fees of a similar nature; (c) sums paid for blueprints, travel and miscellaneous direct charges; (d) general overhead allocated to such contract(s).

It is further understood that for the purpose only of computing the cost of all contracts for professional services to be rendered by the firm, it will be the practice of the firm to consider basic salaries of $_____ per annum for each of the two partners as elements of cost. Such basic salaries for the partners shall be charged directly to the several projects actually worked on by the partners and to general overhead to the extent of that portion of the partners' time which is not directly chargeable to any particular project, such distributions of cost to be computed by the firm's accountant on the basis of time analyses developed from the partners' diaries. It is understood further that general overhead shall include for the purposes hereof: the partners' salaries not chargeable to a particular job; staff salaries, drawings or other compensation to staff members, such as Christmas or year-end bonuses not directly chargeable to a particular job; rent; light; telephone; research; publicity; general travel not chargeable to a particular job; entertaining, and other "scouting" activities; depreciation; general office salaries; and all other general and administrative expenses whether or not specifically previously mentioned and whether or not the same be similar or dissimilar items of expenses; and all taxes other than the personal income tax obligations of the partners. General overhead, however, shall not include: interest expense; charitable contributions; or payments made to key staff representatives to the extent that the same shall represent a share of the firm's net income, as distinguished from payments representing a share of net profits derived from a particular job secured by the Associate. For the purpose of determining general overhead applicable to a particular contract which relates to architectural services or services as a consulting architect, to be performed by the firm, the firm's accountant shall apportion the general overhead of the firm to all contracts of the firm on which direct staff salaries were expended during each fiscal year of the firm, such apportionment to be made at the close of each fiscal year on the basis of the proportion that direct staff salaries on the particular contract bears to the direct staff salaries on all contracts. The computation and determination of the accountant of the firm of the net profits derived by said firm in connection with any such contract(s) described in this paragraph, and the amount, if any, payable to the Associate as additional compensation under this Agreement shall be in accordance with the foregoing terms and conditions and with accepted accounting principles consistently applied and shall be conclusive and binding upon the Associate as well as the firm.

17.2.3   When Employee Receives Salary plus Share in Net Income as Computed for Tax Purposes (Definition III)

III. It is understood, for the purpose of computing the Employer's annual net income, in order to determine the amount of the Associate's participation therein; the Employer's annual net income shall be the aggregate of its annual net income actually received by it and derived solely from its professional activities as architects as computed by the firm's accountant and reported by it, on a cash receipts and disbursements basis, for Federal Income Tax purposes, subject, however, to the following adjustments:

(1) The amount of the Employer's annual net income so reported shall be increased by the amount(s) paid by the Employer to the Associate or any other person(s), to the extent that the same represents a share of the Employer's annual net income.

(2) The amount of the Employer's annual net income so reported shall be decreased by a salary allowance of $_____ per annum payable to each partner in the Employer's firm (irrespective of whether or not same is actually drawn).

17.3   Limiting Outside Activities of Partners. Contracts are the result of mutual assent, and may include any provisions whatever, so long as they are not illegal, immoral, or detrimental to public policy. It is possible to limit the activities of members of a partnership at the discretion of the parties signing the agreement. The following examples of provisions in a partnership agreement illustrate the point:

a. No partner shall be a candidate for any public office, unless he is authorized to do so by partners of the copartnership, pursuant to "Voice in Management Rules"
or
b. Each partner agrees to devote his entire business time and attention exclusively to the business of the copartnership provided that this paragraph of this contract shall in no manner prevent him from acting as a Director on the Board of any Corporation, and devoting such time in connection with the performance of his duties as director as shall be mutually agreeable to all partners.

17.4   Increasing Membership of Firm
17.4.1   Provision Regarding Contracts Already Undertaken. When a
partnership is formed, it is probable that at least the senior partner or partners will have partially completed projects in progress. In order to permit the partners to complete the contracts already undertaken in their own

names, and to consolidate profits or losses on these contracts with the business of the new partnership, a provision such as the following may be considered. It contemplates an existing partnership of architects A and B, expanding to add new partners C and D, and presumes that the original firm of A and B has work in progress, and that D as an individual also has work in progress:

a. It is understood that there is presently in existence an architectural firm known as A and B, in which A and B are the sole partners. Said firm is referred to in this Agreement as the "existing firm." It is the intention and understanding of the parties to this Agreement to permit the existing firm to complete all contracts heretofore taken in its name, and any future contracts for extra or additional work arising out of or relating to any such contracts. The parties recognize that it may be advisable in the future to permit the existing firm to enter into new contracts, in its name, for new work involving the performance of architectural services. However, such new contracts for new work shall not be entered into in the name of the existing firm, unless approved by the partners of the copartnership, pursuant to and in accordance with "Voice in Management Rules." Pending completion of all contracts hereinbefore referred to, it is the intention of the parties to preserve as a legal entity the existing firm, and to preserve the status of A and B as the sole partners thereof. However, to the limited extent hereinafter referred to in (*b*), the profits or losses actually realized by the existing firm on or after January 1, 1978, from the full or partial performance of certain contracts, referred to in (*b*), shall be consolidated, as therein set forth, with the profits or losses of the copartnership.

b. It is understood that the profits or losses of the copartnership shall be computed by consolidating them with the profits or losses of the existing firm (computed on the cash receipts and disbursements basis of accounting), actually realized by the existing firm on and after January 1, 1978, from the full or partial performance, on and after such date, of:

(1) Any contract for architectural or consulting architectural services, heretofore entered into by the existing firm, except those contracts referred to in Schedule _____ annexed hereto and made a part thereof;

(2) Any new contracts referred to in (*a*) hereafter entered into in the name of the existing firm on or after January 1, 1978. As stated in (*a*), no such contracts shall be entered into in the name of the existing firm, during the continuance of the copartnership, unless approved by partners of the copartnership, pursuant to and in accordance with "Voice in Management Rules."

c. It is understood further that the profits or losses of the copartnership shall be computed by consolidating them with the profits or losses of partner D (computed on the cash receipts and disbursements basis of accounting), actually realized by him on and after January 1, 1978, from the full or partial performance on and after such date of:

(1) Those contracts for architectural or consulting architectural services, heretofore entered into by partner D, which are referred to in Schedule _____, annexed hereto and made a part hereof.

(2) Any contracts for architectural or consulting architectural services, hereafter entered into by partner D. However, no such new contracts for new work shall be entered into in the name of D, unless approved by the partners of the copartnership, pursuant to and in accordance with the "Voice in Management Rules."

Any such contracts entered into in the name of D shall be for the benefit of the copartnership and any contracts for new work entered into in the name of the existing firm, in accordance with Section (*a*), shall likewise be for the benefit of the copartnership. On and after January 1, 1978, all contracts for the performance of architectural or consulting architectural services shall be entered into in the name of the copartnership, except as otherwise authorized under the express provisions of this Section or Section (*a*).

17.4.2 *Gradual Contribution to Capital by New Members of Firm.* When new partners are taken into an existing firm, it is quite likely that these younger men, chosen for their talent and promise, will not be able to contribute their full share to the capital of the partnership. In such case, the older members of the firm may be willing to make loans which will permit the new members to make their full contributions to capital over a period of time. This arrangement may be incorporated into the partnership agreement by a provision similar to the one below. It would not be unreasonable to provide that allocations of profits and losses, and cash withdrawals by partners, should also vary proportionately.

As of the first day of January, 1978, the partners of the copartnership shall provide a total capital for the copartnership in the aggregate sum of $68,000.00, and each partner shall contribute a portion thereof, as set forth in Schedule "A" below. On the first day of January of each succeeding fiscal year thereafter, the individual capital account of each partner shall be progressively increased to the respective amounts set forth in said Schedule "A," until the total capital of the copartnership is $140,000.00, and the individual capital account of each partner is in the sum of $35,000, except as hereinafter provided. As of the first day of January, 1978, A and B, individually, shall each loan to the copartnership the sum of $36,000.00, which shall be progressively reduced by the copartnership, in accordance with Schedule "A" or sooner, as hereinafter provided in this Agreement. Said Schedule "A" is as follows:

SCHEDULE "A"

FISCAL YEAR TO BEGIN JANUARY 1, 1978

Name of partner	Initial contribution to capital account	Percentage of initial contribution	Initial loan to be made by partner
A	$23,800.00	35%	$36,000.00
B	23,800.00	35%	36,000.00
C	10,200.00	15%	0.00
D	10,200.00	15%	0.00
Totals	$68,000.00	100%	$72,000.00

FISCAL YEAR TO BEGIN JANUARY 1, 1979

Name of partner	Contribution to capital account to be increased to	Percentage of contribution	Initial loan to be reduced to
A	$27,192.00	33%	$28,800.00
B	27,192.00	33%	28,800.00
C	14,008.00	17%	0.00
D	14,008.00	17%	0.00
Totals	$82,400.00	100%	$57,600.00

FISCAL YEAR TO BEGIN JANUARY 1, 1980

Name of partner	Contribution capital account to be increased to	Percentage of contribution	Initial loan to be reduced to
A	$30,008.00	31%	$21,600.00
B	30,008.00	31%	21,600.00
C	18,392.00	19%	0.00
D	18,392.00	19%	0.00
Totals	$96,800.00	100%	$43,200.00

FISCAL YEAR TO BEGIN JANUARY 1, 1981

Name of partner	Contribution to capital account to be increased to	Percentage of contribution	Initial loan to be reduced to
A	$ 32,248.00	29%	$14,400.00
B	32,248.00	29%	14,400.00
C	23,352.00	21%	0.00
D	23,352.00	21%	0.00
Totals	$111,200.00	100%	$28,800.00

FISCAL YEAR TO BEGIN JANUARY 1, 1982

Name of partner	Contribution to capital account to be increased to	Percentage of contribution	Initial loan to be reduced to
A	$ 33,912.00	27%	$ 7,200.00
B	33,912.00	27%	7,200.00
C	28,888.00	23%	0.00
D	28,888.00	23%	0.00
Totals	$125,600.00	100%	$14,400.00

FISCAL YEAR TO BEGIN JANUARY 1, 1983, AND THEREAFTER

Name of partner	Contribution to capital account to be increased to	Percentage of contribution	Initial loan to be reduced to
A	$ 35,000.00	25%	0.00
B	35,000.00	25%	0.00
C	35,000.00	25%	0.00
D	35,000.00	25%	0.00
Totals	$140,000.00	100%	0.00

17.5 Decreasing Membership of Firm

17.5.1 Voluntary Withdrawal of Partner. If a member of a partnership should withdraw either voluntarily or involuntarily, or become unable, either physically or mentally, to carry on his duties, or if he should die, disagreements are likely to arise regarding his financial interest in the firm. It is advisable to cover such contingencies most explicitly in the partnership agreement, in order to avoid misunderstandings later, at a time when emotions—displeasure with a partner forced to withdraw or pity for a deceased partner's widow—may color judgment. Some contract provisions worthy of consideration are as follows:

VOLUNTARY WITHDRAWAL OF A PARTNER

Any partner may voluntarily withdraw from the firm at the close of any fiscal year by giving to the other partners not less than sixty days' prior written notice of his intention so to do. A partner who shall withdraw from the copartnership voluntarily shall be entitled to receive only the following:

(1) Within one hundred twenty (120) days after the effective date of his withdrawal, the amount of any loans payable to him by the copartnership at the effective date of his withdrawal, whether then due or thereafter to become due under the terms of this agreement.

(2) In addition, within one hundred twenty (120) days after the effective date of his withdrawal, the book value of his capital account, as at the close of business on the effective date of withdrawal, computed on the cash receipts and disbursements basis of accounting. Such book value shall be a sum equal to:

(a) The aggregate sum of his capital contributions from the date he became a partner to effective date of withdrawal, plus or minus, as the case may be:

(b) His share of the firm's net income or loss (computed on the cash receipts and disbursements basis of accounting) credited or charged to him, as the case may be, for each of the fiscal years during which he shall have been a partner, minus:

(c) The aggregate sum of all withdrawals made by him from the date he became a partner to and including the effective date of his withdrawal.

(d) In computing the book value of a partner's capital account, no consideration shall be given to good will, if any.

The aggregate of the sums paid to the withdrawing partner, in accordance with the foregoing provisions, shall constitute full distribution, liquidation, payment and satisfaction of his entire interest in the copartnership, and of all indebtedness of the copartnership to him.

17.5.2   Involuntary Withdrawal of a Partner

INVOLUNTARY WITHDRAWAL OF A PARTNER

Any partner may be required to withdraw from the copartnership as at the close of any fiscal year, if his withdrawal is directed by an affirmative vote in favor of such compulsory withdrawal by partners of the firm possessing not less than 75% of the total "Voice in Management Votes" then entitled to vote thereon and provided there are at least four partners at the time such vote is taken. It is understood, however, that a partner may not be required to withdraw from the copartnership if there are less than four partners at the time a vote is taken.

A partner whose withdrawal from the copartnership is involuntary shall be entitled to receive only the following:

(1) Within sixty days after the effective date of his withdrawal, the amount of any loans payable to him by the firm at the effective date of his withdrawal, whether then due or thereafter to become due under the terms of this agreement.

(2) In addition, within sixty days after the effective date of his withdrawal, the book value of his capital account, as at the close of business on the effective date of withdrawal, computed on the cash receipts and disbursements basis of accounting. Such book value shall be computed in the same manner as is provided in the case of voluntary withdrawal of a partner. [See Section 17.5.1, page 267.]

(3) In addition, in consideration of past services, and to provide for his share of Unrealized Receivables at the effective date of his involuntary withdrawal, a sum equal to one half of his contract participation percentage of net income of the copartnership for the fiscal year immediately following the effective date of his withdrawal, computed on the cash receipts and disbursements basis of accounting. In case of a partnership loss for the fiscal year subsequent to effective date of withdrawal such loss shall be borne by the remaining partners only. For the purposes of this paragraph, the contract participation percentage referred to above shall be the contract participation percentage of the withdrawing partner, as the same existed during the fiscal year, at the close of which his involuntary withdrawal became effective. The amount payable, pursuant to this paragraph shall be paid within sixty days after the close of the fiscal year which immediately follows the effective date of his withdrawal.

The aggregate of the sums paid to the withdrawing partner in accordance with the foregoing provisions of this section shall constitute full distribution, liquidation, payment and satisfaction of his entire interest in the copartnership, and of all indebtedness of the copartnership to him.

17.5.3   Death of a Partner

DEATH OF A PARTNER

Section A. The death of a partner shall not operate as a termination of the copartnership, but the same shall be carried on by the surviving partners until terminated in accordance with the provisions of this Agreement.

Section B. The estate of a deceased partner shall not be entitled to any voice in the management or conduct of the copartnership, and the number of "Voice in Management Votes" possessed by the deceased partner shall immediately be disposed of and apportioned as hereinbefore provided. [See Section 17.1C, page 259.]

Section C. In case of the death of a partner, his estate shall be entitled to receive only the following:

(1) Within one hundred twenty days after the death of a partner, or within twenty days after the appointment of the legal representative(s) for his estate, whichever event shall last occur, the amount of any loans payable by the copartnership to the deceased partner at the date of his death, whether then due or thereafter to become due, under the provisions of this Agreement.

(2) In addition, within one hundred twenty days after the close of the fiscal year in which the death of the partner shall occur, the book value of his capital account, computed on the cash receipts and disbursements basis of accounting, as at the close of the fiscal year in which the death of the partner shall occur. Such book value shall be a sum equal to:

(*a*) The aggregate sum of his capital contributions from the date he became a partner to the date of the death of the partner, plus or minus, as the case may be:

(*b*) His share of the firm net income or loss (computed on the cash receipts and disbursements basis of accounting), credited or charged to him, as the case may be, from the date he became a partner to the close of the fiscal year in which his death shall occur (as though he had lived and had remained a partner until the close of such fiscal year), minus:

(*c*) The aggregate sum of all withdrawals made from the date he became a partner to and including the date of his death, and minus:

(*d*) The aggregate sum of all withdrawals made by his estate between the date of his death and the close of the fiscal year in which said death shall occur; it being understood, however, that during such intervening period (between the date of death and the close of the fiscal year in which the death shall occur), no withdrawals shall be made by the estate of the deceased partner unless such withdrawals are approved by surviving partners of the copartnership pursuant to and in accordance with "Voice in Management Rules" hereinabove referred to.

(*e*) In the computation of such book value, no consideration shall be given to good will, if any.

(3) In addition, in consideration of past services, and to further provide for the deceased partner's share of Unrealized Receivables, at the date of his death, a sum equal to one half of the deceased partner's contract participation percentage of net income of the copartnership (computed on the cash receipts and disbursements basis of accounting), for the fiscal year immediately following the fiscal year in which his death shall occur. In case of a partnership loss for the fiscal year which immediately follows the fiscal year in which the death of a partner shall occur, said loss shall be borne only by the surviving partners. For the purpose of this paragraph, the contract participation percentage referred to above, shall be the contract participation percentage of the deceased partner as the same existed on the date of his death. The amount payable pursuant to this paragraph shall be paid within sixty days after the close of the fiscal year which immediately follows the fiscal year in which the death of a partner shall occur.

The aggregate of the sums paid to the estate of the deceased partner in accordance with the foregoing provisions of this Section, shall constitute full distribution, liquidation, payment and satisfaction of the entire interest of the deceased partner (and his estate) in the copartnership and of all indebtedness of the copartnership to him and his estate.

17.5.4   *Disability of a Partner*

DISABILITY OF A PARTNER

Each partner shall devote his full time and attention to the business of the copartnership. If a partner shall become mentally or physically disabled, and as a result thereof be unable to perform substantially his duties and services as a partner in the copartnership, for a consecutive period not exceeding six months, he shall, nevertheless, be entitled to his full share of the net income of the copartnership during the continuance of such disability, and his full allowable drawings on account thereof. Should such disability continue for a period in excess of six consecutive months, the disabled partner shall be entitled to receive thereafter, during the continuance of such disability, for a further period not in excess of twelve additional months, one half of his pro rata share of the net income of the copartnership, and one half of his then allowable drawings on account thereof. Should such disability continue for more than a total period of eighteen consecutive months from the date of its inception, the disabled partner shall not be entitled to receive after the expiration of said eighteen consecutive months, any share of the net income of the copartnership, nor any sum as a drawing, unless and until he shall be able to substantially perform his duties and services as a partner; and if he is unable to do so within a period of thirty-six months from the date of the inception of his disability, he shall, at the expiration of said thirty-six months, be deemed to have withdrawn from the copartnership. In the latter event, the disabled partner shall be entitled to receive from the copartnership, the same amount he would have received under this Agreement, had he voluntarily withdrawn from the copartnership at the expiration of thirty-six months, except, however, that in computing such amount, his share of net income of the copartnership for the first eighteen months of his disability shall be limited to the extent hereinabove specified; and except further, that he shall not receive any share of the net income of the copartnership for the last eighteen months of his disability, as hereinabove provided. If a partner, following the inception of his disability shall resume his work and duties, but within sixty days thereafter shall become disabled again, then in determining the consecutive period for which his disability endured, the temporary period of resumption shall be disregarded as though he had not resumed his work and duties. It is understood, however, that for the temporary period of resumption, the disabled partner shall receive his full share of the net income of the copartnership. Whenever it shall be necessary to compute, under the above provisions, the full or lesser share of the net income of the copartnership of a disabled partner, for a period of time which is less than a fiscal year, such computation shall be made by the accountant regularly employed by the copartnership. Said accountant, after determining the net income of the copartnership for each fiscal year in which the disability shall continue, in whole or in part, as the case may be, shall apportion the net income of the copartnership thus determined to the several periods of time within such fiscal year that such disability continued, or did not continue, by the use and application of any mathematical formula that he deems appropriate for such purposes. All questions in dispute that may arise under this article shall be settled in accordance with the Construction Industry Rules of the American Arbitration Association, except, however, that there shall be three arbitrators, two of whom shall be architects registered in the State of _____ and one of whom shall be a Certified Public Accountant.

17.5.5 *Suspension of a Partner's Right to Practice*

SUSPENSION OF RIGHT TO PRACTICE

If the right of any partner to practice architecture (engineering) is suspended or revoked, that partner shall be deemed to have withdrawn involuntarily from the partnership as of the date of such suspension or revocation. The value of that partner's interest in the partnership shall be paid to him at the times, and shall be computed in the manner, set forth above for such payment in the event of involuntary withdrawal of a partner. [See Section 17.5.2 page 268.]

CHAPTER 18

Contract Provisions: Joint Ventures, Consultants, and Employment Agreements

A joint venture is a temporary partnership, entered into by professional men usually for the duration of one specific project. The parties to a joint venture may be architects, or engineers, or architects and engineers. Such an association may be desirable because the several parties have varied talents and experience to contribute to the project, in which case specific duties may be expressly allocated to each of the joint venturers by the terms of their agreement with each other. Thus, an architect and an engineer may associate, one to provide architectural services and the other to provide engineering services; or two architects may associate, one to provide the basic design and the other to furnish contract documents and construction supervision.

The agreement between the joint venturers should of course be in writing, and may be more or less extensive, depending upon the relative size and complexity of the project to be done. There follow two sample agreements, one for a large project for the government and the second for a small project. Although a short form, such as example II, may be used for simple projects, it is obvious that many of the conditions concerning the relationships of the parties remain the same whether the project be large or small. Therefore, it is advised that the reader engage experienced legal counsel in the preparation of any joint venture agreement—an admonition applicable to any legal document.

18.1   *Joint Venture Agreements*
18.1.1   *Example I: For a Large Project*

AGREEMENT made and entered into this _____ day of January, 19 _____ between A, a partnership consisting of A1 and A2, of (address), Civil Engineers, and B, a partnership consisting of B1 and B2, of (address), Architects.

WITNESSETH

1. That said parties hereto agree to become and remain associated retroactively from the date the parties have signed a certain Letter of Intent with the United States of America, dated _____, as Joint Venturers, until completion of the professional services therein mentioned, and to be required under the Contract number _____ to be entered into in accordance with said Letter of Intent between the United States of America, acting through _____, as one party, and the parties to this agreement, as the other party.

2. The Joint Venture hereby created shall be known as_____.

3. The said Joint Venture shall be for the purpose only of performing all the Engineering and Architectural services required under the said Letter of Intent and the said Contract to be made and entered into by the parties with the United States of America, through _____, as aforesaid. After said Contract number _____ is executed, this agreement shall apply to all changes and amendments to said contract and pending the execution of said contract, this agreement shall apply to all changes and amendments to said Letter of Intent.

4. Each party to this agreement shall make an initial contribution of $_____ to the capital of the Joint Venture. Thereafter, whenever necessary in the opinion of both parties to this agreement, further contributions to the capital of the Joint Venture shall be made, one-half by each party. All contributions to the capital of the Joint Venture made by either party hereto, and any and all compensation received from the United States of America by the parties hereto in connection with the project identified in said Letter of Intent or the Contract to be executed pursuant thereto, as the same may be modified or amended, or any other funds or monies whatsoever received from any source in connection with or arising out of this Joint Venture shall be deposited in a Bank or Trust Company in the City of _____ selected by the parties jointly.

5. Workmen's Compensation or other necessary insurance covering employees working exclusively for the Joint Venture shall be provided and paid for by the Joint Venture. However, it shall be the obligation of each party of this agreement to provide Workmen's Compensation or other insurance covering its own employees notwithstanding that such employees may perform services as employees of such party hereto in connection with the project described in said Letter of Intent and notwithstanding the further fact that such party shall be reimbursed by the Joint Venture for the premiums paid for said insurance in accordance with the accountants' memorandum hereinafter referred to.

6. All expenses of every kind and nature (as set forth in a memorandum prepared by _____, accountants for the Joint Venture, and approved by the parties) incurred by any of the parties hereto in the performance of said Letter of Intent, the Contract to be executed pursuant thereto or any change or amendment thereof, or incurred by the Joint Venture as such, excluding, however, in any event, compensation for time or services of any of the principals named above as members of any of the partnerships which are parties to this agreement, shall be borne and defrayed by the Joint Venture in the manner set forth in said memorandum.

Accounting procedure governing the treatment of capital contributions, collection of fees from the United States of America, payment and recording of costs and expenses of the Joint Venture and all other items of accounting procedure relating to this Joint Venture shall be in accordance with the aforesaid memorandum prepared by said accountants.

7. The Contract to be entered into with the Government in accordance with said Letter of Intent will provide for the payment of a fixed fee and reimbursement to the Joint Venture of all costs incurred. The costs incurred when received from the Government are to be distributed and paid over to the parties to this agreement in accordance with the memorandum of said accountants.

8. *A.* Whenever the term "home office" is used in this Article 8, it shall mean in the case of A__ (address), and in the case of B__ (address), each said home office to be distinguished from the Joint Venture office at (address).

B. Whenever the term "compensation" is used in this Article 8, such term shall mean salaries and wages at the rates mutually agreed upon by the parties hereto exclusive of overtime premium and exclusive of all bonuses and participation in net income.

C. Whenever the term "overtime premium" is used in this Article 8, such term shall mean compensation paid for overtime in excess of regular rate as distinguished from compensation paid for overtime at regular rate.

D. Each party hereto shall receive that proportion of the net profit of the Joint Venture as its own "home office" direct technical staff payroll, paid or incurred by it in connection with the project, shall bear to the aggregate sum of the "home office" direct technical staff payrolls paid or incurred in connection with the project by both parties hereto, subject to the special adjustments hereinafter mentioned in this Article.

I. For the purpose of computing the division of the net profit of the Joint Venture only, A's own "home office" direct technical staff payroll paid or incurred in connection with the project shall be the sum of the following four parts:

a. Compensation for the time, directly chargeable to the project of those partners and associates of the firm of A enumerated in subsection *E* of this Article, at the rate of $_____ per hour, up to $_____ per day;

b. Compensation paid to the technical staff of the firm of A employed at its "home office," exclusive of partners and associates, for work performed on the project;

c. Compensation paid by the Joint Venture office to those members of its technical staff who were, prior to __(date)__, regular employees or members of the A organization.

d. Compensation actually reimbursed to those subcontractor engineers or other consultants assigned to A on the project with the written consent of both parties hereto.

II. For the purpose of computing the division of the net profit of the Joint Venture only, B's own "home office" direct technical staff payroll paid or incurred in connection with the project shall be the sum of the following four parts:

a. Compensation for the time, directly chargeable to the project, of those partners and associates of the firm of B enumerated in subsection *E* of this Article, at the rate of $_____ per hour, up to $_____ per day.

b. Compensation paid to the technical staff of the firm of B employed at its "home office," exclusive of partners and associates, for work performed on the project;

c. Compensation paid by the Joint Venture office to those members of its technical staff who were, prior to ___(date)___, regular employees or members of the B organization;

d. Compensation actually reimbursed to those subcontractor engineers or other consultants assigned to B on the project with the written consent of both parties hereto.

E. The partners and associates of each of the parties hereto whose time directly chargeable to the project shall enter into the computation of home office direct technical staff payroll at the rate of $_____ per hour are:
In the case of A:

In the case of B:

F. The parties hereto agree that should a disparity exist between the prevailing salary and wage rates experienced in the City of _____ as compared with those experienced in the City of _____ during the performance of the project, then and in such event the computation of the division of the net profit of the Joint Venture made under the foregoing provisions of this Article 8 shall be modified to equalize such disparity in the manner and to the extent mutually agreed upon in writing by _____ and _____, in behalf of the parties hereto. In the event that Messrs. _____ and _____ should be unable to agree upon the appropriate adjustment of such disparity, the question shall then be referred to arbitration in accordance with paragraph 18 hereof.

G. The net losses of the Joint Venture, if any, shall be borne by the parties hereto in the proportions above provided in this Article for the division of profits.

9. The parties hereto acknowledge that up to the date of the signing of this agreement the following subcontractors have been assigned as follows:
To A there have been assigned:

To B there have been assigned:

10. All questions of major policy not otherwise provided for in this agreement shall be determined by mutual agreement of the Joint Venturers. To this end, each of the parties hereto shall designate a representative who shall have authority to establish policies; also an alternate to act in the absence of such designated represent-

ative. Either party may substitute a new representative at any time. Written notice of any designation shall be given by one party to the other party to this agreement.

11. The professional services to be performed pursuant to the Letter of Intent aforementioned and the Contract to be entered into in accordance therewith, or any change or modification thereof, shall be divided so that all inside work including all buildings shall be handled by B, and all outside work by A, unless the parties shall hereafter otherwise agree.

12. All submissions of work under the Contract with the Government will be made upon joint agreement of the parties hereto to represent the collective opinion of the Joint Venturers, but in case of a disagreement as to the relative merits of any of the work to be submitted, the final decision shall rest with the party who shall be required to perform such work as provided for above.

13. Subject to the approval of the Contracting Officer referred to in the Contract to be executed with the Government aforesaid, a subcontract will be entered into with C, Consulting Engineers, for structural engineering of buildings, and with D for mechanical engineering of buildings. No other Engineers or other experts will be retained except with the consent of both parties hereto. All Engineers and other experts employed shall be of recognized reputation and ability in their respective fields of endeavor and any Contract engaging any Engineer or other expert shall be subject to the applicable restrictions and conditions contained in the Prime Contract between the parties hereto and the United States of America.

14. Each party shall keep accurate records of all times and expenses for which reimbursement is sought under the terms of this agreement.

15. The death or disability of any of the partners of either of the parties hereto before the completion of the program shall not dissolve the Joint Venture or affect the rights and duties of the surviving continuing partners of the deceased or disabled partner of partners or their legal representatives.

16. This agreement shall be subject in all respects to the provisions of the aforesaid Contract to be entered into with the Government, except as otherwise expressly set forth herein.

17. Neither party to this agreement shall have the right, power or authority to transfer, pledge or hypothecate all or any part of its or his interest in the said "Government Contract" or in this agreement or any amounts due or to grow due thereon, except by Last Will and Testament or by operation of law, and any such unauthorized transfer, pledge or hypothecation will be void and of no force or effect.

18. The parties hereto agree that all questions or disputes arising between them, respecting any matter pertaining to this agreement, or pertaining to the work, and not covered by this agreement shall be referred to a Board of Arbitrators, consisting of the then President of the _____ Chapter of the American Society of Civil Engineers and the President of the _____ Chapter of the American Institute of Architects and a third party to be selected and agreed upon by the aforesaid Presidents. The decision of a majority of this Board shall be binding and conclusive upon all parties hereto, without exception or appeal; and all right or rights or any action at law or in equity under and by virtue of this agreement, and all matters connected with it, are hereby expressly waived.

IN WITNESS WHEREOF, we, the parties hereto, for ourselves, our heirs, executors, administrators, successors or assigns, hereto have set our hands and seals the day and year first above mentioned.

18.1.2   *Example II: For a Simple Project*

AGREEMENT made this _____ day of September, 19____, as of the _____ day of June, 19____, by and between the firm of A (architects) having its principal place of business at (address) and B (Mechanical Engineer), having his principal place of business at (address)

WITNESSETH

WHEREAS, the parties hereto under date of June _____, 19____, entered into a contract with (Owner), which provides among other things for the performance by them of architectural and engineering services in connection with the proposed design and construction of _____ (the project), for a lump sum of $_____, which includes an allowance of a lump sum of $_____ for structural engineering services to be performed in connection with such project, and

WHEREAS, the parties hereto have agreed and do hereby agree that they shall perform said contract with (Owner) as joint venturers upon the terms and conditions hereinafter set forth,

NOW, THEREFORE, the parties hereto agree as follows:

I. Each of the parties hereto shall be reimbursed for his or its Technical Personnel Salaries.

II. A. Technical Personnel salaries are the sums paid or incurred by a party to this Agreement to his or its Technical Personnel for time (including overtime, if any) actually spent on this project in conferring, inspecting, designing, drafting, writing specifications, checking shop drawings and supervising construction.

B. Technical Personnel salaries shall include also the value of time actually spent on this project, in conferring, inspecting, designing, drafting, writing specifications, checking shop drawings and supervising construction by the following principals:

In the case of A:

In the case of B:

The value of time spent by the principals of A or B is fixed at the rate of $_____ per hour for each hour of time, described above, spent by each of said individuals. There shall be no increase in the aforesaid rates by reason of any overtime on the part of any of the said principals.

III. Each of the parties hereto shall be reimbursed for his or its home office overhead by the payment to him or it of a sum equal to 50% of the total amount calculated and to be paid to him or it pursuant to paragraphs "I" and "II" (A and B) of this Agreement.

IV. From the total lump sum fee to be paid by (Owner) pursuant to the terms of the aforementioned contract, there shall first be deducted:

(A) All sums paid or to be paid to structural engineers.

(B) The items above described in paragraph "I," "II" (A and B) and "III" of this Agreement.

(C) Any other necessary and reasonable costs incurred by the joint venture with the mutual consent of the parties hereto. After making said deductions, the balance remaining, if any, shall constitute the profit of the joint venture which shall be divided between the parties equally.

If the costs and expenses payable by the joint venture are in excess of the lump sum fee received from (Owner), the difference shall constitute a loss of the joint venture and such loss shall be borne by the parties hereto equally.

V. All architectural services shall be performed by A. All mechanical and electrical engineering services shall be performed by B. All structural engineering services shall be performed by C.

VI. All sums received from (Owner) pursuant to the terms of the aforementioned contract shall be deposited in the bank account of A. Rates of compensation paid to employees shall be approved mutually by the parties hereto.

VII. B shall supply A with such architectural employees of B as A may require for the performance of the architectural services under the aforementioned contract with (Owner). Such employees shall continue to remain in the employ of B and B shall be reimbursed by the joint venture for the Technical Personnel salaries paid by him to such employees for any services they may render while working under the supervision of A at A's office, plus a sum equal to 50% of such salaries to cover B's overhead; but no reimbursement for overhead shall be made to B in the case of any employee supplied by him to A, if such employee was not in B's employ on (date).

VIII. Each party hereto shall be reimbursed by the joint venture for his or its Technical Personnel salaries described in paragraphs "I" and "II" (A and B) each month. Reimbursement for overhead, however, shall be made at the end of 19____ and every three months thereafter. The parties hereto acknowledge that the joint venture has received from (Owner) under the terms of aforementioned contract made with said (Owner), the sum of $____ which sum the joint venture has distributed as follows:

To A---$____

To B---$____

The said respective amounts distributed to the parties hereto shall constitute a payment on account to each of them of any sums now or hereafter reimbursable to them respectively under this Agreement. Each party shall on or before October ____, furnish to the other party, a statement of all costs paid or incurred by him up to and including September ____, 19____, for which he or it shall claim reimbursement hereunder and on or before the 15th day of each month thereafter shall furnish to the other party a statement of all costs paid or incurred by him or it up to the last day of the month next preceding the furnishing of such statement for which he or it shall claim reimbursement hereunder.

IX. Each party to this Agreement shall keep complete and accurate records of all time and expenses for which reimbursement is sought by him or it and such records shall be subject to examination and audit at all times by an accountant or other representative engaged by the other party for such purpose.

X. All submissions of work shall be made upon joint agreement of the parties hereto to represent their collective opinion but in case of a disagreement as to the relative merits of any of the work to be submitted, the final decision shall rest with the party who shall be required to perform such work.

XI. Any controversy or claim arising out of or relating to this Agreement or a breach thereof, shall be settled by arbitration in the City of _____, in accordance with the Construction Industry Rules of the American Arbitration Association, except, however, that in any such arbitration, there shall be three Arbitrators, as follows: (1) an Architect: (2) an Engineer; and (3) a Certified Public Accountant.

IN WITNESS WHEREOF, the parties hereto have hereunto executed this Agreement the _____ day of September, 19____, as of the _____ day of June, 19____.

18.2   Architect-Consultant Agreement. It is well to be as specific as possible in establishing the rights and duties of the architect and his consulting engineer in the architect-engineer contract agreement. The following provisions should be considered:

1. In the performance of this subcontract, the Structural [or other] Engineer binds itself to the Architect and to the Owner to comply fully with all the undertakings and obligations, excepting such as do not apply to the Structural (or other) Engineer's services, as are set forth in the principal contract, a copy thereof having been furnished the Structural [or other] Engineer, which is hereby adopted and made a part of this subcontract. Additional copies of the principal contract are on file in the office of _____.

2. It being the intent and purpose of the parties hereto, except as herein otherwise provided, to place the Architect in the same position in regard to this subcontract that the Owner occupies in the principal contract, and to place the Structural [or other] Engineer in the same position in regard to this subcontract that the Architect occupies in said principal contract insofar as same relates to performance of the structural [or other] engineering services, it is expressly stipulated and agreed that the Architect has, and reserves to itself, and the Structural [or other] Engineer grants to said Architect the same rights and powers, in every detail and respect and in the same language and intent that the Owner reserves to itself in the said principal contract insofar as same relates to performance of structural [or other] engineering services; and the Structural [or other] Engineer assumes all the obligations placed upon the Architect by said principal contract insofar as same relates to performance of structural [or other] engineering services and accepts and binds itself faithfully and fully to observe toward the Architect and the Owner each and every term and provision thereof, so as to enable the Architect to fulfill its every obligation to the Owner according to the intent and provisions of said principal contract.

18.2.1   Consultant to Carry Valuable Papers Insurance. If the drawings or specifications prepared by a consulting engineer should be lost or destroyed by fire, the ensuing delay in the progress of the work could be costly to all concerned. It would be wise for the architect to include in the architect-engineer agreement a requirement that his consultants carry valuable papers insurance, namely:

The mechanical [structural, or other] engineer shall obtain valuable papers insurance for the contract documents prepared by him under this agreement in an amount and with such insurance companies as may be approved by the architect.

18.2.2 *Indemnification—Architect by Engineer or Engineer by Architect.*
In many instances an architect is made a party defendant in a lawsuit by reason of his contracting with the owner, where, in fact, the alleged error or omission is attributable to the services of his consulting engineer. The following form is intended to hold the architect harmless in such event. Such a form could be used to hold harmless the engineer were the situation to be reversed.

The Engineer agrees to indemnify and hold the Architect and its partners, employees and agents free and harmless from and against any and all losses, penalties, damages, settlements, costs, charges, professional fees, deductible expenses payable to any insurance company or any other expenses or liabilities of every kind and nature arising out of, or relating to, any and all claims, liens, demands, obligations, actions, proceedings or causes of action of every kind and nature in connection with, or arising directly or indirectly out of, errors and/or omissions and/or negligent acts by the Engineer (including its employees and agents) in the performance of this agreement. Without limiting the generality of the foregoing, any and all such claims, etc., relating to personal injury, death, damage to property, or any actual or alleged violation of any applicable statute, ordinance, administrative order, rule or regulation or decree of any court, in connection with (or arising directly or indirectly out of) errors and/or omissions and/or negligent acts by the consulting engineer, as aforesaid, shall be included in the indemnity hereunder. The consulting engineer further agrees to investigate, handle, respond to, provide defense for and defend any such claims, etc., at his sole expense even if they (claims, etc.) are groundless, false or fraudulent. Notwithstanding the foregoing, the Engineer shall not be liable to indemnify the Architect for damage arising out of bodily injury to persons or damage to property caused by or resulting from the sole negligence of the Architect, its partners, agents or employees.

18.3 *Employment Agreement for Work outside the United States.* Terms
and conditions of employment, when a technical employee is hired for work outside the United States, must be more detailed and specific than is necessary for employment in a home office, because it is impossible to resolve misunderstandings by face-to-face conferences. The following may serve as a checklist of some of the more important items to be included in such an employment agreement.

TERM OF AGREEMENT

The Employee's services will continue during such period as they may be required in connection with the Contract with the Owner mentioned above (herein called the

Contract), commencing on or about _____, and ending on or about _____. By mutual written agreement between the Contractor (Architect) and the Employee, this Employment Agreement may be extended as conditions may require. This Employment Agreement shall terminate in any case if the Contract is terminated by the Owner, in which event the Employee will be notified by telegram and shall go on travel status within 24 hours after receipt of the telegram. This Agreement may also be terminated upon the Contractor giving the Employee not less than seven days' written notice of termination, even though the Contract has not been terminated providing that the Employee works diligently during this termination period and has not been terminated for cause. In the event of any such termination, Employee shall return immediately to New York City, N.Y. Upon such termination Contractor's liability to Employee shall be limited to that portion of Employee's salary which has accrued to date of Employee's return to New York City, N.Y., U.S.A. (or to the date of termination if Employee is already in New York City, N.Y.) then remaining unpaid plus actual expenses incurred by Employee as provided in and limited by this agreement. If Employee quits or if his services are terminated for cause prior to the completion of the performance of this Agreement, Contractor's obligation to Employee will cease on the date of such quitting or termination for cause and Employee shall be liable for the costs and other expenses of his return to New York City, N.Y., U.S.A.

Termination for cause shall include but not be limited to the following: bad temper; the immoderate use of alcoholic drinks; the use of narcotics; contraction or recurrence of venereal disease; carelessness; insubordination; incompetence; failure to travel as scheduled by contractor; failure or refusal to work; setting of a maximum limit on amount of work to be done by Employee or any other employee; any misrepresentation made or concealment of material fact for the purpose of securing this Agreement or in connection with any medical examination relating to it; subversive activity; or any other act of misconduct.

SALARY, OVERTIME AND HOLIDAY PAYMENTS

(a) Employee will be paid at the following straight time rates computed on the basis of the total number of hours devoted to work under this Agreement and in accordance with the policy set forth below.

Foreign   *Stateside*
Rates per Hour   *Rates per Hour*

(b) Employee is guaranteed 54 hours actual work per week while he is in [foreign country] and ready, willing and able to work, and not in travel status.

(c) Hours worked mean:

1. Time actually spent at work in [foreign country].

2. Time spent travelling between job sites or between _____, not exceeding 10 hours in any one day.

For example:

If an employee on any one day had 6 hours of actual work time and 12 hours of actual travel time, he would be paid for 6 hours of work time and 10 hours of travel time, making a total of 16 hours.

If an employee on any one day had 12 hours of actual work time and 6 hours of actual travel time he would be paid for a total of 18 hours.

(d) Employee shall work more than 54 hours per week only if authorized by the Contractor's Chief Coordinator. All work required by the Coordinator and performed in excess of 40 hours per week will be paid for at 1½ times the hourly foreign wage rate above provided. However, Employee shall not work more than 70 hours per week except in an emergency, when by mutual agreement he may work more than 70 hours per week. Saturday, Sunday and Holidays as such, shall not be considered as overtime days. Sunday through Saturday shall constitute the scheduled work week and seven consecutive days at the job sites. Premium time shall not be paid personnel while in travel status or stand-by status.

(e) When travelling from point of hire to destination in [foreign country] and return to point of hire, Employee shall be considered in travel status and shall be paid on the basis of 8 hours per each 24 hour period with a maximum of 40 hours for each continuous 7 day period at the [foreign country] rates. Travel status is defined as one of the following:

1. When travelling from point of hire to [points in foreign country] and return from these locations to point of hire, including all necessary stop-offs for training or inspections of the work at mock up sites.

2. When travelling from [points in foreign country] to New York City or other locations in the United States on direct orders.

3. Travel status starts from time of leaving point of hire to reaching destination.

(f) Time for stand-by and for work performed by Employee in the United States shall be at stateside rates, except when personnel is detached from foreign locations and sent to New York City or other locations in the United States on direct orders; then he shall be paid at foreign rates for the first two weeks, but shall not be paid overtime while in the United States, except when approved in writing. If his stay in the United States exceeds two weeks, the stateside rates shall apply for the entire period. Stand-by status is defined as follows:

1. When an employee is returned from the foreign job sites to the United States during the winter period when it is impractical or inadvisable to work at the foreign job sites, he shall be employed by the Contractor on work in his own office.

2. If, after taking any earned vacation time and any additional vacation time at his own expense, it is impossible to employ him usefully in the above-mentioned capacity he may then be placed on stand-by status to keep him available for future work.

(g) Salary shall be payable by check to such bank and/or individual as the Employee shall designate in writing.

(h) Salary payments shall be subject to deductions required by law of the United States, [foreign country], or deductions authorized by Employee and approved by Contractor.

(i) Employee shall obtain verification of the work hours he has performed.

(j) Employee must take his own cash to site for commissary purchases and be responsible for same.

ALLOWANCES

In addition to his salary, Employee will be provided with the following:

1. Travelling expenses to, from, and between work sites.
2. Reasonable living expenses while in travel status not to exceed $_____ per day within the United States and $_____ per day in [foreign country] unless higher rates are authorized in writing.
3. Transportation of clothing and personal property to a maximum of _____pounds to, from, and between work sites.
4. Transportation facilities between foreign work sites if Employee is required to proceed to said sites; such transportation facilities to be furnished by Contractor.

JOB SITE FACILITIES

(*a*) Board, lodging, laundry, social services and such hospitalization and medical services as in the opinion of the Contractor may be desirable to keep the Employee in condition to render proper services, shall be furnished by Contractor at the job sites. However, in city locations, the Employee shall obtain such facilities and shall be reimbursed for the cost thereof not to exceed $_____ per day unless authorized.

(*b*) Contractor will maintain and operate a commissary at job site where Employees can make purchases on a cash basis.

(*c*) Employee agrees that no claim shall arise against the Contractor for the adequacy of job site facilities furnished hereunder.

LEAVE PRIVILEGES

Employees will be allowed 10 working days paid sick leave per year (if needed) which will accrue at the rate of one day paid sick leave for each five and two-tenths weeks of employment. Sick leave will not be cumulative. Employees will be granted one day paid vacation for each five and two-tenths weeks of employment up to 10 working days per year stateside rate pay. Sick leave which occurs in [foreign country] shall be paid for at foreign rates and sick leave which occurs in the United States will be paid for at stateside rates. If Employee is terminated by the Contractor for cause prior to the completion of performance of the Employment Agreement, or if he quits, or resigns, earned vacation will be forfeited. If however, the Employee's contract is extended so that he works continuously for more than one year, and is terminated for cause in the period succeeding one year's employment, then he shall be entitled to the vacation pay for the year which he has completed under his agreement. If he is terminated because the Contractor's services are terminated, or because the Contractor has given the Employee seven days' notice as required in this Employment Agreement, then his accrued vacation time shall be paid to him as severance pay.

COMPENSATION FOR DISABILITY OR DEATH DUE TO ACCIDENT

(*a*) Compensation insurance benefits shall be paid as provided . . . as the sole remedy for any injury or illness arising out of and in the course of employment under this Agreement.

(b) Any salary payment made to the Employee for the period during which he is entitled to Workmen's Compensation benefits by reason of temporary total, permanent total, or temporary partial disability shall be deemed an advance payment of compensation insurance benefits due the Employee, but only to the extent of such benefits due for the period of disability during which salary is paid.

(c) Should the health of the Employee become so impaired by reason of injuries or illness arising out of and in the course of employment under this Agreement, through no fault of the Employee, as to justify the Contractor, in its opinion and based upon such medical examination as the Contractor may demand, to return the Employee to the point of hire, the Employee will then be returned to such point of hire at the Contractor's expense as herein provided. In such event travel pay and subsistence provisions hereof shall remain applicable until the Employee is returned to the point of hire, at which time all obligations of the Contractor hereunder (except with respect to the payment of compensation insurance if applicable) shall cease. Should the Employee's condition be such as to require hospitalization en route from the site of work to the point of hire, the Contractor will suspend travel pay and subsistence allowance which would accrue during the period of hospitalization.

MEDICAL EXAMINATION AND PERMITS

(a) Before departure from New York City, N.Y., the Employee shall have submitted to such physical examinations and vaccinations and inoculations as required by the Contractor. It is expressly understood that all statements made by the Employee in connection with such examinations shall be deemed material to and a part of this Agreement and any misrepresentation by the Employee in such statements shall relieve the Contractor from any obligations under this Agreement. If the Employee does not, prior to departure from New York City, N.Y., undergo at his own expense such dental or medical treatment as may have been prescribed upon any physical examination provided for herein as a condition of acceptance for employment, this Employment Agreement may be terminated for cause.

(b) The Employee hereby represents and warrants that he is in good health and is fully qualified in training, experience and physical condition to perform work in the classification above at the job sites.

(c) The Employee shall secure all necessary permits and papers required for his departure from and re-entry into the United States.

COMPLIANCE WITH LAWS AND WORKING CONDITIONS

Employee shall comply with all laws, ordinances and regulations both Civil and Military, applicable at the work sites and the vicinity thereof. The Employee shall work and live in harmony with his co-workers and at all times shall conduct himself in an orderly manner, with due regard to the comfort and convenience of his co-workers and shall conform to reasonable standards of personal cleanliness. Employee shall loyally follow directions of assigned superior(s) in matters relating to work.

CLAIMS

The Employee agrees that he will, within 60 days after any claim (other than a claim for compensation insurance) arising out of or in connection with the employment provided for herein, give written notice to the Contractor of such claim, setting forth in detail the facts relating thereto and the basis for such claim; and that he will not institute any suit or action against the Contractor in any court or tribunal in any jurisdiction based on any such claim prior to six months after the filing of the written notice of claim hereinabove provided for, or later than two years after such filing. Any action or suit on any such claim shall not include any item or matter not specifically mentioned in the proof of claim above provided. It is agreed that in such action or suit, proof by the Employee of his compliance with the provisions of this section shall be a condition precedent to any recovery under this Agreement.

DISCLOSURE OF INFORMATION

The Employee is charged with knowledge that disclosure of any secret, confidential or restricted information, to any person not entitled to receive it, or his failure to safeguard any such information, that may come within his knowledge, may subject him to criminal liability under the Federal Espionage Act, and shall be cause for the discharge of the Employee. The Employee shall not disclose any information pertaining to the nature of the work being performed by the Contractor or of the location of such work. Employee agrees not to use camera of any kind at any job site, except by special permission.

TOOLS AND PERSONAL PROPERTY

(a) The Employee shall provide at his own expense all clothing and personal equipment required to enable him to perform work at the job sites. Such clothing and personal equipment shall at a minimum be adequate to allow for outdoor working in the northern states of the U.S.A. in midwinter. Unless authorized in writing by the Contractor, the Employee shall not take with him clothing or other personal property weighing more than _____ pounds and of a value in excess of $_____. Claims for losses will not be considered unless an inventory of such clothing and other personal property has been prepared by the Employee and submitted to the Contractor before the Employee departs from New York City, N.Y., which inventory shall contain an itemized evaluation of the articles listed thereon.

(b) The Contractor is not the insurer of the Employee's personal effects, and will not be responsible or liable for any thefts thereof. Claims for losses while in transit, or as a result of fire, storm or other catastrophe will be determined in the light of the Contractor's liability to the Employee, in accordance with accepted legal principles and subject to the approval of the Contractor. Regardless of the quantity and value of the clothing or other personal property that the Employee takes with him, and regardless of authorization for additional clothing and personal property as provided in (a) above, and regardless of the liability of the Contractor, the Contractor shall in no event reimburse the Employee for loss or damage to clothing and other personal property in an amount exceeding $_____.

(c) The Employee shall be responsible for all tools and other property of the Contractor furnished to him for use in the employment hereunder, and shall satisfactorily account for all such property prior to his departure from the job site, and shall be liable for cost of any such tools and other property which he fails to return or otherwise satisfactorily account for.

METHOD OF PAYMENT OF WAGES

By execution of an appropriate form furnished by the Contractor, the Employee shall designate an individual and/or a bank to whom his earnings for travel to and labor performed at the job site shall be paid. The Employee may provide that all such earnings be paid to an individual or to a bank, or he may provide that part of such earnings be paid to an individual and part be paid to a bank. It is understood, however, that the Employee shall not, without consent of the Contractor, designate more than one individual and more than one bank to receive such earnings at one time. The designation made by the Employee as provided herein, shall remain in effect throughout the term of this Agreement or until written notice of its cancellation and the designation of a different individual and/or bank is furnished to the Contractor and is accepted and acknowledged by it in writing. No assignment or transfers of any amounts payable to the Employee hereunder, other than the designation provided for herein, will be recognized by the Contractor. No change of address of the designee will be recognized by the Contractor unless and until such change is requested in writing by the Employee and accepted and acknowledged by the Contractor in writing.

DISPOSITION OF EMPLOYEE'S REMAINS

In the event of death of the Employee while outside of the United States during the term of this Agreement, the Employee authorizes the Contractor to make appropriate disposition, as shall be deemed best by it under the prevailing circumstances, of the body and personal effects of the Employee. Whenever possible, the Contractor shall at its expense prepare and transport the remains of the Employee to the point of hire or equidistant point indicated by the next of kin.

FINAL SETTLEMENT

On the termination of this Agreement and payment to the Employee of all amounts due to him hereunder, the Employee shall execute and deliver to the Contractor a form furnished by the Contractor, a receipt for said sums and releases of all claims, except such undisposed claims specifically excepted in the release submitted pursuant to the provisions of Section "CLAIMS" hereof. It is understood that in preparing the record of employment on termination, the Employee shall submit to such physical examination both at the job site and after his return to the United States, as the Contractor may deem necessary for the preparation of such record herein required. It is understood that any such physical examinations are at the option of the Contractor and not the Employee.

CHAPTER **19**

Shareholders' Agreement Provisions: Professional Corporations

In the preparation of legal documents, such as one establishing a professional corporation, the professional should seek legal counsel. The following shareholders' agreement provisions, which contemplate two shareholders, indicate some of the points which should be considered by professionals who are planning to incorporate.

19.1 *General*

(a) The authorized capital of the Corporation consists of Two Hundred (200) shares of capital stock, without par value. The number of shares of capital stock issued and outstanding and the names of the beneficial and record owners of such shares are as follows: John Doe—50 shares and Richard Roe—50 shares.

(b) John Doe and Richard Roe are both duly licensed engineers pursuant to the laws of the State of New York and other jurisdictions.

19.2 *Directors and Officers*

The Shareholders each agree that they shall vote for each other as the only Officers and Directors of the Corporation. In the event either Shareholder by reason of death or otherwise fails to qualify or act as an Officer or Director, John Doe or Richard Roe, as the case may be, may designate another person who qualifies under the provisions of the New York Professional Corporation Law, to act as an Officer or Director and the foregoing provision with respect to voting for each other's designee as an Officer and Director shall apply with respect to such person designated.

19.3   Lifetime Restrictions on Transfer of Stock

(a) If any Shareholder during his lifetime wishes to transfer any of his shares of the capital stock of the Corporation, such Shareholder agrees to and shall sell all (and not less than all) of his shares to the Corporation, and the Corporation agrees to and shall purchase all of such shares as hereinafter provided at the price and manner of payments as determined in subsequent paragraphs of this Agreement.

(b) The Shareholder wishing to transfer his shares shall indicate his desire by written notice to that effect to the Corporation and a duplicate notice sent to the other Shareholder at the respective addresses hereinabove set forth.

(c) The Corporation shall promptly notify in writing the Shareholder of a closing date for the purchase and sale of such shares as provided hereafter.

(d) In the event that the Corporation shall fail to purchase all (and not less than all) of the shares of stock of the selling Shareholder, such selling Shareholder shall direct to have the Corporation liquidated in the manner provided under Subparagraph 19.4 (d).

19.4   Death of a Shareholder

(a) Upon the death of any Shareholder, all (and not less than all) of the shares of capital stock of the Corporation owned by the decedent at the time of his death shall be sold by the Executor, Administrator, or other personal representative (collectively referred to as the "legal representative" or "personal representative") of said decedent to the Corporation, and the Corporation shall purchase all of such shares as hereinafter provided at the price and manner of payment as determined in subsequent paragraphs hereinafter set forth.

(b) The legal representative, upon the death of the Shareholder, shall promptly notify the Corporation of the fact of such death, and thereafter the Corporation shall promptly notify the legal representative of a closing date for the purchase and sale of such shares as provided hereafter.

(c) In the event that the Corporation shall fail to purchase all (and not less than all) of the shares of stock of such deceased Shareholder, the legal representative of the deceased Shareholder whose stock is required to have been sold as provided hereinabove shall direct to have the Corporation liquidated in the manner described in Subparagraph 19.4(d) below.

(d) The legal representative, electing to cause the Corporation to liquidate, shall give written notice to that effect to the Corporation and other Shareholders within thirty (30) days following the expiration of the period of time within which the Corporation should have purchased the shares of stock of the decedent. Upon such direction to liquidate, the other Shareholders shall vote their shares (and they hereby designate the legal representative of the deceased Shareholder as their proxy for such purpose) and do any and all things necessary or proper to liquidate the Corporation as soon as practical. The net proceeds of liquidation remaining after the payment in full of all liabilities of the Corporation (excepting liabilities due to the surviving Shareholders) shall, however, be applied first to the payment of the purchase price of the said decedent's shares of stock before any distribution thereof is made to the surviving Shareholders of the Corporation. For the purpose of liquidation and determining the order of payment of liabilities of Corporation in the event of a death, any liabilities of the Corporation due to the surviving Shareholders shall be deemed to be capital contributions.

(e) As used in Paragraphs 19.3, 19.4, and elsewhere in this Agreement, the term "transfer" with respect to any shares of the Corporation includes any sale, exchange, assignment, gift, the creation of any security interest or other encumbrance, and any other disposition affecting title to or possession of any of the shares.

19.5 Disability, Loss, or Suspension of License

(a) If any Shareholder shall be prevented from performing his duties as an Officer by reason of illness or incapacity, physical or mental, he shall continue to receive his regular salary or compensation for a period of ninety (90) days and one-half (½) such salary or compensation for the subsequent period of 90 days of illness or incapacitation and, thereafter, such Shareholder shall not be entitled to receive any such salary or compensation during the period of illness or incapacitation. The aforesaid periods of illness or incapacitation shall relate to any twelve-month consecutive period. Notwithstanding anything herein to the contrary, in the event any Shareholder is prevented from performing his duties as an Officer by such reason of illness or incapacitation for a substantially continuous period consisting of eighteen (18) months, such Shareholder at the written election of the other Shareholder shall be deemed to have offered to transfer his shares of the capital stock of the Corporation as provided in Paragraph 19.3 of this Agreement.

(b) If any Shareholder shall cease to be licensed as a professional engineer pursuant to the laws of the State of New York or shall have his New York license suspended, and by reason thereof thereafter fails for a continuous period of sixty (60) days to qualify as a Shareholder pursuant to the then New York Professional Corporation Law, such Shareholder at the election of the other Shareholder shall be deemed to have then indicated his desire to transfer his shares of the capital stock of the Corporation as provided in Paragraph 19.3 of this Agreement.

19.6 Escrow during Payment Period

(a) If capital stock of a selling Shareholder is purchased by the Corporation under Paragraph 19.3 or 19.4 hereunder, such stock sold by the selling Shareholder or his personal representative shall remain in an escrow to be created at the time of the closing of the transaction and shall be released to the Corporation only upon receipt by the escrowee of a written declaration from the holder of any notes that full payment of the purchase price for all of the shares of stock has been paid. If the Corporation fails to make any timely payment of its notes, evidencing the purchase price, as hereinafter provided, and such failure continues more than ten (10) days, the Corporation shall proceed to liquidate in the manner determined in Paragraph 19.4 and, in particular, Subparagraph 19.4(d) hereof.

(b) The escrowee shall be a reputable financial institution located in New York City or such other person mutually designated by the parties at the time of sale, and any fees and expenses of said escrowee shall be borne equally between the seller and buyer of shares.

(c) Upon payment of the cash and notes hereinafter described in the subparagraphs of Paragraph 19.8, representing the purchase price, the selling Shareholder or, in the event of his death, the personal representative, shall deliver to the Corporation, the certificate or certificates for the shares of capital stock of the Corporation owned by the selling Shareholder, or decedent, as the case may be, properly endorsed for transfer or accompanied by duly executed stock powers in blank, with signatures guaranteed by a bank or trust company or a member firm of the New York Stock Exchange and and accompanied by requisite revenue stamps evidencing payment of all Federal and state transfer taxes, if said taxes are required by law, together with any and all other papers, instruments and documents which reasonably may be required to evidence such purchase, and the Corporation and the remaining Shareholder and the selling Shareholder or legal representative of the decedent, as the case may be, shall exchange general releases to evidence the payment and satisfaction of any obligations running from the Corporation with respect to the purchase and sale to the selling Shareholder or decedent, as the case may be, and vice versa.

19.7 *Purchase Price*

For the purposes of the purchase and sale of the shares of the capital stock of the Corporation, the purchase price shall be an amount equal to the book value of such shares of the calendar month preceding the month in which the offer to transfer such shares of the Corporation determined as at the end of the calendar month preceding the month in which the offer to transfer such shares occurred (referred to sometimes hereinafter as the "Book Value Date"); provided, however, in the event that there is life insurance on the life of a deceased Shareholder with respect to a policy or policies owned by the Corporation and the amount of the proceeds payable thereon exceed the book value of the decedent's shares, then the purchase price hereunder shall be an amount equal to the sum of the insurance proceeds. For purposes of this Agreement, the book value shall be determined by the certified public accountants regularly engaged by the Corporation, in accordance with generally accepted accounting principles and the regular methods and practices used by the Corporation in keeping its books applied on a consistent basis, and further in accordance with, but not limited to, the following provisions:

(a) Good will, if any, and similar intangible assets, including any contracts which the Corporation may have with third parties, shall be deemed to be of no value.

(b) Fixed assets consisting of, but not limited to, furniture, fixtures, machinery and equipment shall be taken at cost less accumulated depreciation.

(c) Accounts receivable shall be stated at the face value thereof less provisions for doubtful accounts and less trade discounts and allowances (if the accounts shall be carried gross upon the books).

(d) The amount of any proceeds realized from any insurance policy owned by the Corporation on the life of any deceased Shareholder shall not be included as an asset on the balance sheet of the Corporation.

(e) Adequate provisions for reserves for Federal, state and local taxes and contingent liabilities to the extent not covered by insurance, shall be accrued and applied as a liability as of the balance sheet date.

(f) Any securities owned by the Corporation shall be taken at the market value thereof if such securities are listed on a national securities exhange or if otherwise publicly traded. Any other securities, except the securities of subsidiary or affiliated corporations, shall be taken at the value at which such securities are carried on the books of the Corporation. Securities of subsidiary or affiliated corporations, shall be valued at their respective book values and in computing such book values for any subsidiary or affiliate the adjustments in this Paragraph 19.7 shall likewise apply.

(g) The net cash surrender value (after reduction for any loans) of life insurance policies owned by the Corporation shall be included as an asset.

The determination of book value by the regular certified public accountants for the Corporation shall be final, conclusive and binding upon all of the parties hereto, including their respective heirs, successors, personal representatives and assigns unless, however, the aggregate book value of the Corporation as determined by such accountants shall be an amount which shall differ by more than 20% from the aggregate book value of the Corporation for the immediately preceding fiscal year as reflected upon the annual statement submitted to the Shareholders. The Shareholders shall see to it that the regular certified public accountants for the Corporation shall promptly after the acceptance of a Shareholder's offer, make a determination of book value for purposes of this Agreement and shall furnish a certificate to the Corporation and to the Shareholders, duly executed by such regular certified public accountants, setting forth such determination of book value pursuant to the provisions of this Agreement.

Notwithstanding anything contained in this Agreement to the contrary, the purchase price as computed hereunder in the event of a purchase and sale during the lifetime of a Shareholder pursuant to Paragraph 19.3 or 19.5 hereof, shall be reduced by a sum equal to the lesser of (1) $30,000.00 or (2) an amount equal to 20% of the aggregate book value of the Corporation.

19.8 Payment of Purchase Price

Payment of the purchase price to be paid by the Corporation for the stock of a selling Shareholder in the circumstances provided for in paragraphs 19.3 and 19.4 shall be made, as follows:

(a) In a purchase under Paragraph 19.3 twenty-five percent (25%) of the purchase price shall be paid by the Corporation at the closing and the balance in thirty-six (36) negotiable promissory notes each in the amount of one thirty-sixth (1/36) of the balance of the purchase price and each dated as of the date of closing.

(b) In a purchase under Paragraph 19.4 and only in the event there is insurance on the life of the deceased Shareholder, the entire amount of insurance proceeds, received under the policy or policies, purchased by the Corporation on the decedent's life shall be paid at the closing fixed by the Corporation, irrespective of whether the amount thereof exceeds the purchase price as determined hereunder, and the unpaid balance, if any, shall be paid in thirty-six (36) negotiable promissory notes in series, each in the amount of one thirty-sixth (1/36) of the said balance and each dated as of the date of closing. It is understood that in the case of a purchase pursuant to Paragraph 19.4, the actual purchase price shall be that provided for in Section 19.7 or the amount of the insurance proceeds, whichever sum shall be greater.

(c) In the case of a purchase under Paragraph 19.4 and there is no life insurance on the life of the deceased Shareholder, then payment of the price shall be made in the manner determined in Subparagraph 19.8(a) hereof.

292   *Special Forms*

(*d*) When notes are given pursuant to paragraphs (*a*), (*b*), or (*c*), above, each note in the series shall bear interest at the annual rate on the unpaid principal sum of six percent (6%) per annum. The first note in said series shall mature one month from the date of such note, and each succeeding note shall mature at one-month intervals thereafter. Each of said notes shall be payable at the bank depository of the Corporation, and each shall contain an acceleration clause in the event of default, a clause permitting prepayment of the said notes without penalty or premium and a clause permitting a reasonable attorneys' fee upon placement for collection after maturity. Each of the said notes shall contain a waiver of notice of dishonor, presentment and protest. The Shareholder who is not transferring his shares hereunder shall make, execute and deliver to the selling Shareholder a separate guarantee of payment with respect of any notes of the Corporation delivered pursuant hereto, subject to the condition, however, that the selling Shareholder shall first proceed to collect said notes from the Corporation.

19.9 *Default*

If any of the following events (hereinafter called "Events of Default") shall occur:

(*a*) If the Corporation shall default in any required payment of the principal of or interest on any of the notes evidencing the balance of the purchase price provided for herein for more than fifteen (15) days after the same shall mature, *or*

(*b*) If the Corporation shall default in the performance of or compliance with any agreement, condition or covenant of this Agreement and such default shall not have been remedied to the reasonable satisfaction of the holders of the said notes thirty (30) days after written notice shall have been received by the Corporation from any holder of any such notes, *or*

(*c*) Upon the death of the surviving shareholder, *or*

(*d*) If the Corporation shall make an assignment for the benefit of creditors or shall audit in writing its inability to pay its debts as they become due or shall file a voluntary petition in bankruptcy or shall file any petition and answer seeking any reorganization, arrangement, composition, readjustment, liquidation, dissolution or similar relief under the present or any future Federal bankruptcy act or other applicable Federal, state or other statute, law or regulation, or shall seek or consent or acquiesce in the appointment of any trustees, receiver, or liquidator of the Corporation or of all or any substantial part of its assets, *or*

(*e*) If the Corporation shall be adjudicated bankrupt or if any proceeding against the Corporation seeking any reorganization, arrangement, composition, readjustment, liquidation, dissolution or similar relief under the present or any future Federal bankruptcy act or other applicable Federal, state or other statute, law or regulation shall remain undismissed or unstayed for an aggregate of sixty (60) days after the commencement thereof or if any trustee, receiver, or liquidator of the Corporation or of all or substantially all of its properties shall be appointed without consent or acquiescence of the Corporation and such appointment shall remain unvacated or unstayed for an aggregate of sixty (60) days, *or*

(*f*) A final judgment for more than twenty thousand ($20,000.00) dollars shall be rendered against the Corporation and shall remain undischarged or unstayed for an aggregate of thirty (30) days after entry thereof, then and in every such event, the holder of any of the aforesaid promissory notes, at the time outstanding, may, at his option, declare by written notice to the Corporation its note or notes to be due and the same shall forthwith mature and become due and payable without presentment, demand, protest or notice of any kind, all of which are hereby expressly waived, anything contained herein or in the notes notwithstanding, and the aforesaid notes shall bear a legend indicating that they are subject to the events of default specified in this Agreement.

19.10 Specific Performance
The capital stock of the Corporation cannot readily be purchased or sold in the open market and for that reason, among others, the Corporation and the Shareholders will be irreparably damaged in the event that this Agreement is not performed. Should any dispute arise concerning the transfer of any shares of capital stock or other provisions of this Agreement, an injunction may be issued restraining such sale or disposition or other action pending the determination of such controversy by arbitration as hereinafter provided. The determination by the arbitrators of any controversy concerning the purchase or sale of any common stock or other provisions herein, shall be enforceable in a court of equity by a decree of specific performance. Such remedy, however, shall be cumulative and not exclusive and shall be in addition to any other remedy which the parties may have.

19.11 Endorsement on Stock Certificate
The certificate or certificates representing the shares of stock issued by the Corporation to any of the parties hereto shall have endorsed upon the face thereof the following legend:

This stock certificate is held subject to the terms of an Agreement dated _____, made by the Corporation and all its Shareholders, a copy of which is on file at the office of the Corporation which restricts the transferability of these shares.

19.12 Personal Representatives
The legal or personal representatives of a deceased Shareholder as that term is used herein, shall mean the executors or administrators of such deceased Shareholder's estate.

19.13 Disputes
Except for injunctive relief and except as provided for herein, any controversy or claim arising out of or relating to this Agreement or any breach or termination thereof, shall be settled by arbitration in the City of New York by a single arbitrator mutually agreed upon by the parties, and judgment upon the award rendered by the arbitrator may be entered in any court having jurisdiction thereof. The parties hereto consent to the jurisdiction of the Supreme Court of the State of New York, and further consent that any process or notice of motion or other application to the said Court or a Judge thereof may be served inside or outside of the State of New York by registered mail, or by personal service, provided a reasonable time for appearance is allowed. In the event that the parties hereto are unable to agree upon an Arbitrator, the party or parties seeking arbitration shall proceed in accordance with the applicable laws of the State of New York pertaining to arbitration.

CHAPTER **20**

Contract Provisions: Owner-Contractor Agreements

20.1 *Provision whereby Contractor Guarantees Maximum Cost of the Work (for Use in Connection with a Cost-plus-Fee Contract)*

The Contractor has estimated that the total cost to the Owner, including the Contractor's fee, for the work completed in accordance with the Contract Documents will not exceed the sum of $_____, which sum, as increased or decreased by extra work or by changes, alterations, additions to or deductions from the work, shall be known as the Guaranteed Total Cost. Should the actual cost of the work as increased or decreased as aforesaid, plus the Contractor's fee, exceed the Guaranteed Total Cost, the Contractor shall pay out of its own funds one hundred percentum (100%) of such excess. Should the actual cost of the work as increased or decreased as aforesaid, plus the Contractor's fee, be less than the Guaranteed Total Cost, then:

[Alternate *A*] All such savings shall revert in full to the owner.

[Alternate *B*] All such savings shall be divided between the Owner and the Contractor in the ratio of two thirds (⅔) to the Owner and one third (⅓) to the Contractor.

(or other options may be adopted.)

20.2 *Supplementary General Conditions.* The following suggested supplementary general conditions should be carefully edited to insure that they reflect the intent of a specific contract, and also to insure that they do not conflict with the general conditions of the contract.

20.2.1 Finality of Architect's (Engineer's) Decision

1. The Architect (Engineer) shall, in all cases, determine the amount and/or quality of the several kinds of work and materials that are to be paid for under this contract and he shall determine all questions in relation to said work and materials and the construction thereof. He shall in all cases decide every question that may arise relative to the execution of this Contract on the part of the Contractor and his estimate and decision shall be final and conclusive upon the Contractor and Owner.

or

2. All work shall be performed to the satisfaction of the Architect (Engineer) and at such times and places, by such methods and in such manner and sequence as he may require, and shall at all stages be subject to his inspection. The Architect (Engineer) will determine the amount, quality, acceptability and fitness of all parts thereof, will interpret the Plans and Specifications, and will decide all other questions in connection therewith. The Architect's (Engineer's) determination shall be final and conclusive. The enumeration of particular instances in which his opinion, judgment, discretion or determination will control, or in which work shall be performed to his satisfaction or subject to his inspection, shall not imply that only the enumerated matters shall be so governed or performed; but without exception all work shall be so governed or performed.

20.2.2 Cleaning Up and Repair

1. The Contractor shall at all times keep the premises free from accumulations or waste material or rubbish caused by his employees or work and at the completion of the work he shall remove all his rubbish from and about the building and all his tools, scaffolding and surplus materials, and shall leave his work "broom clean." In case of dispute, the Owner may remove the rubbish and charge the cost to the several Contractors as the Architect determines to be just. The Contractor for General Construction Work shall clean all glass, exterior and interior, and maintain same in a satisfactory clean condition until the building is turned over to the Owner.

2. At no time shall any rubbish be thrown from the windows of the building.

3. When directed and before the final inspection, the entire exterior and interior of the building and the surrounding areas shall be cleared of all rubbish and thoroughly cleaned by the General Contractor, including the following:

(a) All construction facilities, debris and rubbish shall be removed from the Owner's property.

(b) All new finished surfaces and all surfaces soiled by operations hereunder within the building shall be swept, dusted, washed and polished. This includes cleaning of the work of all finishing trades where needed, whether or not cleaning for such trades is included in their respective specifications.

(c) Access spaces shall be left thoroughly clean.

(d) Install adequate runner strips of building paper on finished floors, to the satisfaction of the Architect.

(e) All equipment shall be new, in an undamaged, bright, clean, polished condition.

(f) All new and replaced glass shall be washed and polished both sides, by a window cleaner specializing in such work.

4. The General Contractor shall be responsible for all breakage of glass from the time the glazier has completed his work until the building is turned over to the Owner. He shall replace all broken glass and deliver the building with all glazing intact and clean.

5. The Contractor shall keep the premises clean and clear of all garbage, refuse and waste matters of any nature which might attract or foster rodents or vermin, and shall provide extermination service if required to keep the premises free from such pests, should this be required.

20.2.3 *Cooperation*

1. The Contractor for General Construction Work and all other Contractors and all Subcontractors shall coordinate their work and shall coordinate with all other trades so as to facilitate the general progress of the work; also to assure correctness and avoid the possibility of accidents to persons and/or damage to the property.

2. The Contractor shall lay out and install his work at such time or times and in such manner as to facilitate the general progress of the project.

3. It is agreed that in the event of any dispute arising as to possible or alleged interference between the various contractors which may retard the progress of the work, the same shall be adjusted by the Architect. His decision as to the parties at fault and as to the manner in which the matter may be adjusted shall be binding and conclusive on all parties.

4. Each trade shall afford all other trades every reasonable opportunity for the installation of their work and for the storage of their materials.

5. If, in the judgment of the Architect, it becomes necessary at any time during the progress of the work to accelerate the work at any particular point, the Contractor or Subcontractor, when ordered or directed by the Architect, shall transfer his men to such point or points and execute such portions of his work as may be required to enable others to hasten and carry on their work.

20.2.4 *Cutting, Patching, and Digging*

1. Each Contractor shall do all cutting, fitting and/or patching in connection with his work that may be required to make its several parts come together properly and fit to receive or be received by work of other contractors as shown upon or reasonably implied by the drawings and specifications for the completed structure.

2. No Contractor, however, shall do any cutting that will impair the strength of the construction and shall report to the Architect any cutting requested by other contractors that he considers too extensive or that will impair the strength of the construction. The size, location, etc., of items requiring an opening, chase or other provisions to receive it in any branch of the work, shall be given by the Contractor requiring same, in ample time to avoid cutting.

3. This will not relieve any Contractor from keeping informed as to such openings, chases, etc., nor from joint responsibility with such other contractors for correctness thereof, nor for cutting and making good after the work is in place. Should

any construction be installed in other than regular and usual working hours (overtime or otherwise), or if on account of strikes, other trades are not at work, then due notice shall be given all other contractors interested, or entire responsibility shall be assumed by the Contractor installing the work for any cutting needed in any work so installed.

4. If through neglect of any Contractor to give required information in regard to cutting of the work of other trades in ample time to prevent unnecessary work, or if, through the delay or mistake of any Contractor, it is necessary to do any additional amount of cutting or replacing of the work, the Contractor requiring the cutting shall pay for such cutting and all necessary patching and repairing in connection with this additional cutting. The Contractor shall not endanger any work by cutting, digging or otherwise and shall not cut or alter the work of any other contractor save with the consent of the Architect.

5. All required cutting, patching and restoring shall be neatly done by mechanics skilled in their trades, and to the satisfaction of the Architect.

6. All work that may be cut, damaged, disturbed or otherwise interfered with during the progress of the work of the various trades shall be fully, properly and carefully patched, repaired and made good in a first-class manner, satisfactory to the Architect, by the Contractor whose work has been cut or damaged and requires repair.

7. Each Contractor shall leave all the work of his contract whole, complete and perfect at the final completion of the building without extra charge.

20.2.5 *Deductions for Uncorrected Work*

If the Owner and Architect deem it inexpedient to correct work injured or work not in accordance with the Contract Documents, an equitable deduction from the Contract Price shall be made therefor, which amount shall be determined by the Architect.

20.2.6 *Grades, Lines, and Levels*

1. The lot lines and bench marks are established on the drawings.

2. All other grades, lines, levels and bench marks shall be established and maintained by the Contractor for General Construction Work who shall be responsible for same.

3. The Contractor for General Construction Work shall verify all grades, lines, levels and dimensions as shown in the drawings and he shall report any errors or inconsistencies in the above to the Architect before commencing work.

4. The Contractor for General Construction Work shall provide and maintain well built batter boards at all corners, and he shall establish bench marks in not less than two widely separated places. As the work progresses he shall establish bench marks at each floor, giving exact levels of the floors.

5. The Contractor for General Construction Work shall employ a licensed surveyor to layout the building, place permanent reference marks on batter boards, establish bench marks and give levels of floors to which all measurements shall be referred.

6. Before starting construction work the Contractor for General Construction Work shall submit to the Architect for approval three (3) blueprint copies of a complete "Construction Stake Layout" of the building at all corners and angles.

7. Upon completion of foundation walls, the Contractor for General Construction Work shall prepare and deliver to the Architect three (3) copies of a certified survey showing that all dimensions, elevations, angles, and location of the building are in accordance with the Architect's drawings.

20.2.7   *Heating during Construction*

All necessary precautions shall be taken by the Contractor for General Construction Work to close up all exterior openings either by permanent glazed windows and doors or by adequate and approved temporary closures. During the period of temporary heating, the Contractor for General Construction Work shall exercise supervisory control of the conditions of the building. Temperature requirements of the various trades shall be maintained. Ventilation and temperatures shall be uniform to prevent shrinkages, cracking or swelling of floors, trim or other work.

A temperature shall be maintained at all times throughout the building for comfortable working conditions, to prevent harmful effects of low temperature and to dry out and keep dry the entire building until it is completed and accepted by the Owner. Should use of the Heating System of the building not be available when temporary heat is required, the Contractor for General Construction Work shall provide heat by other methods approved by the Architect. The temporary heating system shall comply with the regulations of all authorities having jurisdiction over same; and said system shall not cause smudge, defacement or discoloration of finished work, nor shall it be injurious to the workmen. When the Heating System is ready to operate for temporary heat, and upon written authorization of the Architect, the Contractor for General Construction Work shall direct the Heating and Ventilating Contractor to operate the system for temporary heat.

20.2.8   *Heating during Construction—Allowance*

Contractor for General Construction Work shall include in his estimated cost the sum of $_____, which shall be used exclusively for payment of Heating and Ventilating Contractor and the Contractor for Electrical Work for the Operation of the permanent heating plant, in order to provide temporary heat when directed. Payments shall be made as per schedule of rates stated in the form of proposal by the said contractors. Fuel will be paid for by the Owner.

20.2.9   *Insurance (in Addition to the Usual Contractor's Insurance)*

Insurance Covering Special Hazards: Special hazards shall be covered by riders to the Public Liability and/or Property Damage Insurance Policy or Policies herein required, or by separate policies of insurance, in amounts to be approved by the Owner.

Evidence of Insurance: The Contractor shall file with the Architect before commencing work under his Contract, Certificates of Insurance, in triplicate, which certificates shall bear the following information:

1. Name and Address of the insured.

2. Title and location of the operations to which the insurance applies.

3. The number of the policy and the type or types of insurance in force thereunder on the date borne by such certificate.

4. The expiration date of policy and the limit or limits of liability thereunder on the date borne by such certificate.

5. A statement that the insurance of the type afforded by the policy applies to all of the operations on and at the site of the project which are undertaken by the insured during the performance of his contract or subcontract.

6. A statement as to the exclusions of the policy, if any.

7. A statement showing the method of cancellations provided for by the policy. If cancellations may be affected by the giving of notice to the insured by the insurer, the policy shall provide for the lapse of such number of days following the giving of such notice that in the ordinary course of transmission the insured will have actually received such notice at least five (5) days before the cancellation becomes effective.

Notice of cancellation shall be delivered to Owner as well as to the Insured.

20.2.10 *Insurance—Fire [Additional Clause]*

In case of a total loss or a partial loss of the structure by fire before its completion, the Contractor shall proceed with the execution of this Contract and he shall not be relieved from any of his obligations under this Contract, except that the time for completion of the work hereunder shall be extended for such number of days as it may have been (in the opinion of the Architect, evidenced by his certificate in writing, which shall be binding and conclusive upon the Contractor) delayed by reason of any such loss or partial loss by fire.

20.2.11 *Labor*

1. All Contractors and Subcontractors employed upon the work shall and will be required to conform to the "Labor Laws" as amended, of the State, and shall also comply with all rules, regulations and Labor Laws of the Federal government, and the various acts amendatory and supplementary thereto, and all other laws, ordinances and legal requirements.

2. The Contractor shall indemnify and hold harmless the Owner from any and all claims, demands, actions, loss and damage arising by reason of a breach of any of the provisions of this Article. Should such eventuality occur, the Contract may be cancelled or terminated by the Owner and all moneys due or to become due hereunder shall be forfeited by the Contractor.

3. Whenever the provisions of any division of the Specifications may conflict with any agreement or regulations of any kind in force among members of any trade association, union or council which regulates or distinguishes what work shall or shall not be included in the work of any particular trade, the Contractor must make all necessary arrangements of his own to reconcile any such conflict without recourse to the Architect and/or the Owner.

20.2.12 *Light and Power during Construction*

The Electrical Contractor shall include in his base bid the amount of money specified in the Supplementary General Conditions to be used as an allowance, which allowance shall be expended in whole or in part as authorized by the Architect under the conditions hereinafter described.

1. Payment to the Electrical Contractor will be made out of this Temporary Light and Power Allowance only by authorization and direction of the Architect's representative or Project Representative.

2. Compensation to the Electrical Contractor shall be made out of the Allowance for the following:

(*a*) Labor for temporary wiring after regular hours.

(*b*) Labor for installation of additional temporary wiring not shown on the Drawings.

(*c*) Maintenance for temporary wiring after regular hours.

(*d*) Maintenance for motorized heating equipment after regular hours.

3. Reimbursement for authorized labor shall be at cost, plus:

(*a*) Fifteen (15) percent added for taxes, benefits, and supervision.

(*b*) Ten (10) percent added for overhead.

(*c*) Five (5) percent added for profit.

4. Reimbursement for authorized material shall be at cost, plus:

(*a*) Ten (10) percent added for overhead.

(*b*) Five (5) percent added for profit.

5. No labor, material or maintenance for the installation, relocation, extension or removal of special power and light requirements will be paid from this Allowance. The energy cost for temporary light and power at any time is not chargeable to this Allowance. The cost of labor and material for the Temporary Light and Power Installation as shown on the Drawings in the Specifications and the maintenance of same during normal working hours is also not chargeable to the Temporary Light and Power Allowance. All electrical services, materials, etc., not specifically noted in this paragraph shall be furnished and installed under the Electrical Contract and are not chargeable to the Temporary Light and Power Allowance.

6. If required for the maintenance of temporary heating after regular working hours and before the heating equipment is permanently wired up and in operation, the maintenance cost to the Electrical Contractor will be paid out of this Allowance as approved by the Architect.

7. Payment for the work performed under this Allowance will be made after approval of a statement submitted as part of the regular requisition to the Office of the Architect, accompanied by the following:

(*a*) Separate time sheets for the extra electricians' labor, indicating the hours, rates and place where work was done and the name of the party who authorized it.

(*b*) Bills showing actual cost (not list price) of materials furnished and installation with a description of where those materials were used and the name of the person authorizing the installation.

20.2.13   *Light and Power during Construction—Allowance*

The amount of $_____ shall be included in the Electrical Contractor's bid to be used as an allowance to be expended in whole or in part as authorized by the Architect under the conditions described in (Light and Power during Construction, above).

20.2.14 *Maintenance Instructions*

1. The Contractor shall, at the completion of the Contract, deliver to the Architect three (3) copies of a manual presenting for the Owner's guidance full details for the care and maintenance of all visible surfaces and of all equipment included in the Contract.

2. The Contractor shall furnish all literature of the manufacturers relating to equipment, including motors or other manufacturing equipment; also cuts, wiring diagrams, instruction sheets, and all other information pertaining to same that would be useful to the Owner in the operation and maintenance of same.

20.2.15 *Office Facilities*

1. *Contractor's Office:*
The Contractor for General Construction Work shall provide, at the beginning of the work, a Temporary Office of watertight construction, approximately eight feet by ten feet, equipped with windows which operate and door with suitable lock, or hasp and padlock; a wide shelf or table of sufficient length for easy handling and examining of drawings, a file rack for efficient filing and handling of all drawings and details. This office shall be for the use of the Architect and the Contractor's superintendent, where plans and details shall be kept on file for the use of the various contractors and subcontractors engaged in work on the building.

The Contractor shall furnish, at his own expense, heat, light, and telephone service for this office and shall make suitable arrangements with other contractors for the use of the telephone.

2. *Architect's Office:*
The Contractor for General Construction Work shall provide, at the beginning of the work, a separate office, eight feet by eight feet, near the Contractor's office, for the sole use of the Architect. This office shall be built and equipped the same as specified for the Contractor's office, except that the Contractor shall install and maintain a telephone in this office exclusively for the Architect's use from the beginning to the completion of the project, pay all bills in connection with same, and provide the Architect with three keys for this office lock. The Contractor shall also provide one new steel four drawer legal size filing cabinet, full suspension drawers with locking device and keys for the Architect's use and storage of permanent records and drawings.

3. The Contractor shall be responsible for the maintenance of both offices, including the cost of fuel for heating, electric current, phone, janitors' service and other incidentals.

4. The Contractor shall maintain in his Temporary Office all articles necessary for giving "First Aid" and these shall be available for instant use. The Contractor shall also have a standing arrangement for the immediate removal and hospital treatment of any employee or person engaged on the work, who may be injured, or who may become ill.

5. *Business Office:*
The Contractor for each individual contract shall maintain a business office at his regular place of business, with telephone service from 9 A.M. to 5 P.M. on all working days.

20.2.16   *Progress Schedule*

1. Within two (2) weeks after signing his Contract, the Contractor shall submit to the Architect for his review and approval, a tentative outline schedule of progress expected to be made by the Contractor in the various stages of the work covered by the Contract. The schedule, when approved, shall be submitted to the Architect in quadruplicate.

2. The schedule, when approved, shall be strictly adhered to, overtime work being performed by the Contractor without additional payment if necessary to maintain the progress of the schedule unless it can be conclusively shown that the delay or interference resulted from the acts or omissions of other contractors and beyond the control of the Contractor whose schedule is interfered with.

3. Where such delay or interference of other contractors is caused, the amount of time extended to the Contractor whose time has been interfered with, will be only equal to the time he lost.

4. Adherence to the various stages of progress by the Contractor as set forth in the approved schedule of progress, shall be understood as a requisite and precedent to the issuance of certificate for partial payments.

5. In case the schedule, as originally approved, cannot be adhered to as so scheduled, the Contractor shall furnish with the monthly requisitions a revised schedule showing revisions, with a statement for causes of delays.

20.2.17   *Progress Meetings*

1. The Contractor agrees that if and when he is requested by the Architect or by the Owner to do so, he will attend and cause his subcontractors and/or their representatives to attend any and all meetings called by the Architect or the Owner, to accelerate or discuss the progress of the work under his contract.

2. Failure of the Contractor, his subcontractors or their representatives to be present at the meetings may be cause for cancellation of their contract.

20.2.18   *Progress Photographs*

The day the operation is started and with each monthly application for payment, the Contractor for General Construction Work shall have photographs made and submitted, in duplicate; four (4) views shall be taken, always from the same points, as directed by the Architect, to show the progress of the work until the building is enclosed. Each negative shall be numbered and dated and shall have the name of the Architect, of the building, and bear the project number. Photographs shall be 8×10 inches, mounted on linen, and provided with a binding edge.

20.2.19   *Protection of Work and Property*

1. Whenever a serious or fatal accident occurs at the site during construction, the Contractor shall immediately notify the Architect, and cause an investigation to be conducted at once into the cause of such accident and full testimony shall be taken together with photographs, tests, etc., to determine completely the cause thereof.

2. The Contractor for General Construction Work shall employ and retain one or more competent watchmen, to guard the premises at night and at all times (day and night) on Saturdays, Sundays, holidays and any other day on which the Contrac-

tor for General Construction Work is not represented on the project until the entire operation is complete and/or the Owner has taken charge of the building. In the event that the Architect or Owner at any time deems the watchman's service inadequate or incompetent, the Contractor for General Construction Work shall increase or change the watchman personnel. It is also the intention of this paragraph that the Contractor for General Construction Work shall employ and retain one or more competent watchmen to provide 24 hour protection to the project at all times when for any reason it becomes necessary to shut down the work and discontinue temporarily the continuance of the project. Such causes as inclement weather, strike, inability to obtain materials, etc., are construed as being within the intent of this paragraph.

20.2.20 Samples

1. The Contractor shall furnish, for written approval, all samples as directed. The work shall be in accordance with approved samples.

2. Samples shall be submitted in triplicate of sufficient size or number to show the quality, type, range of color, finish and texture of the material.

3. Each set of samples shall be labeled, bearing the name and quality of the material, the Contractor's name, date, contract and project, and a notation as to its intended placement.

4. A letter of transmittal, in triplicate, from the Contractor requesting approval must accompany all samples.

5. Transportation charges to the Architect's office must be prepaid on all samples forwarded.

6. In case the samples are disapproved, other samples shall be submitted until satisfactory and approved.

7. Samples and other required information shall be submitted in sufficient time to permit proper consideration and action without delaying any operation of the project. Materials, equipment and/or appliances shall not be ordered until approval is received in writing from the Architect. All materials, equipment and/or appliances shall be furnished equal in every respect to the approved samples.

8. The approval, in writing, of any sample will be given as promptly as possible, and shall be only for the characteristics, color, texture, strength or other features of the material named in such approval and no other. When this approval is issued by the Architect, it is done with the distinct understanding that the materials to be furnished will fully and completely comply with the specifications. Use of materials will be permitted only as long as the quality remains equal to the approved samples, and complies in every respect with the specifications.

9. No approval of a sample shall be taken in itself to change or modify any of the requirements of the Contract.

10. The disapproval of samples or delay in submitting or resubmitting samples shall not be deemed cause for an extension of time.

20.2.21 Separate Contracts

If, before completion of the work contemplated herein, it shall be deemed necessary by the Owner to do any other or further work in or about the building or structure than is provided for in the Contract, the Contractor shall not in any way interfere with or molest such person or persons as the Owner may employ, by contract or otherwise, to do such work, and the Contractor shall suspend such part of the work herein specified, or shall carry on the same in such manner as to afford all reasonable facilities for doing such further work; and no damage or claim by the Contractor by reason thereof shall be allowed except such extensions of the time specified in the Contract for the performance thereof as the Owner may deem reasonable.

20.2.22   Sanitary Facilities

1. The Contractor for General Construction Work shall not allow any sanitary nuisances to be committed in or about the work, and shall enforce all sanitary regulations of the local and state health authorities.

2. The Contractor for General Construction Work shall post notices, take such precautions as may be necessary, remove all excrement deposited in or about the building and do any cleaning necessary to the building and/or premises to keep same in a sanitary condition.

3. The Contractor for General Construction Work shall, at the beginning of the work, provide on the premises where directed a suitable temporary convenience and enclosure for the use of all workmen on the job, and maintain same in a sanitary condition and remove same and all its contents at the completion of building operations or when directed by the Architect.

20.2.23   Signs

1. The Contractor shall not display, or permit to be displayed, on or about the premises any sign, trademarks, posters or other advertising device. He shall enforce the Architect's instructions regarding advertisements, fire and smoking.

2. The Architect will furnish a sketch of a sign for identification of Architect at the job site. The Contractor for General Construction Work shall furnish material for and have the sign painted and displayed as directed.

3. Before final payment the Contractor shall remove all surplus materials, falsework, temporary structures, plant of any description and debris of every nature resulting from his operations, and put the site in a neat and orderly condition.

20.2.24   Suspension

The Owner reserves the right to suspend the whole or any part of the work herein contracted to be done, for a reasonable time, without compensation to the Contractor for such suspension. The time for completing the work shall be extended by such number of days as the Contractor was delayed by the suspension.

20.2.25   Temporary Facilities

1. *Stairs and Hatchways:*
The Contractor for General Construction Work shall provide and maintain substantial temporary plank stairways or ramps with handrails and guards connecting with every floor of the construction, guard rails to all hatchways and/or openings at the various floor levels, and temporary planks securely fastened to steel undertreads of stairs for the protection of stair nosing.

2. *Ventilation:*

During construction and up to the date of final acceptance, the Contractor for General Construction Work shall be responsible for and pay for all labor required for the opening and closing of windows and doors as may be necessary for the drying out of plaster and/or finished work and to keep the rain and snow out of the building. In case the Contractor shall fail to make satisfactory arrangements for the performance of this item of the work, the Owner shall have the right to have the same done at the Contractor's expense.

3. *Storage Sheds:*

The Contractor shall erect ample storage shed space for the building materials requiring shelter from the weather, and locate same to make the best use of the space available on the property. Where street space is used, he shall secure the necessary permits and conform to all local requirements. Upon completion and conclusion of all contract work or when directed by the Architect, he shall take down and remove all temporary field structures built and used by him and restore the site occupied by same to the satisfaction of the Architect.

20.2.26   *Trial Usage*

1. The temporary or trial usage by the Owner of any mechanical device, machinery, equipment or any work or materials supplied under the Contract, before final completion and written acceptance by the Architect shall not be construed as an evidence of acceptance of same. The Owner shall have the privilege of such temporary and trial usage for such reasonable length of time as the Architect shall deem proper for making a complete and thorough test of same, and no claim for damage shall be made by the Contractor for the injury to or breaking of any parts of such work which may be caused by weakness or inaccuracy of structural parts or by defective materials or workmanship. If the Contractor so elects, he may, at his own expense, place a competent person or persons satisfactory to the Architect to make such trial usage.

2. The trial shall be under the supervision of the Architect or his duly authorized representative.

Case References

[1] Chapel v. Clark, 117 Mich. 617, 76 N.W. 62 (Mich. 1898).

[2] Osterling v. Alleghany Trust Co., 260 Pa. 64, 103 A. 528 (Pa. 1918).

[3] Fitzgerald v. Walsh, 107 Wis. 92, 82 N.W. 717 (Wis. 1900).

[4] Jovis v. Charben Inc., 199 N.Y.S.2d (N.Y. 1960).

[5] Vaky v. Philips, 194 S.W. 601 (Tex. 1919).

[6] Stevens v. Fanning, 59 Ill. App. 2d 285, 207 N.E.2d 136 (Ill. 1965).

[7] Wagaschal Associates v. West, 362 Mich. 676, 107 N.W.2d 874 (Mich. 1961).

[8] Mitterhausen v. Wisconsin Conf., 245 Wis. 353, 14 N.W.2d 19 (Wis. 1944).

[9] Tsoi v. Ebenezer Baptist Church, 153 So.2d 592 (La. 1963); also Caldwell v. U.P.C., 20 Ohio Op. 2d 364, 88 L. Abs. 323, 180 N.E.2d 638 (Ohio 1961).

[10] Capitol Hotel Co. Inc. v. Rittenberry, 41 S.W.2d 697 (Tex. 1931).

[11] Higgins v. G. Piel Company, Inc., 208 App. Div. 729. 202 N.Y.S. 874 (N.Y. 1924).

[12] Spalding County v. Chamberlin, 130 Ga. 649, 61 S.E. 533 (Ga. 1908).

[13] Audubon v. Andrews, 187 Fed. 254 (D.N.Y. 1911).

[14] New Era Homes v. Forster, 299 N.Y. 303, 86 N.E.2d 757 (N.Y. 1949).

[15] Integrity Flooring, Inc. v. Zandor Corp., Inc., 130 N.J.L. 244, 32 A.2d 507 (N.J. 1943).

17 Jacobberger v. School Dist. No. 1, 122 Or. 124, 256 P. 652 (Or. 1927).

18 Smith & English v. Board of Education of the City of Liberal, 115 Kansas 155, 222 P. 101 (Ka. 1924).

19 Adamant Manufacturing Company of America v. Bach, 26 App. Div. 255; *aff'd*, 163 N.Y. 555, 57 N.E. 1103 (N.Y. 1900).

20 Wood & Company v. Alvord & Swift, 232 App. Div. 603, 251 N.Y.S. 35; *aff'd*, 258 N.Y. 611 (N.Y. 1932).

21 MacKnight Flintic Stone Co. v. The Mayor, 160 N.Y. 72, 68 N.E. 1119 (N.Y. 1899).

22 Early v. O'Brien, 51 App. Div. 569 (N.Y. 1900).

23 Dearstine v. Dunckel, 130 Misc. 281, 223 N.Y.S. 234; *rev'd*, 223 App. Div. 795, 228 N.Y.S. 191 (N.Y. 1928).

24 Whitney-Dierks Heating Corp. v. State, 207 Misc. 423, 139 N.Y.S.2d 34; *aff'd*, 3 App. Div. 2d 948, 162 N.Y.S.2d 370 (N.Y. 1957).

25 Shapiro v. Driscoll Co., 266 App. Div. 260, 42 N.Y.S.2d 94; *aff'd*, 292 N.Y. 519, 54 N.E.2d 205 (N.Y. 1944).

26 Cauldwell-Wingate Co. v. State, 276 N.Y. 365, 12 N.E. 443 (N.Y. 1938).

27 Hubert v. Aitken, 5 N.Y.S. 839; *affirming*, 2 N.Y.S. 711, 15 Daly (N.Y.) 237; *aff'd*, 123 N.Y. 655, 25 N.E. 954 (N.Y. 1890).

28 Burke v. Ireland, 166 N.Y. 305, 59 N.E. 914 (N.Y. 1901).

29 Petersen v. Rawson, 34 N.Y. 370 (N.Y. 1866).

30 Bloomsburg Mills v. Sordonic Const. Co., 401 Pa. 358, 164 A.2d 201 (Pa. 1960).

31 Scott v. Potomac Insurance Co. of Dist. of Columbia, 217 Or. 323, 341 P.2d 1083 (Or. 1959).

32 Hasbrouck v. Rymkevitch, 25 App. Div. 2d 187, 268 N.Y.S.2d 604 (N.Y. 1966).

33 Alexander v. Hammarberg, 103 Cal. 2d 872, 230 P.2d 399 (Cal. 1951).

34 Shine v. Hagemeister, 169 Wis. 343, 172 N.W. 750 (Wis. 1919).

35 Carrols Equities Corp. v. Villnave, 350 N.Y. Supp. 2d 90 (N.Y. 1973).

36 County of Broome v. Smith, Inc., 78 Misc. 2d 889 (N.Y. 1974).

37 Davis, Brody, Wisniewski v. Barrett, 253 Iowa 1178, 115 N.W.2d 839 (Iowa 1962).

38 Fry v. Kent, 62 Wash. 2d 953, 385 P.2d 323 (Wash. 1963).

39 D'Luhosch v. Andros, 109 N.Y.S.2d 491 (N.Y 1951).

40 Dick Weatherston's Associated Mechanical Services, Inc. v. Minnesota Mutual Life Insurance Company, 257 Minn. 184, 100 N.W.2d 819 (Minn. 1960).

41 Di Silvestri v. Golden Crest Motel Corp., 148 Conn. 121, 167 A.2d 857 (Conn. 1961).

42 Dane v. Brown, 70 F.2d, 164 (2d Cir. 1934).

[43] Cantrell v. Perkens, 177 Tenn. 47, 146 S.W.2d 134 (Tenn. 1941).

[44] Markel v. Fla. State Bd. of Architecture, 268 So.2d 374, 58 A.L.R. 3d 538 (Fla. 1972).

[45] MacPherson v. Buick Motor Co., 217 N.Y. 382, 111 N.E. 1050 (N.Y. 1916).

[46] Inman v. Binghamton Housing Authority, 3 N.Y.2d 137, 164 N.Y.S.2d 699; 143 N.E.2d 895 (N.Y. 1957).

[47] Olsen v. Chase Manhattan, 9 N.Y.2d 829, 175 N.E.2d 350 (N.Y. 1961).

[48] Ramos v. Shumavon, 21 A.D. 2d 4 (N.Y. 1964).

[49] Miller v. DeWitt, 37 Ill. 2d 273, N.E.2d 630 (Ill. 1967).

[50] Day v. National U.S. Radiator Corp., 241 La. 288, 128 So.2d 660 (La. 1961).

[51] Krafchik v. Hiltner, 66 Montg. Co. L.R. 112, 64 York 18 (Pa. 1950).

[52] Rozny v. Marnul, 250 N.E.2d 656 (1969).

[53] Dore v. LaPierre et al.; 226 N.Y.S.2d 949 (N.Y. 1962).

[54] Stem v. Warren, 185 App. Div. 823, 174 N.Y.S. 30; mod'g 96 Misc. 362, 161 N.Y.S. 247; mod. 227 N.Y. 538, 125 N.E. 811 (N.Y. 1920).

[55] Matter of Baker (Board of Education), 309 N.Y. 551, 132 N.E.2d 837 (N.Y. 1956).

[56] White v. Corliss, 46 N.Y. 467 (N.Y. 1871).

[57] Geremia v. Boyarksy, 107 Conn. 387, 140 A. 749 (Conn. 1928).

[58] Stewart v. Newbury, 220 N.Y. 379, 115 N.E. 984 (N.Y 1917).

[59] Lord Construction Co. v. United States to Use of Sexton, 28 F.2d 340 (2d Cir. 1928).

[60] Shields v. City of New York, 84 App. Div. 502, 82 N.Y.S. 1020 (N.Y. 1903).

[61] Fetterolf v. S & L Construction Co., 175 App. Div. 177, 161 N.Y.S. 549 (N.Y. 1916).

[62] Martini v. Elade Realty Co., 293 N.Y. 778, 58 N.E.2d 519 (N.Y. 1944).

[63] New England Foundation Co. v. Commonwealth, 327 Mass. 587, 100 N.E.2d 6 (Mass. 1951).

[64] Witmer v. Vulcan Methods, Inc., 41 Misc. 2d 41, 244 N.Y.S.2d 825 (N.Y. 1963).

[65] Bethlehem Steel v. Turner Const. Co., 2 N.Y.2d 456, 141 N.E.2d 590 (N.Y. 1957).

[66] Doehler Metal Furniture Co. v. U.S.; 149 F.2d 130 (2d Cir. 1945).

[67] U.S. v. Axman, 234 U.S. 36 (1914).

[68] Vernon Lumber v. Harcen Construction Co., 60 Fed. Supp. 555 (N.Y. 1945).

[69] Hammaker v. Schleigh, 157 Md. 652, 147 A. 790 (Md. 1929).

[70] Connors v. Town of Tewksbury, 318 Mass. 615 (Mass. 1945).

[71] Jacobs v. Kent, 230 N.Y. 239, 129 N.E. 889 (N.Y. 1921).

[72] Bellizi v. Huntley Estates, 3 N.Y.2d 112, 143 N.E.2d 802 (N.Y. 1957).

[73] Southwestern Engineering Co. v. U.S., 341 Fed.2d 998 (Mo. 1965).

74 Moon v. Wilson, 100 Fla. 791 (Fla. 1930).

75 Reetz v. Stackler, 24 Misc. 2d 291, 201 N.Y.S.2d 54 (N.Y. 1960).

76 Benjamin v. Toledo Plate & Window Glass Co., 8 Ohio L. Abs. 264 (Ohio 1929).

77 Wood-Hopkins Contracting Co. v. Masonry Contractors, Inc. (1970 Fla. App.) 235 So.2d 548, 61 A.L.R. 3d 786.

78 Brandt Corp. v. City of New York, 14 N.Y.2d 217, 199 N.E.2d 493 (N.Y. 1964).

79 Fredburn Construction Corp. v. City of N.Y., 280 N.Y. 402, 21 N.E.2d 370 (N.Y. 1939).

80 United States v. Wunderlich, 342 U.S. 98 (1951).

81 United States of America v. Hammer Contracting Corporation and Aetna Insurance Corporation, 331 F.2d 173 (2d Cir. 1964).

82 Garbis v. Apatoff, 192 Md. 12 (Md. 1948).

83 Kerr v. Milwee, 202 Md. 235 (Md. 1952).

84 Helm v. Speith, 298 Ky. 225 (Ky. 1944).

85 Montrose v. Westchester, 80 F.2d 841 (2d Cir. 1963); also Adams v. Tri-City Amusement Co., 124 Va. 473 (Va. 1919); and Kerr v. Milwee, 202 Md. 235, 96 A.2d 1 (Md. 1952).

86 City of Hazard Municipal Housing Commission v. Hinch, 411 S.W.2d 686 (Ky. 1967).

87 Caspersen v. LaSala Bros., Inc. and Omaha Realty Company, Inc., 253 N.Y. 491 (N.Y. 1930).

88 Dudar v. Milef Realty Corp., 258 N.Y. 415 (N.Y. 1932).

89 Semanchuck v. Fifth Ave., etc., 290 N.Y. 412, 49 N.E.2d 507 (N.Y. 1943).

90 Tipaldi v. Riverside Memorial Chapel, 273 App. Div. 414; aff'd, 298 N.Y. 686, 82 N.E.2d 585 (N.Y. 1948).

91 General Obligations Law, Art. 5 Sec. 322.1, McKinneys Consolidated Laws of N.Y. Book 23A.

92 Jordan v. City of New York, 3 App. Div. 2d 507; aff'd, 5 N.Y.2d 723 (N.Y. 1958).

93 General Obligations Law, Art. 5 Sec. 324, McKinneys Consolidated Laws of N.Y. Book 23A.

94 Trecartin v. Mahony-Troast, 18 N.J. Super. 380, 87 A.2d 349 (N.J. 1952).

95 Broderick v. Caldwell Wingate, 301 N.Y. 182, 93 N.E.2d 629 (N.Y. 1950).

96 Zucchelli v. City Construction Co., 4 N.Y.2d 52 (N.Y. 1958).

97 Schwartz v. Merola, 290 N.Y. 145, 48 N.E. 299 (N.Y. 1943).

98 Dow v. Holly Mfg. Co., 49 Cal. 2d 720, 321 P.2d 736 (Cal. 1958).

99 Pastorelli v. Associate Engrs., 176 Fed. Supp. 159 (R.I. 1959).

100 Spano v. Perini Corp., 25 N.Y.2d 11 (N.Y. 1969).

101 20 E. 74th St. v. Minskoff, 308 N.Y. 407, 126 N.E. 507 (N.Y. 1955).

102 Brody v. Mayor of N.Y.C., 20 N.Y. 312 (N.Y. 1859).

103 McNutt v. Eckert, 257 N.Y. 100 (N.Y. 1931).

[104] Gerzof v. Sweeney, 16 N.Y.2d 206, 211 N.E. 826 (N.Y. 1965).

[105] Gaskell v. Maslenka, 33 Misc. 2d 88, 225 N.Y.S.2d 442 (N.Y. 1962).

[106] Hodges v. Burns, 23 Misc. 2d 318 (N.Y. 1960).

[107] Soley v. Jones, 208 Mass. 561, 95 N.E. 94 (Mass. 1911).

[108] Afgo Engr. v. State, 244 App. Div. 395, 279 N.Y.S.2d 512; *aff'd*, 268 N.Y. 716, 198 N.E. 573 (N.Y. 1935).

[109] Koppelon v. Ritter Flooring, 97 N.J.L. 200, 116 A. 491 (N.J. 1922).

[110] Murphy v. U.S. Fidelity, 100 App. Div. 93 (N.Y. 1905).

[111] J. K. Welding Co. v. Shanahan Construction, New York Law Journal March 27, 1963, Page 19.

[112] American Bridge v. State of New York, 245 App. Div. 535, 283 N.Y.S. 577 (N.Y. 1935).

[113] Baker v. State of New York, 267 App. Div. 712 (N.Y. 1944).

[114] Norcross v. Wills, 198 N.Y. 336, 91 N.E. 803 (N.Y. 1910).

[115] Vonasek v. Hirsch and Stevens, 221 N.W.2d 815 (Wis. 1974).

[116] Marcus and Nocka v. Julian Goodrich Architects, Inc., 127 Vt. 404, 250 A.2d 739 (Vt. 1969).

[117] Peter Kiewet Sons Co. v. Iowa Southern Utilities Co. et al., 355 F. Supp. 376 (Iowa 1973).

[118] Albert Simon v. Omaha Public Power District, 189 Neb. 183 (Sup. Ct. Neb. 1972), 202 N.W.2d, 157.

[119] Regulations of Connecticut State Agencies, 320-289-11-c-3.

[120] New York State Education Law, 6509—Definitions of Professional Misconduct.

[121] Schipper v. Levitt and Sons, 44 N.J. 70, 207 A.2d 314 (N.J. 1965).

[122] Hartley v. Ballou, 201 S.E.2d 712 (N.Car. 1974).

[123] Avner v. Longridge Estates, 272 Cal. App. 695, 77 Cal. Rptr. 633 (Cal. 1969).

[124] Damora v. Stresscon International, Inc., 324 S.2d 80, Supreme Court of Fla., Nov. 1975.

[125] Jackson v. City of Walla Walla, 130 Wash. 96, 226 P.487 (Wash. 1924).

[126] Sweet v. Morrison, 116 N.Y.19 (N.Y. 1889).

[127] Tufano v. Port of N.Y. Authority, 18 App. Div. 2d 100; *aff'd*, 13 N.Y.2d 848, 242 N.Y.S.2d 489, 192 N.E.2d 270 (N.Y. 1963).

[128] Matter of Riverdale Fabrics Corp., 306 N.Y. 288, 118 N.E.2d 104 (N.Y. 1954).

[129] Application of Spectrum Fabrics Corporation, 285 A.D. 710, 139 N.Y.S.2d 612; *aff'd*, 309 N.Y. 709, 128 N.E.2d 416 (N.Y. 1955).

[130] Edgar H. Wood Associates v. Alex J. Skene, 347 Mass. 351, 197 N.E.2d 886 (Mass. 1964).

[131] Shanahan v. Macco Constr. Co., 224 Cal. App. 2d 327, 36 Cal. Rptr. 584 (Cal. 1964).

[132] Read v. Turner, 239 Cal. App. 2d 504, 48 Cal. Rptr. 919 (Cal. 1966).

[133] Ashworth v. Glover, 20 Utah 2d 85, 433 P.2d 315 (Utah 1967).

[134] Shaw v. Williamsville Manor, 38 A.D. 2d 442 (N.Y. 1972).

[135] Gendell v. Orr, 13 Phila. 191 (Pa. 1897).

[136] Kirk v. Poston, Court of Appeals, First App. Dist. of Ohio, No. 11979 (Ohio 1972).

[137] Nucor Corp. v. Tennessee Forging Steel Service, Inc., 476 F.2d 386 (Tenn. 1973).

[138] Henry Holt and Co. v. Liggett and Myers Tobacco Co., 23 F. Supp. 302 (Pa. 1938).

[139] Ames v. Dyer, 41 Me. 397 (Me. 1856).

[140] Turck v. Allard, 87 N.J.L. 721; 94 A. 583 (N.J. 1915); also Mutual Benefit Life Insurance Company v. Rowand, 26 N.J.Eq. 389 (N.J. 1875).

[141] Bralus Corp. v. Berger, 282 App. Div. 959, 125 N.Y.S.2d 786; *aff'd*, 307 N.Y. 626, 120 N.E.2d 829 (N.Y. 1954).

[142] A. P. Lee v. Du-Rite, 366 Pa. 548 (Pa. 1951).

[143] C. H. Heist Ohio Corp. v. Bethlehem Steel Company, 20 App. Div. 2d 201, 246 N.Y.S.2d 15 (N.Y. 1964).

[144] Marchetti v. Sleeper, 100 Conn. 339, 37 C.B.J. 215 (Conn. 1924).

[145] Chesnow v. Gorelick, 246 Mich. 571, 225 N.W. 4 (Mich. 1929); also 9 Mich. Bar Journal 189.

[146] Berger v. Turnblad, 98 Minn. 163, 107 N.W. 543 (Minn. 1906); Lamoreaux v. Andersch, 128 Minn. 261, 150 N.W. 908 (Minn. 1915).

[147] Robert V. Clapp Co. v. Fox, 124 Ohio St. 331, 178 N.E. 586 (Ohio 1931).

[148] Fosmire v. National Surety Company, 229 N.Y. 44, 127 N.E. 472 (N.Y. 1920).

[149] Daniel-Morris Co., Inc. v. Glens Falls Indemnity Co., 308 N.Y. 464, 126 N.E.2d 760 (N.Y. 1955).

[150] Fort Worth Independent School Dist. v. Aetna Casualty & Surety Co., 48 F.2d 1 (2d Cir. 1931).

[151] State, for Use of National Surety Corp. v. Malvanoy et al., 72 So.2d 424 (Miss. 1954).

Index